How does his interp of 3 Thess
change if it were indeed written
first (e.g. p 166)

THE NEW INTERNATIONAL
GREEK TESTAMENT COMMENTARY

Editors
I. Howard Marshall
and
W. Ward Gasque

THE EPISTLES TO THE THESSALONIANS

The New International Greek Testament Commentary

THE EPISTLES TO THE
THESSALONIANS

A Commentary on the
Greek Text

by

CHARLES A. WANAMAKER

WILLIAM B. EERDMANS PUBLISHING COMPANY
GRAND RAPIDS, MICHIGAN

THE PATERNOSTER PRESS
EXETER

Library of Congress Cataloging-in-Publication Data

Wanamaker, Charles A.
The Epistles to the Thessalonians: a commentary on the Greek text /
by Charles A. Wanamaker.
p.   cm.   — (The New International Greek testament commentary)
ISBN 0-8028-2394-7
1. Bible. N.T. Thessalonians—Commentaries. I. Title. II. Series: New international Greek
testament commentary (Grand Rapids, Mich.)
BS2725.3W35   1990
227'.8107—dc20   90-36510
                                          CIP

DEDICATION

The letters of Paul to the newly founded Christian community at Thessalonica hold a special place within the Christian tradition as they are very possibly the earliest extant Christian writings. For Christians living in oppressive societies such as contemporary South Africa they hold another significance. Among the communities established by Paul, the church at Thessalonica appears to have been the only one to have suffered serious external oppression. As I have argued in the commentary, following the lead of several other scholars, the initial oppression of the Christians at Thessalonica very probably resulted from the challenge that their new faith posed to Roman imperial ideology: in principle, either the imperial claims of Rome and its emperors or the claims of Christians regarding their Lord, Jesus Christ, who was to come from heaven to assert his sovereignty, had to be honored. The Christians at Thessalonica chose Jesus as their Lord, not Caesar, and so paid the price for rejecting the ideology of the dominant culture.

Many Christians in apartheid South Africa have recognized a similar challenge, the more insidious by virtue of the State's claim to be founded on Christian principles. The example of the Thessalonian Christians, who refused to bow to coercive oppression of the idolatrous dominant society, has been emulated not only by such well-known Christian opponents of apartheid as Archbishop Desmond Tutu, Reverend Allan Boesak, and Reverend C. F. Beyers Naudé, but also by hundreds and thousands of unknown Christians who have lived courageously, often suffering, sometimes even dying for their belief that Jesus' Lordship means freedom and justice for all. In so doing, they stand in the tradition of the Christians at Thessalonica, of Paul, who was no stranger to state oppression (2 Cor. 11:23-25), of the Jewish Christians in Judea who suffered from Jewish nationalist hostility (1 Thes. 2:14-16), and ultimately of Jesus himself, who died as an enemy of Rome. This commentary is dedicated to all those Christians who have suffered in the past, are suffering at present, or who will be called on to suffer in the future to bring about the justice and peace of God in South Africa.

CONTENTS

COMMENTARY ON 1 THESSALONIANS

COMMENTARY ON 2 THESSALONIANS

CONTENTS

INDEXES

FOREWORD

While there have been many series of commentaries on the English text of the New Testament in recent years, it is a long time since any attempt has been made to cater particularly to the needs of students of the Greek text. It is true that at the present time there is something of a decline in the study of Greek in many traditional theological institutions, but there has been a welcome growth in the study of the New Testament in its original language in the new evangelical schools, especially in North America and the Third World. It is hoped that *The New International Greek Testament Commentary* will demonstrate the value of studying the Greek New Testament and help toward the revival of such study.

The purpose of the series is to cater to the needs of students who want something less technical than a full-scale critical commentary. At the same time, the commentaries are intended to interact with modern scholarship and to make their own scholarly contribution to the study of the New Testament. There has been a wealth of detailed study of the New Testament in articles and monographs in recent years, and the series is meant to harvest the results of this research in a more easily accessible form. The commentaries will thus include adequate, but not exhaustive, bibliographies. They will attempt to treat all important problems of history, exegesis, and interpretation that may arise.

One of the gains of recent scholarship has been the recognition of the primarily theological character of the books of the New Testament. This series will, therefore, attempt to provide a theological understanding of the text, based on historical-critical-linguistic exegesis. It will not, however, attempt to apply and expound the text for modern readers, although it is hoped that the exegesis will give some indication of the way in which the text should be expounded.

Within the limits set by the use of the English language, the series aims to be international in character; the contributors, however, have been chosen not primarily in order to achieve a spread between different countries but above all because of their specialized qualifications for their particular tasks. This publication is a joint venture of The Paternoster Press, Exeter, England, and Wm. B. Eerdmans Publishing Company, Grand Rapids, USA.

The supreme aim of this series is to serve those who are engaged in the ministry of the Word of God and thus to glorify his name. Our prayer is that it may be found helpful in this task.

I. Howard Marshall
W. Ward Gasque

PREFACE

Over the last two decades the nature of New Testament Studies has changed dramatically with the introduction of new approaches to complement traditional forms of literary and linguistic analysis, historical criticism, and theological interpretation. The invitation to write this commentary coincided with a shift in my own work as I began to incorporate what, for want of a better description, may be called a social science approach to my studies. This has had enormous implications for the writing of this commentary, as the reader will see.

In the past my attention would have focused on the history of ideas, that is, on the origin and interconnection of Paul's theological thought with Jewish and Hellenistic thought and the reconstruction of the historical processes giving rise both to Christianity at Thessalonica and to Paul's writing of 1 and 2 Thessalonians. Central to my exegesis would have been a careful linguistic analysis of the text. This would have provided a basis for making historical judgments about the meaning intended by Paul as he composed the text and how the text would have been interpreted by its original recipients. This approach has dominated the work of previous commentators on 1 and 2 Thessalonians, from whom I have learned a great deal.

For my part, I have not ignored the traditional approach to writing a commentary, and in fact at several points I believe that I have been able to make a contribution to the questions raised by traditional exegesis. At the same time, however, I have attempted to go beyond previous commentaries on the Thessalonian correspondence by taking seriously the social dimensions both of Christianity at Thessalonica and of the texts of 1 and 2 Thessalonians. I have sought to understand Pauline Christianity at Thessalonica as a socio-religious movement in the first-century Greco-Roman world and have attempted to grasp the social character and functions of Paul's letters within this context. The reader must judge how successful I have been in my efforts to blend traditional exegetical methods with the newer approaches.

My debt to scholars past and present is enormous and is reflected in references throughout the commentary. Unfortunately, the recent work of Frank Hughes (*Early Christian Rhetoric*, 1989) arrived too late to do it justice. I have, however, incorporated several of his valuable suggestions regarding the rhetoric of 2 Thessalonians and have provided a few remarks to indicate my considerable disagreement with his historical conclusions.

One scholar not mentioned in the text has had a significant impact on my thinking about 1 and 2 Thessalonians and deserves special mention. In a chance conversation at a conference we were both attending, Professor Robert Fortna mentioned that he had long held the view that the authenticity of 2 Thessalonians could only be maintained if it were considered the first rather than the second letter of Paul to the Thessalonians. His comment caused me to reassess in a critical way my views on the sequence of the letters. To my amazement I found myself compelled by the evidence to assume the priority of 2 Thessalonians over 1 Thessalonians. The arguments for my position will be found in the second main section of the Introduction. Since scholarly opinion is often conservative about accepting ideas that run counter to widely held views, and rightly so, I have written the commentary in such a way as to enable readers to use the commentary regardless of what their position is vis-à-vis the question of epistolary sequence.

I owe a debt of thanks to many people who have in one way or another contributed to the writing of this volume. First, I would like to thank Professors W. Ward Gasque and I. Howard Marshall for inviting me to participate in this series and for their helpful comments regarding my manuscript. I would also like to thank Dr. John W. Simpson, Jr., of Eerdmans for his careful editing of my manuscript and his encouragement of my work. Second, I owe a debt of gratitude to my colleagues and students in the Department of Religious Studies at the University of Cape Town, as well as the Department's support staff, for their help and encouragement. A special word of appreciation is due to Mrs. Arlene Stephenson for proofreading the manuscript and to my post-graduate students Ms. Mary Armour, who read the penultimate version of the manuscript with the careful eye of an editor, making many valuable suggestions, and Ms. Jeanette Matthews, who produced the indexes with great care. I would also like to express my thanks to the Research Committee of the University of Cape Town for generous financial support and especially for a year's research leave, during which the bulk of the commentary was written.

Finally, a word of thanks is due to my family. My children, Kristianna and Geoffrey, have taken an interest in the progress of my work and have often encouraged me. My wife, Helena, has been a constant source of support and encouragement. In the midst of her own busy career she has always taken time to serve as a sounding board for my ideas. Her comments have often forced me to rethink important issues and to bring greater precision to their expression. For this I am indeed grateful.

Charles A. Wanamaker

ABBREVIATIONS

Textual notes are from *UBSGNT*. Works cited by author or author and short title are listed in the Bibliography.

BOOKS OF THE BIBLE

Gn., Ex., Lv., Nu., Dt., Jos., Jdg., Ru., 1, 2 Sa., 1, 2 Ki., 1, 2 Ch., Ezr., Ne., Est., Jb., Ps(s)., Pr., Ec., Ct., Is., Je., La., Ezk., Dn., Ho., Joel, Am., Ob., Jon., Mi., Na., Hab., Zp., Hg., Zc., Mal., Mt., Mk., Lk., Jn., Acts, Rom., 1, 2 Cor., Gal., Eph., Phil., Col., 1, 2 Thes., 1, 2 Tim., Tit., Phm., Heb., Jas., 1, 2 Pet., 1, 2, 3 Jn., Jude, Rev.

OTHER ANCIENT SOURCES

Apocrypha and Septuagint

1, 2, 3, 4 Kgdms.	1, 2, 3, 4 Kingdoms
Tob.	Tobit
Wis.	Wisdom of Solomon

Pseudepigrapha, Dead Sea Scrolls, and Rabbinic Literature

2 Bar.	*Syriac Apocalypse of Baruch*
1 Enoch	*Ethiopic Enoch*
Gn. Rab.	*Genesis Rabbah*
Jub.	*Jubilees*
Mart. Is.	*Martyrdom of Isaiah*
Pss. Sol.	*Psalms of Solomon*
Sib. Or.	*Sibylline Oracles*

Classical and Hellenistic Literature

Ann.	*Annals* (Tacitus)
Ant.	*Jewish Antiquities (Antiquitates Judaicae)* (Josephus)
Ap.	*Against Apion (Contra Apionem)* (Josephus)
Diog. Laert.	Diogenes Laertius
El.	*Electra* (Sophocles)
Ep.	*Epistulae Morales* (Seneca)
Hdt.	Herodotus
Hist.	*History of the Peloponnesian War* (Thucydides)
Il.	*Iliad* (Homer)
Leg. All.	*Legum Allegoriae* (Philo)

Mor.	*Moralia* (Plutarch)
Spec. Leg.	*De Specialibus Legibus* (Philo)
War	*The Jewish War (Bellum Judaicum)* (Josephus)

Early Christian Literature

Apoc. Mos.	*Apocalypse of Moses*
Barn.	Letter of Barnabas
Did.	Didache
Ep. Diog.	Epistle to Diognetus
Pol.	Polycarp, *To the Philippians*
Smy.	*Letter to the Smyrnaeans* (Ignatius)

REFERENCE WORKS, PERIODICALS, AND SERIES

AB	Anchor Bible
AGJU	Arbeiten zur Geschichte des antiken Judentums und des Urchristentums
AnBib	Analecta Biblica
ANRW	*Aufstieg und Niedergang der römischen Welt*
ASNU	Acta seminarii neotestamentici upsaliensis
ASR	*American Sociological Review*
ATR	*Anglican Theological Review*
BAGD	Walter Bauer, William F. Arndt, F. Wilbur Gingrich, and Frederick Danker, *A Greek-English Lexicon of the New Testament and Other Early Christian Literature*. Chicago: University of Chicago, ²1979.
BDF	F. Blass and A. Debrunner, *A Greek Grammar of the New Testament and Other Early Christian Literature*, tr. and rev. Robert W. Funk. Chicago: University of Chicago, 1961.
BEvT	Beiträge zur evangelischen Theologie
BFCT	*Beiträge zur Förderung christlicher Theologie*
Bib	*Biblica*
BJRL	*Bulletin of the John Rylands University Library, Manchester*
BNTC	Black's New Testament Commentaries (= Harper's New Testament Commentaries)
BZNW	Beihefte zur *Zeitschrift für die neutestamentliche Wissenschaft*
CBQ	*Catholic Biblical Quarterly*
CNT	Commentaire du Nouveau Testament
ConB	Coniectanea biblica
DNTT	*New International Dictionary of New Testament Theology*, ed. Colin Brown. Three volumes; Grand Rapids: Zondervan, 1975-78.
DTT	*Dansk teologisk tidsskrift*
ÉBib	Études bibliques
EKKNT	Evangelisch-katholischer Kommentar zum Neuen Testament
ETL	*Ephemerides theologicae lovanienses*
EvQ	*Evangelical Quarterly*

ABBREVIATIONS

ExpTim	*Expository Times*
FRLANT	Forschungen zur Religion und Literatur des Alten und Neuen Testaments
HNT	Handbuch zum Neuen Testament
HTR	*Harvard Theological Review*
ICC	International Critical Commentary
Int	*Interpretation*
JBL	*Journal of Biblical Literature*
JSNTSS	Journal for the Study of the New Testament Supplement Series
JTS	*Journal of Theological Studies*
JTSA	*Journal of Theology for Southern Africa*
LCL	Loeb Classical Library
LEC	Library of Early Christianity
LSJ	H. G. Liddell and R. Scott, *A Greek-English Lexicon,* revised and augmented by H. S. Jones and R. McKenzie. Oxford: Clarendon Press, 1968.
MNTC	Moffatt New Testament Commentary
NCBC	New Century Bible Commentary
NEB	*New English Bible*
Neot	*Neotestamentica*
Nestle-Aland[26]	*Novum Testamentum Graece,* ed. Kurt Aland, Matthew Black, Carlo M. Martini, Bruce M. Metzger, and Allen Wikgren; critical apparatus by Kurt Aland and Barbara Aland. Stuttgart: Deutsche Bibelstiftung, 1979.
NICNT	New International Commentary on the New Testament
NIV	*New International Version*
NovT	*Novum Testamentum*
NovTSup	Novum Testamentum Supplements
NTD	Das Neue Testament Deutsch
NTS	*New Testament Studies*
RHPR	*Revue d'histoire et de philosophie religieuses*
RSV	*Revised Standard Version*
RTR	*Reformed Theological Review*
SANT	Studien zum Alten und Neuen Testament
SBLDS	Society of Biblical Literature Dissertation Series
SBLSP	Society of Biblical Literature Seminar Papers
SBS	Stuttgarter Bibelstudien
SBT	Studies in Biblical Theology
SNT	Studien zum Neuen Testament
SNTSMS	Society for New Testament Studies Monograph Series
ST	*Studia Theologia*
SUNT	Studien zur Umwelt des Neuen Testaments
TDNT	*Theological Dictionary of the New Testament,* ed. Gerhard Kittel and Gerhard Friedrich; tr. Geoffrey W. Bromiley. Ten volumes; Grand Rapids: Eerdmans, 1964-76.
TEV	*Today's English Version (Good News Bible)*

TZ	*Theologische Zeitschrift*
UBSGNT	*The Greek New Testament,* ed. Kurt Aland, Matthew Black, Carlo M. Martini, Bruce M. Metzger, and Allen Wikgren. New York: United Bible Societies, [3]1975.
VD	*Verbum domini*
WBC	Word Biblical Commentary
WMANT	Wissenschaftliche Monographien zum Alten und Neuen Testament
ZB	Zürcher Bibelkommentare
ZNW	*Zeitschrift für die neutestamentliche Wissenschaft*
ZTK	*Zeitschrift für Theologie und Kirche*

BIBLIOGRAPHY

The works listed here are cited by author's name and short title, except commentaries on the Thessalonian Epistles, which are cited by author's name only (Best, Bruce, Dibelius, von Dobschütz, Findlay, Frame, Friedrich, Holtz, Marshall, Marxsen, Masson, Milligan, Morris, Neil, Rigaux, and Trilling).

Aberle, David, "A Note on Relative Deprivation Theory as Applied to Millenarian and Other Cult Movements," *Reader in Comparative Religion: An Anthropological Approach,* ed. W. A. Lessa and E. Z. Vogt, 537-541. New York: Harper & Row, 1964.

Aune, David E., *The New Testament in Its Literary Environment.* LEC 8; Philadelphia: Westminster, 1987.

Aus, Roger D., *Comfort in Judgment: The Use of Day of the Lord and Theophany Traditions in Second Thessalonians 1.* Unpublished Ph.D. Dissertation; New Haven: Yale University, 1971.

_____, "God's Plan and God's Power: Isaiah 66 and the Restraining Factors of 2 Thess 2:6-7," *JBL* 96 (1977) 537-553.

_____, "The Liturgical Background of the Necessity and Propriety of Giving Thanks according to 2 Thess 1:3," *JBL* 92 (1973) 422-438.

_____, "The Relevance of Isaiah 66:7 to Revelation 12 and 2 Thessalonians 1," *ZNW* 67 (1976) 252-268.

Bailey, John A., "Who Wrote II Thessalonians?" *NTS* 25 (1978-79) 131-145.

Baltensweiler, Heinrich, "Erwägungen zu 1 Thess 4,3-8," *TZ* 19 (1963) 1-13.

Bammel, Ernst, "Judenverfolgung und Naherwartung: Zur Eschatologie des Ersten Thessalonicherbriefs," *ZTK* 56 (1959) 294-315.

_____, "Preparation for the Perils of the Last Days: I Thessalonians 3:3," *Suffering and Martyrdom in the New Testament: Studies Presented to G. M. Styler by the Cambridge New Testament Seminar,* ed. W. Horbury and B. McNeil, 91-100. Cambridge: Cambridge University, 1981.

Barnouin, M., "Les problèmes de traduction concernant II Thess. II.6-7," *NTS* 23 (1976-77) 482-498.

Barrett, Charles Kingsley, *A Commentary on the First Epistle to the Corinthians.* BNTC; London: Black, 1968.

_____, *A Commentary on the Second Epistle to the Corinthians.* BNTC; London: Black, 1973.

_____, "Shaliah and Apostle," *Donum Gentilicium: New Testament Studies in Honour of David Daube,* ed. E. Bammel, C. K. Barrett, and W. D. Davies, 94-102. Oxford: Clarendon, 1978.

Bassler, Jouette M., "The Enigmatic Sign: 2 Thessalonians 1:5," *CBQ* 46 (1984) 496-510.

Baumgarten, Jörg, *Paulus und die Apokalyptik. Die Auslegung apokalyptischer Überlieferungen in den echten Paulusbriefen.* WMANT 44; Neukirchen-Vluyn: Neukirchener, 1975.

Beauvery, R., "Πλεονεκτεῖν in 1 Thess. 4.6a," *VD* 33 (1955) 78-85.

Beck, Norman A., *Mature Christianity: The Recognition and Repudiation of the Anti-Jewish Polemic in the New Testament.* London: Associated University Press, 1985.

Beker, J. Christiaan, *Paul the Apostle: The Triumph of God in Life and Thought.* Edinburgh: Clark, 1980.

Berger, Peter, *The Social Reality of Religion.* Harmondsworth: Penguin, 1973.

_____ and Thomas Luckmann, *The Social Construction of Reality: A Treatise in the Sociology of Knowledge.* London: Lane, 1967.

Best, Ernest, *A Commentary on the First and Second Epistles to the Thessalonians.* BNTC; London: Black, 1977[2].

_____, *One Body in Christ: A Study in the Relationship of the Church to Christ in the Epistles of the Apostle Paul.* London: SPCK, 1955.

Betz, Hans Dieter, *Galatians: A Commentary on Paul's Letter to the Churches in Galatia.* Hermeneia; Philadelphia: Fortress, 1979.

_____, "The Literary Composition and Function of Paul's Letter to the Galatians," *NTS* 21 (1975) 353-379.

Bjerkelund, Carl J., *Parakalô: Form, Funktion und Sinn der Parakalô-Sätz in den paulinischen Briefen.* Bibliotheca Theologica Norvegica 1; Oslo: Universitets-forlaget, 1967.

Boers, Hendrikus, "The Form-Critical Study of Paul's Letters: 1 Thessalonians as a Case Study," *NTS* 22 (1975-76) 140-158.

Borgen, Peder, "God's Agent in the Fourth Gospel," *Religions in Antiquity: Essays in Memory of E. R. Goodenough,* ed. J. Neusner, 136-148. Leiden: Brill, 1968.

Bouttier, Michael, *En Christ.* Paris: Presses Universitaires de France, 1962.

Braun, Herbert, "Zur nachpaulinischen Herkunft des zweiten Thessalonicherbriefes," *ZNW* 44 (1952-53) 152-156.

Bruce, Frederick F., *1 and 2 Thessalonians.* WBC; Waco, Texas: Word, 1982.

_____, *New Testament History.* Garden City, New York: Doubleday, 1972.

Buck, Charles, and Greer Taylor, *Saint Paul: A Study of the Development of his Thought.* New York: Scribner's, 1969.

Burridge, Kenelm, *New Heaven, New Earth: A Study of Millenarian Activities.* Oxford: Blackwell, 1969.

Bussmann, C., *Themen der paulinischen Missionspredigt auf dem Hintergrund der spätjüdischen-hellenistischen Missionsliteratur.* Bern: Lang, 1971.

Collins, Adela Yarbro, *Crisis and Catharsis: The Power of the Apocalypse.* Philadelphia: Westminster, 1984.

_____, "Persecution and Vengeance in the Book of Revelation," *Apocalypticism in the Mediterranean World and the Near East. Proceedings of the International*

Colloquium on Apocalypticism, Uppsala, August 12-17, 1979, ed. David Hellholm, 729-749. Tübingen: Mohr, 1983.

_____, "Vilification and Self-Definition in the Book of Revelation," *HTR* 79 (1986) 308-320.

Collins, John J., *The Apocalyptic Imagination: An Introduction to the Jewish Matrix of Christianity.* New York: Crossroads, 1984.

Collins, Raymond F., "A propos the Integrity of 1 Thes.," *ETL* 55 (1979) 65-106.

_____, "Paul, as seen through his own eyes. A Reflection on the First Letter to the Thessalonians," *Louvain Studies* 8 (1980) 348-381. = Collins, *Studies on the First Letter to the Thessalonians,* 175-208. Bibliotheca Ephemeridum Theologicarum Lovaniensium 66; Louvain: Peeters/Louvain University, 1984.

_____, "Tradition, Redaction and Exhortation in 1 Th 4,13–5,11," *L'Apocalypse johannique et l'Apocalyptique dans le Nouveau Testament,* ed. J. Lambrecht, 325-343. Bibliotheca Ephemeridum Theologicarum Lovaniensium 53; Gembloux: J. Duculot, 1980. = *Studies on the First Letter to the Thessalonians,* 154-172.

Conzelmann, Hans, *An Outline of the Theology of the New Testament.* London: SCM, 1969.

Cranfield, Charles E. B., *A Critical and Exegetical Commentary on the Epistle to the Romans.* Two volumes, ICC; Edinburgh: Clark, 1975, 1979.

Cullmann, Oscar, "Le caractère eschatologique du devoir missionaire et de la conscience apostolique de S. Paul," *RHPR* 16 (1936) 210-245.

Dalbert, Peter, *Die Theologie der hellenistisch jüdischen Missionsliteratur unter Auschluss von Philo und Josephus.* Hamburg-Volksdorf: Reich, 1954.

Davies, William D., *Paul and Rabbinic Judaism: Some Rabbinic Elements in Pauline Theology.* Philadelphia: Fortress, 1980[4].

_____, "Paul and the People of Israel," *NTS* 24 (1977-78) 4-39. = Davies, *Jewish and Pauline Studies,* 123-152. Philadelphia: Fortress, 1984.

Deissmann, Adolf, *Light from the Ancient East.* London: Hodder and Stoughton, 1927[2].

Demke, Christoph, "Theologie und Literarkritik im 1. Thessalonicherbrief: Ein Diskussionsbeitrag," *Festschrift für Ernst Fuchs,* ed. G. Ebeling, E. Jungel, and G. Schunack, 103-124. Tübingen: Mohr, 1973.

Dibelius, Martin, *Die Briefe des Apostels Paulus. II. Die Neun Kleinen Briefe.* HNT; Tübingen: Mohr, 1913.

Dobschütz, Ernst von, *Die Thessalonicher-Briefe.* Nachdruck der Ausgabe von 1909. Mit einem Literaturverzeichnis von Otto Merk, herausgegeben von Ferdinand Hahn; Göttingen: Vandenhoeck & Ruprecht, 1974.

Donfried, Karl Paul, "The Cults of Thessalonica and the Thessalonian Correspondence," *NTS* 31 (1985) 336-356.

_____, "Paul and Judaism: I Thessalonians 2:13-16 as a Test Case," *Int* 38 (1984) 242-253.

Doty, William G., *Letters in Primitive Christianity.* Philadelphia: Fortress, 1973.

Dunn, James D. G., *Unity and Diversity in the New Testament: An Inquiry into the Character of Earliest Christianity.* London: SCM, 1977.

Eckart, Karl-Gottfried, "Der zweite Brief des Apostels Paulus an die Thessalonicher," *ZTK* 58 (1961) 30-44.

Edson, Charles, "Cults of Thessalonica," *HTR* 41 (1948) 153-204.

_____, "Macedonia," *Harvard Studies in Classical Philology* 51 (1940) 125-136.

Elliger, Winfried, *Paulus in Griechenland: Philippi, Thessaloniki, Athen, Korinth.* SBS 92/93; Stuttgart: Katholisches Bibelwerk, 1978.

Ellis, E. Earle, *Prophecy and Hermeneutic in Early Christianity.* Grand Rapids: Eerdmans, 1978.

Enslin, Morton Scott, *The Ethics of Paul.* New York: Harper & Brothers, 1930.

Evans, Robert M., *Eschatology and Ethics: A Study of Thessalonica and Paul's Letters to the Thessalonians.* D.Th. Dissertation (1967); Princeton: McMahon, 1968.

Faw, Chalmer E., "On the Writing of First Thessalonians," *JBL* 71 (1952) 217-232.

Festinger, Leon, *A Theory of Cognitive Dissonance.* Stanford: Stanford University, 1957.

_____, Henry W. Riecken, and Stanley Schachter, *When Prophecy Fails: A Social and Psychological Study of a Modern Group that Predicted the Destruction of the World.* New York: Harper & Row, 1964 reprint (1956).

Findlay, George G., *The Epistles of Paul the Apostle to the Thessalonians.* Cambridge Greek New Testament for Schools and Colleges. Grand Rapids: Baker, 1982 reprint (1904).

Frame, James E., *A Critical and Exegetical Commentary on the Epistles of St. Paul to the Thessalonians.* ICC; Edinburgh: Clark, 1912.

Freyne, Sean, "Vilifying the Other and Defining the Self: Matthew's and John's Anti-Jewish Polemic in Focus," *"To See Ourselves as Others See Us": Christians, Jews, "Others" in Late Antiquity,* ed. Jacob Neusner and Ernest S. Frerichs, 117-143. Atlanta: Scholars, 1985.

Friedrich, Gerhard, "1-2 Thessalonians," in Jürgen Becker, Hans Conzelmann, and G. Friedrich, *Die Briefe an die Galater, Epheser, Philipper, Kolosser, Thessalonicher und Philemon: Übersetzt und Erklärt.* NTD; Göttingen: Vandenhoeck & Ruprecht, 1981.

_____, "1. Thessalonicher 5,1-11, der apologetische Einschub eines Späteren," *ZTK* 70 (1973) 288-315.

_____, "Ein Tauflied hellenistischer Judenchristen: 1. Thess. 1,9f," *TZ* 21 (1965) 502-516.

Funk, Robert W., "The Apostolic *Parousia:* Form and Significance," *Christian History and Interpretation: Studies Presented to John Knox,* ed. William R. Farmer, C. F. D. Moule, and R. Richard Niebuhr, 249-268. Cambridge: Cambridge University Press, 1967. = "The Apostolic Presence: Paul," Funk, *Parables and Presence,* 81-102. Philadelphia: Fortress, 1982.

Furnish, Victor Paul, *The Love Command in the New Testament.* New York: Abingdon, 1972.

_____, *II Corinthians: Translation with Introduction, Notes, and Commentary.* AB; Garden City, New York: Doubleday, 1984.

Gager, John G., *Kingdom and Community: The Social World of Early Christianity.* Englewood Cliffs, New Jersey: Prentice-Hall, 1975.

Georgi, Dieter, *The Opponents of Paul in Second Corinthians*. Edinburgh: Clark, 1986.

Gerhardsson, Birger, *Memory and Manuscript: Oral Tradition and Written Transmission in Rabbinic Judaism and Early Christianity*. ASNU 22; Lund: Gleerup, 1964^2.

Giblin, Charles H., *The Threat to Faith: An Exegetical and Theological Re-examination of 2 Thessalonians 2*. AnBib 31; Rome: Pontifical Biblical Institute, 1967.

Goguel, Maurice, *Introduction au Nouveau Testament*. Four volumes; Paris: Leroux, 1925.

Gregson, R., "A Solution to the Problem of the Thessalonian Epistles," *EvQ* 38 (1966) 76-80.

Haenchen, Ernst, *The Acts of the Apostles: A Commentary*. Oxford: Blackwell, 1971.

Harnisch, Wolfgang, *Eschatologische Existenz. Ein exegetischer Beitrag zum Sachanliegen von 1 Thessalonicher 4,15–5,11*. FRLANT 110; Göttingen: Vandenhoeck & Ruprecht, 1973.

Hartman, Lars, *Prophecy Interpreted: The Formation of Some Jewish Apocalyptic Texts and of the Eschatological Discourse, Mark 13 Par*. ConB, NT Series 1; Lund: Gleerup, 1966.

Havener, Ivan, "The Pre-Pauline Christological Credal Formulae of 1 Thessalonians," SBLSP 20 (1981) 105-128.

Heirich, Max, "Change of Heart: A Test of Some Widely Held Theories about Religious Conversion," *American Journal of Sociology* 83 (1977) 653-680.

Hemberg, Bengt, *Die Kabiren*. Uppsala: Almquist & Wiksell, 1950.

Hendrix, Holland L., *Thessalonicans Honor Romans*. Ph.D. thesis. Harvard University, 1984.

Hengel, Martin, *Between Jesus and Paul: Studies in the Earliest History of Christianity*. London: SCM, 1983.

Hewett, J. A., "1 Thessalonians 3.13," *ExpTim* 87 (1975-76) 54-55.

Hock, Ronald F., "Paul's Tentmaking and the Problem of His Social Class," *JBL* 97 (1978) 555-564.

_____, *The Social Context of Paul's Ministry: Tentmaking and Apostleship*. Philadelphia: Fortress, 1980.

_____, "The Workshop as a Social Setting for Paul's Missionary Preaching," *CBQ* 41 (1979) 438-450.

Holladay, Carl R., *THEIOS ANER in Hellenistic-Judaism: A Critique of the Use of this Category in New Testament Christology*. SBLDS 40; Missoula, Montana: Scholars, 1977.

Holmberg, Bengt, *Paul and Power: The Structure of Authority in the Primitive Church as Reflected in the Pauline Epistles*. Philadelphia: Fortress, 1980 (1978).

Holtz, Traugott, *Der erste Brief an die Thessalonicher*. EKKNT 13; Zürich: Benziger, 1986.

_____, " 'Euer Glaube an Gott': Zu Form und Inhalt von 1 Thess 1,9f," *Die Kirche des Anfangs. Für Heinz Schürmann*, ed. Rudolf Schnackenburg, Joseph Ernst, and Joseph Wanke, 459-488. Freiburg: Herder, 1978.

_____, "Traditionen im 1. Thessalonicherbrief," *Die Mitte des Neuen Testaments: Einheit und Vielfalt neutestamentlicher Theologie. Festschrift für Eduard*

Schweizer zum siebzigsten Geburtstag, ed. Ulrich Luz and Hans Weder, 55-78. Göttingen: Vandenhoeck & Ruprecht, 1983.

Holtzmann, Heinrich J., "Zum zweiten Thessalonicherbrief," *ZNW* 2 (1901) 97-108.

Hughes, Frank Witt, *Early Christian Rhetoric and 2 Thessalonians.* JSNTSS 30; Sheffield: JSOT, 1989.

Hyldahl, N., "Auferstehung Christi—Auferstehung der Toten (1 Thess. 4,13-18)," *Die Paulinische Literatur und Theologie: Anlässlich der 50. jährigen Gründungs-Feier der Universität von Aarhus,* ed. Sigfred Pedersen, 119-135. Teologiske Studier 7. Göttingen: Vandenhoeck & Ruprecht, 1980.

Jensen, J., "Does *Porneia* Mean Fornication? A Critique of Bruce Malina," *NovT* 20 (1978) 161-184.

Jeremias, Joachim, *Unknown Sayings of Jesus.* London: SPCK, 1964.

Jewett, Robert, "The Agitators and the Galatian Congregation," *NTS* 17 (1970-71) 198-212.

_____, *A Chronology of Paul's Life.* Philadelphia: Fortress, 1979.

_____, "The Form and Function of the Homiletic Benediction," *ATR* 51 (1969) 18-34.

_____, *Paul's Anthropological Terms: A Study of Their Use in Conflict Settings.* AGJU 10; Leiden: Brill, 1971.

_____, *The Thessalonian Correspondence: Pauline Rhetoric and Millenarian Piety.* Foundations and Facets; Philadelphia: Fortress, 1986.

Judge, Edwin A., "The Decrees of Caesar at Thessalonica," *RTR* 30 (1971) 1-7.

Käsemann, Ernst, *Commentary on Romans.* Grand Rapids: Eerdmans, 1980.

Kaye, Bruce N., "Eschatology and Ethics in 1 and 2 Thessalonians," *NovT* 17 (1975) 47-57.

Kemmler, Dieter Werner, *Faith and Human Reason: A Study of Paul's Method of Preaching as Illustrated by 1–2 Thessalonians and Acts 17,2-4.* NovTSup 40; Leiden: Brill, 1975.

Kennedy, George A., *The Art of Persuasion in Greece.* Princeton: Princeton University, 1963.

_____, *New Testament Interpretation through Rhetorical Criticism.* Chapel Hill: University of North Carolina, 1984.

Kern, Friedrich H., "Über 2. Thess 2,1-12. Nebst Andeutungen über den Ursprung des zweiten Briefs an die Thessalonicher," *Tübinger Zeitschrift für Theologie* 2 (1839) 145-214.

Knopf, Rudolf, *Das nachapostolische Zeitalter. Geschichte der Christlichen Gemeinden vom Beginn der Flavierdynastie bis zum ende Hadrians.* Tübingen: Mohr, 1905.

Koester, Helmut, *Introduction to the New Testament.* Vol. II. *History and Literature of Early Christianity.* Philadelphia: Fortress, 1982.

_____, "I Thessalonians—Experiment in Christian Writing," *Continuity and Discontinuity in Church History* (G. H. Williams Festschrift), ed. F. F. Church and T. George, 33-44. Leiden: Brill, 1979.

Kümmel, Werner Georg, *Introduction to the New Testament.* London: SCM Press, 1975[2].

_____, "Das literarische und geschichtliche Problem des ersten Thessalonicherbriefes," *Neotestamentica et Patristica: Eine Freundesgabe O. Cullmann zum 60. Geburtstag,* ed. W. C. van Unnik, 213-227. NovTSup 6; Leiden: Brill, 1962.

Larsen, J. A. O., "Roman Greece," *An Economic Survey of Ancient Rome,* IV, ed. T. Frank, 259-498. Baltimore: Johns Hopkins, 1938.

Laub, Franz, *Eschatologische Verkündigung und Lebensgestaltung nach Paulus: Eine Untersuchung zum Wirken des Apostels beim Aufbau der Gemeinde in Thessalonike.* Münchener Universitäts-Schriften: Katholisch-Theologische Fakultät; Regensburg: Pustet, 1973.

Lightfoot, Joseph Barber, *Saint Paul's Epistle to the Galatians.* London: Macmillan, 1884[8].

Lindemann, Andreas, "Zum Abfassungszweck des Zweiten Thessalonicherbriefes," *ZNW* 68 (1977) 35-47.

Lofland, John, and Rodney Stark, "Becoming a World-saver: A Theory of Conversion to a Deviant Perspective," *ASR* 30 (1965) 862-874.

Lohfink, Gerhard, *Die Himmelfahrt Jesu: Untersuchungen zu den Himmelfahrts- und Erhöhungstexten bei Lukas.* SANT 26; Munich: Kösel, 1971.

Lohmeyer, Ernst, "Probleme paulinischer Theologie," *ZNW* 26 (1927) 158-173.

Longenecker, Richard N., "Ancient Amanuenses and the Pauline Epistles," *New Dimensions in New Testament Study,* ed. Richard N. Longenecker and Merrill C. Tenney, 281-297. Grand Rapids: Zondervan, 1974.

_____, "The Nature of Paul's Early Eschatology," *NTS* 31 (1985) 85-95.

Lüdemann, Gerd, *Paul: Apostle to the Gentiles. Studies in Chronology.* London: SCM, 1984.

Lütgert, Wilhelm, "Die Volkommenen im Philipperbrief und die Enthusiasten in Thessalonich," *BFCT* 13 (1909) 547-654.

Luz, Ulrich, *Das Geschichtsverständnis des Paulus.* BEvT 49; Munich: Kaiser, 1968.

Lyons, George, *Pauline Autobiography: Toward a New Understanding.* SBLDS 73; Atlanta: Scholars, 1985.

MacMullen, Ramsay, *Paganism in the Roman Empire.* London: Yale University, 1981.

_____, *Roman Social Relations: 50 B.C. to A.D. 284.* London: Yale University, 1974.

Malherbe, Abraham J., "Exhortation in First Thessalonians," *NovT* 25 (1983) 238-256.

_____, " 'Gentle as a Nurse': The Stoic Background to 1 Thess. II," *NovT* 12 (1970) 203-217.

_____, *Moral Exhortation, A Greco-Roman Sourcebook.* LEC 4; Philadelphia: Westminster, 1986.

_____, *Paul and the Thessalonians: The Philosophical Tradition of Pastoral Care.* Philadelphia: Fortress, 1987.

Manson, Thomas W., "St. Paul in Greece: The Letters to the Thessalonians," *BJRL* 35 (1952-53) 428-447.

Marshall, I. Howard, *1 and 2 Thessalonians.* NCBC; London: Marshall, Morgan, and Scott, 1983.

_____, *Last Supper and Lord's Supper.* Exeter: Paternoster, 1980.

Martyn, J. L., "Apocalyptic Antinomies in Paul's Letter to the Galatians," *NTS* 31 (1985) 410-424.

Marxsen, Willi, "Auslegung von 1 Thess 4,13-18," *ZTK* 66 (1969) 23-37.

_____, *Der erste Brief an die Thessalonicher.* ZB; Zürich: Theologischer Verlag, 1979.

_____, *Introduction to the New Testament: An Approach to its Problems.* Oxford: Blackwell, 1968.

_____, *Der zweite Thessalonicherbrief.* ZB; Zürich: Theologischer Verlag, 1982.

Masson, Charles, *Les deux Épîtres de Saint Paul aux Thessaloniciens.* CNT; Neuchâtel: Delachaux et Niestlé, 1957.

Mearns, Christopher L., "Early Eschatological Development in Paul: The Evidence of I and II Thessalonians," *NTS* 27 (1980-81) 137-157.

Meeks, Wayne A., *The First Urban Christians: the Social World of the Apostle Paul.* New Haven: Yale University, 1983.

_____, *The Moral World of the First Christians.* LEC 6; Philadelphia: Fortress, 1986.

_____, " 'Since Then You Would Need to Go Out of the World': Group Boundaries in Pauline Christianity," *Critical History and Biblical Faith: New Testament Perspectives,* ed. Thomas J. Ryan, 4-39. College Theology Society Annual Publication Series; Villanova, Pennsylvania: Villanova University, 1979.

_____, "Social Function of Apocalyptic Language in Pauline Christianity," *Apocalypticism in the Mediterranean World and the Near East. Proceedings of the International Colloquium on Apocalypticism. Uppsala, August 12-17, 1979,* ed. David Hellholm, 687-705. Tübingen: Mohr, 1983.

Metzger, Bruce M., *The Text of the New Testament.* Oxford: Oxford University, 1964.

_____, *A Textual Commentary on the Greek New Testament: A Companion Volume to the United Bible Societies' Greek New Testament (third edition).* New York: United Bible Societies, 1971.

Meyer, Ben F., *The Aims of Jesus.* London: SCM, 1979.

Milligan, George, St. *Paul's Epistles to the Thessalonians.* London: Macmillan, 1908.

Morris, Leon, *The First and Second Epistles to the Thessalonians: The English Text with Introduction, Exposition and Notes.* NICNT; Grand Rapids: Eerdmans, 1959.

_____, "Καὶ ῞Απαξ καὶ Δίς," *NovT* 1 (1956) 205-208.

Moule, Charles Francis Digby, *The Origin of Christology.* Cambridge: Cambridge University, 1977.

Munck, Johannes, *Paul and the Salvation of Mankind.* Richmond: John Knox, 1959.

Munro, Winsome, *Authority in Paul and Peter: The Identification of a Pastoral Stratum in the Pauline Corpus and 1 Peter.* SNTSMS 45; Cambridge: Cambridge University, 1983.

Nebe, G., *"Hoffnung" bei Paulus: Elpis und ihre Synonyme im Zusammenhang der Eschatologie.* SUNT 18; Göttingen: Vandenhoeck & Ruprecht, 1983.

Neil, William, *The Epistles of Paul to the Thessalonians.* MNTC; London: Hodder and Stoughton, 1950.

Nickle, Keith F., *The Collection: A Study in Paul's Strategy.* SBT 48; London: SCM, 1966.

O'Brien, Peter T., *Introductory Thanksgivings in the Letters of Paul.* NovTSup 49; Leiden: Brill, 1977.

Okeke, G. E., "I Thessalonians 2:13-16: The Fate of the Unbelieving Jews," *NTS* 27 (1980-81) 127-136.

Orchard, J. B., "Thessalonians and the Synoptic Gospels," *Bib* 19 (1938) 19-42.

Otzen, P., " 'Gute Hoffnung' bei Paulus," *ZNW* 49 (1958) 283-285.

Papazoglu, Fanoula, "Quelques aspects de l'histoire de la province de Macédoine," *ANRW* 2.7.1., ed. H. Temporini and W. Haase, 302-369. Berlin: de Gruyter, 1979.

Pearson, Birger A., "1 Thessalonians 2:13-16: A Deutero-Pauline Interpolation," *HTR* 64 (1971) 79-94.

Peel, M. L., "Gnostic Eschatology and the New Testament," *NovT* 19 (1970) 141-154.

Pereira de Queiros, Maria Isaura, "Messianic Myths and Movements," *Diogenes* 90 (1975) 78-99.

Petersen, Norman R., *Rediscovering Paul: Philemon and the Sociology of Paul's Narrative World*. Philadelphia: Fortress, 1985.

Pfitzner, V. C., *Paul and the Agon Motif*. NovTSup 16; Leiden: Brill, 1967.

Plevnik, Joseph, "1 Thess 5,1-11: Its Authenticity, Intention and Message," *Bib* 60 (1979) 71-90.

_____, "The Parousia as Implication of Christ's Resurrection (An Exegesis of 1 Thess 4,13-18)," *Word and Spirit: Essays in Honor of D. M. Stanley on his 60th Birthday*, ed. Joseph Plevnik, 199-277. Toronto: Regis College, 1975.

_____, "The Taking Up of the Faithful and the Resurrection of the Dead in 1 Thessalonians 4:13-18," *CBQ* 46 (1984) 274-283.

Price, S. R. F., *Rituals and Power: The Roman Imperial Cult in Asia Minor*. Cambridge: Cambridge University, 1984.

Refshauge, Ebba, "Literaerkritiske overvejelser: Til de to Thessalonikerbreve," *DTT* 34 (1971) 1-19.

Reicke, Bo, "Judaeo-Christianity and the Jewish Establishment, A.D. 33-66," *Jesus and the Politics of his Day*, ed. Ernst Bammel and Charles Francis Digby Moule, 145-152. London: SCM, 1984.

Rigaux, Béda, *Saint Paul: Les Épitres aux Thessaloniciens*. ÉBib; Paris: Gabalda, 1956.

_____, "Tradition et Rédaction dans 1 Th. V.1-10," *NTS* 21 (1974-75) 318-340.

The Road to Damascus: Kairos and Conversion. Johannesburg: Skotaville, 1989.

Robinson, J. Armitage, *St Paul's Epistle to the Ephesians*. London: Macmillan, 1909[2].

Sanders, Edward P., *Paul and Palestinian Judaism: A Comparison of Patterns of Religion*. London: SCM, 1977.

Sanders, Jack T., "The Transition from Opening Epistolary Thanksgiving to Body in Letters of the Pauline Corpus," *JBL* 81 (1962) 348-362.

Schillebeeckx, Eduard, *Jesus: An Experiment in Christology*. New York: Seabury, 1979.

Schippers, R., "The Pre-Synoptic Tradition in 1 Thessalonians II 13-16," *NovT* 8 (1966) 223-234.

Schmidt, Daryl, "The Authenticity of 2 Thessalonians: Linguistic Arguments," *SBLSP* 22 (1983) 289-296.

_____, "1 Thess 2:13-16: Linguistic Evidence for an Interpolation," *JBL* 102 (1983) 269-279.

Schmidt, Johann Ernst Christian, *Vermutungen über die beiden Briefe an die Thessalonicher*. Bibliothek für Kritik und Exegese des Neuen Testaments und ältesten Christengeschichte 2/3; Hadamar: Gelehrtenbuchhandlung, 1801.

Schmithals, Walter, *Paul and the Gnostics*. Nashville: Abingdon, 1972.

Schubert, Paul, *Form and Function of the Pauline Thanksgivings*. BZNW 20; Berlin: Töpelmann, 1939.

Schürer, Emil, *The History of the Jewish People in the Age of Jesus Christ (175 B.C.–A.D. 135)*, III/1 rev. and ed. G. Vermes, F. Millar, and M. Goodman. Edinburgh: Clark, 1986.

Schüssler Fiorenza, Elisabeth, *In Memory of Her: A Feminist Theological Reconstruction of Christian Origins*. New York: Crossroads, 1983.

Scroggs, Robin, *The Last Adam: A Study in Pauline Anthropology*. Oxford: Blackwell, 1966.

Sharot, Stephen, *Messianism, Mysticism, and Magic: A Sociological Analysis of Jewish Religious Movements*. Chapel Hill: University of North Carolina, 1982.

Snow, David A., and Cynthia L. Phillips, "The Lofland-Stark Conversion Model: A Critical Reassessment," *Social Problems* 27 (1979-80) 430-447.

Spicq, Ceslaus, *Les Épîtres pastorales*. ÉBib; Paris: Gabalda, 1947.

_____, "Les Thessaloniciens 'inquiets' etaient ils des paresseux?" *ST* 10 (1956) 1-13.

Stern, Menahem, "The Jewish Diaspora," *The Jewish People in the First Century: Historical Geography, Political History, Social, Cultural and Religious Life and Institutions*, ed. Samuel Safrai and Menahem Stern, 117-183. Compendia Rerum Iudaicarum ad Novum Testamentum 1; Philadelphia: Fortress, 1974.

Stowers, Stanley K., *Letter Writing in Greco-Roman Antiquity*. LEC 5; Philadelphia: Westminster, 1986.

_____, "The Social Sciences and the Study of Early Christianity," *Approaches to Ancient Judaism. Volume V: Studies in Judaism and Its Greco-Roman Context*, ed. William S. Green, 149-181. Brown Judaic Studies 32; Atlanta: Scholars Press, 1985.

_____, "Social Status, Public Speaking and Private Teaching: The Circumstances of Paul's Preaching Activity," *NovT* 26 (1984) 59-82.

Strelan, J. G., "Burden-Bearing and the Law of Christ: A Re-examination of Galatians 6:2," *JBL* 94 (1975) 266-276.

Strobel, A., *Untersuchungen zum eschatologischen Verzögerungsproblem auf Grund der spätjüdisch-urchristlichen Geschichte von Habakuk 2,2ff.* NovTSup 2; Leiden: Brill, 1961.

Talmon, Yonina, "Millenarian Movements," *Archives européennes de sociologie* 7 (1966) 159-200. = "Millenarism," *International Encyclopedia of the Social Sciences* X, ed. by D. L. Sills, 349-362. New York: Macmillan, 1968.

Theissen, Gerd, *The Social Setting of Pauline Christianity: Essays on Corinth*, ed. and trans. and with an Introduction by John H. Schütz. Philadelphia: Fortress, 1982.

Thurston, Robert W., "The Relationship between the Thessalonian Epistles," *ExpTim* 85 (1973-74) 52-56.

Tiede, David L., *The Charismatic Figure as Miracle Worker*. SBLDS 1; Missoula, Montana: Scholars Press, 1972.

Townsend, John T., "II Thessalonians 2:3-12," *SBLSP* 19 (1980) 233-250.

Trilling, Wolfgang, *Untersuchungen zum zweiten Thessalonischerbrief.* Leipzig: St. Benno, 1972.

_____, *Der zweite Brief an die Thessalonicher.* EKKNT 14; Zürich: Benziger, 1980.

Turner, Nigel, *A Grammar of New Testament Greek* (by James Hope Moulton), vol. III: *Syntax.* Edinburgh: Clark, 1963.

Vielhauer, Philipp, *Geschichte der urchristlichen Literatur: Einleitung in das Neue Testament, die Apokryphen und die Apostolischen Väter.* Berlin: W. de Gruyter, 1978².

Wanamaker, Charles A., "Apocalypticism at Thessalonica," *Neot* 21 (1987) 1-10.

_____, "A Case Against Justification by Faith," *JTSA* 42 (1983) 329-337.

Weiss, Johannes, *Earliest Christianity: A History of the Period A.D. 30-150,* vol. I, trans. and ed. Fredrick C. Grant. New York: Harper & Brothers, 1959 (1937).

Wengst, Klaus, *Christologische Formeln und Lieder des Urchristentums.* SNT 7; Gütersloh: Mohn, 1972.

Wenham, David, "Paul and the Synoptic Apocalypse," *Gospel Perspectives: Studies of History and Tradition in the Four Gospels,* vol. II, ed. Richard T. France and David Wenham, 345-375. Sheffield: JSOT, 1981.

West, J. C., "The Order of 1 and 2 Thessalonians," *JTS* 15 (1914) 66-74.

White, John L., *The Form and Function of the Body of the Greek Letter.* SBLDS 2; Missoula, Montana: Scholars, 1972.

_____, *Light from Ancient Letters.* Foundations and Facets; Philadelphia: Fortress, 1986.

Whittaker, Molly, *Jews and Christians: Graeco-Roman Views.* Cambridge Commentaries on Writings of the Jewish and Christian World 200 BC to AD 200; Cambridge: Cambridge University, 1984.

Wichmann, W., *Die Leidenstheologie: Eine Form der Leidensdeutung im Spätjudentum.* Stuttgart: Kohlhammer, 1930.

Wiles, Gordon P., *The Significance of the Intercessory Prayer Passages in the Letters of St Paul.* SNTSMS 24; Cambridge: Cambridge University, 1974.

Wilson, Bryan, *Religion in Sociological Perspective.* Oxford: Oxford University, 1982.

Witt, Rex E., "The Egyptian Cults in Ancient Macedonia," *Ancient Macedonia,* ed. B. Laourdas and C. Makaronas, I, 324-333. Thessaloniki: Institute for Balkan Studies, 1970.

_____, "The Kabeiroi in Ancient Macedonia," *Ancient Macedonia,* ed. B. Laourdas and C. Makaronas, II, 67-80. Thessaloniki: Institute for Balkan Studies, 1977.

Wrede, William, *Die Echtheit des zweiten Thessalonicherbrief untersucht.* Leipzig: Henrichs, 1903.

Wuellner, Wilhelm, "Greek Rhetoric and Pauline Argumentation," *Early Christian Literature and the Classical Intellectual Tradition. In Honorem Robert M. Grant,* ed. William R. Schoedel and Robert L. Wilken, 177-188. Théologie Historique 54; Paris: Beauchesne, 1979.

Zerwick, Maximilian, *Biblical Greek: Illustrated by Examples,* English edition by J. Smith. Rome: Scripta Pontificii Instituti Biblici, 1963.

INTRODUCTION

PAUL AND THE FOUNDING OF THE CHURCH AT THESSALONICA

THE HISTORY OF THESSALONICA TO THE TIME OF THE PAULINE MISSION

Thessalonica, modern-day Salonica, was founded around 315 BC by Cassander, the king of Macedonia. He named the city for his wife, Thessalonica, the half-sister of Alexander the Great. The city, built on the site of ancient Therme, was located at the head of the Gulf of Therme on the best natural harbor of the Aegean Sea (Elliger, *Paulus in Griechenland*, 78). This location made Thessalonica the chief port city for the whole of Macedonia. In Roman times its location was particularly important because it lay on the Via Egnatia, the main land route for both commerce and military movements between Asia Minor and the Adriatic port of Dyrrachium. Across the Adriatic Sea lay the port of Brundisium (modern-day Brindisi) and the Via Appia, which led directly to Rome. As a result of this strategic position Thessalonica was the largest and most important city of Macedonia in Roman times and served as the Roman provincial administrative center during those periods when Macedonia was a separate province, as it was at the time of Paul's mission to Thessalonica.

As a result of the support it lent to the Second Triumvirate in the civil war after Julius Caesar's murder, Thessalonica was made a free city in 42 BC by Marcus Antonius (Mark Antony). This had several important consequences, as Jewett (*Thessalonian Correspondence*, 123) observes. First, it meant that the city was given a degree of local autonomy, as well as the right to mint both its own and imperial coins (see Larsen, "Roman Greece," 449). Second, the city was promised freedom from military occupation and granted certain tax concessions. Third, it meant that the city did not become a Roman colony. This had two important effects: (1) *Ius Italicum*, which would have replaced local legal institutions, was not imposed, and (2) Thessalonica did not have to absorb a large settlement of demobilized Roman soldiers as happened at Philippi, Cassandra, and elsewhere. This naturally left the local ruling elite in control of the city with its traditional institutions intact.

Edson ("Macedonia," 133) has plausibly suggested that Thessalonica established the cult of the goddess Roma and the Benefactor Romans at this time in appreciation for its newly acquired status. This was clearly a political act on the part of those who controlled the city. They sought to cement the good relations with Rome that materially benefitted them. What is interesting to note is the close connection between political issues and religious practices: In the ancient world religion and politics were overtly linked because religion was recognized as a powerful force in legitimating the position of dominant groups within society.

Greece, and Macedonia in particular, bore much of the brunt of the Roman civil wars that raged from 44 to 31 BC, not only because a number of major battles were fought in the region but also because the various combatants recruited soldiers, requisitioned supplies for their troops, and ultimately pillaged in the area to supply themselves. After the turmoil, depredations, and depopulation of the civil war period, which ended with the victory of Octavian (Augustus) over the forces of Marcus Antonius and Cleopatra at Actium in 31 BC, Thessalonica, like the other cities of Macedonia, entered into a period of unparalleled peace and generally improving economic circumstances as commercial activity underwent considerable development (see Papazoglu, "Quelques aspects," 357; Larsen, "Roman Greece," 465). This situation continued well beyond the time of Paul.

By the time of Paul the population of Thessalonica was cosmopolitan. The original Macedonian population had long been assimilated with Greek immigrants from the south, giving the city a distinctively Greek character. In the period after Actium significant numbers of Latin-speaking people settled in Thessalonica, particularly merchants and imperial administrators. While we lack evidence except from the account in Acts 17 and some possible Jewish inscriptional evidence from a later period (see Schürer, *History* III/1, 66-68), it seems highly likely that a significant Jewish community existed at Thessalonica as in other major cities of the eastern Mediterranean in the early imperial period (Stern, "Jewish Diaspora," 114-117). The city's position as a port on the Via Egnatia, the main east-west land route between the Aegean and the Adriatic Seas, made it a natural commercial center for the province of Macedonia, as well as a major access point for the northern part of the Balkan Peninsula. Agriculture and timber were probably the main local products. Jewett (*Thessalonian Correspondence*, 121) suggests that mining products were also important to Thessalonica, but evidence for this is lacking in the imperial period, as Larsen indicates ("Roman Greece," 486-488).

Paul would have encountered a variety of religious competitors in Thessalonica. Acts 17 suggests that the Jewish community was one of the most serious competitors. But that Thessalonica was also rich in pagan religious cults is revealed even by his claim that the majority of his converts had been pagan worshippers (cf. 1 Thes. 1:9). Archaeological and inscriptional evidence indicates that Thessalonica had the usual complement of mystery cults, including those that had Dionysus, Sarapis, and Cabirus as their tutelary deities (see Edson, "Cults"; Donfried, "Cults"). The Dionysian and Cabirian cults were state-sponsored, as the likenesses of their deities on coins minted by the city indicate.

During the first century AD, the cult of Cabirus was becoming the chief city cult (see Hemberg, *Kabiren*, 205-210 on the Cabirus cult). It had the approval and patronage of the city's social elite or aristocracy—the wealthiest members of society (landowners, merchants, and traders) who were responsible for the day-to-day governance of the city. The city's aristocracy intended the cult to be a unifying force in the life of Thessalonica, giving a sense of common identity to all its citizens. To attack the cult and its deity was tantamount to an attack on the community itself and could result in mob violence (cf. MacMullen, *Roman Social Relations,* 66). Like other such cults throughout the Roman world it undoubtedly served the important social function of reinforcing the hierarchical character of the society. Honoring the noble god of the cult led the masses to honor the local nobles who demonstrated their largesse by providing for the cultic feasts and festivals, which played such an important role in civic life (MacMullen, *Paganism,* 59, cf. 172n.32; MacMullen bases this assertion on a remark by Plutarch in *Mor.* 822B).

Apart from the mystery cults and the cult to Roma and the Benefactor Romans, Thessalonica also embraced the imperial cult from a very early stage in the aftermath of Actium and the establishment of the Empire in 27 BC. Inscriptional evidence from the reign of Augustus shows that the offices of priest and ἀγωνοθέτης (president) of the Caesar cult, as well as a temple to Caesar, already existed during the time of Augustus (Edson, "Macedonia," 132). On the basis of numismatic evidence it is clear that the imperial cult began as a cult dedicated to Julius Caesar, whose head appears on a coin dating from perhaps as early as 29-28 BC (Edson, *loc. cit.*). On this coin Caesar is designated as god and on the reverse a head of Augustus appears with the city's legend. This clearly relates Augustus (the adopted son of Julius Caesar) to his deified adoptive father and implies the status of *divi filius* (son of the deified), a designation adopted by Augustus for himself. This title with the status it gave to its bearer came to play an important role in the imperial cult (cf. Donfried, "Cults," 346).

Politically, the establishment of the imperial cult made good sense because it cemented Thessalonica's relations with Rome and the emerging imperial order. But Price (*Rituals and Power,* 239-248) has demonstrated that the founding of imperial cults in the Greek east had a more fundamental significance: It served as a means of defining the relation of power existing between the emperor and his subjects through the use of the traditional Greek symbolic system, which represented power as divine in origin. The importance of this becomes clear when we recognize that any attack on the imperial cult, which persisted from the time of Augustus until the Constantinian period,

5

threatened the carefully constructed symbolic order mediating Roman imperial power to the social order of the city where the cult had been established. This was clearly a danger that a missionary like Paul who propagated an alien religion like Christianity needed to guard against in the Greek cities of the Roman Empire. As we will see later, this may help explain the difficulties experienced by the Christian community in Thessalonica.

PAUL'S MISSION AT THESSALONICA

The Acts Account

We have only two major sources of information regarding the Pauline mission at Thessalonica: the two letters to the church from Paul and his co-missionaries Silvanus and Timothy, and the account of the founding of the church in Acts 17:1-10. According to the Acts narrative, after he was expelled by the city magistrates at Philippi, Paul came to Thessalonica by way of Amphipolis and Apollonia, which lay on the Via Egnatia between Philippi and Thessalonica. Acts reports that he began his mission in Thessalonica by entering the Jewish synagogue on the sabbath according to his usual practice. For three sabbaths he reasoned with the people in the synagogue, seeking to prove from the OT that the messiah must suffer and die (an idea that was not a standard belief among Jews of the time) before being raised from the dead by God. This argument was then presumably linked to the historical facts regarding Jesus' life in order to demonstrate that Jesus was the messiah. The account suggests that Paul's primary success was among the God-fearers, Gentiles who attached themselves to the synagogue, participated in Jewish worship, and observed to varying degrees Jewish purity and ritual practices. (See Schürer, *History* III/1, 150-176 on the God-fearers and their relationship to Judaism.) Acts 17:4 suggests that it was leading Gentile women of the city in particular who were attracted to the Christian message. Luke portrays Paul's success as leading to jealousy in the Jewish community, a theme which recurs on several occasions in Acts (see 13:45, 50; 14:19; 18:12-17). According to 17:5 the Jews incited the city rabble against Paul and his fellow Christians. When they were unable to find Paul, a Christian named Jason, who appears from the Acts account to have been Paul's patron, and other unnamed Christians were hauled before the politarchs, the local officials responsible for the administration of the city. Jason and his fellow believers were accused of disturbing the general peace and acting against the decrees of Caesar by claiming that there was another king, Jesus. This charge naturally troubled the city officials who took security from Jason and the others to ensure that they would keep the peace. Immediately following this episode Paul and Silas (Silvanus of the Pauline letters) were promptly smuggled out of town and sent on their way to Beroea.

The Acts account is not without certain difficulties. Luke appears to have condensed the details of Paul and his fellow missionaries' stay at Thessalonica. On the surface Acts 17:1-10 suggests that Paul and Silas left after only three sabbaths. 1 Thes. 2:9 gives the impression, however, that Paul was located at Thessalonica long enough to establish himself in his trade and provide the Christians there with a model for their behavior. A period of three or four weeks hardly seems sufficient for this, and in any case in Phil. 4:15f. Paul mentions that the church at Philippi sent financial aid more than once while he was at Thessalonica. It seems unlikely that the stay of three sabbaths implied in Acts 17, even if it had stretched to four weeks, would have necessitated or even allowed time for such active support, given the distances involved (approximately 150 kilometers).

Another difficulty is that the narrative in Acts places the focus of Paul's missionary work solely on the synagogue, where he supposedly converted a number of God-fearers. In neither 1 nor 2 Thessalonians does Paul indicate that he preached in the synagogue. Hock (*Social Context*, 37-42) has shown that the workshop was very probably one of the key places from which Paul conducted his missionary work, a point confirmed by 1 Thes. 2:9. Another factor weighing against the possibility that the majority of Paul's converts came from the already existing group of Gentile God-fearers who identified with the Jewish synagogue is that Paul says to the Thessalonian Christians, "You turned to God from idols" (1 Thes. 1:9). Such a remark would seem inappropriate if the majority of his Gentile converts had already turned their backs on pagan religious practices by affiliating with the Jewish synagogue. Moreover, if the majority of Paul's converts had come from the synagogue, it would be indeed strange that Paul makes no direct reference to the OT at any point in either 1 or 2 Thessalonians. Even when he builds an argument from the OT, as he does in 2 Thes. 1:6-12, he gives no indication of the source of his argument. At the very least Marshall (p. 5) is correct when he maintains that the Gentiles, including pagan Gentiles, constituted a larger grouping in the church than Acts would appear to suggest.

A further question sometimes raised in regard to the Acts report concerns the source of the trouble which drove Paul out of Thessalonica. Haenchen (*Acts,* 513), following Loisy, asks whether or not a person reading 1 Thessalonians without knowing the Acts report would conclude that the Jewish community at Thessalonica was responsible for persecuting the Christians there. Acts 17:5 blames the jealousy of the Jewish community for the trouble at Thessalonica. 1 Thes. 2:14, on the other hand, places responsibility for the persecution on the Thessalonians' fellow citizens. This difference between Acts and Paul's words, however, should not be overplayed. Acts 17:5 does after all imply that the public acts of opposition were conducted by non-Jews, and Paul for his part immediately connects the problems experienced by the Thessalonians with the persecution suffered by Judean Christians at the hands of their fellow Jews. Paul's reference to the situation certainly does not preclude a certain degree of Jewish involvement, and 1 Thes. 2:15 may even indicate that it was Jewish opposition which forced Paul to leave Thessalonica (Malherbe, *Paul and the Thessalonians,* 62). One further point should be borne in mind: Paul and his converts presumably were not immune to Jewish opposition, as 2 Cor. 11:24 demonstrates. Without this verse we would never have known this from the Pauline letters themselves; thus we should not be too hasty in rejecting some Jewish involvement in the troubles which emerged at Thessalonica. I will return to the question of the opposition experienced at Thessalonica later.

The Character of Paul's Mission

One important point needs to be made from the outset regarding the Pauline mission. Paul did not carry out his missionary work alone; rather he operated with a small team of coworkers. This is why many of Paul's letters are addressed from himself together with one or more missionary colleagues (cf. 1 Cor. 1:1; 2 Cor. 1:1; Phil. 1:1). In 1 and 2 Thessalonians three people are mentioned: Paul, Silvanus, and Timothy. Given the use of the first person plural in passages like 1 Thes. 2:1-12 that refer to the actual mission at Thessalonica, we must assume that Silvanus, who is referred to in Acts 17:4 as Silas, and Timothy, who is not mentioned in the Acts report of the work in Thessalonica, were coworkers with Paul in the founding of the church there. While Timothy was clearly subordinate to Paul, as his role as emissary for the apostle indicates (cf. 1 Thes. 3:1-6), Silvanus was probably considered a peer of Paul in the missionary enterprise. He may in fact have gone with Paul as the official representative of the mother church at Jerusalem. Certainly nothing in the Pauline letters indicates that Silvanus did Paul's bidding in the way that Timothy did. Thus when we think of the Pauline mission to Thessalonica we must see it as a team effort. Paul may have been the dominant personality, but Silvanus was his equal, at least in terms of status (see comments on 1 Thes. 1:1, pp. 68f.).

The Acts account of the mission is probably correct in suggesting that Paul began by preaching in the synagogue. However, the large number of pagans who seem to have converted to Christianity at Thessalonica according to 1 Thes. 1:9 would not have been reached by this means. As suggested above, the workshop formed one locus of missionary activity outside the synagogue. The workshop of an artisan was commonly a place for intellectual discourse, and in fact Hock (*Social Context,* 38-41) shows that at the time of Paul it was so used by Cynic philosophers. As Paul and his colleagues largely supported themselves in their missionary work at Thessalonica (1 Thes. 2:9; 2 Thes. 3:8), it is reasonable to assume that much of Paul's time was spent in a small shop where people interested in his message could come and talk with him while he worked at his trade.

8

The homes of some of his converts and sympathizers formed another possible site of missionary activity. Stowers ("Social Status," 65-68) has demonstrated that private homes were an important arena in antiquity for teaching and other forms of intellectual discourse. He has further suggested that they provided Paul with a degree of legitimacy and security for his missionary work which was not available to him in more public forums such as marketplaces and synagogues. The fact that Paul's churches were formed around households (cf. 1 Cor. 16:15; Rom. 16:23) provides strong evidence for Stowers's contention. In the case of Thessalonica, where the majority of Paul's converts came from outside the synagogue, it seems probable that the household of someone like Jason, who is specifically mentioned in Acts 17:5, served as a forum for Paul's missionary preaching and teaching.

Acts 17 indicates that Paul's message to his synagogue audience concerned the Jewish messiah, Jesus, whom he claimed had died and been raised from the dead according to the Jewish scriptures. Preaching to a Jewish audience that the messiah had come was entirely appropriate, even if it did require proof since the fate of Jesus did not correspond to normal messianic expectations. This message, however, was inappropriate for a Gentile audience having no contact or sympathy with the Jewish community. Not surprisingly, therefore, the gospel that Paul proclaimed to the largely pagan audience in Thessalonica had a different character from his proclamation in a synagogue context.

According to the apostle's own account of his mission to the Thessalonians in 1 Thes. 1:9f., his converts "turned to God from idols to serve the living and true God and to await God's son from heaven, whom God raised from the dead, Jesus the one saving us from the coming wrath." If this is what the Christians at Thessalonica were converted to, then we may reasonably assume that it reflects the major components of Paul's preaching to them.[1] Three points stand out.

First, Paul proclaimed the monotheistic faith which he had inherited from Judaism. In this respect his preaching probably did not differ significantly from the message of other Hellenistic Jewish missionaries of the period (see Dalbert, *Theologie der hellenistisch jüdischen Missionsliteratur*; Bussmann, *Themen*).

Second, as we would expect, he proclaimed the death and resurrection of Jesus, but probably not as the fulfillment of Jewish expectations. Pagan Gentiles would hardly have been interested in a Jewish messiah.

---

1. 1 Thes. 1:9-10 is widely regarded as a typical extract from mission preaching to pagans in the Hellenistic world (see Malherbe, *Paul and the Thessalonians*, 30), but see Holtz (" 'Euer Glaube' ") and the comments below on these verses for criticism of this view. Rom. 1:18-32 adds considerably to the outline found in 1 Thes. 1:9-10 and probably reflects the normal content of Paul's preaching to pagans.

Third, and perhaps most interestingly, the significance of Jesus was explained in terms of deliverance from impending divine judgment against the ungodliness and wickedness that characterized the present age. In other words, eschatological salvation from imminent divine judgment formed a key part of Paul's mission preaching. In light of recent studies that have stressed the apocalyptic character of all of Paul's thought (such as Baumgarten, *Paulus und die Apokalyptik*; Beker, *Paul the Apostle*), it should come as no surprise that an apocalyptic worldview played a major role in Paul's missionary preaching. The essence of Paul's apocalyptic worldview consisted in his belief that he lived at the end of the present age of rebellion from God, that God had acted decisively to bring about eschatological or end-time salvation in Jesus Christ, and that soon the Lord Jesus Christ himself would come from heaven to render judgment to the wicked and to consummate salvation for the elect of God.

The importance of this component in Paul's preaching at Thessalonica becomes clear when we recognize that over a quarter of 1 Thessalonians and nearly half of 2 Thessalonians deal with problems and issues regarding the parousia or coming of Christ from heaven. This has led Meeks ("Social Function," 689-695) and Jewett (*Thessalonian Correspondence*, 161-178; cf. Wanamaker, "Apocalypticism") to portray the Pauline mission at Thessalonica as a "millenarian movement," a term used by social scientists, particularly anthropologists. Gager (*Kingdom and Community*, 21) lists five principal characteristics of millenarian movements that can be correlated with aspects of Pauline Christianity: (1) belief in imminent salvation (1 Thes. 1:9f.; 1 Cor. 7:29-31), (2) belief that the present social order will be transformed (Gal. 6:14f.; Rom. 8:18-23; 1 Cor. 7:29-31), (3) release of emotional energy (Gal. 3:5; 1 Cor. 12:4-11; 14:1-5), (4) brevity of the movement's existence (this is more difficult to demonstrate, but it is widely agreed that the apocalyptic outlook of Paul was largely replaced in the second and third generation of Christianity), and (5) the central role of a prophetic figure who articulates the new set of beliefs and practices (in this sense Paul was clearly a prophet).

The object of Paul's missionary preaching and teaching was twofold. He sought to gain converts to the distinctively Christian beliefs and behavior patterns which he proclaimed, and then he sought to form his converts into a new community in order to provide them with a context in which their new faith and commitment to God could develop and mature. Both of these aspects of Paul's mission deserve further comment.

In considering how Paul managed to convert pagans to the Christian way of life several factors need to be given attention. First, why would pagan Thessalonians be interested in becoming Christians, especially in light of the fact that doing so obviously created tensions between them and their fellow citizens (cf. 1 Thes. 1:6; 2:14)? Although we lack detailed knowledge of the social and psychological situation of the Thessalonian Christians in their pre-Christian days, recent studies into millenarian movements offer help at this point. Social scientists have shown that people who are attracted to movements promising imminent salvation and the transformation of the present social order, as Pauline Christianity did, are often predisposed to do so by their social situation (Talmon, "Millenarian Movements," 181-192). Perhaps the most important of these factors is what Burridge (*New Heaven*, 13) calls "dissatisfaction with the current system." This arises when a negative discrepancy exists between people's legitimate expectations or past situation and their current experience within society. Aberle ("Note," 209) calls this "relative deprivation," since it is based on people's perceived sense of deprivation rather than their experience of absolute deprivation. A wide variety of factors such as political oppression, economic hardship, social disorder, low status, or a feeling that the current social and symbolic system has lost its meaning may precipitate a sense of dissatisfaction in individuals and groups within a given society. It is this which makes them open to suggestions that the existing social order with its values, means of measuring success, and structures of power will be overthrown in the near future and replaced by a new order in which they will occupy favored positions at the expense of those who hold such positions in the existing social order.

Meeks (*First Urban Christians*, 173f.) has suggested that Paul's converts were attracted to the new millenarian form of religion which he espoused because they suffered from status inconsistency. By this he means that those members of the Pauline communities about whom we have information regarding their socio-economic status (those with relatively greater wealth and status) show signs that their "achieved status" (wealth and/or power that they gained in their own right) was greater than their "attributed status" (the social position which they were thought to occupy by their contemporaries; cf. Meeks, 73). Meeks thinks that their experience of status inconsistency made them receptive to the apocalyptic or millenarian message of Paul because their social experience created cognitive dissonance.[2] According to Meeks (174), people suffering from the emotional distress of status inconsistency,

> who find themselves in an ambiguous relation to hierarchical structures, might be receptive to symbols of the world as itself out of joint and on the brink of radical transformation. They might be attracted to a group that undertook to model its own life on that new picture of reality.

2. Cognitive dissonance theory is used in social psychology to refer to mental distress arising from contradictions between one's deeply held beliefs and/or expectations and the actual state of affairs. The theory postulates that when such contradictions exist the individual or group experiencing the dissonance must find some way to overcome it. The theory was originally developed by Festinger, Riecken, and Schachter (*When Prophecy Fails*; see also Festinger, *Theory of Cognitive Dissonance*).

Cutler

The cognitive dissonance theory tentatively put forward by Meeks is problematic for explaining the situation at Thessalonica and why people there were attracted to Christianity. We have almost no information about individuals at Thessalonica on which to base conclusions regarding their possible status inconsistency. Besides this, even 1 Corinthians, from which most of the evidence on status inconsistency is drawn, would not support the idea that a majority of people in the Corinthian congregation were suffering from cognitive dissonance induced by status inconsistency or from falling status caused by a deteriorating economic position. At an analytical level, Meeks's use of cognitive dissonance theory is of little value because of imprecision in formulating its relevance to the specific situation at Thessalonica. Moreover, as Stowers ("Social Sciences," 170f.) has pointed out, the theory itself is of dubious worth since it "obscures all of the critical questions about beliefs, intentions, and motives" and in the end is "muddled and incoherent."

Jewett (*Thessalonian Correspondence*, 165-168), who also understands Pauline Christianity at Thessalonica in millenarian terms, offers an alternative explanation of why some Thessalonians were attracted to the Christian faith. Building on research into the Cabirus cult, the most popular mystery cult among the Thessalonians (see especially Edson, "Cults"; Hemberg, *Kabiren*; Evans, *Eschatology and Ethics*; Witt, "Egyptian Cults," "Kabeiroi"), Jewett postulates that its co-optation into the civic cult during the first century may have "resulted in emptying it of the power to provide solace for handworkers facing economic and social pressure under Roman rule" (*op. cit.,* 165). The transformation of what had been a popular cult offering protection and aid to the poor into a civic cult controlled by the city's ruling elite may well have left some lower-class devotees of Cabirus with a sense of frustration and loss as their special protector came to be identified with those from whom they needed protection. This in turn may have made them open to the apocalyptic Christ proclaimed by Paul, because, as Jewett (128) has shown, a structural similarity existed between the Cabirus figure and the Christ as proclaimed by Paul. Two of the similarities are particularly worth mentioning. Cabirus, like Christ, was a martyred hero who on occasion returned to life to aid his followers, and worship of Cabirus apparently involved an initiation process in which sins were confessed and the initiates were cleansed through baptism in water and "symbolic immersion in the blood of the martyred god" (Jewett, 129). Thus the frustration of the laboring classes at the co-optation of their tutelary deity and the similarities of the religion proclaimed by Paul probably made Christianity an attractive alternative, at least for some pagan Thessalonians. As Jewett (165f.) puts it:

> The expectation of a returning Cabirus who would aid the poor and defend them against their oppressors was transformed and revitalized in the new and more compelling form of Christ who was present in the congregation as their

12

redeemer and the source of their ecstasy, and who was also proclaimed as coming again in wrath against the wicked.

Jewett (167) notes one other important factor which may have predisposed the Thessalonians to Paul's apocalyptic eschatology. He draws on the work of Pereira de Queiros ("Messianic Myths"), who has observed that modern-day messianic movements in Brazil and other places often originate among a "pariah people," that is, a marginalized group within a society. A "pariah people" experiences oppression and believes that its grievances cannot be righted by the existing socio-economic system in which polarization and stratification are occurring as a result of colonization. Of particular interest to Jewett is Pereira de Queiros's claim that an important condition associated with the emergence of messianic movements is the social polarization of a society previously based on family connections.

Jewett finds a close correlation between this and the Thessalonian situation. Originally Thessalonica had been created by amalgamating a number of villages which continued to keep their separate identities in the new city over a long period of time. Jewett assumes that the original structure of the city lent itself to the preservation of family and clan ties as they had existed in the villages. But in the imperial period, during which Paul lived, the social fabric of Thessalonica began to alter dramatically with the arrival of Roman officials and Latin and Greek immigrants who came for commercial reasons. Jewett suggests that in this situation some of the families who had long-standing roots in the city were socially dispossessed and unable to gain access to the new social elite. In such a situation the promise of an alternative world soon to emerge, as proclaimed by Paul, would have proved particularly attractive to people who were not successfully competing against new arrivals.

Although Jewett's views of the factors predisposing the Thessalonians to accept the apocalyptic message announced by Paul and his colleagues cannot be confirmed from 1 and 2 Thessalonians, they have considerably more plausibility than those of Meeks. This is so because Jewett roots the Pauline mission in the known socio-religious environment of Thessalonica and in social processes that were occurring at the time. If Jewett's views are accepted, it would help to explain why 1 and 2 Thessalonians are more clearly dominated by apocalyptic themes than any of Paul's other extant writings. That is to say, the situation at Thessalonica enabled and perhaps required Paul to emphasize those apocalyptic features of early Christianity, such as the return of the martyred Lord from heaven, which correlated with the pre-Christian religious outlook of his converts and addressed their feelings of alienation from the dominant society.

Even without Jewett's attempt at concretizing the millenarian hypothesis at Thessalonica, we are still obligated to posit a millenarian situation because of what we know about the Christianity that emerged at Thessalonica from the Pauline letters to the Christians there. Although we can never be certain about the specific factors predisposing the Thessalonians to accept Paul's apocalyptic eschatology, that they did, in the face of considerable opposition and disapproval from their fellow citizens (1 Thes. 2:14), indicates that they were fundamentally dissatisfied with their situation (see Wanamaker, "Apocalypticism," 4f.).

While those Thessalonians who became Christians were probably predisposed to the type of message announced by Paul and his colleagues because of their social circumstances, this does not actually help us in understanding how conversion took place or, put somewhat differently, what constituted conversion. In the first place Paul clearly saw the hand of God in the conversion of the Thessalonians. Thus he reminds them that the gospel was not communicated to them merely in spoken words, but also with divine power and the Holy Spirit. When they became followers of Christ they did so with great joy given by the Spirit (1 Thes. 1:4-6). At the same time, however, a careful reading of the Thessalonian correspondence reveals another dimension to the conversion of the Thessalonians of which Paul himself seems to have been aware.

Recent studies of the phenomenon of conversion have stressed that in all but the most exceptional cases conversion is not an instantaneous decision for some alternative belief system, but a socio-psychological process whereby an individual is inducted into a new social world with its own particular beliefs and practices (Lofland and Stark, "Becoming a World-saver"; Heirich, "Changes of Heart,"; Snow and Phillips, "Lofland-Stark Conversion Model"). Berger and Luckmann (*Social Construction*, 176-182), among others, refer to conversion as a process of resocialization because it usually consists of an individual becoming engaged with a new set of significant others who possess an alternative understanding of life and participate in an alternative social world with its own distinctive knowledge, roles, values, and attitudes. Conversion occurs when an individual is inducted into an alternative social world through a process of socialization that on the one hand undermines or symbolically annihilates the social world from which he or she has come and on the other replaces it with the new one of the group into which the person is being inducted. This is precisely what happened to the Thessalonians under the guidance of Paul and his fellow missionaries.

Paul, Silvanus, and Timothy belonged to the Christian social world with its distinctive beliefs about God and Christ, its ethical values, and its alternative social structures centering on the community of faith, the Church. Through their preaching and Christian lifestyle the missionaries went about making this world meaningful for their prospective converts and inducting them into it. At the same time they symbolically destroyed the world out of which their converts had come. For example, the language in 1 Thes. 5:4-9 about "children of the dark and of the night" who are destined to suffer the

14

wrath of God constituted a symbolic annihilation of the Thessalonians' pre-Christian experience. On the other hand, the language about the "children of light and of the day" served to confirm the Christian way of life as that which would lead to salvation for the followers of Christ at Thessalonica.

Although socialization and resocialization are clearly modern analytical categories, there is evidence within 1 Thessalonians itself to indicate that Paul had a clear grasp of the phenomena of conversion as a resocialization process. Perhaps the clearest evidence is in 1 Thes. 2:1-12, where Paul reminds his readers of the character of his apostolic ministry to them. In vv. 11f. Paul claims that he and his associates treated the Thessalonians "like a father treats his own children." The patriarchal father in the ancient world took responsibility for the moral instruction and behavior of his offspring (cf. 1 Cor. 4:14) and, in theory at least, assumed the leading role in socializing his children into the socio-economic, religious, and cultural way of life to which they were born. In 1 Thes. 2:11f. Paul acknowledges that he played just such a role toward the Thessalonians with regard to the new beliefs, the new way of life, and the new social world of Christian existence to which they were converted. V. 12 states that the readers had been called by God into the divine dominion, into the social world where God's will and rule operate. By implication they had been called out of their previous social world, where God's authority was not accepted (cf. 5:1-11). Three participles, παρακαλοῦντες, παραμυθούμενοι, and μαρτυρόμενοι, are used by Paul in v. 11 to describe his fatherly activity. They refer respectively to his exhortation to adopt the Christian way of life which he described and exhibited to them, to his comforting them in their tribulation by explaining its significance and purpose within the framework of the Christian worldview, and to his insistence that they think and act like Christians at all times. By doing these things, as a father would for his own children, Paul and his fellow missionaries resocialized the pagan Thessalonians into the Christian understanding and world of experience.

Alongside the activity of making converts among the Thessalonians, Paul and his coworkers engaged in another related task, that of building a community. Without a community to reinforce the new beliefs and values and to encourage proper Christian behavior and practice, it is unlikely that Paul's converts would have survived as Christians. The importance of Christian community cannot be overestimated. Gager (*Kingdom and Community*, 129-132, 140) argues that it was the sense of community with its implications for "absolute and exclusive loyalty," and its concern "for every aspect of the believer's life" that gave Christianity the decisive edge over all of its religious competitors, with the obvious exception of Judaism, from which Christianity derived its radical sense of community. Unlike Judaism, however, Christianity was inclusive rather than exclusive, that is, it was open to outsiders, who were freely welcomed into the community to participate on equal terms with everyone else (cf. Gal. 3:28).

15

The process of community formation is indeed a complex matter to which I can give only brief attention. Perhaps the most important contribution of Paul to the formation of the Christian community in Thessalonica was that he gave converts a new sense of identity as Christians. This was accomplished at a symbolic level by what Meeks (*First Urban Christians*, 84-96) terms "the language of separation," that is, symbolic annihilation of their previous world-view, and "the language of belonging." The language of separation occurs with regularity in the Thessalonian correspondence (1 Thes. 1:9; 4:5, 7, 12, 13; 5:5f.; 2 Thes. 1:7f.; 2:11f.; 3:6, 14f.) and serves in a negative way to mark the boundary between those who belong to the Christian community and those who do not, thereby encouraging the new Christian identity. Similarly, the language of belonging is also prominent in the Thessalonian correspondence (1 Thes. 1:4; 2:12; 5:5; 2 Thes. 1:11-12; 2:6, 13-15; 3:16) and functions positively to reinforce converts in their identity as members of the new community. Building the community at the symbolic level by creating a Christian identity among converts, including the idea that they constituted a new family, whence the language about love of the brothers (and sisters; cf. 1 Thes. 3:12; 4:9f.), was matched at a practical level by the ethical requirement that converts demonstrate their love and commitment to one another in their actions (cf. 1 Thes. 4:1-11; 5:12-15; 2 Thes. 3:14f.).

By the time Paul and his colleagues left Thessalonica they had formed their converts into a community capable of carrying on the process of evangelization and community-building that they had begun, even in the face of serious opposition. This of course did not mean that Paul had no further worries about them. Paul and his coworkers, it would appear, were forced to leave Thessalonica under duress. This seems to be the implication of 1 Thes. 2:17, where he chooses the term ἀπορφανισθέντες ("being made orphans") to describe his separation from his converts. Best (124) points out that the term connotes a forced separation as opposed to a voluntary one. Judging by what Paul says in 3:1-3, it would appear that he left at a time when the community was suffering from external pressure, and it is reasonable to assume that this was an important factor in his withdrawal, as Acts 17:5-10 suggests. Paul did not consider his task complete at the time of his departure. By sending Timothy as his emissary and through his written communications Paul sought to continue the process of resocialization and community-building which he had begun during his stay in Thessalonica (cf. Holmberg, *Paul and Power*, 80f.). I will discuss below (pp. 53-63) Paul's continuing relations with the church at Thessalonica and the historical setting of the Thessalonian correspondence.

LITERARY QUESTIONS REGARDING 1 AND 2 THESSALONIANS

In the modern period a number of literary questions have been debated with respect to 1 and 2 Thessalonians. Here I will focus on four issues. Perhaps the most debated question at present is that of the authenticity of 2 Thessalonians, though there is also considerable contention about the literary integrity and unity of both letters. A third issue, which in my opinion has received far too little serious attention, is that of the sequence of the letters. Also to be considered are recent efforts to analyze the letters using ancient rhetorical theory. As the question of authenticity is currently the most vexed area of debate, I will begin with it.

THE QUESTION OF AUTHENTICITY

The Nineteenth-Century Debate

Although Pauline authorship of 1 Thessalonians was occasionally questioned in the nineteenth century, particularly by F. C. Baur and his school of NT criticism,[1] no contemporary scholars of repute seem to doubt the authentic Pauline character of the letter. The same, however, is certainly not true of 2 Thessalonians, and in fact in the last two decades the balance of expressed opinion has tilted decisively against the authenticity of 2 Thessalonians.

The first scholar to question the Pauline origin of 2 Thessalonians as we have the letter appears to have been J. E. C. Schmidt in his essay *Vermutungen über die beiden Briefe an die Thessalonicher,* written around 1800. Schmidt thought that 2 Thes. 2:1-12 was an interpolation into an otherwise authentic letter. He based this conclusion on two considerations. First, an apparent contradiction exists between the eschatological expectation found in 2 Thes. 2:1-12, which posits a sequence of events before the parousia of Christ, and 1 Thes. 4:13–5:11, which concerns the sudden occurrence of the parousia.

---

1. For a survey of the nineteenth-century debate regarding the authenticity of 1 Thessalonians see Rigaux, 120-124.

Schmidt also found the Antichrist fantasy in 2:1-12 un-Pauline in character. His thesis lacks credibility, however, because if 2:1-12 is removed from the letter as an interpolation, then the letter becomes nothing more than an empty shell.

Schmidt's claim that tension exists between the eschatological expectations of 1 Thessalonians and 2 Thessalonians has been a recurring feature of the argument for inauthenticity ever since his day (cf. Masson, 7; Marxsen, *Introduction*, 42f.; Hughes, *Early Christian Rhetoric*, 81-83). This position is, however, untenable on several accounts. In the first place, the early Christians were perfectly capable of juxtaposing their belief in the sudden parousia of Christ (1 Thes. 5:1-11) with signs of its coming (2 Thes. 2:3-12), as Mk. 13:14-37 conclusively demonstrates. Second, much of the seeming contradiction in eschatological expectation between the two letters is based on a failure to grasp the function of 2 Thes. 2:3-12 and the meaning of 1 Thes. 5:1-4.

2 Thes. 2:3-12 was not intended to list events expected to precede the day of the Lord, as though an eschatological timetable were available to predict when the day could be expected.[2] Rather it served as a proof that the day of the Lord, which some at Thessalonica seem to have thought had come (2:2), had not yet occurred. Neither does 1 Thes. 5:1-4 teach that the day of the Lord was to come suddenly and unexpectedly for the Thessalonian Christians, contrary to what is commonly said (cf. Hughes, *Early Christian Rhetoric*, 81). On careful inspection it teaches that the day of the Lord was to come suddenly on *those who were not Christians* (vv. 2f.). At the same time, however, the text makes clear that Paul's converts were not ignorant about the coming of Christ's parousia (vv. 1, 4). They knew enough about "the times and seasons" (v. 1) to ensure that it would not overtake them "like a thief" (v. 4). This suggests strongly that they knew how and when to anticipate the parousia of Christ.

The debate begun by Schmidt was taken a step forward with the work of Kern ("2. Thess 2,1-12," published in 1839). He maintained that 2 Thessalonians showed signs of literary dependence on 1 Thessalonians and argued that 2 Thes. 3:17 was an attempt by a forger to gain acceptance for his work.

---

2. Hughes (*Early Christian Rhetoric*, 58) develops a four-stage timetable:

1. "now": Restraint; 2. "first": Rebellion; 3. "then": Revelation of the Man of Lawlessness; 4. (immediately upon #3): Appearance of Jesus to destroy the Man of Lawlessness.

This timetable is at one major point incorrect and in general is misleading. The writer of 2 Thes. 2:3f. does not say "first rebellion, and *then* the revelation of the lawless one." He speaks of the rebellion and the manifestation of the lawless one as one complex event. Since this complex event is immediately followed by the parousia, the readers are not given a useful timetable for discerning the signs of the time in vv. 3-8, nor is there any reason to conclude that the parousia is being delayed by the necessity of a series of events taking place. Only one complex event precedes the day of the Lord, and it precedes it immediately.

The arguments of Kern against the Pauline authorship of 2 Thessalonians were accepted as normative for much of the remainder of the nineteenth century (Kümmel, *Introduction,* 261).

From Wrede to Trilling

While the issue of authenticity was widely discussed both by those who favored it and by those who rejected it in the wake of Kern's work (see Rigaux, 124-128 on the debate), the next major contribution to the debate came from Wrede *(Echtheit).* His work dominated the debate from its appearance until Trilling's monograph appeared in 1972. Taking his cue from a brief essay by Holtzmann ("Zweite Thessalonicherbrief"), which had sought to apply the methods of literary criticism to the problem of authenticity, Wrede focused attention on the literary relationship between 1 and 2 Thessalonians. Accepting the Pauline authorship of 1 Thessalonians, he argued that 2 Thessalonians shows slavish dependence on it, covering the same themes in almost identical order and mirroring the literary style of the first letter right down to verbal repetition. He concluded that the similarity of 2 Thessalonians to 1 Thessalonians, a similarity greater than between any other two Pauline letters, could only be explained by deliberate forgery.

Wrede then went a step further by attempting to locate the *Sitz im Leben* of the supposed forgery. He claimed, without much evidence, that sometime after the death of Paul, probably between AD 100 and 110, 2 Thessalonians was written to overcome a false understanding of eschatology. He believed that this error, which maintained that the day of the Lord had already come (2 Thes. 2:2), had arisen from an incorrect interpretation of 1 Thes. 5:1-11. The forger, according to Wrede, sought to discredit 1 Thessalonians as a Pauline letter and to replace its faulty eschatological perspective with what he believed to be the true Pauline perspective on eschatology. From Wrede's point of view 2 Thes. 2:2 and 3:17 were intended to inculpate 1 Thessalonians as a forgery.

Wrede's proposal regarding the origin of the forgery is improbable, however, because there is no evidence for a resurgence of imminent eschatological expectation at the beginning of the second century. As Jewett (*Thessalonian Correspondence,* 6) has pointed out, this places a question mark beside his case for inauthenticity since any "forgery theory is credible only if it succeeds in placing a document in a period that corresponds with the views and issues revealed therein." It is also difficult to see how 1 Thes. 5:1-11, which after all is part of the eschatological discussion begun in 4:13, could ever have led anyone to conclude that the day of the Lord had already come. In addition, Best (53f.) has pointed out that the structural similarities between 1 and 2 Thessalonians are not as great as Wrede supposed and that the cumulative value of the minor points of similarity found by him are also less than totally convincing. As I will show later, the rhetorical genre and structure of the two letters is fundamentally different as well.

From the time of Wrede to the publication of Trilling's work in 1972, the debate regarding authenticity primarily centered around the issues raised by Wrede and those raised by Schmidt and Kern in the nineteenth century. Minor exceptions to this were the work of Braun ("Nachpaulinische Herkunft") and Marxsen (*Introduction*). Braun (152-156) argued that 2 Thessalonians was not Pauline because it betrays signs of post-apostolic theological concerns. For example, he claims that the judgment has been moralized in 2 Thessalonians because it is no longer based on acceptance or rejection of the gospel but on whether one is persecuted or a persecutor. He also sees a shift from the use of the word "God" to the term "Lord" in such passages as 2:13, 16; 3:3, 5, 16, and maintains that the parousia has been shifted to an indefinite future. These features, according to him, are typical of a period after Paul. His arguments seem dubious, however, since there is nothing inherently un-Pauline about the use of the term "Lord" in 2 Thessalonians, nor does 2 Thes. 1:7 seem to allow for an indefinite delay of the parousia. Finally, the theme of the salvation of the persecuted over against the condemnation of the persecutors is a natural extension of the Pauline understanding of the wrath of God being directed against all who are unrighteous and oppose God (cf. Rom. 2:5-10).

Marxsen (*Introduction,* 37-44) begins with the assumption that 2 Thes. 2:2, with its reference to the idea of the day of the Lord having come, reflects a later Gnostic perversion of eschatology. He concludes that 2 Thessalonians must have been written at a very different time from 1 Thessalonians, placing it after AD 70. He, like Braun, finds several elements in 2 Thessalonians that he claims are post-Pauline in character. Among these are fundamental differences in eschatological perspective between the two letters and an un-Pauline emphasis on apostolic authority in 2 Thes. 2:15. As I have indicated above, the eschatological differences scholars like Marxsen find between 1 Thes. 4:13–5:11 and 2 Thes. 2:1-12 largely result from their failure to understand the function of the material in 2 Thes. 2:3-12. In any case the eschatological differences found by Marxsen are no greater than those between other letters of Paul. For example, the immediacy of the eschatological expectation in 1 Thes. 5:1-11 contrasts rather sharply with the divine eschatological plan which Paul unfolds in Romans 9–11. Rom. 11:25f. requires the conversion of the full number of Gentiles before final salvation can come to the people of Israel. Marxsen's assertion that the eschatology of 2 Thessalonians, which is future in character, lacks the present orientation found in 1 Thessalonians appears questionable. 2 Thes. 2:13f. alludes to both present and future dimensions of eschatological salvation. That 2 Thessalonians emphasizes Paul's apostolic authority in an un-Pauline way is fundamentally incorrect. One need look no further than 1 Thes. 2:1-13 to see that Paul emphasized his own authority to the Thessalonians when he was present with them. Other letters of Paul make it clear that they were vehicles of his apostolic authority (cf. 1 Cor. 5:3-5; 7:12; 16:1-4; Gal. 1–2). In light of the above considerations Marxsen's position fails to convince.

Trilling's Arguments against Authenticity

The impetus for viewing 2 Thessalonians as inauthentic has increased dramatically since the appearance of Trilling's *Untersuchungen* in 1972. He begins with a survey of the debate up to the time he wrote and arrives at several important conclusions (p. 45). The most significant of these are: (1) no single argument against the authenticity of 2 Thessalonians can be convincing by itself, but only the sum of several arguments; (2) the unique relation between 1 and 2 Thessalonians produces the principal difficulty in understanding the peculiarities of 2 Thessalonians, and only the person who can explain this acceptably has the prospect of success; and (3) all other questions are of secondary importance. In the light of these conclusions he offers a new approach to the problem by focusing attention on three areas in which he claims to find significant factors that demonstrate that 2 Thessalonians is not a genuine Pauline letter. Because he claims that only the sum of the several arguments against the authenticity of the letter can prove the case, it is necessary to consider his arguments in detail in order to assess the overall strength of his case.

Trilling directs the first part of his own argument to stylistic considerations. He begins by attempting to negate the findings of Rigaux (76-111), who used stylistic factors to support his claim that 2 Thessalonians was a genuine Pauline letter. Trilling claims that the vocabulary, which has been shown to be Pauline, is indecisive for the authenticity debate. In terms of Trilling's attempts to show a consistent pattern of stylistic differences, however, similarities in vocabulary between 2 Thessalonians and other authentic Pauline letters must be taken as favoring its Pauline origin. Somewhat similar to the question of vocabulary is the matter of unusual expressions in 2 Thessalonians. Trilling (*Untersuchungen*, 48-51) takes up a list of forty unique expressions in 2 Thessalonians that Rigaux borrowed from Frame (Frame, 32f.). He does not maintain that these demonstrate that 2 Thessalonians is non-Pauline; as he recognizes, similar lists can be drawn from other Pauline letters. He does contend, however, that certain of the unique expressions, particularly those of an apocalyptic character, add weight to the "linguistically transformed usage of the whole of II [Thessalonians]" (my translation), implying that this indicates the work is not from Paul. This ignores the fact that the subject matter of 2 Thessalonians may have been responsible for a number of the unusual expressions, just as one finds that the subject matter of 1 Corinthians 15 required unusual expressions.

Following the evidence of Rigaux, Trilling next looks at the relative frequency of chiasms, parallelisms, antithetical formulations, word groupings of two and three members, word plays, pleonasms, and metaphors in 1 and 2 Thessalonians. He concludes that the evidence does not allow for a final judgment regarding authenticity or inauthenticity, but he believes that it favors inauthenticity. He bases this conclusion on the fact that 2 Thessalonians is relatively poorer in many of the features mentioned above than 1 Thessalonians. His position, however, is unconvincing. He assumes, incorrectly, that in matters of style a comparison between the frequency of certain stylistic features in 1 and 2 Thessalonians is sufficient for determining what is and is not authentic Pauline style. For his line of argument to carry conviction he would need to show that the levels of frequency in 1 Thessalonians are more typical of the authentic Pauline letters than those found in 2 Thessalonians. Until this is done, it is inadmissible to draw any conclusions from a comparison of 1 and 2 Thessalonians.

Having finished with the stylistic features discussed by Rigaux, Trilling introduces further characteristics that he thinks militate against the authenticity of 2 Thessalonians. He first looks at supposed fullness of expression, including compound words, the frequent use of "all," and unusual combinations of substantives and adjectives. All of these can be shown to occur in Paul's authentic letters, so that no significant conclusions can be drawn from their appearance in 2 Thessalonians. Trilling thinks otherwise. Because of the repeated use of "all," he concludes that the letter is consciously generalizing, and therefore does not reflect a concrete situation. If Trilling were correct in his assumption that a high frequency of "all" indicates a lack of concrete situation, then 1 Thessalonians and Philippians, among others, must be understood in the same way since they too have a relatively high frequency of the use of "all." Since this runs against the received wisdom regarding these two letters, it seems a highly dubious argument for establishing that 2 Thessalonians was written for a general rather than a specific situation. Even if one were to conclude that 2 Thessalonians is somewhat generalizing on other grounds, it would not provide any significant proof of a lack of authenticity. One can think of reasons why an authentic letter from Paul might appear to be generalizing. For example, Paul might not have been well-informed about the precise situation that he was addressing, a point that I will later show has a bearing on our understanding of 2 Thessalonians.

Trilling proceeds to list striking expressions and favored words and word groups, as well as certain key terms which are repeated. But these are of little or no relevance to the debate on authenticity since the same phenomena occur in other authentic Pauline letters, and therefore he makes little of them. He does, however, point out two further stylistic considerations which he sees as important. First, he claims that the letter has an "official tone," which he implies is incompatible with the tone of 1 Thessalonians and which leads him to infer that the style and thought patterns of the letter may come from someone other than Paul. Second, he observes that certain typical Pauline features such as diatribe, rhetorical questions, brief sentences, terse imperatives, and parenetic series are absent. This results in the letter reading like a formal doctrinal writing, in contrast with Paul's usual style. In taking this position Trilling rejects without any supporting argument the views of von Dobschütz (43f.), who attributes the formal tone to situational factors. Whether or not von Dobschütz is correct in his analysis of the situation that prevailed when 2 Thessalonians was written, there can be no denying that all Paul's letters are contextually determined, as Beker *(Paul the Apostle)* has decisively demonstrated. This means that the formal tone and various stylistic features mentioned by Trilling may be attributable to the situation that Paul sought to address.

On the basis of our discussion it seems fair to conclude that the first point of Trilling's argument for inauthenticity does not carry much weight. As both Marshall (34) and Jewett (*Thessalonian Correspondence,* 11) note in connection with various elements of Trilling's arguments about style and vocabulary, a series of weak arguments based on marginal evidence does not add up to a strong case.

In the second part of his argument Trilling attempts what he calls a form-critical investigation of 2 Thessalonians (*Untersuchungen,* 67-108). He proceeds by looking at the individual structural units of the book, often comparing them with similar material in 1 Thessalonians. He first argues that the close similarity in wording between the prescripts of 1 and 2 Thessalonians is unusual since no two other prescripts are so similar. On the other hand, he finds the additional phrase "from God the father and the Lord Jesus Christ" in 2 Thes. 1:2 ponderous, while claiming that the prescript of 2 Thessalonians lacks the overall richness in formulation of such prescripts as those of Romans, 2 Corinthians, and Galatians. Such observations, however, are of little or no value for the question of authenticity since nothing in the prescript is inherently un-Pauline, nor should the similarity between the prescripts of 1 and 2 Thessalonians surprise us. The two letters were written closer in time to one another than any other two Pauline letters that we possess.

Trilling next turns to the introductory thanksgiving. He begins by claiming that the long thanksgiving sentence of 2 Thes. 1:3-12 only formally conforms with the normal Pauline thanksgiving, taking 1 Thes. 1:2-10 as normative. He then maintains that the thanksgiving in 2 Thessalonians is so general that it does not appear to be addressed to a concrete congregational situation. Instead it reads like a didactic exposition concerning the ideas of judgment and parousia. He comes to a somewhat similar conclusion regarding the thanksgiving found in 2 Thes. 2:13-14 as well. This line of argument, however, is unsound. In the first place, Trilling has failed to establish that 1 Thessalonians can be regarded as normative. There is no necessary or prescribed style of thanksgiving in the Pauline letters. Galatians, for example, does not even have a thanksgiving, but no one to my knowledge has called into question its authenticity because of this. Just as the situation that prevailed in Galatia led to Paul's deviation from his normal epistolary style, so also the deviation of the thanksgiving in 2 Thessalonians from the thanksgivings in 1 Thessalonians and other Pauline letters may be explicable in terms of the prevailing situation. Furthermore, as Marshall (35) notes, a didactic and even parenetic component can be found in other Pauline thanksgivings (cf. 2 Cor. 1:3-7). It is also the case that the thanksgiving lacks a specific congregational situation only to the extent that one denies that the recipients actually were experiencing some form of oppression. In light of these facts, it would be precarious to draw any conclusions about authorship from the nature of the thanksgiving in 2 Thessalonians.

Trilling (*Untersuchungen*, 75-93) offers an interesting tradition-historical analysis of the apocalyptic material in 2 Thes. 2:1-12, arguing that the writer used traditional apocalyptic material (vv. 3f. and 8-10a) and placed this material in his own didactic/parenetic structure through the interpretative additions of vv. 5-7 and 10b-12. Anyone familiar with this section will realize that 2:1-12 clearly contains traditional material along with the author's own interpretative comments, and Trilling may be correct in his delineation of the two types of material. But this tells us nothing about the question of authorship since it is well-known that Paul used this mode of composition elsewhere in his writings (cf. Phil. 2:1-11; 1 Cor. 15:1-11).

Trilling's comments in the fourth section of his chapter on form-critical analysis concern the prayers of 2 Thessalonians in general, with special attention to the prayer in 3:3-5. This prayer, he claims, shows literary dependence upon the prayer in 1 Thes. 3:11-13, but lacking a concrete letter situation, it is more formal and general in character. But while it may lack some of the personal warmth of 1 Thes. 3:11-13, it does have a concrete situation within the letter in that it prepares for the parenetic section that follows. Once again no serious conclusions about authorship can be drawn on the basis of this material.

The same is also true of the parenesis in 2 Thes. 3:6-15. Trilling shows that 3:6-15 differs markedly from the exhortation in 1 Thes. 5:13-22. But no real conclusions can be drawn from this since Trilling fails to take seriously the possibility that the circumstances at the time of writing may have dictated different approaches in the two letters. Trilling can assert that no real concrete situation is manifest in the instructional material (*Untersuchungen*, 96f.; 100f.) only by minimizing the importance of 2 Thes. 3:11, which clearly does have an explicit situation in mind. Similarly he fails to provide evidence for his allegation that the text reflects the lax Christian practices of a later, post-apostolic period.

The final section in Trilling's discussion of form criticism (*Untersu-*

chungen, 101-108) deals with the epistolary conclusion of 2 Thessalonians. He finds that 2 Thes. 3:17 lacks the personal warmth of other concluding greetings where Paul explicitly identifies himself as writing the greeting in his own hand. The personal character of the usual Pauline concluding greeting is replaced by emphasis on the authoritative nature of the greeting and signature, which is, according to Trilling, intended to stress that 2 Thessalonians is an authoritative apostolic writing. Trilling argues that these points fit into the impersonal and authoritative pattern of the letter and are indicative of the letter's non-Pauline authorship. Once again Trilling's position is questionable. If we were to apply the same criterion for authenticity to others of Paul's letters we would have to exclude Romans, on the grounds that it is essentially impersonal, and Galatians, which lays much more stress on apostolic authority than 2 Thessalonians.

That the individual forms of 2 Thessalonians deviate from the authentic Pauline letters as Trilling suggests in his overall conclusions on form criticism does not adequately take into account that Paul's letters are not a homogeneous set of writings holding to a standard pattern (cf. Jewett, *Thessalonian Correspondence*, 12f.). Rather, they are highly situational, and this has enormous significance for their manner and style of presentation, not to mention their content.

The third major component of Trilling's case for the non-Pauline origin of 2 Thessalonians concerns the theology of the letter. He examines the letter's theology in terms of its relation to the Pauline tradition, its understanding of the Christian life, and its conception of God and Christ (*Untersuchungen*, 109-132), concluding that it contains instruction of an OT and Jewish nature and formal language that on the one hand preserves aspects of Pauline theology but on the other lacks important details. According to Trilling, the key contribution of the pseudonymous author of 2 Thessalonians was his attempt to employ Paul, through a process of reinterpretation, to address the pressing eschatological questions of his own day. The evidence that Trilling marshals in support of these conclusions is not nearly so clear-cut as he suggests, as we will show in relation to three broad areas of discussion.

In the first place, Trilling's attempts to differentiate between a variety of genuine Pauline terms and concepts and their post-Pauline usage in 2 Thessalonians is unconvincing because he uses the available evidence in a highly selective manner. For example, he finds that the term "gospel" in 2 Thes. 1:8 lacks the powerful and comprehensive character of the term elsewhere in Paul. This, according to Trilling, indicates that 2 Thessalonians does not come from Paul (*Untersuchungen*, 110f.). But "gospel" is not always used in a comprehensive sense elsewhere in Paul. In Gal. 1:7, for instance, the word simply refers to Paul's message about Christ without any further specification. Similarly in 1 Thes. 2:2, 4, 8, and 9 "gospel" remains undifferentiated. Trilling further claims that the way in which 2 Thes. 1:8 and 10 imply that the gospel is contained in the witness of Paul reflects a later period when the apostle's witness had become identical with doctrine and tradition (112). But the identification of the witness of Paul with the gospel of Christ is not a post-Pauline phenomenon. The apostle himself can speak of divine judgment taking place "according to my gospel" in Rom. 2:16 (cf. 16:25), implying that his particular testimony regarding Christ is the gospel (cf. 1 Thes. 2:1-9). Trilling also asserts that the understanding of "the truth" in 2 Thes. 2:10-12 is narrower than the Pauline concept of truth and lacks its nuances. He sees in that passage the same sort of perception of truth as in the Pastoral Epistles, where the "truth" concerns sound doctrine. Trilling can only come to such a conclusion by ignoring Pauline texts like Rom. 1:18; 2:8; 3:5, 7; and 1 Cor. 13:6, in which Paul contrasts truth with unrighteousness as in 2 Thes. 2:10 and 12.

The same difficulties manifest themselves in Trilling's treatment of tradition and the example of Paul. For instance, Trilling observes in 2 Thes. 2:15 an understanding of tradition that he believes was characteristic of the post-Pauline period when Church doctrine or instruction was viewed as tradition from the earlier apostolic period (*Untersuchungen*, 117f.). This is to read more into the passage than seems permissible. The conception of tradition found in 2:15 is not so very different from that found in other Pauline texts like 1 Cor. 11:2 and especially 1 Thes. 2:13; 4:1f.; 5:1f. That Paul's spoken word and his letters were considered normative was not only true of the post-Pauline period, but also true of Paul's own perception of his oral and written instruction. Trilling's contention (118) that the letter reflects a later period than Paul's, because the life of the apostle has become a normative example in 3:6-12, is possible only if passages like 1 Thes. 1:6; 1 Cor. 4:16; and 11:1 are ignored. As these texts demonstrate, Paul admonished his converts to imitate his behavior as a matter of course.

In the second place, Trilling's discussion of what he terms the Christian life as seen in 2 Thessalonians represents a doubtful analysis of the data. He claims (*Untersuchungen*, 122) that the lack of joy and expectation in the letter reflects a situation typical of the later NT writings. Jewett (*Thessalonian Correspondence*, 13) challenges this assertion on two grounds. First, if joy and expectation are characteristic of Pauline letters, then Galatians, which is singularly lacking in joy and for that matter eschatological expectation, would also have to be classified as post-Pauline. Second, and more importantly, 2 Thes. 1:5-12 concerns the apocalyptic joy of anticipated triumph over the readers' current enemies (cf. 1 Thes. 2:14-17).

Trilling (*Untersuchungen*, 123) further contends that the missionary power and apostolic spirit of the earlier period remains only a vestige in 2 Thessalonians. But 2 Thes. 3:1 requests prayers from the readers for the rapid and successful progress of the Pauline mission. That a forger put such a request in to give the letter the appearance of authenticity seems improbable.

Trilling's discussion of the themes of parousia and judgment (*Untersuchungen*, 124-127) reflects similar inadequacies. He attempts to eliminate the definite situation presupposed by 2 Thes. 2:2, whatever the exact character of the situation may have been, because he wishes to claim that 2 Thessalonians is not a genuine letter but a religious tract (cf. Jewett, *Thessalonian Correspondence*, 14). He further maintains that 2 Thessalonians places its concept of the parousia under the theme of judgment, deviating from Paul by the strong emphasis on retribution. This, Trilling believes, reflects the point of view of later NT writers. Here he fails to consider the social function of the language about retribution when directed toward the situation of persecution presupposed by 2 Thessalonians, a situation we know existed at Thessalonica from 1 Thessalonians. Such language promises vindication to the victims of oppression by assuring them of the reversal of roles between oppressors and oppressed on the day of God's judgment. In doing so it is intended positively to give courage to those who are currently experiencing persecution and negatively to provide a strong warrant against withdrawal from the community. Meeks ("Social Function," 689) accurately describes the social function of the judgment theme when he says of 2 Thes. 1:7-10 that "it serves primarily to emphasize the group's distinctiveness as a persecuted minority, and their ultimate superiority to those who are now opposing them." Meeks claims, rightly, that "if we pay strict attention to the functions that the apocalyptic language most likely serves in this letter [2 Thessalonians], then many of the reasons for doubting Pauline authorship become less persuasive" (689).

In the third place, Trilling's views regarding the image of God and Christ in 2 Thessalonians add little to his general argument. Perhaps his most important statement in this regard is that the portrayal of Christ as "Lord" reflects the progressive transfer of OT attributes of God to Christ, which he regards as typical of a period later than that of Paul (*Untersuchungen*, 128). But the Pastoral Epistles, to which Trilling seeks to relate 2 Thessalonians at times, show no similarity in their pattern of usage regarding the designation "Lord." More importantly, the pattern of usage is closer between 1 and 2 Thessalonians than any other two Pauline letters. Trilling takes no account of the possibility that the context may have played a significant role in the presentation of Christ as Lord in 2 Thessalonians. That 2 Thessalonians stresses that Jesus will return to vanquish all opposition undoubtedly accounts for the way in which he is designated as Lord.

In the end, Trilling is unable to propose a known setting within the early Church in which to locate 2 Thessalonians. He does set forth a hypothetical setting, saying that a renewal of apocalypticism led to the writing of the letter, which was intended to act as a brake on expectations regarding the coming of Christ.

Trilling began with the claim that no single argument against the authenticity of 2 Thessalonians was sufficient to demonstrate the matter and therefore only the sum of several arguments could do so. I have shown that there are significant difficulties with various details in each of his three main lines of argument. Three problematic lines of argument taken together simply do not add up to a compelling argument. In spite of this, since its publication Trilling's book has been the foundation stone for most writers' opposition to the authenticity of 2 Thessalonians (cf. Friedrich, 252-257; Vielhauer, *Geschichte*, 89-102; Koester, *Introduction* II, 241-246).[3]

Jewett (*Thessalonian Correspondence*, 16f.) offers a judicious assessment of the authorship question at present: "The evidence concerning the authenticity of 2 Thessalonians is equivocal, with the likelihood remaining fairly strongly on the side of Pauline authorship." The principal reasons for this are twofold. First, the letter claims to be an authentic Pauline writing, and there is nothing inherent in the thought, language, or style of the letter that requires a different conclusion when proper account is taken of the contextual nature of all of Paul's writings. Second, no forgery hypothesis so far has been able to offer a credible explanation for the origin of the letter and its relation to 1 Thessalonians, as Marshall (40-45) has demonstrated.[4]

Nevertheless, this is not to say that the traditional understanding of 2 Thessalonians as Paul's second letter to the church at Thessalonica is completely satisfactory. One of the least examined presuppositions regarding 2 Thessalonians, both by those who hold that Paul was the author and by those who claim that he was not, concerns the belief that the letter was written after 1 Thessalonians. I shall examine this matter in detail later, but first attention must be given to the question of the literary integrity and unity of the Thessalonian correspondence.

---

3. One scholar who seems to have subsequently sought to demonstrate the inauthenticity of 2 Thessalonians without knowledge of Trilling's work is Bailey ("Who Wrote . . . ?"). But he adds very little, if anything, that is new to the debate.

4. Hughes (*Early Christian Rhetoric*, 84-95) has proposed a novel solution to the problem of the origin of 2 Thessalonians. He claims that "a traditionally-minded, late first-century Pauline Christian who had internalized the words and theology of 1 Thessalonians" wrote to refute the fulfilled eschatology ascribed to Paul by Colossians and Ephesians (91). Hughes assumes that what twentieth-century scholars have come to call realized or fulfilled eschatology is incompatible with future eschatology. John's Gospel demonstrates that the two existed side by side in early Christianity (cf. Jn. 5:22-29). What is perhaps more significant is the presence of futurist eschatology in such passages as Eph. 1:21; 2:7; Col. 1:22f., 27; 3:4. This clearly indicates that the writer(s) of Ephesians and Colossians, whether Paul or others, could not have maintained that the day of the Lord had already come, the heresy that Hughes claims is being refuted in 2 Thessalonians 2.

THE LITERARY INTEGRITY AND UNITY OF 1 AND 2 THESSALONIANS

During the twentieth century a number of studies have raised questions concerning the literary integrity and unity of 1 and 2 Thessalonians. R. F. Collins ("Integrity") has provided an excellent survey of the various contributions on these issues up to the late 1970s. In the scholarly literature of the last three decades three types of hypothesis have been presented regarding the integrity and unity of 1 and 2 Thessalonians. The simplest of these are the theories which hold that discrete units of material have been interpolated into the original Pauline text. More complex is the theory of Schmithals. He claims that 1 and 2 Thessalonians are the products of redactional processes. The most complex hypotheses are those which combine redaction and interpolation theories. In what follows each of these three types of hypothesis will be discussed in order to assess its validity.

Interpolation Hypotheses

Several writers, most notably of late, Pearson ("1 Thessalonians 2:13-16"), Boers ("Form-Critical Study"), D. Schmidt ("1 Thess 2:13-16"), and Koester (*Introduction* II, 113), have proposed that 1 Thes. 2:13-16 is an anti-Jewish interpolation from a period after the fall of Jerusalem. The idea of an interpolation or gloss has been associated with this passage for a long time. Knopf (*Nachapostolisches Zeitalter,* 139 n. 1) thought that 2:16b originated as a marginal gloss written after the destruction of Jerusalem in AD 70, while Goguel (*Introduction,* 305-307) believed that 2:14-16 was an interpolation because of its anti-Jewish tone. The contemporary debate, however, is heavily dependent on the work of Pearson, who launched a new stage in its development by providing a carefully worked-out argument that the whole of 1 Thes. 2:13-16 is an interpolation (cf. Eckart, "Zweite Brief").

Pearson begins with v. 16c, which speaks of divine wrath having come upon the Jews to the end. The only event in the first century catastrophic enough to account for the finality of the view expressed in v. 16c, according to Pearson, was the destruction of Jerusalem in AD 70. Pearson implies that since v. 16c serves as the conclusion to the participial clauses of vv. 15 and 16a, b, which in turn modify the words τῶν Ἰουδαίων of v. 14, the whole of vv. 14-16 is suspect.

Other historical and theological considerations also call into question the authenticity of vv. 15f. (Pearson, "1 Thessalonians 2:13-16," 85f.). Among other things, Pearson finds the anti-Judaism of vv. 15f., which is typical of the Greco-Roman Gentile world, incompatible with the thought of Paul. Paul the Jew, according to Pearson, could never have written the *ad hominem* remarks of v. 15 asserting that the Jewish people do not please

God and that they oppose everyone, nor does Paul ever ascribe the death of Jesus to the Jewish people as vv. 14f. do. That the Jewish people were subjected to the wrath of God with finality, as v. 16 states, contradicts the view expressed by Paul in such texts as Rom. 9:1 (presumably Pearson means 9:4) and 11:26.

On historical and theological grounds Pearson considers v. 14 problematic as well (86-88). He makes the point that we have no evidence for the persecution of Jewish Christians in Judea, as v. 14 claims happened, prior to AD 62, when James the brother of Jesus was murdered in Jerusalem. It is also unlikely that Paul would have used the Judean Christians as an example for Gentiles as v. 14 does. Moreover, the usage of the *mimesis* terminology contradicts his normal insistence that his congregations imitate him alone.

To these historical and theological arguments, Pearson (88-91) adds a form-critical observation that he believes casts doubt on the authenticity of the whole of vv. 13-16. Structurally, 2:11-12 introduces what Funk ("Apostolic *Parousia*") calls the "apostolic parousia," but the apostolic parousia itself only begins in 2:17. When seen in this light the resumption of the thanksgiving period in 2:13-16 appears to interrupt the original flow of the text, a clear sign of an interpolation.

In the concluding part of his article, Pearson (91-94) isolates what he perceives as the *modus operandi* and historical motivation of the interpolator. Words and phrases drawn from the introductory thanksgiving in 1 Thes. 1:2-10 are employed to create a seemingly Pauline framework for the interpolator's message. This message was intended to encourage persecuted Christians by the example of the "embattled Christians of Palestine." The interpolator thus sought to unite all Christians against the Jews who had become hostile toward them in the period after the fall of Jerusalem.

Although Pearson's argument appears sound at first glance, on closer inspection it has several serious flaws. First, the historical setting in the period after AD 70 suggested by Pearson is unnecessary. The first Jewish-Roman War, which culminated in the destruction of Jerusalem, was undoubtedly the greatest catastrophe to overtake the Jewish people in the first century, but it certainly was not the only one of major proportions. The death of the Jewish King Agrippa in AD 44, the revolt of Theudas in 44-46, the famine in Judea in 46-47, and the expulsion of the Jews from Rome in 49 were all major crises for the Jewish people. If 1 Thessalonians was written around 50, a date most scholars are agreed on, the riot in Jerusalem during the passover of 49 may well be in mind, as Jewett ("Agitators," 205 n. 5) has suggested. Josephus (*Ant.* 20.112 and *War* 2.225) claims that twenty to thirty thousand people were killed in the riot. Even if his figures are considerably inflated, as seems likely, this would have appeared to contemporary Jewish people to have been a major disaster, one that Paul might have interpreted as divine punishment for the oppression of Christians in Palestine,[5] as Jewett points out.

Although the charge in v. 15 that the Jews were responsible for Jesus' death is unique in Paul, it is paralleled in the later traditions of Acts and Matthew. At an historical level it can hardly be denied that the Jerusalem ruling elite were guilty of complicity in Jesus' death. To the extent that Jewish nationalists were oppressing Jewish Christians in Palestine when 1 Thes. 2:13-16 was written, it is only to be expected that distinctions between varying Jewish agents of oppression (in the case of Jesus, the ruling elite, and in the case of the Jewish Christians, ardent nationalists) are not brought to the fore by Paul. From his and his contemporaries' viewpoint, the persecution of the Christians in Judea represented a continuation of the phenomenon going back to the prophets of the OT period and recently manifested in the experiences of Jesus and Paul himself (cf. 2 Cor. 11:24).

That Paul was incapable of the scurrilous *ad hominem* attack against the Jewish people in v. 15, as Pearson believes, is questionable (cf. Phil. 3:2). Davies ("Paul and the People of Israel," 9) argues that 1 Thes. 2:13-16 reflects the "unsophisticated, perhaps the unreflecting (and impetuous?) reaction of an early Paul, not to the Jewish people as a whole but to Jews who were violently opposing the preaching of the gospel to Gentiles and thus hindering the divine purpose."

Pearson's references to Rom. 9:1 (presumably 9:4) and 11:26 to prove that Paul never contemplated the final rejection of the Jewish people implied in 1 Thes. 2:16 is problematic on two counts. In the first place, Pearson's understanding of ἔφθασεν δὲ ἐπ' αὐτοὺς ἡ ὀργὴ εἰς τέλος is incorrect, as Donfried ("Paul and Judaism," 249-252) has shown. In both 1 Thessalonians itself and also Romans "wrath" has present and future references. Thus the passage does not exclude the possibility that God may finally be gracious to the Jewish people. Εἰς τέλος does not imply the finality of the wrath that has come upon the Jewish people but that wrath has come upon them "until the end." In the second place, Pearson appears to assume that Romans 9–11 represents a fixed piece of Pauline theology on the subject of Israel which the apostle held throughout his ministry. But Romans 9–11 is a contextually-determined presentation of Paul's thoughts about the Jewish people written

---

5. Pearson ("1 Thessalonians 2:13-16," 86-87) citing Hare, Brandon, and Goppelt, contends that there was no persecution of Christians in Palestine between AD 44 and the period of the Jewish-Roman War. The studies of Jewett ("Agitators," 204-208) and Reicke ("Judeo-Christianity"), which approach the problem from different perspectives, argue forcefully and convincingly that persecution of Jewish Christians did occur in the prewar period. Gal. 6:12 is clear evidence for the existence of Jewish nationalist-inspired persecution of Jewish Christians, as Jewett has demonstrated (cf. also Gal. 4:21-31). It is also worth noting at this point that the claim by Paul in 1 Thes. 2:15 that he too had been persecuted by his fellow Jews is borne out by 2 Cor. 11:24.

when the gospel was beginning to spread more rapidly among Gentiles than it was among the chosen people of God.

Pearson's discussion of the *mimesis* terminology in v. 14 is misdirected. Paul does not instruct the Thessalonians to become imitators of the Judean Christians, as Pearson implies. Instead he tells the Thessalonians that they have already become imitators of the Judean Christians by virtue of having suffered oppression from their fellow citizens. In the light of this it is not surprising that the term for imitation is used in a different fashion than is customary in Paul.

Pearson's final claim that the letter is better structured without 2:13-16 is a matter of individual opinion. With Marshall (9) and Jewett (*Thessalonian Correspondence*, 38), I would argue that 2:13-16 is a necessary component of the letter, though rhetorically it may be termed a digression (see commentary). On the one hand it emphasizes the readers' response to Paul's preaching of the gospel as portrayed in 2:1-12, and on the other it explains why Paul was so anxious to revisit the Thessalonians, as he recounts in 2:17-20. Without 2:13-16 it would not be at all clear why Paul was so concerned about his converts. Undoubtedly, 2:13-16 does not tell the whole story, but it would most likely have been adequate for the original readers, who had shared in the untimely separation from Paul implied in v. 17.

The subsequent work of Boers ("Form-Critical Study," 150-152) and Koester (*Introduction* II, 113) has added little to Pearson's arguments. Schmidt ("1 Thess 2:13-16"), however, has offered a new approach to the problem which he sees as complementing Pearson's work. He adduces linguistic evidence, based on an analysis of the syntax of 1 Thes. 1:2–3:10, to support the claim that 2:13-16 is an interpolation. The primary thrust of his argument is that the syntax of 2:13-16 deviates significantly from that of the surrounding context. Although this is true, the same may also be said of 1:2-7 and many other Pauline texts such as 2 Cor. 11:23-28. Thus while Schmidt's analysis of the linguistic patterns of the text is essentially correct, the conclusions that he draws from his analysis are suspect. Before Schmidt can legitimately conclude that the differences in the linguistic patterns of 2:13-16 signal an interpolation, he will need to analyze a much wider sample of the Pauline corpus to demonstrate that the level of stylistic difference exceeds the normal Pauline range. With Jewett (*Thessalonian Correspondence*, 41), I am doubtful that a thoroughly comparative study will support Schmidt's contentions, because Paul shows a high degree of stylistic originality throughout his letters. Even if it were to be shown that 2:13-16 is unique within the Pauline corpus, other factors would need to be considered. For example, many scholars recognize that the material in vv. 15f. was already traditional by Paul's day (see Schippers, "Pre-Synoptic Tradition"; Collins, "Integrity," 100-103; Donfried, "Paul and Judaism," 248f.). If Paul took it over as a pre-formed tradition, then a major component of Schmidt's argument would fall away. The unusual level of embedded clauses, pointed out by Schmidt, would be explicable without recourse to the interpolation hypothesis. Until Schmidt produces more comparative evidence his argument must be judged inconclusive at best.

Although excising 1 Thes. 2:13-16 from the Pauline canon as an interpolation would remove one of the most virulent anti-Jewish statements of the NT, a thought not far from the mind of Pearson ("1 Thessalonians 2:13-16," 78) and others such as Beck (*Mature Christianity*, 46), the evidence for the whole section being interpolated is far from convincing. Unless and until further evidence is forthcoming in support of the interpolation hypothesis, it should be assumed that 2:13-16 formed part of the original text of the letter (cf. Lyons, *Pauline Autobiography*, 202-207).

The only other text in 1 Thessalonians which has received serious consideration as an interpolation is 5:1-11. Friedrich ("1. Thessalonicher 5,1-11") has argued that the thought of 5:1-11 is inconsistent with the preceding section of the letter. In 4:13-18 Paul attempts to reassure his readers that their dead loved ones will share with them in the parousia of Christ. This implies a sense of imminent expectation of the eschatological events. By way of contrast, according to Friedrich, 5:1-11, but especially vv. 1-3, imply that a diminution of the parousia expectation, which was characteristic of a later period, had taken place. The interpolator sought to correct this by claiming that people had a false sense of security (vv. 2f.). Friedrich finds that in 5:10 the interpolator tries to overturn the clear implication of 4:15 that Paul would survive to the parousia by allowing for the possibility that he would not. To this line of argument Friedrich adds two further points. First, 5:1-11 contains a considerable amount of non-Pauline material, and second, some of the Pauline expressions in 5:1-11 are used in ways not characteristic of Paul.

These arguments of Friedrich have failed to convince other scholars for several reasons (cf. Rigaux, "Tradition et Rédaction," 320; Plevnik, "1 Thess 5,1-11," 71-90; Marshall, 12f.). To begin with, it is obvious that from the beginning of the Christian movement a tension existed between imminent expectation of the end and interest in when the parousia would actually occur (see Plevnik, 72f.). Second, 5:1-11 does not indicate that the writer faulted his readers for a diminished sense of expectation as Friedrich suggests. Vv. 3 and 5 make it clear that it is outsiders who have a false sense of security, not the Christian readers. Third, 5:10 should not be contrasted with 4:15, because it simply seeks to reassure the readers that they, like their dead fellow believers, will share in the life to come. Fourth, most scholars agree that 5:1-11 contains a considerable amount of traditional material that Paul has taken up and redacted for his own purposes (see Rigaux, "Tradition et Rédaction"; Plevnik, esp. 80-90; R. F. Collins, "Tradition," 334-343; Holtz, "Traditionen," 66-71). Thus it is unnecessary to appeal to the interpolation hypothesis to account for the unusual character of the material.

Schmithals's Compilation Hypothesis

Schmithals (*Paul and the Gnostics,* 123-218) accepts the authenticity of all the material in both 1 and 2 Thessalonians (though see p. 180 of *Paul and the Gnostics* on 1 Thes. 2:15f.), but maintains that the two letters were actually composed from four original letters to the Thessalonians. These, he contends, were later redacted into the two canonical letters which we now have. The four original letters according to Schmithals were:

> Letter A: 2 Thes. 1:1-12 and 3:6-16, written when Paul first learned that the community was being disturbed by Gnostic interlopers,
>
> Letter B: 1 Thes. 1:1–2:12 and 4:2–5:28, written when Paul learned that the interlopers were making headway with the community, in part by disparaging his apostleship,
>
> Letter C: 2 Thes. 2:13f., 2:1-12, 2:15–3:3(-5), and 17f., written when Paul heard that the Gnostics were inculcating the belief that the day of the Lord had already come, basing their claim on a letter which he had reputedly written, and
>
> Letter D: 1 Thes. 2:13–4:1, written after Timothy had returned to Paul with the good news that the community was resisting the Gnostics.

This reconstruction is based on the observations that 1 Thes. 2:13 looks like a separate introductory thanksgiving, that 3:11–4:1 appears as though it could be the conclusion of a letter, that 2 Thes. 2:13f. also contains a thanksgiving period, and that 2:15–3:3 is reminiscent of the close of a letter.

This partitioning of the canonical letters into a collection of four original letters has received little or no support from other scholars, and for good reasons. Form-critical studies of the Pauline letters render the theory implausible on several counts. First, whether one accepts the view of Schubert *(Form and Function)* that the formal opening thanksgiving section extends from 1 Thes. 1:2 to 3:13 or that of J. T. Sanders ("Transition") that 2:13 introduces a second thanksgiving section into the letter, it is unnecessary to assume that a second statement of thanksgiving is sufficient for concluding that the material which follows was originally part of the introductory section of a separate letter. Moreover, the form of Schmithals's proposed fourth letter (1 Thes. 2:13–4:1) is without precedence among Paul's letters. It consists only of an opening thanksgiving with no letter body and parenesis following a concluding doxology, neither of which occurs in any other Pauline letter (see Best, 33f.). In effect, Schmithals's solution to the double thanksgiving of 1 Thessalonians creates bigger problems than those it was intended to resolve. Bjerkelund (*Parakalô,* 125-140) undermines Schmithals's claims regarding 1 Thes. 4:1 by providing evidence that this verse is an integral part of the pericope 4:1-12. Similar problems exist with Schmithals's partition of 2 Thessalonians as well. In any case, apart from the form-critical considerations, the very content of Schmithals' proposed letters makes his thesis of little use. His letters make little or no sense historically or rhetorically, as Jewett (*Thessalonian Correspondence*, 34-36) shows.

Combined Theories of Redaction and Interpolation

Several scholars have developed complicated theories involving redaction and interpolation. The earliest of these is the theory of Eckart ("Zweite Brief"), who argues that 1 Thes. 2:13-16; 4:1-8, 10b-12; and 5:12-22 as well as the redactional seams of 3:5; 4:18; and 5:27 are non-Pauline on the basis of vocabulary, style, and content. He then asserts that two authentic letters can be extracted from what remains:

> Letter A: 1:1–2:12; 2:17–3:4; 3:11-13 and
> Letter B: 3:6-10; 4:13–5:11; 4:9-10a; 5:23-26; 5:28.

Eckart's thesis has been subjected to a devastating critique by Kümmel ("Literarische und geschichtliche Problem"), who shows conclusively that the vocabulary, style, and content of Eckart's supposed interpolations are Pauline and that Eckart's hypothesis fragments cohesive units of material like 2:17–3:13 and 4:1–5:11. Besides this, the two authentic letters which Eckart finds in 1 Thessalonians make little or no sense in terms of Paul's normal epistolary style. For these reasons, Eckart's hypothesis has never been taken very seriously.[6]

Demke ("Theologie und Literarkritik") has proposed a different redaction and interpolation theory by applying two criteria for separating redactional material from authentic material. These criteria are differing vocabulary and differing ideological outlook from authentic Pauline letters. He isolates five Pauline fragments within 1 Thessalonians: 2:17–3:2a; 3:5b-11; 4:9-10a; 4:13-17; and 5:1-22. These, he claims, a redactor has supplemented with 1:2–2:16; 3:2b-5a; 3:12-4:8; and 5:23-27 in order to present Paul as an example of true faith (chaps. 1–3) and to give instruction in devout living based on the apostolic tradition (chaps. 4–5).

Without entering into a detailed analysis of Demke's argument, it is possible to say that it rests on two false premises. First, differing vocabulary and even variations in the usage of the same terms in the Pauline corpus are not in themselves evidence of redactional material. Paul's letters show considerable variation in vocabulary, a fact not surprising since they were written over a period of at least half a decade by a reasonably literate individual.

---

6. Another radical proposal involving redaction and a form of interpolation has come from Refshauge ("Literaerkritiske overvejelser"). I have not seen this work, but judging from the discussions of R. F. Collins ("Integrity," 76-77, 95, 103-104) and Jewett (*Thessalonian Correspondence*, 43-44) it is a singularly implausible theory.

Moreover, terms like παρουσία (1 Thes. 3:13; 5:13) and ἔμπροσθεν (2:19; 3:13), which Demke uses to isolate non-Pauline material, occur elsewhere in undisputed parts of undisputed Pauline letters (see 1 Cor. 15:23 and 2 Cor. 5:10). Second, Demke takes no account of the contextual nature of Paul's writings and his theological thought, let alone the possibility that his theology developed. The uniformity that Demke attempts to superimpose on Paul's thought is simply not borne out by the evidence.

The most recent attempt at a comprehensive theory of redaction and interpolation in the composition of the Thessalonian correspondence comes from Munro (*Authority,* 82-94). Her project is by far the most ambitious of those examined so far. She attempts to argue that the whole of the original ten-letter Pauline/deutero-Pauline corpus underwent ecclesiastical redaction sometime between AD 90 and 140. To Paul's original letters redactors added what Munro (148) calls the "pastoral stratum," characterized by its emphasis on "authority and subjection to it." While reserving her judgment regarding the Pauline authorship of 2 Thessalonians, she finds 2 Thes. 2:15; 3:4; and 3:6-15 to be interpolated material emanating from the later pastoral stratum. In the case of 1 Thessalonians she discovers the later stratum in 1:5b, 6a, 7; 2:1-16; 4:1-12; 5:12-15, 21b, 22. The rest of the material in the letter appears to be earlier, though she does not commit herself to the exclusive Pauline provenance even of this material. She employs the usual criteria of theological and stylistic differences, along with the existence of contextual abruptions to distinguish the interpolations of the later stratum from the original material. In the case of both 1 and 2 Thessalonians she declares virtually every single verse which contains patterns for or instructions about ethical behavior as well as injunctions regarding Church order to be from the later stratum.

It would appear that Munro begins with the notion that ethical issues and considerations regarding Church order were only of interest to the later Church. But is it a credible thesis to maintain that Paul offered no ethical models or instruction and no guidelines about Church order to his converts when he wrote? This seems totally improbable because elsewhere in Paul's letters ethical instruction is made normative for governing Christian existence (cf. Gal. 5:16-26). Furthermore, Munro has a curious way of positing that content parallels between earlier writings and later writings must be explained in terms of interpolations into the earlier works. For example, she identifies 1 Thes. 4:4 with Eph. 5:21-23 because both are concerned with sexual relations. Since the latter is part of the later stratum, according to her analysis, the former is as well. But no justification is offered as to why sexual relations could not have been a concern of Paul's. That themes in the authentic Pauline writings, like sexual ethics, were picked up by the later tradition is a much less cumbersome concept to explain the similarities than Munro's reverse influence hypothesis, which requires her elaborate redaction/interpolation theory.

Another element in Munro's argument that is particularly problematic is her main stylistic criterion employed to isolate interpolated material. She contends that material containing antithetical parallelism of a noneschatological sort reflects the later stratum and repeatedly makes reference to this in her analysis of 1 and 2 Thessalonians. But this entails a very questionable assumption. Because one finds antithetical parallelism in later material, this hardly proves that it was not characteristic of Paul. Malherbe (*Moral Exhortation*, 136-138) has shown that antithetical presentations were typical of parenetic material and the setting out of ethical examples in Greco-Roman moral exhortation. Paul, versed in both the rhetorical tradition and the moral philosophy of the Greco-Roman world, almost certainly appropriated the antithetical style for himself from this source. To use its presence as a criterion for isolating later tradition, as Munro does, is to decide on a priori grounds that antithetical material is post-Pauline. Thus Munro's argument turns out to be circular. In effect, she does not prove her thesis; she assumes that it is correct and then interprets 1 and 2 Thessalonians in light of it. For this reason her whole thesis is completely undermined at a methodological level.

From the above discussion it is clear that the only serious case for interpolation into the text of the Thessalonian correspondence turns out to be the one for 1 Thes. 2:13-16. But even this one falls short of carrying conviction when the arguments are considered carefully. Therefore, until more convincing arguments are offered, we may assume the essential literary integrity of both 1 and 2 Thessalonians.

THE SEQUENCE OF THE THESSALONIAN CORRESPONDENCE

Although this runs contrary to prevailing scholarly opinion, I am convinced that one of the principal stumbling blocks to a solution regarding the relationship of 2 Thessalonians to 1 Thessalonians lies in the assumption of the priority of 1 Thessalonians. If it can be shown that a strong case exists for the priority of 2 Thessalonians, many of the problems associated with the relation between the two letters can be resolved.

The question of the date and setting of 1 and 2 Thessalonians is complex and hinges on the wider problem of the general chronology of Paul's life, which itself is a much debated issue, as the works of Jewett *(Chronology)* and Lüdemann *(Paul: Apostle to the Gentiles)* reveal. It is beyond the scope of this commentary to enter into this debate. Suffice it to say that at this stage I am not convinced by Lüdemann's fairly radical reworking of Pauline chronology, and therefore I adopt a more traditional understanding of Pauline chronology, fully recognizing that it too has problems, especially where Paul's letters and Acts appear to be at variance with one another.

Within the traditional framework most scholars, for example, Kümmel (*Introduction*, 257-260), Best (7-13), Koester (*Introduction* II, 112f.), and

Marshall (20-23), maintain that 1 Thessalonians was written from Corinth a few months after the founding of the church at Thessalonica.[7] 1 Thes. 3:1-6 indicates that Paul sent Timothy from Athens to Thessalonica (this visit of Paul to Athens is usually identified with the one mentioned in Acts 17:16-34), and most scholars believe that by the time Timothy returned to Paul, the apostle had moved on to Corinth, from which the letter was written shortly after Timothy's arrival. Most scholars assume that 2 Thessalonians was written after 1 Thessalonians, and because of the similarity in themes it is usually held that the time between the two letters was short. 2 Thessalonians, it is thought, was intended to resolve an aberration in the Thessalonians' eschatological understanding that had arisen in the wake of 1 Thessalonians and to call a halt to the idleness and unruly behavior of some of the church's members. This latter trouble was already present at the time 1 Thessalonians was written and had persisted, perhaps becoming worse.

The traditional view has not gone unquestioned. There is no a priori reason why the canonical order should necessarily be the historical order. As Bruce (xli) notes, the canonical sequence of the Pauline letters was generally determined on the basis of length rather than any critical considerations about historical sequence. A number of scholars over the years, for example, West ("Order of 1 and 2 Thessalonians," 66-74), Weiss (*Earliest Christianity*, 286-291), Manson ("St. Paul in Greece," 428-447), Gregson ("Solution," 76-80), Buck and Taylor (*Saint Paul*, 140-145), and Thurston ("Relationship," 52-56) have challenged the priority of 1 Thessalonians.

Manson (438-446) has made the best case for the priority of 2 Thessalonians. He argues that 2 Thessalonians was written while Paul was in Athens and that Timothy delivered it to the Thessalonians at the time of the visit mentioned in 1 Thes. 3:1-6. 1 Thessalonians was then written from Corinth when Timothy returned to Paul after having delivered 2 Thessalonians. Following the lead of Weiss, Manson gives five principal reasons for the priority of 2 Thessalonians over 1 Thessalonians: (1) The persecution that seems to be happening in the present according to 2 Thes. 1:4-7 appears to be a thing of the past in 1 Thessalonians (cf. 1 Thes. 2:14). (2) The problem regarding disorder emerging in the church appears to be a new development in 2 Thes. 3:11-15, while it is treated as though it were a known problem in 1 Thes. 4:10-12. (3) The closing in 2 Thes. 3:17, in which mention is made that Paul's signature is the mark of all his genuine letters, is pointless unless 2 Thessalonians is the first letter. (4) The remark in 1 Thes. 5:1 that the readers have no need for instruction regarding the time of the end seems particularly

---

7. Jewett (*Thessalonian Correspondence*, 49-60) holds a similar view though he comes at the problem from a different perspective than the traditional one. He, unlike those mentioned in the text, accepts John Knox's critical principle that no information from Acts can be used in reckoning chronology if it is in conflict with data from Paul's letters.

appropriate if they had already read 2 Thes. 2:1-12. (5) The expression "now concerning," which occurs in 1 Thes. 4:9, 13 and 5:1, appears to be a common formula to introduce answers to questions raised earlier by the intended recipients (cf. 1 Cor. 7:1). In each case Manson shows that the subject introduced in 1 Thessalonians arises from a question raised by the Thessalonians regarding an earlier discussion of the subject in 2 Thessalonians. Thus 1 Thes. 4:9-13, which deals with orderly behavior, arises from the earlier discussion of the issue in 2 Thes. 3:6-15; the question concerning the fate of those who die before the parousia, which lies behind 1 Thes. 4:13, appears to be a response to anxieties created by 2 Thes. 2:1-12, which deferred the parousia to an indefinite future; and the question apparently addressed in 1 Thes. 5:1 regarding the time of the parousia seems also to arise from 2 Thes. 2:1-12, where Paul indicates that the day of the Lord is still in the future (cf. Thurston, "Relationship," 54-55).

Manson's arguments are normally dismissed on two principal grounds. First, they are inconclusive. Scholars like Best (43f.), Marshall (26), and Jewett (*Thessalonian Correspondence*, 24f.) point out that the discussions in 2 Thessalonians regarding persecution, disorderly behavior, and the problem of the parousia, which Manson believes reflect the intensity of the initial situation at Thessalonica, might just as well mirror a deteriorating or unstable situation after 1 Thessalonians. They also maintain that the words in 2 Thes. 3:17, "this greeting is in my own hand, Paul's, which is a mark in every letter of mine," give us an ambiguous piece of evidence. No other letter of Paul has a similar statement of authentication, so 2 Thes. 3:17 is problematic whether 2 Thessalonians is the first or second letter (so Best, 43). Jewett (*Thessalonian Correspondence*, 27f.) goes so far as to claim that if we did not have 1 Thessalonians, which concludes with a greeting from Paul (1 Thes. 5:27), "we would have to hypothesize a letter like it containing such a closing greeting" since the authentication statement in 2 Thes. 3:17 only makes sense if the recipients had a previous letter with a closing greeting that authenticated it. With respect to the questions that led to 1 Thes. 4:9, 13 and 5:1, Best, Marshall, and Jewett agree that there is no necessary connection with material to be found in 2 Thessalonians. The questions to which Paul is responding might just as easily have arisen on their own after his departure.

The second principal reason for dismissing Manson's position is found in the apparent references in 2 Thes. 2:2, 15; 3:17 to a previous letter by Paul to the Thessalonians. But of these only 2 Thes. 2:15 is strong evidence for a previous letter. I will later show that even this piece of evidence is equivocal.

Rather than attempting to refute the counter-arguments to Manson's position at this stage, it will be more helpful to ask what is the basis of the position of those who insist on the priority of 1 Thessalonians. If a clear case can be made for the priority of 1 Thessalonians, then we may take the counter-arguments against Manson as implicitly proven. There would be, therefore, no point in trying to argue for a reversal of the canonical sequence. On the other hand, if the case for the priority of 1 Thessalonians cannot be made in a convincing fashion, then the case for the precedence of 2 Thessalonians must be taken seriously.

When we turn to the arguments of those favoring the priority of 1 Thessalonians it is striking how little evidence they have actually adduced for their position. For the most part scholars like Kümmel (*Introduction*, 264), Best (45), and Marshall (25f.) have been content with offering a refutation of the arguments in favor of the reverse sequence of the letters while providing several cursory reasons for their own position. The only scholar of whom I am aware who has seriously argued for the priority of 1 Thessalonians is Jewett (*Thessalonian Correspondence*, 26-30), who incorporates most of the evidence presented by others who defend the canonical sequence.

Jewett develops three lines of evidence. First, he looks at the three possible references in 2 Thessalonians to a previous letter of Paul (2:2, 15; and 3:17), pointing out that no such references exist in 1 Thessalonians (*Thessalonian Correspondence*, 27f.). In the case of 2 Thes. 2:2 he argues that Paul's reference to a letter "as from us" purporting to prove that the day of the Lord had come can only be explained in one of two ways: either the letter alluded to was a forgery or it was an authentic Pauline letter prior to 2 Thessalonians that was being misused by some people in the community. Jewett rejects the possibility of a forgery because we have no other evidence for its existence. This leaves him with the conclusion that it must refer to an authentic Pauline letter, with 1 Thessalonians as our only available candidate.

But we need not assume that a forgery actually existed. Paul may have merely thought that one did or simply considered the possibility. Alternatively, he may have included the reference for rhetorical affect, that is, he may have simply been listing possible sources of confusion without seriously believing that a forged letter actually did lead to the problem at Thessalonica regarding the parousia (cf. Best, 279). Furthermore, 1 Thes. 4:13–5:11 precludes the possibility of the misinterpretation suggested in 2 Thes. 2:2 by identifying the day of the Lord with the parousia of Christ, the resurrection of dead believers, and the ascension of both living and dead Christians. Best (279), who accepts the priority of 1 Thessalonians, is undoubtedly correct when he maintains that if Paul had thought that 1 Thessalonians was being misunderstood he would have responded by redefining his views as he does, for example, in 1 Cor. 5:9-13. For this reason it is almost certain that 2 Thes. 2:2 does not refer to 1 Thessalonians.

In 2 Thes. 2:15 Paul writes, "Hold fast to the traditions that you were taught (ἐδιδάχθητε), whether through word of mouth or through our letter." Jewett believes that this is a clear reference to 1 Thessalonians since the aorist passive verb ἐδιδάχθητε implies that the letter referred to was in existence when 2 Thessalonians was written, and the only extant candidate is 1 Thessalonians. This is the single strongest piece of evidence in favor of the priority of 1 Thessalonians, but it is far more ambiguous than Jewett acknowledges.

First, even if ἐδιδάχθητε is to be taken with "through our letter," which is not altogether certain, it does not necessarily prove the priority of 1 Thessalonians. It is not beyond the realm of possibility that Paul had written another letter to the Thessalonians prior to either our 2 Thessalonians or our 1 Thessalonians.

Second, ἐδιδάχθητε ("you were taught") is amenable to at least two other interpretations than the one given by Jewett. (a) The verb may function as an epistolary aorist in relation to the expression "through our letter" since the teaching in question precedes the verb in the letter. (b) BAGD (s.v., 2c) suggests that the verb may have the sense of a perfect passive. If this is correct then it would represent a natural way of including both the apostle's original oral teaching and the immediately antecedent instruction within the letter.

Third, the singular form of "letter" (ἐπιστολῆς) would appear to exclude the possibility that another letter already existed, since Paul undoubtedly intended his readers to hold fast to his teaching regarding the parousia in the immediately preceding verses (cf. Lindemann, "Abfassungszweck," 37). If the Thessalonians possessed a previous letter from Paul we would expect the plural "letters" in order to include the teaching in both letters.

Fourth, the reference to "our letter" is certainly more vague than we might have expected had Paul intended a reference to 1 Thessalonians. On every other occasion when Paul alludes to an earlier letter he does so in a way that identifies the letter either by its content or its result (cf. 1 Cor. 5:9; 2 Cor. 2:3f.; 7:8). This point takes on added weight if we interpret 2 Thes. 2:2 as implying that Paul considered the possibility that a forged letter existed. The vague allusion in 2:15 to a previous letter could actually be used to support the authority of a forged document.

According to Jewett, the third reference to a previous letter is found in 2 Thes. 3:17, where Paul indicates that his own handwriting authenticates all of his letters. This, Jewett contends, presupposes that the Thessalonians had access to at least one other letter from Paul. A different interpretation of 3:17 is preferable. In light of 2:2, which implies that a forgery may have existed, it is more probable that Paul wished to give his readers a way of testing any letter that might claim to be from him. In any case, if the readers already had a letter of Paul, it is strange that there is no direct mention of it in 3:17, since clearly the verse would have the intention of authenticating a previous letter, if such a letter existed.

The second line of evidence adduced by Jewett (*Thessalonian Correspondence*, 28f.) to prove the priority of 1 Thessalonians concerns the "rhetorical implications of the references" to persecution. Jewett begins by denying that we can determine anything about the chronology of the letters from the way in which persecution is dealt with in the two letters. Instead he argues that the rhetoric of the letters indicates that the canonical sequence is also the correct historical sequence. This conclusion is based on the presence in 1 Thessalonians of "an elaborate explanation of the apocalyptic significance of persecution," which suggests that the readers had not yet accepted such an understanding of persecution. On the other hand, 2 Thessalonians merely serves to strengthen the readers' already existing "sectarian, apocalyptic outlook that understands persecution as a sign of belonging to the new age rather than the old." This implies that they had accepted the doctrine by the time 2 Thessalonians was written. Rhetorical logic requires that the elaboration of the doctrine of eschatological persecution precedes its acceptance, and therefore 1 Thessalonians is prior to 2 Thessalonians.

This second argument for the priority of 1 Thessalonians is unconvincing for several reasons. First, the objective evidence of the text, which Jewett dismisses, weighs heavily against his position. When 2 Thessalonians was written the community was undergoing persecution, as the present tense verbs of 2 Thes. 1:4-6 show, but there is no indication either that this was a new outbreak of persecution or an old problem that had reemerged. By way of contrast, when 1 Thessalonians was written the persecutions were a thing of the past, as the aorist tense of 1 Thes. 2:14 demonstrates. Best (42), however, contends that 1 Thes. 3:3 implies that the persecution of the Thessalonians was continuing at the time 1 Thessalonians was written and that therefore nothing can be made of the present tenses in 2 Thes. 1:4-6. This represents a serious misunderstanding of 1 Thes. 3:3. The verse refers to what Paul thought was happening at Thessalonica when he sent Timothy back there, not to what he believed was happening at the time 1 Thessalonians was written. This has important implications. Like most of those who maintain the priority of 2 Thessalonians, I would argue that 2 Thessalonians was delivered by Timothy during the visit mentioned in 1 Thes. 3:1-5. This means that a clear correlation can be made between the contents of 2 Thessalonians regarding the presence of persecution and the situation that Paul thought prevailed at Thessalonica when Timothy was sent there (see the discussion of this below, pp. 57-60).

Jewett's second line of evidence for the canonical sequence is doubtful for another reason. 1 Thes. 3:3f. demonstrates that Paul had taught the Thessalonians the "apocalyptic significance" of persecutions at the time of their conversion. For this reason it would have been perfectly natural for Paul to assume that his converts understood the eschatological significance of persecution when 2 Thessalonians was written, if it was written prior to 1 Thessalonians. Whether they did or not is another matter, of course. From what has been said above it is fair to say that the "rhetorical implications of the references" to persecution put forward by Jewett do not necessitate the priority of 1 Thessalonians. In fact they may favor 2 Thessalonians as the first letter on the grounds that it was only after Timothy's visit (when, according to my view, 2 Thessalonians was delivered) that Paul realized that the Thessalonians had not fully understood the implications of their persecution.

Jewett's third argument for the priority of 1 Thessalonians, like his second, is based on a consideration of rhetoric. He maintains (*Thessalonian Correspondence*, 29f.) that in epistolary rhetoric it is normal to refer back to the preceding stages of a relationship and that allusions to previous contact should customarily be understood as referring to the last contact between the parties unless there is evidence to the contrary. This is because it is considered "unnatural in an epistolary situation to refer to distant phases of a relationship without taking into account the intervening phases that alter the relationship or add critical new information." On the basis of his examination of the Thessalonian correspondence, Jewett claims that a striking fact emerges. All references to Paul's direct contact with the community in 1 Thessalonians concern the founding mission (cf. 1 Thes. 1:5, 9f.; 2:17) and especially Paul's conduct at that time (2:1-12). 1 Thes. 3:1-10 also mentions Paul's most recent contact, which was by means of his personal representative Timothy, whom he had sent to learn how the church was faring and whose return precipitated the writing of 1 Thessalonians. What is missing, Jewett argues, especially in 1 Thes. 2:1-12, where we might expect it, is a reference to an intervening letter, if such a letter existed. On the other hand, the only allusion in 2 Thessalonians to the founding mission, according to Jewett, occurs in 2:15, a passage that in his view mentions a previous letter. This is, he argues, exactly what we should expect from the point of view of epistolary rhetoric, since the initial stage of the relationship is referred to along with an allusion to the most recent stage, namely, Paul's first letter to the community.

But on careful inspection Jewett's third argument is vulnerable at several key points. To begin with, as was shown earlier, 2 Thes. 2:15 is equivocal evidence for the existence of another letter. Furthermore, 2:15 is not the only mention of the founding mission in the letter. In 3:6-10 Paul invokes his and his coworkers' behavior at the time of their founding mission as an example of how the Christians at Thessalonica should conduct themselves. Paul concludes the same passage by reminding his readers of the command that he gave when he was with them that no one should eat who was unwilling to work. The apostle does this, however, without any reference to 1 Thessalonians, which deals with the same general theme in 2:1-12 and more specifically in 4:10-12 where a command is given that is strikingly similar to the one mentioned in 2 Thes. 3:10. On the basis of Jewett's own premises this constitutes a powerful argument for the priority of 2 Thessalonians, because we would expect Paul to mention the intervening correspondence precisely at this point—if 1 Thessalonians existed at the time. That he does not mention it indicates that it did not exist, according to Jewett's understanding of what we should expect in epistolary references to the relationship between writer and addressees. In fact Manson ("St. Paul in Greece," 442) may be correct in maintaining that 1 Thes. 4:10-12 is an allusion to the injunction in 2 Thes. 3:12.

It is true, as Jewett says, that there is no *direct* reference to 2 Thessalonians in 1 Thessalonians. But two factors suggest that 1 Thes. 3:1-5 presupposes the existence of 2 Thessalonians. First, Funk ("Apostolic *Parousia*") has demonstrated that Paul's letters were a form of apostolic parousia, that is, that Paul's authority was communicated over distance and time by means of his letters. White (*Light*, 216) points out that it was a common practice in Paul's day to send a letter with a trusted representative who was authorized to interpret and elaborate the contents of the letter being delivered. For this reason it is not altogether surprising that Paul should mention sending Timothy, rather than the letter that Timothy carried with him, if Timothy did take a letter with him.

Second, careful examination of 2 Thessalonians corresponds remarkably with Paul's statement in 1 Thes. 3:1-5 regarding Timothy's mission to Thessalonica on Paul's behalf. To begin with, 2 Thes. 1:4-6 indicates that the readers were undergoing oppression from people outside the community at the time the letter was written, but 1 Thes. 2:14 makes it clear that by the time 1 Thessalonians was written the persecution was a thing of the past. Since nothing in 2 Thessalonians remotely suggests that the persecution represented a renewed outbreak after the period of tranquility implied by 1 Thes. 2:14 or an intensification after the writing of 1 Thessalonians, as Marshall (26) proposes, 2 Thessalonians would seem to reflect the earlier situation that prevailed at the time Timothy returned to Thessalonica (cf. Weiss, *Earliest Christianity*, 289f.; Manson, "St. Paul in Greece," 438-441).

Similarly, Paul's concern in 2 Thessalonians for strengthening the faith of his converts and encouraging them reflects one of the reasons for Timothy's return visit. In fact Paul employs the same terms, στηρίξαι and παρακαλέσαι, in his wish-prayer for his readers in 2 Thes. 2:17 as he employs in 1 Thes. 3:2 to describe his intention in sending Timothy back. Since the wish-prayer functions as a summary of the main theme of 2 Thessalonians, its correspondence with the purpose of Timothy's visit is particularly striking.

Furthermore, von Dobschütz (264) has noted that the infinitive σαλευθῆναι ("to be shaken") in 2 Thes. 2:2 accords with σαίνεσθαι ("to be shaken") in 1 Thes. 3:3. 2 Thes. 2:1-2 indicates that one of Paul's primary purposes in writing was to keep his converts from being disturbed by claims that the day of the Lord had come. Whatever the problem was, it arose in the context of their persecution (see Best, 277; Marshall, 186). 1 Thes. 3:3 explicitly states that Timothy was sent to prevent the Thessalonians from being disturbed by their experience of persecution. Thus both 2 Thessalonians and Timothy's visit had the same purpose, which suggests rather strongly that Timothy took 2 Thessalonians with him when he returned to Thessalonica.

From this examination of Jewett's arguments we can draw two significant conclusions. First, the case for the canonical sequence of the Thessalonian correspondence has been inadequately demonstrated. The strongest piece of evidence, in fact virtually the only evidence of any real merit for the precedence of 1 Thessalonians, turns out to be the possible reference to a previous letter in 2 Thes. 2:15. On careful analysis, however, this supposed reference appears to be highly equivocal on several grounds. I have shown that the most likely interpretation of the passage is that it refers to 2 Thessalonians itself rather than to a previous letter (which in any case need not be our 1 Thessalonians). Second, Jewett's two arguments based on epistolary rhetoric, far from favoring the canonical sequence, on closer examination actually support the priority of 2 Thessalonians. In light of this discussion, we can say that the available evidence actually supports the priority of 2 Thessalonians.

This conclusion has implications for two other major questions regarding the Thessalonian letters. Many of the arguments for the non-Pauline origin of 2 Thessalonians are based on the assumption that 1 Thessalonians was written earlier than 2 Thessalonians, whoever wrote the latter. Therefore, those who wish to maintain that 2 Thessalonians is not Pauline must begin by demonstrating the priority of 1 Thessalonians or lose a considerable portion of the cumulative evidence on which they depend. Second, reversal of the canonical sequence enables us to understand more clearly the historical situation in which the two letters were written, as will be shown below (pp. 53-63).

THE RHETORIC OF THE THESSALONIAN CORRESPONDENCE

Thematic and Epistolary Approaches to 1 and 2 Thessalonians

In most commentaries on the Thessalonian correspondence the writers attempt to analyze the letters thematically in order to set out their structures in outline form. This approach has an inherent weakness. It tends to fragment the letters into sequences of themes without sufficient attention to the unity of their argumentation and the rationale for their overall structure. It also ignores the literary reasons for the inclusion of indivdual themes and their relationship to one another. Jewett (*Thessalonian Correspondence*, 68) further criticizes the thematic approach for lending itself to uncontrolled "theological biases" on the part of commentators who allow favorite doctrines to dominate their thematic analysis.

A different approach from thematic analysis has been to examine Paul's letters in terms of their epistolary forms (see, e.g., White, *Form and Function*; Doty, *Letters*; O'Brien, *Introductory Thanksgivings*). Scholars practicing epistolary analysis have isolated components of Paul's letters such as prescripts, introductory thanksgivings, main bodies, apostolic parousia segments, exhortative sections, and letter closings. They have not succeeded, however, in explaining the relationships between the individual components or the logic of the letters as integrated literary productions. The concentration on the letter openings and closings of Paul's letters has also obscured the nature and function of the main bodies of the letters, and the body is after all the heart of every letter (cf. Stowers, *Letter Writing,* 22).

Both 1 and 2 Thessalonians have proved particularly resistant to epistolary analysis because their thanksgivings do not fit into the normal pattern of the thanksgiving period occurring at the conclusion of the letter opening. 1 Thessalonians has three distinct thanksgivings scattered throughout the first three chapters, and 2 Thessalonians has two in the first two chapters. Epistolary analysis has been unable to explain this aberration in a convincing way.

In addition to these problems both thematic and epistolary analysis are inadequate from a methodological viewpoint. As Jewett (*Thessalonian Correspondence,* 68) maintains, they lack "sufficient grounding in the conceptual framework of ancient letter writing."

The Rhetorical Genres of 1 and 2 Thessalonians

An alternative to the two approaches just discussed is to examine Paul's letters from the perspective of Greco-Roman letter-writing theory, which was closely connected with ancient rhetorical theory. In a society in which letters formed the principal means of communication between people separated from one another, letters functioned in a variety of ways depending upon the situation.

According to ancient rhetorical theory going back to Aristotle there were three genres of rhetoric: judicial rhetoric, deliberative rhetoric, and demonstrative or epideictic rhetoric. These designations originally were applied to types of public oratory, but as Kennedy (*New Testament Interpretation,* 19) points out, they have applicability to any form of discourse. In terms of classical rhetorical theory judicial rhetoric was employed when a speaker or author attempted to persuade an audience to make a decision about the correctness or incorrectness of some past event. As its name implies, it was the rhetoric of the law court. Deliberative rhetoric was directed to persuading people regarding the course of action to be followed in the future. Epideictic rhetoric sought through praise and blame to lead people into appropriate behavior in the present. Stowers (*Letter Writing,* 51f.) contends that letters can be found that conform to each of these genres, but this approach to classifying letters is not completely satisfactory because the schema is not sufficiently nuanced. Stowers (49-117), drawing on the epistolary handbooks of antiquity, presents a sixfold typology of letters based on their social functions: (1) letters of friendship, (2) family letters, (3) letters of praise and blame, (4) letters of exhortation and advice (which may be subdivided into parenetic letters, letters of advice, protreptic letters, letters of admonition, rebuke, reproach, and consolation), (5) letters of mediation, and (6) accusing, apologetic, and accounting letters.

Paul's letters to the Thessalonians may be classified in terms of either the standard rhetorical genres or Stowers's system of epistolary classification. The two systems have in common that they both help us to assess the literary intention of the author. This in turn sheds light on the socio-historical situation that the author addressed. Using the traditional rhetorical genres, Kennedy (*New Testament Interpretation,* 142) categorizes 1 Thessalonians as deliberative rhetoric, recognizing that it is essentially an exhortative letter. He appears to choose this heading on the grounds that deliberative rhetoric involves an argument concerning "self-interest and future benefits" (20). The characterization of 1 Thessalonians as deliberative rhetoric with a parenetic intention implies that Paul was seeking to *persuade* the Thessalonians to adopt or maintain the style of life inculcated by the letter. On close inspection, however, it is clear that 1 Thessalonians is filled with praise for the readers because of their exemplary behavior (see 1:2-3, 6-10; 2:13-14, 19-20; 3:6-9; 4:1-2, 9-10).

Jewett (*Thessalonian Correspondence,* 71-72) and Lyons (*Pauline Autobiography,* 219-221) are therefore correct in identifying 1 Thessalonians as a "demonstrative/epideictic" letter because such letters are devoted to praise (or blame) of people's behavior (cf. Kennedy, *New Testament Interpretation,* 73-85 on epideictic rhetoric).[8] To the extent that praise dominates, the parenesis is not persuasive but affirmative in character. Paul's encomium of his readers served to encourage them in their new Christian point of view and behavior. It thereby functioned to maintain the boundaries and distinctive features of the Christian world that the Thessalonians had come to inhabit through their conversion (cf. Stowers, *Letter Writing,* 77-81 on the use of praise and blame in maintaining socially constructed realities in the ancient world). The fact that the letter is demonstrative in character rather than deliberative is significant. It indicates Paul's relative satisfaction with the progress of the Thessalonians and the absence of serious problems requiring correction.

Stowers (*Letter Writing,* 94-106) and Aune (*Literary Environment,* 206), following the lead of Malherbe ("Exhortation in First Thessalonians"), identify 1 Thessalonians as a parenetic letter (cf. Meeks, *Moral World,* 125-130). This classification overlaps to some extent with the rhetorical genre classification of demonstrative rhetoric as understood by Jewett and Lyons.

---

8. Parenesis or exhortation was not given much treatment by rhetoricians (Stowers, *Letter Writing,* 51f.). When it was discussed it was related to both deliberative and demonstrative rhetoric depending upon whether the motive was one of persuasion or praise (Lyons, *Pauline Autobiography,* 220). The element of persuasion is clearly absent in 1 Thessalonians 1–3, and therefore the parenetic material of 2:1-12 is most naturally related to the demonstrative theme of praise. It should perhaps be noted that the parenetic quality of Paul's self-praise in 2:1-12 owes more to the tradition of moral philosophy in antiquity than to rhetoric.

It fails, however, to provide clarity about the intention of the exhortation or parenesis since parenesis may either be directed to confirming people in their present form of behavior, the function of demonstrative rhetoric in parenetic contexts, or to altering people's behavior, the function of deliberative rhetoric in parenetic contexts. As was suggested above, the preponderant element of praise in 1 Thessalonians reflects Paul's general satisfaction with the recipients of the letter and indicates that the parenesis was intended to reinforce them in their current forms of behavior rather than direct them to a different pattern of behavior.

Hughes (*Early Christian Rhetoric*, 55), Jewett (*Thessalonian Correspondence*, 82) and Kennedy (*New Testament Interpretation*, 144) identify 2 Thessalonians as a piece of deliberative rhetoric because it seeks to persuade the readers to think and act differently in the future. This seems to be the appropriate category. Unlike 1 Thessalonians, in which the readers are praised and exhorted to continue in their present beliefs and practices, 2 Thessalonians seeks to persuade its readers to adopt a different understanding of the day of the Lord than the one that they seem to hold (2:1-12) and to act against the disruptive influence of the idle (3:6-15). The decisions that Paul hopes to elicit from his readers clearly affect their future beliefs and practices, as well as their future well-being. Thus the letter conforms to the nature of deliberative rhetoric.

Neither Stowers nor Aune classifies 2 Thessalonians in terms of the epistolary typology that he adopts. The fact that Paul calls for a change in beliefs regarding the day of the Lord (2:1-12) and a different behavior pattern indirectly on the part of the idle and directly on the part of the responsible members of the community (3:6-15) fits with the primary characteristic of Stowers's letter of advice (see Stowers, *Letter Writing*, 107f.). Since the letter of advice in its pure form was understood to be deliberative in character, this reflects an overlap in the two systems of categorization. The use of deliberative rhetoric by Paul in 2 Thessalonians reflects his concern about the situation in the church and his desire to bring about important changes among its members.

Rhetorical Analysis

Ancient rhetoric was concerned with more than mere functional classifications of discourse. Kennedy (*New Testament Interpretation*, 3) explains the significance of rhetoric in the following way:

> Rhetoric is that quality in discourse by which a speaker or writer seeks to accomplish his [or her] purpose. Choice and arrangement of words are one of the techniques employed, but what is known in rhetorical theory as "invention"—the treatment of the subject matter, the use of evidence, the argumen-

48

tation, and the control of emotion—is often of greater importance and is central to rhetorical theory as understood by Greeks and Romans.

Paul's letters clearly demonstrate that he was reasonably well-educated in the art of rhetoric. For this reason it is possible to analyze his letters from the standpoint of rhetoric in order to understand their structure, argumentation, use of evidence, and control of emotion. By doing so it takes us beyond the usual thematic approach to the letters found in most commentaries to a conception of the principles used by Paul himself in constructing his letters and their argumentation.

From a rhetorical point of view 1 Thessalonians can be divided into the following structural units:

1. Epistolary Prescript (1:1)
2. *Exordium* (1:2-10)
3. *Narratio* (2:1–3:10)
   3.1 First Part of the *Narratio* (2:1-12)
   3.2 *Digressio* (2:13-16)
   3.3 Second Part of the *Narratio* (2:17–3:10)
4. *Transitus* (3:11-13)
5. *Probatio* (4:1–5:22)
6. *Peroratio* and Epistolary Closing (5:23-28)[9]

The epistolary prescript and closing effectively serve as the context into which the rhetorical structure is placed. The *exordium* is intended to elicit the sympathy of the audience, which it does through praise, and to set out the main themes of the letter. 1:2-3 and 6-9 thus introduce the theme of praise, which has a parenetic goal throughout the letter (cf. 2:13; 3:6-10; 4:1, 9-10; 5:11). 1:5 announces the theme of Paul's ministry to the Thessalonians and his apostolic character, which is the primary subject of the *narratio* (cf. 2:1-12 and 2:17–3:10). The theme of persecution in v. 6 prepares for the *digressio* in 2:13-16 where the same subject is discussed in greater detail (cf. also 3:3-4). 1:9-10 points forward to chaps. 4–5 where Paul treats the subjects of Christian behavior and eschatological expectation, while serving as a transition to 2:1 where Paul speaks of his mission to the Thessalonians.

In the *narratio* (2:1–3:10) Paul skillfully interweaves two types of classical rhetorical proof.[10] Much of the material is directed to establishing

---

9. Those familiar with the rhetorical analysis of 1 Thessalonians given by Jewett (*Thessalonian Correspondence*, 71-78) will recognize my debt to him, though at certain crucial points I differ from him.

10. Kennedy (*New Testament Interpretation*, 15) points out that according to Aristotle there were three modes of artistic proof available: *ethos,* which inhered in the speaker or writer, *pathos,* which inhered in the audience, and *logos,* which inhered in the discourse. *Ethos* refers

Paul's *ethos* or credibility with his readers by demonstrating what kind of missionary he had proved to be when working among the Thessalonians and later when separated from them. This then is a demonstration of Paul's statement in 1:5 regarding his claim that the Thessalonians knew what sort of people their missionaries were and knew by implication that they were people who could be trusted. This gives the *narratio* its philophronetic quality in overcoming the distance separating Paul and his friends at Thessalonica and leads to its parenetic value.[11] Some of the material in the *narratio* and in the *digressio,* which occurs in the middle of the *narratio,* functions to evoke *pathos* in the readers. Proof of a speaker's or writer's position could be achieved through arousing a strong emotional response in the audience. Paul's repeated praise of the Thessalonians has the effect of affirming them in their conversion to the Christian beliefs and practices that he inculcated, in spite of the persecution that came in the wake of their acceptance of Christ.

Having effectively reestablished his relationship with his converts in the *narratio,* Paul appropriately concludes with a wish-prayer to be able to visit his converts at Thessalonica and then introduces the theme of parenesis in the *transitus* (3:11-13). This becomes the subject of the second main part of the letter (4:1–5:22). Jewett (*Thessalonian Correspondence,* 75, 78) calls this section the *probatio.* The *probatio* consists in a series of proofs broadly parenetic in character. The topics dealt with in the proofs seek to strengthen the Thessalonians in their current beliefs and practices through encouragement and clarification. The parenetic quality of the material is underscored by the repeated use of παρακαλεῖν and its counterpart ἐρωτᾶν, words referring to exhortation (cf. 4:1, 10, 18; 5:11, 12, 14). Paul's argument in this section is that his readers have received the necessary information about how they should behave and please God, and therefore they should simply do what they are already doing with renewed fervor (4:1-2).

The *peroratio* and epistolary closing (5:23-27) emphatically recapitulates the principal theme of the letter, parenesis directed toward Christian living, and enjoins that the letter be read to the whole community. The letter ends with a typical Pauline benediction.

As a piece of deliberative rhetoric, the structure of 2 Thessalonians differs markedly from 1 Thessalonians because deliberative rhetoric did not

---

to the credibility that authors or speakers seek to create in their discourses in order to gain the trust of their audiences. *Pathos* concerns the emotional reactions which the communicator elicits from the audience. *Logos* relates to the logical arguments of a discourse that seek to demonstrate probable proof.

11. If my thesis is correct that 2 Thessalonians preceded 1 Thessalonians, the rhetorical situation envisaged by 1 Thessalonians may have arisen from the coolness of 2 Thessalonians, which lacks the friendly tone and praise of the readers characteristic of 1 Thessalonians. In 1 Thessalonians Paul may have been attempting to overcome resentment or a possible sense of rejection caused by his first letter, our 2 Thessalonians.

normally include a narration (Kennedy, *New Testament Interpretation,* 24). The following outlines the rhetorical structure of 2 Thessalonians:

1. Epistolary Prescript (1:1-2)
2. *Exordium* (1:3-12)
3. *Partitio* (2:1-2)
4. *Probatio* (2:3-15)
   4.1 First Proof (2:3-12)
   4.2 Second Proof (2:13-15)
5. *Peroratio* (2:16-17)
6. *Exhortatio* (3:1-15)
7. Epistolary Closing (3:16-18)

As with 1 Thessalonians, the rhetorical structure of 2 Thessalonians is bracketed by an epistolary prescript and closing, which give the document its formal character as a letter. The *exordium* begins with praise for the readers' progress in the faith under trying circumstances (1:3f.). This leads to the introduction of the main theme of the letter, the future occurrence of the day of the Lord, in 1:5-10. The prayer report in vv. 11f. solicits the goodwill of the readers (Hughes, *Early Christian Rhetoric,* 54) and prepares both for 2:13-17 and for the parenesis in 3:1-15.

Jewett (*Thessalonian Correspondence,* 86) and Hughes (*Early Christian Rhetoric,* 56) correctly designate 2:1-2 the *partitio.* Jewett does so because it announces what he believes to be the two principal arguments of the letter. Hughes agrees with this but adds that according to Cicero the *partitio* may also list points of disagreement with one's opponents. He then sees the question whether "the day of the Lord has come" as the major issue in dispute. Hughes's view is based on his belief that a post-Pauline writer is combating heretics and thus is involved in a polemic against them in 2 Thessalonians. I have already shown that the evidence for this thesis is far from compelling. Paul is not actually in dispute with opponents; he is, rather, engaged in correcting a serious misconception. For this reason it is best to speak simply of two proofs being announced in the *partitio.*

2:1-2 indicates that the fundamental proof of the *probatio* is a demonstration that the day of the Lord or the parousia has not come. Two proofs are offered in the *probatio.* Vv. 3-12 demonstrate that the events preceding the parousia of Christ have not occurred. Hughes (*op. cit.,* 57) has suggested that the second proof is found in vv. 13-15 and is connected with v. 2a, where Paul urges his readers not to be disturbed by the misconception that the day of the Lord has already come. According to Hughes the purpose of this second proof is to encourage "the readers' personal and doctrinal stability." This analysis seems correct in that the second proof provides a demonstration of why the readers should not be troubled in their beliefs regarding the day of the Lord.

Hughes designates vv. 16f. as a *peroratio* that summarizes the two proofs of vv. 3-15. This fits with Giblin's observation (*Threat to Faith*, 43) that Paul regularly uses ἄρα οὖν ("therefore then") as a concluding phrase. Since this phrase occurs in v. 15 and v. 16 begins a wish-prayer, it is likely that v. 15 concludes the *probatio*. The *peroratio* invokes God and the Lord Jesus Christ "to do to or for the readers what the proofs have sought to persuade them to do" (Hughes, 62). In the process it appeals to the readers' emotions by expressing Paul's concern for them and reiterates what they are to do.

While an element of exhortation regarding perseverance until the parousia is introduced in the conclusion of the *probatio,* the main exhortation of the letter is found in 3:1-15 and hence the designation of this section as an *exhortatio.*[12] The deliberative character of the rhetoric in 2 Thessalonians is especially clear in this section as Paul seeks to persuade his readers to take a particular course of action regarding the idle members of the community.

Having considered the various literary issues relating to 1 and 2 Thessalonians, I will turn now to a brief reconstruction of the situations in which the two letters were written. Drawing on the essentially literary arguments I have put forward in favor of the priority of 2 Thessalonians and the insights gained from rhetorical analysis, it will be possible to offer what I believe is a more plausible explanation of the situation in which the two letters originated than has heretofore been possible.

12. See Hughes (*Early Christian Rhetoric,* 63f.) on the place of exhortation within the epistolary tradition and in relation to deliberative rhetoric.

THE HISTORICAL SETTING OF
1 AND 2 THESSALONIANS

Our understanding of Paul's continuing relation with the church at Thessalonica after he left and the historical situation in which 1 and 2 Thessalonians were written depends to a great extent on two key factors: the order in which the letters are believed to have been written and the view that is taken regarding the types of problems that Paul sought to address. I have shown above that good grounds exist for accepting the reverse sequence of the letters. Here I will begin by examining some of the major theories regarding possible problems within the Thessalonian church and then attempt to reconstruct the historical setting of each letter in connection with Paul's continuing relation with the Thessalonian church.

PROPOSALS REGARDING PROBLEMS IN THE THESSALONIAN CHURCH

Over the years researchers have posited a number of different congregational situations to explain the particular set of issues apparently addressed by 1 and 2 Thessalonians. Often this has been done on the basis of theories that attempt to locate opposition to Paul throughout his missionary activity within one group.

In the nineteenth century, F. C. Baur and the Tübingen school defended the view that Paul confronted Judaizers (those who sought to require Gentiles to become Jews before they could be fully Christian) at Thessalonica, just as he did everywhere else, according to this theory. This view has no contemporary defenders. The evidence of the two letters simply does not support the theory. None of the central issues like law, circumcision, and justification by faith, which play a decisive role in the debate in Galatians, is found in the Thessalonian letters.

More recently Schmithals (*Paul and the Gnostics,* 123-218) has attempted to fit the Thessalonian correspondence into his general thesis that Paul continually fought off Gnostic intruders into his missionary congregations. Schmithals considers Paul's remarks in 1 Thes. 1:5, 9 and 2:1-12 as a defense of his apostolic ministry against a number of supposed Gnostic charges, such as that Paul's ministry lacked spiritual power and was characterized by deceit and greed (140-151). In 4:3-8 Schmithals (155-158) believes that Paul attacks Gnostic libertinism in sexual matters, while in 4:9-12 he sees Paul criticizing Gnostic enthusiasm, which encouraged idleness (158-160). In 4:13-18 he finds Paul defending the resurrection against its denial by Gnostic agitators (160-164), and in 5:1-11 he claims that Paul asserts Christian eschatology against Gnostics who denied all eschatological events (164-167).[1] According to Schmithals (167-169), 5:12-13 reflects Paul's attempt to bolster the authority of the community leaders against the Gnostic interlopers.

Schmithals's Gnostic hypothesis has failed to convince most scholars for several reasons. In the first place, none of the features singled out by Schmithals are necessarily Gnostic in character. For example, Malherbe ("'Gentle as a Nurse'"; *Moral Exhortation,* 54f.) has shown that 1 Thes. 2:1-12 is an attempt by Paul to show that he behaved impeccably toward his converts, like an ideal moral philosopher among the Stoics or the Cynics. Consequently, the passage need have nothing to do with a defense against Gnostic attacks. Similarly, there is nothing in the letters to suggest that the Thessalonians denied the resurrection or other eschatological events, though clearly they were confused about Paul's eschatological teachings. Secondly, the letters contain no evidence whatsoever to suggest that Paul thought that he was dealing with interlopers, whether Gnostic or otherwise. Had intruders been present we would expect some form of reference, undoubtedly of a caustic nature, like we find in Gal. 5:12 and 2 Cor. 11:12-15. The absence of this is a clear indication that whatever troubles may have existed in the church were not brought in from the outside. Thirdly, as Jewett (*Thessalonian Correspondence,* 149) remarks, a number of "distinctive features of Gnosticism . . . are conspicuously absent in Thessalonica." Among these he mentions "dualism of flesh and spirit, christological speculation, the speculative use of Genesis 1–3," and "the enactment of libertinistic behavior." In light of these considerations we may safely exclude the possibility of Gnostic opponents.

Another general theory regarding Paul's opponents was applied specifically to the Thessalonian situation by Lütgert ("Volkommenen"). He found reason to believe that the source of most of the problems at Thessalonica arose from a radicalization of what Paul had taught. This radicalization led to spiritual enthusiasm on the part of some and brought in its wake libertinism and indolence by those who felt themselves to be spiritually superior. The key component in the enthusiasts' reinterpretation of Paul's teaching was their belief that in receiving the spirit they had experienced the eschatological event

---

1. Harnisch *(Eschatologische Existenz)* has taken up the views of Schmithals regarding 1 Thes. 4:13–5:11 and offered slight modifications, but essentially his position is the same as that of Schmithals.

of the parousia of the Lord. For such people the benefits of the resurrection had become a present reality (see Lütgert, 632-638). Numerous scholars have employed the essential thrust of Lütgert's thesis, emphasizing that spiritual enthusiasm gave rise to a form of realized eschatology among the spiritual elite at Thessalonica (see Jewett, *Thessalonian Correspondence*, 142-147).

In a sense, a close connection exists between Lütgert's position and the position of Schmithals. It is mainly a matter of degree. Both Schmithals and Lütgert rely on the same basic evidence to prove that the troubles at Thessalonica involved either a deeschatologized version of Christianity (Schmithals; cf. Harnisch, *Eschatologische Existenz*) or a realized eschatology (Lütgert). Moreover, both scholars claim that the targets of Paul's criticism practiced a form of spiritual elitism that resulted in libertarian behavior and idleness. The strength of the enthusiast interpretation over Schmithals's Gnostic hypothesis is that it does not require outside intervention, for which there is no evidence, and it attempts to bring together a variety of evidence into a coherent position.

But it is not without difficulties, as Jewett (*Thessalonian Correspondence*, 147), one of its former exponents, has recognized. Perhaps the greatest weakness resides in the lack of evidence in the letters themselves for a clear connection between the problems associated with eschatology and the possession of the Spirit. Nowhere are the two associated in the letters, and in fact the assumption that Paul was dealing with a self-conscious belief in realized eschatology is not borne out by careful exegesis (see the comments below on 1 Thes. 4:15; 2 Thes. 2:2). Furthermore, the Thessalonian letters, when compared with 1 Corinthians, where spiritual gifts were a serious issue of contention, simply do not provide sufficient evidence of the existence of spiritual enthusiasm. Certainly 1 Thes. 5:19-22, the only injunction regarding spiritual gifts in either letter, cannot sustain the weight of the hypothesis, because it could have been construed by spiritual enthusiasts to favor their basic activity (for further criticism see Best, 19-22).

In his recent monograph Jewett attempts to develop a new theory about the opposition confronted by Paul in the letters (*Thessalonian Correspondence*, 149-157). He claims that something like a "divine man ideology" was at work. By this he means that some people in the community believed themselves to have transcended the normal bounds of human experience. He offers four types of evidence that point to this conclusion.

First, through a comparison of Paul's missionary behavior (1 Thes. 2:1-12) with that of the ἄτακτοι (2 Thes. 3:6-15; 1 Thes. 5:14; cf. 1 Thes. 4:11f.; Jewett understands this term as referring to "disorderly members of the community"), he purports to find details that correlate, to a certain extent, with the divine man profile adduced by scholars in the past (151f.). These details include Paul's denial of πλάνη, ἀκαθαρσία, and δόλος (error, immorality, and deceit) on his part in 1 Thes. 2:3, which Jewett believes were characteristic of the behavior of the ἄτακτοι, at least from Paul's perspective. Also Paul's positive claim to having acted gently (vv. 6-7) and in a pious and upright manner (v. 10) is antipodal to the exploitative and scandalous (4:11-12) behavior of the ἄτακτοι.

Jewett's second and third types of evidence are based on correlations that he makes with information in 2 Corinthians regarding Paul's opponents, whom he also understands in terms of divine man ideology. He begins by pointing to the behavior of Paul's opponents in Corinth. The apostle seems to imply that they used deceit for the purpose of monetary gain. He also accuses them of domineering behavior and of demanding recognition of their superior ecstatic gifts. These factors have been associated by Georgi with controversies regarding the divine man in the Greco-Roman world (*Opponents*, 229-246). Jewett (153) finds here a parallel with the behavior of the ἄτακτοι in 1 and 2 Thessalonians. He further finds that some of the claims of Paul in 1 Thes. 2:1-12 show "a kind of competitive correlation with specific features of a divine man ideology" as they appear in 2 Corinthians (*Thessalonian Correspondence*, 153f.). Among these are Paul's claims to boldness (1 Thes. 2:2) and approval by God (2:4; cf. 2 Cor. 10:18; 13:3-7; 3:1-3), as well as his claim to have shared not only the gospel but also himself with his converts (1 Thes. 2:8; cf. 2 Cor. 4:5).

Jewett's fourth type of evidence consists in "general similarities between the Thessalonian radicals and divine men." Employing the model of the divine man reconstructed by scholars earlier in the century, he notes the tendency of divine man ideology to emphasize ecstasy as evidence of divinity on the part of its missionary claimants (154). He sees a correspondence with the self-understanding of the ἄτακτοι at this point, whom he contends were conscious of having "transcended time and trouble in their ecstatic experiences" even to the point of transcending death. This consciousness, according to Jewett, gave rise to shock and despair when the community experienced persecution in spite of living in the "apocalyptic triumph of the spirit."

Having set out the evidential basis for a connection between divine man ideology and the Thessalonian situation, Jewett (155f.) acknowledges that the thesis has certain problems. In the first place, a number of English-speaking scholars have provided extensive critiques of the divine man concept as it has been reconstructed primarily by German-speaking scholars (e.g., Tiede, *Charismatic Figure;* Holladay, *THEIOS ANER*). Secondly, in relation to the Thessalonian correspondence, the divine man ideology only correlates with 1 Thes. 2:1-12 and a few other passages where Jewett thinks that the behavior of the ἄτακτοι is under discussion. Moreover, he recognizes that such aspects as invading missionaries who assert their superiority over Paul, peculiar allegorical interpretations of scripture, and the Hellenistic Jewish background posited by Georgi are all problematic. But in spite of this Jewett (*Thessalonian Correspondence*, 156f.) believes that the divine man model adds to our understanding of the ἄτακτοι and offers parallels to the practices of the Cabiric cult that existed in Thessalonica.

Unfortunately, Jewett's line of reasoning is a house of cards. Nowhere in the text of the letters is a connection made between the ἄτακτοι and the practice of error, immorality, or deceit. In the case of 1 Thes. 4:11f., the issue is not the "scandalous libertinism" of the ἄτακτοι but the need for Christians to live quiet, orderly, and circumspect lives that would be beyond reproach from outsiders. By this injunction Paul sought to minimize the possibility of renewed oppression, not to combat a major "theological" deviation within the community. As will be shown in my discussion of 2 Thes. 3:6-15, Jewett has misunderstood the question of the ἄτακτοι by not considering the proper social origin of the problem. Jewett recognizes the basic disparity between the situation at Corinth and Thessalonica, including the clear differences between the ἄτακτοι, who originated in the church at Thessalonica, and the "superlative apostles," who were interloping missionaries at Corinth. There is, therefore, no justification for correlating the evidence from the two situations, even if the divine man ideology were conclusively shown to be applicable to the Corinthian situation.[2] Finally, Jewett's "mirror" reading of 1 Thes. 2:1-12, that is, his assumption that behind Paul's antithetical statements we can discern the position of his opponents, constitutes a misunderstanding of the rhetoric of autobiography in the Greco-Roman world, as Lyons (*Pauline Autobiography,* 95-112, 183f.) has forcibly demonstrated.

If Paul was not facing Judaizers, Gnosticizing tendencies, spiritual enthusiasts, or a type of divine man ideology, then what was the congregational situation on the two occasions when he wrote to the Christian community at Thessalonica? A careful analysis of the two letters and the historical data provided by Paul regarding his ongoing relation with the community yield a very different image than those so far discussed.

THE SITUATION PRESUPPOSED BY 2 THESSALONIANS

1 Thes. 2:17–3:6 provides us with a narrative of Paul's relationship with the church at Thessalonica after his departure up to the time at which 1 Thessalonians was written. After Paul's apparently hasty departure from Thessalonica (1 Thes. 2:17; cf. Acts 17:5-10) a period of time passed before he had further contact with the church. On at least two occasions Paul wanted to revisit his converts but was unable to do so (1 Thes. 2:18). Finally when he was overcome with anxiety about the Thessalonians, he sent Timothy to

---

2. Theissen, *Social Setting,* 27-53 offers a much more plausible analysis of the situation at Corinth than Georgi when he claims that the troubles arose because of competing types of missionary strategy.

establish and encourage them (3:1-2). At the time he sent Timothy, Paul believed that the Thessalonians were being persecuted and that they were in danger of being shaken in their faith (3:3). This fear turned out to be unfounded (v. 6). I have shown earlier that a number of these details relating to Timothy's visit correlate with the contents of 2 Thessalonians to such a degree that it is reasonable to assume that Timothy took 2 Thessalonians with him when he paid the visit mentioned in 1 Thes. 3:1-5. With this in mind I shall now attempt to reconstruct the congregational setting of 2 Thessalonians.

The first point to note regarding the congregational situation at the time 2 Thessalonians was written is that we know very little about it. Paul himself does not appear to have been well-informed about circumstances in Thessalonica when he wrote the letter. A careful reading suggests that Paul had three principal concerns regarding the church: he believed that the church was undergoing oppression (2 Thes. 1:4-6); he was worried that his converts were deviating from a correct understanding of the day of the Lord (2:1-12); and he was troubled by a report that some members of the community were indolent and exercising a disruptive influence on the community (3:6-15). Only in respect to the last point does he indicate that his comments were based on information that he had received, but even this indication (3:15) is very vague.

Paul does not specify his source of information, nor does anything in the letter indicate his source. This is of some interest. In both 1 Corinthians (cf. 1 Cor. 7:1, 25; 8:1; 12:1; 16:1) and 1 Thessalonians (cf. 4:9, 13; 5:1) Paul uses the expression "now concerning" (περὶ δέ) when answering questions raised in communications from his converts. The absence of this expression in 2 Thessalonians suggests that he was not responding to a direct communication from the church. This impression is further confirmed by the fact that he does not seem to know the origin of his readers' false understanding regarding the day of the Lord, as 2 Thes. 2:2 shows. If these observations are correct, they lead to another correlation between 2 Thessalonians and Timothy's urgent visit to the church at Thessalonica. Paul says in 1 Thes. 3:5 that he sent Timothy to *learn* whether the Thessalonians were remaining faithful when he could no longer tolerate his ignorance in the matter. In the case of both 2 Thessalonians and Timothy's return to Thessalonica Paul appears to have had little firsthand information about the church, but clearly for some reason he was anxious about the community.

If Paul had no direct information from the church, why did he address the three principal issues dealt with in 2 Thessalonians? The most reasonable explanation for this is that a report had come from Christians outside the community at Thessalonica mentioning difficulties that they had heard were taking place in the community. A possible source of this information may have been the church at Philippi. The Christians there appear to have maintained close contact with Paul after he left. I have already mentioned that Phil.

4:16 states that they sent support to Paul on at least two occasions during the time he was conducting his mission at Thessalonica. In the preceding verse, Phil. 4:15, he comments that the Philippians were the only church group to enter into a reciprocal relation of giving and receiving after he left Macedonia. Anyone coming by land from Philippi to Athens, where Paul was when he sent Timothy back to Thessalonica (1 Thes. 3:1), would have passed through Thessalonica, perhaps spending the night with someone in the Christian community there. From such limited exposure the messenger may have gained impressions about the problems in the church there, but would still not have detailed information. This scenario can never be proven, but something like it must be assumed to explain on the one hand why Paul wrote when he did and on the other why he is so vague about the source of the disturbance regarding the parousia of Christ. Paul's lack of information about the circumstances explains why he felt compelled to send Timothy along with the letter even though he apparently would have preferred not to (cf. 1 Thes. 3:1).

This explanation of the situation leading to the writing of 2 Thessalonians runs contrary to the prevailing assumptions made about the matter, but it has an important advantage. Most recent commentators believe that 1 Thessalonians conveys a sense of Paul's relative satisfaction with the progress of the church (cf. Rigaux, 57-62; Best, 15f.; Marxsen, 28; Marshall, 9f.). Because Paul adopts a more critical and argumentative line in 2 Thessalonians, those who believe that Paul wrote it posit that circumstances deteriorated between the two letters (cf. Best, 59; Marshall, 23-25). But this poses a problem noted by Jewett (*Thessalonian Correspondence,* 91f.): "the more serious difficulties of 2 Thessalonians appear to have arisen from a completely unproblematic congregational situation a few months earlier."

If the view suggested above is correct, the problem posed by Jewett lies in a faulty understanding of the relation between the two letters. Paul wrote 2 Thessalonians when he received a secondhand report of troubles in the church. After sending Timothy and our 2 Thessalonians to his converts he was pleased to discover that matters were not as precarious as he had been led to believe. In fact, when Timothy returned, Paul was overjoyed to learn that the Thessalonians had not deviated from the faith that he had given to them (1 Thes. 3:6-10). He was also pleased with their moral progress on the whole. Both 1 Thes. 4:2 and 10 give the impression that Paul was satisfied with their Christian behavior and only wished to encourage them to continue doing what they were already doing.

But Jewett solves the problem he has posed differently, with the claim, based on rhetorical analysis, that 1 Thessalonians reflects serious problems (*Thessalonian Correspondence,* 92). This is a strange claim. Earlier in his monograph (71f.) Jewett rightly identifies 1 Thessalonians as a piece of epideictic or demonstrative rhetoric. Epideictic rhetoric was devoted to either praise or blame in order to encourage people to "hold or reaffirm some point of view in the present" (Kennedy, *New Testament Interpretation,* 19). Unlike deliberative rhetoric it was not intended to persuade people to change their minds or their behavior (see Kennedy, 19). As the element of praise predominates through out 1 Thessalonians and the element of blame is almost totally absent, it is difficult to see in the letter concern on Paul's part about a troubled congregational situation that would eventually necessitate his writing 2 Thessalonians. Moreover, if things were already as problematic as Jewett thinks when 1 Thessalonians was written, then epideictic rhetoric would have been the wrong rhetorical approach. Paul could hardly have called on his readers to hold on to their current beliefs and practices if he believed that serious deviations in these areas were emerging in the church. Rather he would have been forced to persuade his readers to change their theology and behavior through the use of deliberative rhetoric (cf. Lyons, *Pauline Autobiography,* 219-221).

THE SITUATION PRESUPPOSED BY 1 THESSALONIANS

The circumstances both of Paul and his converts that lie behind the writing of 1 Thessalonians are much clearer than those for 2 Thessalonians. In 1 Thes. 3:1-10 Paul explains his reasons for sending Timothy back to the congregation and then his own experience of relief and joy upon learning from Timothy about the perseverance and progress of the Thessalonians in the Christian faith. V. 6 makes it clear that the letter was written almost immediately upon Timothy's return. This suggests that Paul's intention was to clarify any issues raised by the Thessalonians with Timothy as well as to address any problems that Timothy may have discerned in the life of the Christian community at Thessalonica.

The letter creates the overall impression that Paul was pleased with the progress of his converts in Thessalonica given the adverse circumstances that they had endured. Many attempts to infer from the text the exact nature of the congregational situation have led to misunderstandings. Perhaps the most important misreading involves the interpretation of 2:1-12. This section is normally described as an apology for the character of the apostolic mission to the Thessalonians. Many scholars assume that if Paul describes his activity in antithetical terms, as he does in this section (see vv. 1f., 3-4b, 5-7, and 8), then someone was impugning his integrity and his apostolic authority through negative criticism (e.g., Frame, 90; Schmithals, *Paul and the Gnostics,* 142-155; Marshall, 61; Jewett, *Thessalonian Correspondence,* 92, 102-104; Holtz, 92-95). Against this, Laub (*Eschatologische Verkündigung,* 133-136) has shown that this view often results from foisting the situation in 2 Corinthians onto 1 Thes. 2:1-12 (Schmithals, 142-155, does exactly this). Holtz (93f.) avoids this criticism by arguing that Paul was responding to a charge leveled by his non-Christian opponents, probably at the instigation of the Jews in Thessalonica. The opponents sought to discredit Paul in the eyes of his converts by linking him to the self-aggrandizing practices of the wandering Cynic preachers of the day.

Against the view of Holtz and others who look for historical reasons for the antithetical formulations of 2:1-12, Lyons (*Pauline Autobiography*, 184; cf. Malherbe, " 'Gentle as a Nurse,' " 217) has convincingly argued:

> Antithetical constructions require a literary and rhetorical rather than a historical explanation. They were far too common in the normal synagogue preaching of Hellenistic Judaism and the moral discourses of itinerant Cynic and Stoic philosophers in clearly non-polemical settings to assume, as the consensus of New Testament scholarship has done, that Paul's antithetical constructions uniformly respond to opposing charges.

Lyons (189-221) goes on to demonstrate conclusively that the function of the autobiographical material in 1 Thes. 2:1–3:13 is parenetic. Paul offers his own conduct as a moral example of how a Christian should behave, as the connections between 2:1–3:13 and the exhortative material in 4:1–5:22 show. Malherbe ("Exhortation in First Thessalonians," 240f.) makes the same point, noting that "a major part of ancient paraenesis was the offering of a model to be imitated . . . , the delineation of which is done antithetically." While I am convinced of the essential correctness of Lyons and Malherbe's position, it may be that a subsidiary motivation in the autobiographical material was to demonstrate for the readers Paul's continuing concern for them. This may have the intention of overcoming possible disappointment that Paul himself had not managed to come back to them. Such an understanding would account both for the highly affectional language of the passage and for Paul's claim that Satan had thwarted his desire to revisit the Thessalonians on several occasions (2:17-20).

Once it is accepted that Paul was not faced with serious opposition within the community, the focus of attention shifts from chaps. 1–3 to chaps. 4–5. Although Paul offers exhortation and instruction regarding a number of themes, it lacks the intensity characterizing such material in other letters of his (e.g., compare 1 Thes. 4:4-8 with 1 Cor. 5:1-5; see Lyons, *Pauline Autobiography*, 220). In both 4:1 and 4:10 Paul encourages his readers to continue in their moral progress and abound in it without offering any serious correction of their behavior. This implies a situation in which there were no pressing ethical deviations requiring reproach. Instead, as Malherbe ("Exhortation in First Thessalonians," 250-256) has demonstrated, much of the ethical exhortation and even the eschatological material in 4:13-18 have a basis in traditional parenesis. This should warn us of the need to exercise considerable caution in trying to reconstruct the congregational situation from such material.

The only major issues in the congregation would appear to be related to their eschatological outlook. In 4:13 Paul writes: "Now we do not want you to be ignorant concerning those who sleep. . . ." This looks like an issue that the Thessalonians raised with Timothy, as the expression δὲ . . . περί ("now concerning") seems to indicate (see the comments on this construction). The problem would appear to have resulted from either the readers' failure to understand Paul's eschatological teaching at the time he was with them or Paul's failure to explain the full implications of the parousia of Christ at that time.

Paul's primary concern is not to correct a doctrinal aberration but to provide consolation for his readers regarding the participation of their deceased love ones in the parousia (4:18). Although we lack sufficient information to know how the two might connect together, it may be that this problem was related to the issue discussed in 2 Thes. 2:1-12. For example, the Thessalonians might have believed that the day of the Lord had come for their deceased loved ones. They may have evolved this belief to explain how their dead loved ones could share in the assumption to heaven that was to occur at the coming of Christ. Paul's lack of knowledge about this at the time 2 Thessalonians was written (see above) may explain why 2 Thessalonians failed to address the matter and why he needed to speak again to the issue in 1 Thes. 4:13-18.

The Thessalonians also appear to have requested clarification about a second matter pertaining to eschatology. In 5:1-2 Paul says, "Now concerning the times and dates, you have no need [for us] to write to you, for you yourselves know well that the day of the Lord comes as a thief in the night." This new topic, similarly to 4:13-18, begins with περὶ δέ. Whatever the precise question is that Paul seeks to clarify, it does not reflect a major aberration in the beliefs of the Thessalonians, as Paul simply reminds them of what they already know. His intention, according to 5:11, is for the Thessalonians to encourage one another about the need for watchfulness in light of the eschatological times in which they live. As in 4:13-18, the question raised by the Thessalonians may follow on the trouble that Paul deals with in 2 Thes. 2:1-12. As I will show in the comments on 1 Thes. 5:1-2, that passage does not contradict the eschatological scenario of 2 Thes. 2:1-12, when properly understood. What 1 Thes. 5:1-11 does clearly demonstrate is that Paul encouraged his converts to ethical rigor through the belief that the parousia of Christ was imminent.

One further point needs to be mentioned. In both 4:11-12 and 5:14 Paul's exhortation seems to deal with the problem of the idle, a theme treated with marked urgency in 2 Thes. 3:6-15. In 1 Thessalonians, however, the urgency has gone out of the discussion. Manson ("St. Paul in Greece," 442) long ago observed that the exhortations in 4:11-12 and 5:14 have force only when read against the original exhortation in 2 Thes. 3:11-15. This indicates that the disturbance caused by the idle was largely under control after Timothy's visit and therefore only necessitated a fairly gentle reminder from Paul.

If my views are correct, we actually know relatively little about the community in Thessalonica at the time that Paul wrote 1 Thessalonians. The reason is that there were no major crises that Paul sought to address and no major ethical deviations that Paul felt compelled to correct. Lyons (*Pauline Autobiography*, 219) takes a similar position and makes the interesting point that:

> Perhaps compensating for our loss of certainty as to the historical situation in Thessalonica, is the possibility that we have in 1 Thessalonians an indication of what Paul actually considers ethically momentous, and not simply an illustration of how he responds to ethical failures on the part of his converts.

This is indeed an important gain in our understanding of Pauline Christianity. The dearth of information available for reconstructing a nuanced portrait of the congregational situation in the case of both 1 and 2 Thessalonians should lead to a renewed interest in the character and function of the letters themselves against their socio-religious background in the first-century Greco-Roman world.

COMMENTARY ON 1
THESSALONIANS

EPISTOLARY PRESCRIPT: 1:1

Letters in the Greco-Roman world, like modern letters, followed a standard format that included a prescript or salutation, body, and conclusion. The salutation in Greek letters almost always included three elements: the sender's name, the addressee, and a pro forma greeting: *A to B: greetings* (with a verb like "sends" being understood). This could be extended to include additional greetings and a wish for good health. For example: Θέων Ἡρακλείδη τῷ ἀδελφῷ πλεῖστα χαίρειν καὶ ὑγιαίνειν ("Theon to his brother Herakleides many greetings and good health"; see White, *Light*, 118 for this and other examples; cf. Est. 8:13 [12a, LXX]; 1 Macc. 10:18; 2 Macc. 10:22). 1 Thessalonians begins with the shortest and simplest prescript of any of the extant Pauline letters and conforms closely to the unelaborated salutations of contemporary Greek letters, with one significant modification, as we shall see.

1:1 1 Thessalonians, like 1 and 2 Corinthians, Philippians, Colossians, Philemon, and 2 Thessalonians, purports to have been sent by Paul and one or more of his coworkers. The senders of 1 Thessalonians, as in the case of 2 Thessalonians, identify themselves as Paul, Silvanus, and Timothy. To what extent Silvanus and Timothy actively participated in the composition of the letter is impossible to say, but in conformity with the prescript, the first person plural is used throughout the letter with very few exceptions.

Three passages in particular, however, suggest that the letter should be read primarily as an embodiment of Paul's thought. In 2:18 the first person plural is replaced by the first person singular in the second part of the verse where Paul specifically identifies himself: διότι ἠθελήσαμεν ἐλθεῖν πρὸς ὑμᾶς, ἐγὼ μὲν Παῦλος καὶ ἅπαξ καὶ δίς ("wherefore we wished to come to you, I Paul, once and again"). A few verses later, in 3:5, the first person singular occurs again. Given Paul's self-assertion in 2:18, we must assume that κἀγὼ ... ἔπεμψα ("and I ... sent") in 3:5 also refers to Paul himself. This impression is further confirmed by the fact that the passage in question concerns an occasion when Timothy was sent as a substitute for the person who stands behind the "I." From other letters of Paul we know that this is precisely how Paul employed Timothy (cf. 1 Cor. 4:17; 16:10; Phil. 2:19). The other text in which the first person singular occurs is 5:27, where the author of the letter "adjures" his readers to ensure that the letter is read to "all the brothers." The sheer authoritativeness of this injunction implies an author of the stature of

Paul who could impose such a demand on his readers (see R. F. Collins, "Paul," 351-353 for further discussion of the "I" passages).

If in fact Paul is the real author of 1 Thessalonians, why has he included the names of his fellow workers Silvanus and Timothy in the salutation? Two answers may be given. In the first place, Silvanus and Timothy shared in the missionary work at Thessalonica, and therefore as Paul's colleagues they had a stake in the development of the church there. Their inclusion as co-senders of the letter thus strengthens the authority of the document by implying unanimity among Paul and his coworkers regarding the situation of the Thessalonians. Doty (*Letters,* 30) has suggested a second reason. In Hellenistic letters the carrier who was to deliver the letter was often mentioned in order to link him with the writer and thereby "guarantee that what he had to say in interpreting the letter was authorized by the writer." Since Paul used various colleagues in this way, including Timothy, this may help explain the inclusion of Silvanus and Timothy in the prescript if one or both of them was to deliver the letter (see 3:1-5 on the use of Timothy as an emissary and substitute for Paul's apostolic parousia or presence).

In most of his letters Paul begins by identifying himself as an apostle (Rom. 1:1; 1 Cor. 1:1; 2 Cor. 1:1; Gal. 1:1) or as the slave or prisoner of Christ (Phil. 1:1; Phm. 1). The absence of such a self-identification in 1 Thessalonians (and 2 Thessalonians) is therefore noticeable but can perhaps be explained in terms of the situation. In the case of Romans, 1 and 2 Corinthians, and Galatians, Paul's status and authority were to some degree in question. In the case of Philippians and Philemon the self-description was intended to evoke respect and possibly sympathy from the recipients. Nothing in 1 Thessalonians indicates that Paul's authority or status was in doubt among his readers, and Paul's personal situation was certainly not as precarious at the time of writing as it was when Philippians and Philemon were written.

Details of Paul's life and apostleship are known well enough not to require elaboration here. The same is not true, however, of Silvanus and Timothy. Σιλουανός is almost certainly the person whom Acts refers to as Σιλᾶς (Acts 15:22, 27, 32 and nine times in 15:40–18:5). Σιλουανός is probably the Latinized form of his name while Σιλᾶς is the Grecized version, both perhaps derived from Aramaic Šᵉʾîlaʾ (BDF §125.2; see Bruce, 6 for an alternative possibility). Paul mentions Silvanus in the prescript of both 1 and 2 Thessalonians and in 2 Cor. 1:19, where he states that Silvanus shared in the mission work at Corinth. Acts 17:1-9 indicates that he did so at Thessalonica as well.

Acts tells us several other things about Silas that may help explain his role with Paul. After the Jerusalem conference recorded in Acts 15, Silas and a man named Barsabbas, both "leading men among the brothers" at Jerusalem (v. 22), were sent with a letter to the Gentile converts in Antioch, Syria, and Cilicia specifying certain moral and ritual purity practices that the Gentile Christians were to adhere to (vv. 22-34). According to 15:36-41, when Paul and Barnabas fell out over whether John Mark should accompany them on a second missionary journey, Paul took Silas with him. While we are unable to confirm these details from Paul's own letters, it is not beyond the realm of possibility that Paul took Silvanus along precisely because he was a representative of the mother church in Jerusalem. By doing so he perhaps hoped to ensure the support of Jerusalem for his missionary activity and to emphasize the unity of his work with the mother church.

Nickle (*Collection*, 18-22) has argued that one of the "apostles of the churches" referred to in 2 Cor. 8:23 was Silvanus. Whether his identification of Silvanus can be maintained or not, 2 Cor. 8:17-24 does indicate that Paul on some occasions was accompanied by representatives of Jerusalem. That Silvanus was an apostle seems likely. As Holmberg (*Paul and Power*, 65) has observed, if Paul intended plural ἀπόστολοι in 1 Thes. 2:7 to be taken seriously, then he acknowledged Silvanus as an apostle. From Paul's perspective this meant that Silvanus was a witness to the resurrected Jesus, and therefore his status was comparable to that of James the brother of Jesus and of Paul himself (1 Cor. 15:3-8). This fits well with the impression created by Acts, which claims that Silas was a prominent member of the Jerusalem church. Thus we should think of Silvanus, not as an underling of Paul like Timothy, but as "a respected colleague almost the equal of Paul himself" (Holmberg, 65).

The name Τιμόθεος occurs in all the letters of the Pauline corpus except Galatians and Ephesians. In six letters Timothy is named as Paul's co-writer (1 Cor. 1:1; Phil. 1:1; Col. 1:1; 1 Thes. 1:1; 2 Thes. 1:1; Phm. 1). 1 Cor. 4:17 and 16:10; Phil. 2:19-23; and 1 Thes. 3:1-6 make it clear that Timothy served as Paul's special assistant and emissary to the churches when Paul was unable to be present. As Funk ("Apostolic *Parousia*," 255-258) has shown, Timothy exercised Paul's apostolic parousia, that is, he embodied Paul's apostolic authority and power to the churches in Paul's absence (see 1 Thes. 3:2). Phil. 2:19-22 indicates that Paul considered him his most trusted assistant and confidant, while 1 Cor. 4:17 reveals a strong sense of warmth on Paul's part toward Timothy, whom he calls his "faithful and beloved child in the Lord."

According to Acts 16:1-3, Timothy was a disciple from Lystra whose mother was a Jewish Christian and whose father was a Gentile and very possibly a nonbeliever as well. When Paul selected Timothy to accompany him on his second missionary journey, he had him circumcised because it was known in the local Jewish community that his father was a Gentile. Acts 20:4 indicates that he traveled with Paul on his last journey to Jerusalem, and the prescripts of both Philippians and Philemon show that he was with Paul in his imprisonment, presumably at Rome. Elsewhere in the NT he is mentioned as the recipient of two letters, 1 and 2 Timothy, that claim to have been written by Paul. He is also named in Heb. 13:23, which may have given rise to the ascription of Hebrews to Paul in the ancient Church.

The prescript of 1 Thessalonians specifies that the letter was addressed ἐκκλησίᾳ Θεσσαλονικέων ("to the church of the Thessalonians"). "Church" probably has more meaning for us than ἐκκλησία had for the Thessalonians. The Greek word was used of a summoned assembly, for example, a regularly summoned political body (cf. Josephus, *Ant.* 12.164) or a public gathering of a more general sort (cf. Acts 19:32). The word was also used in the LXX for the solemn gathering of the people of Israel as a religious assembly (cf. Dt. 31:30; 1 Kgdms. [1 Sa.] 17:47). Because the Christian community constituted the new people of God who assembled regularly for worship and fellowship, the word was taken over by Paul and others as a designation for any local Christian community (cf. 1 Cor. 4:17; Gal. 1:22), for the wider Christian community (cf. 1 Cor. 12:28), and even for house churches (Rom. 16:5). Use of ἐκκλησία for the assembly of the Christian community may also reflect the desire for a distinctively "Christian" identity in the face of Jewish use of συναγωγή for local Jewish congregations (cf. Acts 6:9).

ἐν θεῷ πατρὶ καὶ κυρίῳ Ἰησοῦ Χριστῷ ("in God the Father and the Lord Jesus Christ") specifies which assembly is being addressed, as in about twenty percent of the other occurrences of ἐκκλησία in Paul's letters (cf. 1 Cor. 1:2; 15:1; Gal. 1:13). What is unusual, however, is the idea that the church is somehow "in God." Paul characteristically uses "in *Christ*" to indicate the incorporation of the Christian into Christ's life in all its dimensions (cf. Rom. 6:11; see Best, *One Body*; Bouttier, *En Christ*; Moule, *Origin of Christology*, 47-96 on the use of "in Christ" in Paul's letters), but he does not use "in God" in a similar spatial sense, except, as here, with ἐκκλησία. For this reason Best (*Commentary,* 62) suggests that "in God" should be understood instrumentally and that the whole phrase should be rendered "the Christian community brought into being by God the Father and our Lord Jesus Christ." Bruce (7) on the other hand argues that if "in . . . the Lord Jesus Christ" has its customary meaning here, then "in God the Father" should be understood in the same fashion. No definitive solution to this question can be offered on grammatical grounds. It is certain, however, that whether the instrumental or the spatial sense of ἐν was intended, Paul sought to link the Christian community in Thessalonica to both God and Christ because it had its origin in divine activity, its existence was to be determined by God the Father and the Lord Jesus Christ, and its members were to live out their lives in the presence of the divine.

The theological importance of the name and nature of the church at Thessalonica should not cause us to lose sight of the fact that the Christian ἐκκλησία was first and foremost a community, a social institution, without which Christianity would never have succeeded in becoming the dominant religion of the Roman Empire. This was the cardinal advantage that it enjoyed over its religious competitors in the Roman world, which, with the exception of Judaism, did not generally organize adherents into religious communities (see Gager, *Kingdom and Community,* 140). The communal character of

Christianity provided the context in which converts were resocialized from the pagan or exclusively Jewish worlds to the new Christian world with its distinctive sets of beliefs and values. (See the Introduction, pp. 14f. above, for a further discussion of religious conversion as a socialization process.) It was also the basis for separating those who professed faith in the one God and Father and in the one Lord Jesus Christ (cf. 1 Cor. 8:6) from the rest of humanity by reinforcing the new Christian social identity. In other words the Christian community or church helped to establish group boundaries between saved and unsaved humanity. This was essential for sustaining its identity and that of its members in a hostile world (see Meeks, " 'Since then . . . ,' " 4-29; *First Urban Christians,* 84-106 on group boundaries in Pauline Christianity).

χάρις ὑμῖν καὶ εἰρήνη ("grace to you and peace") concludes the prescript of the letter by offering a somewhat abbreviated form of the standard Pauline greeting. It differs markedly from the greeting in the normal Greek letter, where some form of χαίρειν ("greetings" or "rejoice") is used, but it has some correspondence to the normal Jewish greeting, "peace." In 2 Macc. 1:1 we find a combination of the typical Greek greeting, χαίρειν, with the traditional Jewish greeting, εἰρήνη. What is interesting about this example is that "peace" is part of a formulaic prayer for the well-being of the recipients that occurs after the formal greeting. *2 Bar.* 78:2 employs "mercy and peace" in a similar fashion, and Doty (*Letters,* 29f.) notes that this was typical of Jewish letters.

Thus Paul's "grace and peace," which in all of his other undisputed letters is qualified by some variant of the words "from God our Father and the Lord Jesus Christ," constitute a formulaic prayer for the addressees of his letters. For this reason Lohmeyer ("Probleme," 159) may be correct when he says that the formula was primarily liturgical in character. While there is always a danger of reading too much into isolated occurrences of words, Paul undoubtedly intended "grace and peace" to evoke in his readers a sense of divine blessing upon their lives characterized by God's freely given favor and the sense of completeness or wholeness (the root idea of the Hebrew word *šālôm*) that results from reconciliation with God through Christ's death. In this way Paul shows his grounding in the OT understanding of God's dealings with the people of Israel.

EXORDIUM: 1:2-10

Since the early form-critical work of Paul Schubert *(Form and Function),* it has become common to speak of the thanksgiving period of the Pauline letters as a specific structural component in the apostle's letters. With the exception of Galatians, all of the Pauline letters addressed to churches have a thanksgiving section immediately following the prescript (cf. Rom. 1:8-15; 1 Cor. 1:4-9; Phil. 1:3-11; Col. 1:3-8; 2 Thes. 1:3-12). 2 Cor. 1:3-7 and Eph. 1:3-14 are not exceptions to this rule even though neither εὐχαριστῶ nor any of its cognates occurs. In those two letters "blessed (εὐλογητός) be the God and Father of our Lord Jesus Christ" clearly serves to introduce a section having the same function as the other opening thanksgiving sections in the letters of Paul. This has led Doty *(Letters,* 32) to suggest that we should speak of "thanksgiving and/or blessing segments" in the Pauline letters. Paul's opening thanksgivings seem to function as substitutes for the common wish for well-being or mention of supplication on behalf of the recipient(s) that occur in Hellenistic letters (cf. White, *Light,* 219; Stowers, *Letter Writing,* 73).

The case of 1 Thessalonians is peculiar, however, because of the further expressions of thanksgiving in 2:13 and in 3:9f., on the basis of which Schubert (17-27) claims that the introductory thanksgiving stretches as far as 3:13. In 2:13 Paul returns to the theme of thanksgiving by offering thanks for his readers' conversion immediately after his description in vv. 1-12 of the nature of his ministry among them that led to their conversion. In 3:9f. the apostle summarizes the theme of his continuing concern for his converts (2:17–3:8) by means of a thanksgiving statement. O'Brien *(Introductory Thanksgivings,* 144), following the lead of Schubert, explains the diffuse character of the thanksgiving in 1 Thessalonians by claiming that Paul includes "personal and official details in and around his thanksgiving or petitionary prayer reports." Though Schubert and O'Brien have both struggled to explain the atypical form and function of the thanksgiving section in 1 Thessalonians, they have clearly not succeeded because they have not offered a satisfactory explanation for the large sections of material that occur between the three thanksgiving statements.

Several other scholars have recognized the structural unity of 1:2–3:13 implied in the work of Schubert and O'Brien (cf. Frame, 12-17; Rigaux, 33-37; Lyons, *Pauline Autobiography,* 175-221; Jewett, *Thessalonian Corre-*

spondence, 68-78). Lyons and Jewett (see also Kennedy, *New Testament Interpretation*), in particular, have offered a new way forward by their application of rhetorical analysis to the letter. Jewett describes 1:1-5 as the *exordium* or introduction to the letter. According to rhetorical theory the *exordium* or *prooemium* was intended to make the audience "well-disposed, attentive, and tractable" toward the communicator (Kennedy, *Art of Persuasion,* 121; cf. *idem, New Testament Interpretation,* 23f.). According to Jewett the *exordium* of 1 Thessalonians announces thanksgiving as the principal theme of the letter. The *narratio* section of 1:6–3:10 then narrates the reasons for Paul's thanksgiving to God.

While Jewett is essentially correct, it is more appropriate to speak of 1:2-10 as the *exordium* of the letter. Good reason exists for doing so. The *exordium,* in addition to evoking a sympathetic response from its readers, was intended to announce the main themes of the letter. The theme of thanksgiving is clearly set forth in vv. 2f. But a variety of subthemes are also introduced in vv. 4-10.

Beginning in v. 4 and continuing to v. 10 Paul takes up the conversion of his readers. This theme is elaborated upon in the narration in 2:1-12, which is followed by Paul's thanksgiving for his readers' conversion in 2:13. In v. 6 Paul mentions the persecution experienced by the Thessalonians at the time of their conversion and how it led to their becoming imitators of himself and the Lord. This provides the theme of the digression in 2:14-16 as well as the underlying motif in the continuation of the narration found in 2:17–3:5. The second part of the narration furnishes the basis for the third thanksgiving in 3:6-10. Similarly, the subject of eschatological expectation, of central importance in 4:13–5:11, is first announced in 1:9f. At first sight parenesis, an important theme of the letter in 2:1-12, where it is implicit, and 4:1–5:22, where it is explicit, appears to be missing from the *exordium.* This initial perception is not proven correct on closer reflection. Paul's implied praise of the readers in vv. 6-9 is parenetic in character because it serves to affirm the Thessalonians in their Christian way of life (cf. 4:1-12). In addition the implied praise of the readers and the reference to their fame among other Christians in 1:6-10 clearly function to create a sympathetic audience for what follows, as one would expect of a well-constructed *exordium* (cf. Kennedy, *New Testament Interpretation,* 142). Finally, it should be noted that the true *narratio* seems to begin in 2:1. Beginning in 2:1 the outline found in 1:4-10 is repeated and expanded. If 1:6-10 is treated as the start of the *narratio,* then the repetition of material from it in 2:1–3:10, a section more or less corresponding to a chronological history of relations between Paul and the Thessalonians, becomes somewhat disjointed.

1:2 Paul immediately affirms his readers by telling them: εὐχαρι-στοῦμεν τῷ θεῷ πάντοτε περὶ πάντων ὑμῶν ("we give thanks to God always concerning all of you"). Grammatically περὶ πάντων ὑμῶν ("concerning all of you") could go either with εὐχαριστοῦμεν ("we give thanks"), which precedes it, or with μνείαν ποιούμενοι ("making mention"), which follows it. On the basis of 1 Cor. 1:4, where περὶ ὑμῶν goes with the preceding εὐχαριστῶ (cf. 2 Thes. 1:3), it seems best to take it with εὐχαριστοῦμεν here and then understand ὑμῶν with μνείαν ποιούμενοι (cf. Rigaux, 359). In fact a number of manuscripts, including ℵ², C, D, F, and G, add ὑμῶν between μνείαν and ποιούμενοι (see the apparatus of Nestle-Aland²⁶ for this).

When Paul affirms that he and his colleagues give thanks for the Thessalonians and adds μνείαν ποιούμενοι ἐπὶ τῶν προσευχῶν ἡμῶν ("making mention [of you] in all our prayers"), this is not a mere rhetorical remark or epistolary nicety. As a Jew brought up in the custom of regular prayer, he undoubtedly did offer continual thanks to God in his prayers for his converts and their faith in Christ. πάντοτε suggests that thanksgiving for the Thessalonians was an ongoing part of Paul's prayer life, and it is this that differentiates the apostle's assertion concerning the giving of thanks for the Thessalonians from a mere rhetorical device written in a pro forma way at the beginning of a letter, as in many of the Hellenistic letters from the period. That Paul placed considerable importance on thanksgiving in prayer is shown by the fact that he enjoined this practice on his converts (5:17f.). O'Brien (*Introductory Thanksgivings*, 146) may be correct in claiming that plural εὐχαριστοῦμεν indicates that Paul, Silvanus, and Timothy met together regularly to share in corporate prayer with thanksgiving to God for the conversion of the Thessalonians.

The main clause of v. 2, "we give thanks always concerning you," is followed by three dependent participial constructions: μνείαν ποιούμενοι . . . μνημονεύοντες . . . εἰδότες ("making mention . . . remembering . . . knowing"). These give a rhythmic quality to the material in vv. 2-4. The participles are not, however, logically parallel since "making mention in our prayers" does not constitute grounds for giving thanks to God, while "remembering your work of faith . . ." and "knowing your election" do.

ἀδιαλείπτως ("without ceasing") at the end of v. 2 may go either with the preceding words, μνείαν ποιούμενοι ("making mention") or with the following words, μνημονεύοντες ὑμῶν τοῦ ἔργου τῆς πίστεως κτλ. ("remembering your work of faith . . ."), at the beginning of v. 3. In opposition to *UBSGNT* and many commentators (e.g., Findlay, 19; Frame, 75; Friedrich, 211) it seems better to link this word with what precedes it since this is less disruptive to the rhythmic flow of the sentence (Rigaux, 361; cf. Best, 66). It then serves a parallel function to the πάντοτε of the main clause by explaining the manner in which Paul and the others "always give thanks" for the Thessalonian Christians, namely, by "*constantly* mentioning" them in their prayers.

1:3 When Paul gives thanks to God for his readers he does so because he remembers their response to the gospel: μνημονεύοντες ὑμῶν τοῦ ἔργου τῆς πίστεως καὶ τοῦ κόπου τῆς ἀγάπης καὶ τῆς ὑπομονῆς τῆς ἐλπίδος ("remembering your work of faith, toil of love, and steadfastness of hope"). This thanksgiving statement clearly serves as a word of praise. Rhetorically it is intended to create a positive emotion or *pathos* in the readers (on the use of *pathos* in rhetoric see Kennedy, *New Testament Interpretation*, 15) in order to make them well disposed to Paul's parenetic advice (cf. Stowers, *Letter Writing*, 80). The well-known triad of faith, love, and hope recurs often in Pauline and other early Christian literature (cf. 1 Thes. 5:8; Rom. 5:1-5; 1 Cor. 13:12; Gal. 5:5f.; Col. 1:4f.; Eph. 4:2-5; Heb. 6:10-12; 10:22-24; 1 Pet. 1:3-8, 21f.; Barn. 1:4; 9:8; Pol. 3:2f.). Paul uses it here to express the essence of his readers' experience as Christians. He does this by using each member of the triad as a subjective genitive to the verbal idea contained in the governing noun. Thus Paul remembers "their work that proceeds from their faith," "their labor that proceeds from their love," and "their steadfastness that proceeds from their hope." No significant difference in meaning can be distinguished between ἔργος and κόπος in v. 3. Both, in connection with their respective subjective genitives, refer to activities that mark the addressees as Christians in a pagan and hostile world.

"Your work of faith" (ὑμῶν τοῦ ἔργου τῆς πίστεως) is of particular interest in the context of Pauline theology. The radical disjunction that Martin Luther claimed to have found in Paul's writings between faith and human striving (work) and that led him to reject the letter of James as a "strawy epistle" needs careful qualification. In Galatians where Paul attacks "works" most vigorously and contrasts them with "faith," he has a particular type of "works" in mind. He condemns those works proceeding from the Jewish Torah and what E. P. Sanders *(Paul and Palestinian Judaism)* calls "covenantal nomism" (cf. Gal. 2:15f.; 3:2-5). His attack on "works of the law" in Galatians was a theological polemic designed to distinguish the new religion to which he belonged from the mother religion from which it and he had come (though obviously Paul would not have articulated it this way). The loss of the original context of the debate, especially since the Reformation, has led to a fundamental misunderstanding of Paul and Pauline theology (see Wanamaker, "Case"). Our text clearly indicates that Paul did not conceive of Christian faith as radically opposed to works. For him Christian activity proceeds from faith, and thus he would probably have endorsed the views of Jas. 2:14-17. Paul does not specify what the "work of faith" consisted in here, but his readers probably would have understood it in terms of the totality of their new Christian life-style that distinguished them from the pagans around them and from their own past.

The expression "labor of love" (κόπου τῆς ἀγάπης), like the preceding phrase "work of faith," cannot easily be given a specific content. Like much theological language it is evocative and allows the reader to fill in the detail from his or her own experience. Nevertheless, we may safely say that the love that Paul refers to is both his converts' love for God and their love for one another (cf. 1 Thes. 4:9; 2 Thes. 3:5). Love was neither a mere emotion for Paul nor simply a social virtue, as Enslin (*Ethics,* 74) describes it. Instead, as Furnish (*Love Command,* 94) points out, for Paul love was "the necessary manifestation within Christ's body of the new creation already underway in the working of God's Spirit," and like faith, it was inextricably linked to the activities that proceeded from it. It would appear from 4:10 that the Thessalonians had shown their Christian love toward their fellow believers in Macedonia (cf. 2 Cor. 8:1-5), and this may have been the specific fact in Paul's mind as he wrote of their "labor of love." Whether this is correct or not, Paul's inculcation of love among his converts had an important social function, as we shall see later (see on 3:12).

The choice of ὑπομονῆς ("steadfastness") to go with ἐλπίδος ("of hope") would appear to have particular significance in the context of 1 Thessalonians. The letter makes it abundantly clear that Paul's readers had experienced serious opposition from their fellow citizens (cf. 2:14). Nevertheless, they had remained faithful to the gospel (cf. 3:6) because their hope was fixed on the Lord Jesus Christ. Thus Paul uses the objective genitive phrase τοῦ κυρίου ἡμῶν Ἰησοῦ Χριστοῦ ("our Lord Jesus Christ") with the verbal idea contained in the noun ἐλπίδος: their hope was in Jesus, whom they believed would soon return from heaven to bring about their deliverance (cf. 1:10; 2 Thes. 1:3-10). Therefore, from Paul's perspective it was their firmly fixed hope in Jesus Christ that gave them the strength to persevere in their new Christian beliefs and behavior in spite of considerable adversity from their non-Christian fellow citizens.

The concluding words of v. 3, ἔμπροσθεν τοῦ θεοῦ καὶ πατρὸς ἡμῶν ("before our God and Father"), may go either with the preceding words "the hope of our Lord Jesus Christ" or with the participle "remembering" at the beginning of the verse. Bruce (12f.) argues in his comment on 1:3 that "before our God and Father" is too far removed from the participle to be taken with it and therefore takes it with "work of faith," "labor of love," and "steadfastness of hope." But when he comments on 3:9, where "before our God" occurs in a context concerning prayer, he refers back to 1:3 and implies that the phrase relates in 1:3 to the participle "remembering" (68). This seems the better choice because, if the phrase is taken with μνημονεύοντες, it becomes clear that Paul's "remembering" of the Thessalonians "before our God and Father" refers specifically to his prayers of thanksgiving for them. Thus v. 3 provides part of the grounds for his thanksgiving to God concerning the Thessalonians.

1:4 The second reason that Paul gives thanks to God for his readers is that he knows of their election by God. His knowledge of their election is based on the transformation that took place in their lives when he and his colleagues preached Christ to them. By placing εἰδότες, ἀδελφοὶ ἠγαπημένοι ὑπὸ [τοῦ] θεοῦ, τὴν ἐκλογὴν ὑμῶν ("knowing your election, brothers [and sisters], beloved by God") after the statement concerning their "work, labor, and steadfastness" Paul is able to reinforce the connection between their new Christian way of life and the certainty of their salvation at the parousia or public manifestation of Christ.

ἀδελφοί ("brothers") is used here and throughout the letter when Paul wishes to address his readers directly. This usage is common in the Pauline letters (cf. Rom. 1:13; 7:1, 4; 1 Cor. 1:10, 11, 26; 2 Cor. 1:8; 8:1; Gal. 1:11; 3:15; Phil. 1:12; 3:1; 2 Thes. 1:3, etc.) and in fact is Paul's favorite form for direct address of his readers. The choice of this word to designate members of the Christian community has considerable importance. "Brother" was used in Judaism to express group identity or a loose sense of group kinship (e.g., Dt. 15:3, 12; Philo, *Spec. Leg.* 2.79f.; Josephus, *Ant.* 10.201), and it was undoubtedly from there that it was taken over by the early Christians. With the Christians it fitted neatly with several symbolic relationships that were part of their new self-identity. They called God their "father" (Gal. 4:6; Rom. 8:15), professed themselves to be his adopted children (cf. Gal. 3:26; 4:4-7; Rom. 8:14-23), and understood Christ, the son of God, to be their brother (cf. Rom. 8:29). This logically made them brothers and sisters (cf. 2 Cor. 6:18) of one another and contributed to the emergence of a strong sense of kinship among them. In this way they gained a new social identity as former kinship and social ties broke down under the demands of their new religious commitments.

Paul extends the address by adding the words "beloved by God," which are intended to evoke a strong sense of belonging to God and undoubtedly had the effect of assuring the readers that whatever abuse and rejection they experienced at the hands of family, friends, or fellow citizens was worth it because of the standing they had gained with the one true and living God. In effect these underscored Paul's assertion of his readers' "election" to salvation because the Thessalonians' sense of election by God singled them out from those non-Christians around them whom they believed were destined for divine wrath (cf. 1:10).

The idea of election to salvation, like the idea of being part of a family, had its roots in the OT and in Judaism (see Dt. 7:6-11 and cf. Rom. 9:11; 11:5, 7, 28), although the word ἐκλογή ("election") does not occur in the LXX and is used by Paul of Christians only in this passage (however, compare his use of the adjective ἐκλεκτός in Rom. 8:33; 2 Thes. 2:13, 16; and Col. 3:12). The doctrine of community election had an important social function for Paul and his converts. Paul's use of ἐκλογή here serves a similar function to the family language of which the terms "brothers and sisters" are a part. It is what Meeks (*First Urban Christians,* 85) calls "the language of belonging." Such language helps to create a sense of group identity and, one might add, superiority for a community setting itself over against the wider society of which it is a part. The sense of exclusiveness that belief in divine election engendered among early Christians was one of the powerful internal factors giving Christianity an advantage over its religious competitors like the mystery religions and philosophical competitors like the Stoics and Cynics, who were not exclusivistic and therefore generally failed to create a strong sense of community identity among their adherents (cf. Gager, *Kingdom and Community*, 131f.). Thus the belief of the Thessalonians in their election by God was of tremendous social significance, since on the one hand it gave them a new identity and sense of belonging to the saved community of God, while on the other it helped symbolically to annihilate the world of their previous social existence, an important and necessary step if they were to remain converted (see pp. 14-16 above).

1:5 The exact relation of v. 5 to what precedes is unclear because the connective particle ὅτι could be taken either in a causal sense, yielding a meaning like "we know your election *because* . . . ," or in an epexegetical sense, yielding a meaning like "we know your election, *that is, how*. . . ." The latter interpretation requires that "your election" in v. 4 be understood as meaning "the manner of your election" (Best, 73). This seems unlikely, however, because it was probably not the manner of the Thessalonians' election that caused Paul to give thanks, but the fact of their election. Therefore it seems better to take ὅτι in a causal sense with Rigaux (372f.) and O'Brien (*Introductory Thanksgivings*, 151f.), among others. Paul was sure of his readers' election because of the results achieved by the gospel preaching that he and his fellow missionaries had done. This starting point, however, is forgotten to some extent in v. 5 as Paul elaborates on the manner of the apostolic preaching to the Thessalonians. It is only in vv. 6-10 that Paul gives the positive reason why he is certain of the election of the Thessalonians.

He describes the preaching by himself and his fellow missionaries as τὸ εὐαγγέλιον ἡμῶν ("our gospel"). "Gospel" (εὐαγγέλιον) occurs some 60 times in the Pauline corpus and is the apostle's favorite term for describing the message that he proclaimed. It most probably passed into the Christian tradition from the preaching of Jesus, who used texts like Is. 52:7, where the verbal form εὐαγγελιζόμενος occurs, to define his own activity (see Meyer, *Aims*, 129-137). But in Paul the content of the gospel has become the report about Jesus Christ as God's son and agent in bringing about eschatological salvation. By extension it refers to the totality of the Christian message as proclaimed by Paul. However, it can also refer to the act of preaching (2 Cor. 8:18; cf. G. Friedrich, *TDNT* II, 729; Best, 74). While the content of preaching can never be divorced fully from the act of preaching, this verse seems to refer to the manner in which Paul and his fellow missionaries preached among the readers. Therefore the primary nuance of εὐαγγέλιον in this verse concerns the act of delivering the gospel rather than its content. For this reason "our gospel" should be understood as meaning "our gospel preaching": "our" should not be understood as a possessive pronoun but as a subjective genitive to the verbal idea in "gospel."

According to Paul, his preaching to the Thessalonians was οὐκ... ἐν λόγῳ μόνον ἀλλὰ καὶ ἐν δυνάμει καὶ ἐν πνεύματι ἁγίῳ καὶ [ἐν] πληροφορίᾳ πολλῇ ("not in word only but also in power and in the Holy Spirit and in great conviction"). Paul is not contrasting preaching as mere human speech with preaching in power and the Holy Spirit and therefore does not make an absolute contrast, as in 1 Cor. 2:4, where he seems to be denying the charge that he was a sophist in his preaching. Rather he insists here that his preaching consisted in both the words that were spoken and the power that was manifested to the Thessalonians at the time. The οὐκ μόνον... ἀλλὰ καὶ... formula is used here then for intensification, not contrast (Kemmler, *Faith and Human Reason*, 159).

From passages like Gal. 3:5 and especially Rom. 15:18f. and 2 Cor. 12:12f. we know that Paul's apostolic work was accompanied by manifestations of power. He does not tell us in 1 Thes. 1:5 in what the manifestation of "power" consisted. In Rom. 15:18f., however, he speaks of Christ working through him for the conversion of the Gentiles ἐν δυνάμει σημείων καὶ τεράτων ("in power of signs and wonders"). We should probably understand δύναμις ("power") in 1 Thes. 1:5 in a similar way as referring to the miraculous signs and wonders that accompanied the preaching of the gospel. In this context we may perhaps think of the gifts of the Spirit that Paul enumerates in 1 Cor. 12:8-10 as manifestations of what the apostle meant by "power." This power undoubtedly carried considerable ability to convince people of the truth of his preaching because its manifestations were interpreted as divine acts (cf. Holtz, 47), just as Christian faith healers in the modern world use "miracles" in their preaching of the gospel to convince their audiences.

It is difficult to separate "in power" from the subsequent words "in the Holy Spirit," because the source of this power for Paul was the Holy Spirit. The absence of the article with πνεύματι ἁγίῳ does not mean that Paul is simply referring to a divine spirit that inspires people (contra Turner, *Syntax* III, 175 and Best, 75, who accepts Turner's view). Paul frequently does not include the article when he uses πνεῦμα ἅγιος in prepositional phrases where the context indicates that he is referring to the Holy Spirit (cf. Rom. 5:5; 9:1; 14:17; 15:16; 1 Cor. 12:3; 2 Cor. 6:6; see BDF §§255; 277 on the definite nature of anarthrous nouns in prepositional phrases).

Although πληροφορία might conceivably mean "fullness" (Rigaux, 377-379), the words [ἐν] πληροφορίᾳ πολλῇ are best translated "in great conviction" (cf. Holtz, 47). Bruce (14) suggests that this conviction was on the part of the Thessalonians, but this seems unlikely. Like the two preceding phrases this one concerns the manner of Paul's preaching of the gospel. This view is confirmed by the subsequent words. The καθώς ("just as") continues the discussion of how Paul came across to the Thessalonians, while only in v. 6 does Paul turn to the effect of the mission on his readers.

With the clause καθὼς οἴδατε οἷοι ἐγενήθημεν [ἐν] ὑμῖν δι' ὑμᾶς ("just as

79

you know what sort of people we were among you for your sakes"), Paul makes the first of a number of direct appeals in the letter to the recollection of the Thessalonians to confirm the accuracy of what he is telling them (cf. 2:1-12; 3:3f.; 4:2; 5:2). This is typical of parenetic letters that assume that the recipients are "already substantially living and acting in the right way" (Stowers, *Letter Writing*, 103) and fits the designation of the letter as a piece of epideictic or demonstrative rhetoric (see above, pp. 46-48). As far as Paul was concerned, his apostolic manner of life was lived for the sake of his converts (δι' ὑμᾶς) and was totally in keeping with the message that he and his colleagues had declared to the Thessalonians. In fact it was part of the gospel preaching itself, as this verse indicates. With the final words of v. 5 Paul introduces a theme that he subsequently elaborates in considerable detail in 2:1-12. At the same time he prepares for v. 6 where he speaks of the Thessalonians' imitation of himself and his colleagues.

1:6 As was indicated in connection with v. 5, v. 6 is closely related to v. 4 and provides the most tangible evidence of the Thessalonians' election by God. It also relates to v. 5 because it gives an indication of the result of Paul's missionary preaching among the Thessalonians and the impact of his and his fellow missionaries' manner of living on their converts. Rhetorically, v. 6 returns to the theme of praise of the addressees that Paul began in vv. 2f. The intention of this praise was to elicit a positive response from the audience that would make them more willing to receive the parenesis of the letter. But this material has another intention. Behind the praise of the Thessalonians implied in v. 6 is a subtle piece of parenesis inculcating perseverance in all circumstances through imitation of Paul and the Lord Jesus. (On the use of personal examples in parenesis see Malherbe, *Moral Exhortation*, 125, 135-138.)

The theme of imitation is found in several of Paul's letters. In such passages as Phil. 3:17; 1 Cor. 4:16; and 11:1 Paul urges his converts to become imitators of himself (cf. Gal. 4:12; Phil. 4:9; 2 Thes. 3:7, 9). In 1 Cor. 11:1 he specifies that the Corinthian Christians should imitate him just as he imitates Christ. This creates the impression that Paul understood his own life as a form of mediation between Christ and his converts. His life provided the model of a Christ-like life for those who had no firsthand knowledge of Christ (cf. Marxsen, 38f.).

In the present verse, however, the theme of imitation is more limited since it appears to be concerned with the Thessalonians' initial experience as Christians: καὶ ὑμεῖς μιμηταὶ ἡμῶν ἐγενήθητε καὶ τοῦ κυρίου, δεξάμενοι τὸν λόγον ἐν θλίψει πολλῇ ("and you became imitators of us and of the Lord, receiving the word in great distress"). The aorist participle δεξάμενοι ("having received") alludes to the fact that it was in connection with receiving the gospel report under great duress from their own fellow citizens (see 2:14) that they became imitators of Paul and the Lord. It needs to be asked whether the participle is temporal or instrumental. Did the readers become imitators of the missionaries "*when* they received the gospel in great distress" or "*by* receiving the gospel in great distress"? Put another way, was their imitation achieved by the way in which they received the gospel (instrumental) or did their imitation consist in their experience of considerable opposition at the time that they became converts (temporal)? The problem with the instrumental understanding is that it makes the imitation consist in the way in which they received the word. While it is conceivable that Paul might have meant that he received the word in tribulation, as some commentators suggest (e.g., Best, 77; Marshall, 54), it is considerably more difficult to know what Paul might be referring to with τοῦ κυρίου, since the Lord presumably did not receive the word under duress, though he certainly experienced oppression in his life. For this reason it is better to understand the participle as temporal. The Thessalonians' imitation of Paul and the Lord consisted in their experience of great distress accompanied by the "joy of the Holy Spirit" at the time of their conversion.

The expression "you became imitators of us and the Lord" has a significant rhetorical function within the letter. Stowers (*Letter Writing,* 95f.) has pointed out that parenetic letters require the writer to be "the recipient's friend or moral superior." Paul does not speak of his apostleship in the prescript or the *exordium* of 1 Thessalonians, but the phrase "you became imitators of us" asserts Paul's position as the superior in the relationship with his converts. It thereby legitimates his right to guide and instruct his readers in the ways of Christ.

Malherbe (*Paul and the Thessalonians,* 48) maintains that the θλῖψις suffered by the Thessalonians was "the distress and anguish of heart experienced by persons who broke with their past as they received the gospel" rather than some form of external duress applied to dissuade them from converting to the Christian faith. This seems unlikely for three reasons: (1) In 3:3 Paul uses θλῖψις of external oppression that his readers have undergone. It is questionable whether the same word would be used in two very different senses in the same general context of the letter. (2) It is improbable that Paul meant that his converts had become imitators of the Lord by virtue of their inner sense of conflict at the time of their conversion. Paul would hardly have wanted to suggest such internal ambivalence on the part of the Lord, whom they were imitating. (3) In v. 7 Paul proceeds to say that the Thessalonians' experience of "much distress" resulted in their becoming an example for all the believers in Macedonia and Achaia. This implies very strongly that in v. 6 Paul was speaking about more than mere "distress and anguish of heart." After all, every convert to the new faith could be said to undergo "distress and anguish of heart" in the sense suggested by Malherbe. Since the cause and nature of the distress experienced by the recipients of the letter has great significance for understanding the development of Christianity at Thessalonica, I will come back to this problem in the discussion of 2:14, where Paul says that the Thessalonians' persecution occurred at the hands of their fellow citizens. At present it suffices to say with Holtz (49) that the Thessalonian Christians underwent some form of social oppression at the time of their conversion.

The final words of the verse, μετὰ χαρᾶς πνεύματος ἁγίου ("with the joy of the Holy Spirit") are particularly important. They remind the readers of the tangible proof of their election. It was not only in that they received the word in distress that they became imitators of Paul and the Lord, but also in that they had a sense of joy in this situation that could not be accounted for in human terms. Their joy was, according to Paul, inspired by the Holy Spirit.

Their joy undoubtedly did rest on several objective considerations. To begin with, they were now part of a new community, the people of God, which could look forward to imminent salvation when Jesus would return, and second, their oppressors and all others outside their community would be subject to the wrath of God at the coming of Christ (cf. 1:10). Without this fundamental belief in future vindication and salvation in the face of persecution, a belief characteristic of early Christians (cf. 1 Pet. 1:6f.; 2:20f.; Mt. 5:11f.) that later gave rise to the cult of the martyrs, the powerful emotion of joy in the face of opposition would be inexplicable. The communal nature of the Pauline churches provided a context in which such beliefs could be stated and reinforced (see pp. 15f. above on the importance of the community in maintaining the Christian symbolic world). A final factor bears mentioning. In all probability Paul and his converts believed that distress or tribulation was a precursor to the coming of Christ (see the comments on 3:2-4; 2 Thes. 1:5-10). The experience of distress was a sign that the parousia with its promise of final redemption was close at hand. Thus we can see how Paul's theological statement regarding the divinely inspired joy in the face of persecution was grounded in the belief structure, or symbolic world, which he had given to his converts.

1:7 V. 7 is a dependent clause expressing one of the important results (ὥστε) of the experience of the Thessalonians in converting to the Christian message that Paul had proclaimed. Because their conversion had occurred in spite of opposition and distress and they had remained faithful in the face of continuing opposition (cf. 3:1-5), their persistence served as a source of encouragement and inspiration to other groups of believers in their region. Just as they had become imitators of Paul and the Lord, they in turn became τύπον πᾶσιν τοῖς πιστεύουσιν ἐν τῇ Μακεδονίᾳ καὶ [ἐν] τῇ Ἀχαΐᾳ ("an example to all the believers in Macedonia and Achaia"). τύπον ("example") is singular because Paul alludes to the experience of the community as a whole. Apparently, the hostility directed toward the Thessalonians was not the common experience of other Christian communities in the Roman provinces of Macedonia, where Thessalonica was located, and Achaia, which included Corinth, at least to begin with (but see 2 Cor. 8:1f.). This accounts for the unique esteem in which the community at Thessalonica was held by Paul and his mission congregations.

At the level of epistolary rhetoric, the verse is yet another item in praise of the recipients. Like the previous verse and the verses that immediately follow, it helps to create *pathos,* or a positive emotional reaction in the audience, by affirming their unique standing within the wider Christian community.

1:8 V. 8, loosely connected with the preceding verse by γάρ, continues the idea of the previous sentence: not only did the Thessalonians become an example for other Christians, but also from them ἐξήχηται ὁ λόγος τοῦ κυρίου οὐ μόνον ἐν τῇ Μακεδονίᾳ καὶ [ἐν τῇ] Ἀχαΐᾳ, ἀλλ᾽ ἐν παντὶ τόπῳ ("the word of the Lord has sounded forth not only in Macedonia and [in] Achaia, but in every place"). The expression ὁ λόγος τοῦ κυρίου ("the word of the Lord") derives from the OT (cf. Gn. 15:1, 4; Is. 1:10; Je. 2:4, etc.) and is unusual in Paul. It occurs only here and in 2 Thes. 3:1, though it appears frequently in Acts (8:25; 12:34; 13:44, 48; 15:35, 36; 19:10). In keeping with the OT usage it emphasizes that the message, in this case of divine salvation, not judgment, originates from the Lord. For Paul, however, "the Lord" is not God as in the OT but Jesus Christ.

The verb ἐξήχειν is found only here in the NT and provides the image of something, like sound, going forth in all directions. Just what Paul means by this is not clear. Possibly he means that the Thessalonians immediately began to engage in their own missionary work, but this appears unlikely since their activity would surely not have been as widespread as this verse suggests. It seems much more probable that Paul means something like "the report concerning what the Lord has done among you" had gone out to the wider Christian community, first in the Roman provinces of Macedonia and Achaia (here thought of as one region if ἐν τῇ, which is absent before "Achaia" in many manuscripts, is not original) but also beyond this to other areas as well. "In every place" is clearly hyperbolic, though undoubtedly the report concerning the Thessalonians' response to the gospel in the face of opposition did spread widely, particularly if most other Christian congregations did not suffer oppression from their local communities at this time. This interpretation is supported by the fact that the ἀλλά ("but") clause offers a geographical extension to the idea of the preceding clause. ἡ πίστις ὑμῶν ἡ πρὸς τὸν θεὸν ἐξελήλυθεν ("your faith toward God has gone out") is parallel to "the word of the Lord rings out" and interprets it; "the word of the Lord has sounded out from you" means little more than that the report of their faith went forth.

As a result of their fame (ὥστε) Paul could say, μὴ χρείαν ἔχειν ἡμᾶς λαλεῖν τι ("we have no need to say anything"). Naturally, he means that it was unnecessary for him and his colleagues to "say anything," that is, to other Christians about the Thessalonians. 2 Thes. 1:4, however, indicates that he in fact did hold up the Thessalonian community as an example to other churches because of their unique experience and faithful response to the gospel (cf. 2 Cor. 8:1-5). This seeming contradiction is explained if we assume the priority of 2 Thessalonians, as I have argued in the Introduction. As a result of Paul's initial reports regarding the Thessalonians, which were intended to encourage perseverance in other congregations, by the time 1 Thessalonians was written it was no longer necessary for the apostle to recount the faithfulness of the Thessalonians in the face of external adversity. It had become a well-known fact. According to Stowers (*Letter Writing,* 99) reference to the testimony of others was a common practice in parenetic letters. By affirming his readers' accomplishments and the fame that it brought them, Paul continues through praise to create *pathos* in his readers. This device was intended to make the recipients receptive to the exhortation and advice offered by the letter.

1:9-10   These two verses must be taken together because the versification in this case is highly arbitrary and separates two parallel infinitives dependent upon the same main verb. In addition, it is widely assumed that these two verses contain a pre-Pauline formula summarizing missionary preaching to the Gentiles, which the apostle has taken over to describe the nature of his mission to the Thessalonians.

From a grammatical point of view γάρ ("for") in v. 9 indicates that the following clause explains the reason why Paul did not have to say anything about the Thessalonians and their conversion to other Christian congregations. According to Paul, believers in the various communities reported two things concerning the mission to the Thessalonians. First, he says: αὐτοὶ περὶ ἡμῶν ἀπαγγέλλουσιν ὁποίαν εἴσοδον ἔσχομεν πρὸς ὑμᾶς ("they report what manner of welcome we had with you"). At first sight it is a little surprising that Paul should describe the report as focusing on himself and his colleagues. But the point of the statement concerns their reception by the Thessalonians. εἴσοδος may refer to the act of entering or more generally to the whole visit itself. Here, as in 2:1, which takes up the theme of this clause, it embraces the whole visit rather than just the manner of entry. The way in which the Thessalonians had received and responded to the Pauline mission under very trying circumstances had probably become a piece of missionary propaganda used to demonstrate the truth of the Christian message to others.

The second part of the report concerning the Thessalonians circulated among the other Christian communities dealt with their actual response to the missionaries' activity among them. It is this material that is thought to contain the pre-Pauline formula. The formula is usually said to be a summary of the mission preaching to the Gentiles. This view is based on the belief of many scholars that the passage contains uncharacteristic Pauline linguistic usage and that the thought is not typically Pauline (see Best, 85-87, who argues for this position and offers a convenient summary of it).

A number of factors, however, argue against this understanding of vv. 9b-10 (cf. Holtz, "'Euer Glaube'"; *idem, Erster Brief,* 54-64 for what follows). In the first place it is for the most part a misnomer to speak of "pre-Pauline" material. Paul's missionary activity went back to the very earliest days of the Christian faith (see Hengel, *Between Jesus and Paul,* 30-47), and we know of no organized mission to the Gentiles in the earliest period except for the one carried out by Paul (cf. Gal. 2:7-9).

Secondly, the supposed formula lacks the careful construction and balance that we would normally expect of such a formula. For example, the change from second person plural (ἐπεστρέψατε, "you turned") to first person plural (ἡμᾶς, "us") at the end of v. 10 disrupts the statement grammatically. Also the repetition of "God" in ἐπεστρέψατε πρὸς τὸν θεὸν ἀπὸ τῶν εἰδώλων δουλεύειν θεῷ ζῶντι καὶ ἀληθινῷ ("you turned to God from idols to serve the living and true God") is clumsy. Furthermore, ὃν ἤγειρεν ἐκ [τῶν] νεκρῶν ("whom [God] raised from the dead") interrupts the thought flow of v. 10. (Havener, "Pre-Pauline Formulae," 105f. attempts to overcome these problems by completely redefining what constitutes the original formula.)

As I will show in what follows, the grounds for maintaining that the linguistic usage is uncharacteristic of Paul are not altogether convincing, though Holtz ("'Euer Glaube,'" 472-482) is probably correct in saying that there are similarities to the language of Hellenistic Jewish missionary literature. This is not surprising since Paul may well have been a Jewish missionary before he became an apostle of Christ (cf. Gal. 1:14). With regard to the claim that the statement is atypical of Paul's thought, it should be noted that this view rests on the assumption that the passage is in fact a formula, the very thing requiring proof.

Paul says that the various church communities report concerning the Thessalonians' response to his mission preaching πῶς ἐπεστρέψατε πρὸς τὸν θεὸν ἀπὸ τῶν εἰδώλων ("how you turned to God from idols"). ἐπιστρέφειν ("turn"), often said to be unusual for Paul, occurs in Gal. 4:9 and 2 Cor. 3:16. While it is used by Paul only here in the way in which it is commonly used in Acts (9:35; 11:24; 14:15; 15:19; 26:20), all three instances in Paul allude to some form of conversion either to or away from God. Paul's description of his readers' conversion as consisting in their turning "from idols to God" indicates that the Thessalonian church was primarily composed of Gentiles who had previously been pagans (cf. 2:13), not Jews or so-called God-fearers (cf. Jewett, *Thessalonian Correspondence,* 118f.). Even if the passage is thought to be a formula, this conclusion still stands since Paul presupposed that the Thessalonians would recognize their own experience in what he was writing.

Paul speaks on occasion of idols. In 1 Cor. 8:4 he denies their real existence, though in 1 Cor. 10:19f. he argues that food offered to them by pagans is in reality offered to demons. Our text, like 1 Cor. 8:4-7, emphasizes the monotheistic faith of Christianity by contrasting the living and true God of the Christian faith with idols. In 1 Thes. 1:9 Paul uses the expression "you turned from idols" in a very broad sense to define the Thessalonians' turning away from their pre-Christian religion. The word "idols" has symbolic significance here because it embraces the totality of the religious experience of his readers (and by implication their social existence) before their conversion, just as the expression "to God," in conjunction with the first infinitive phrase, "to serve the living and true God," embraces the totality of their Christian religious (and social) experience. In effect, Paul draws attention to the two antithetical forms of religion and social existence that the Thessalonians had known in such a way that he may deprecate their past and affirm their present existence. This has an essentially parenetic function. By stressing the nature of the separation between the readers and those of their neighbors and relatives who continued to worship dead and false gods in the form of idols, Paul sought to encourage this separation (cf. Meeks, *Moral World*, 125f.).

Best (85) has questioned the Pauline character of δουλεύειν θεῷ ζῶντι καὶ ἀληθινῷ ("to serve the living and true God"), claiming that it is unusual for Paul to use "serve" (δουλεύειν) with God instead of Christ. "Serve" is used with a variety of terms in Paul, such as "sin" (Rom. 6:6), "spirit" (Rom. 7:6), "law" (Rom. 9:25), and "those which by nature are not God" (Gal. 4:8), but with "Christ," which Best identifies as characteristic Pauline usage, on only three occasions (Rom. 14:18; 16:18; Col. 3:24). This evidence demonstrates that there is no standard application of the word in Paul's writings.

Just as turning to the "living and true God" implied a new mode of existence in the present for the Thessalonians, so it also implied a new future hope for them as they awaited the Son of God from heaven. The infinitive ἀναμένειν ("to await") is a *hapax legomenon* not only in Paul but also in the NT as a whole. The idea, however, occurs on several occasions in Paul's letters where he speaks of Christians as waiting (ἀπεκδεχέσθαι) for the coming of Christ (cf. Rom. 8:19; 1 Cor. 1:7; Phil. 3:20).

The christological designation υἱὸν αὐτοῦ ("his son") is found only here in 1 Thessalonians, but elsewhere plays an important role in Paul's thought. In several key contexts he describes the gospel that he preaches as the gospel of God's son (cf. Rom. 1:3f., 9; 2 Cor. 1:19), and he goes so far as to identify his call to apostleship as a revelation of God's son to him in order that he should preach Christ to the Gentiles (Gal. 1:15f.). In other passages he employs the designation to indicate the close relationship between God and Christ as God's agent for bringing about eschatological salvation (cf. Rom. 5:8-11; 8:3, 32; Gal. 2:20; 4:4f.; see also 1 Cor. 15:24-28). It performs a somewhat similar function here in 1 Thes. 1:10. The emphasis on God in v. 9 led Paul to refer to God's son in order to identify together the one whom his readers expectantly awaited to rescue them with God, to whom they had turned at the time of their conversion. The sonship connection also explains why

Jesus may be relied upon to rescue them from the wrath of God that is about to come. (For a close parallel to the thought of v. 10, including the sonship designation, see Rom. 5:9f.)

The son of God is to come "from heaven" (ἐκ τῶν οὐρανῶν), the place of his present rule as Lord. Scholars such as Best (83) who claim that the language in vv. 9f. is not typical of Paul point to the plural form of the word οὐρανῶν as part of the evidence for this. This is hardly a weighty consideration. Paul uses the plural form of the word on a number of occasions (cf. 2 Cor. 5:1; Phil. 3:20; Col. 1:5, 16, 20), even though he uses the singular more frequently. In Jewish thought heaven was divided into a number of levels on which different things took place, hence the use of the plural form "the heavens." Paul's acceptance of this concept can be clearly seen from 2 Cor. 12:2, where he describes a man whom he knew—probably himself—who was taken up to the third heaven in a rapture experience.

Part of Paul's mission proclamation included the promise of the return of Jesus from heaven to complete the eschatological events begun with his resurrection. This was a foundational belief both of Paul's apocalyptic theology (see Beker, *Paul the Apostle*, 135-181) and of earliest Christianity in general (see Hengel, *Between Jesus and Paul*, 48-64, esp. 60; Schillebeeckx, *Jesus*, 410-416). It enabled the early Christians to maintain that Jesus was the messiah in spite of his failure to actualize his messianic rule during his earthly lifetime. Mearns ("Early Eschatological Development") clearly misunderstands this phenomenon, which is not unique to Christianity (see Sharot, *Messianism, Mysticism, and Magic*, 115-129), when he argues that futuristic eschatology was a later development rather than part of the initial élan of early Christianity. It is possible to go further. Had the early followers of Jesus not believed that he would soon return from heaven as the messianic Lord, Christianity would almost certainly not have come into existence. Belief in the parousia of Christ is what gave the resurrection its real significance by promising the realization of Christ's messianic rule on the plane of human history.

The flow of v. 10 as well as the grammatical structure is badly disrupted by the relative clause ὃν ἤγειρεν ἐκ [τῶν] νεκρῶν ("whom he raised from the dead"). This suggests that it may have been an afterthought by which Paul sought to identify God's son who was to come from heaven as the same person as the one "whom," Christians maintain, "he raised from the dead." It also has another possible function. To the extent that the Thessalonians accepted the resurrection as an act of God, it would give them confidence in the prospect of Christ's coming in power. This would seem to substantiate the point made above about the connection between the resurrection and the parousia in early Christian thought.

The final part of v. 10 specifies more closely whom the Thessalonians expected from heaven and what his role was to be at the eschaton. The use of the personal name "Jesus" was probably elicited by the need to relate the participial construction τὸν ῥυόμενον ἡμᾶς ἐκ τῆς ὀργῆς τῆς ἐρχομένης ("the one saving us from the coming wrath") back to the words "his son" after the break in thought progression caused by the relative clause "whom he raised from the dead." It also makes explicit the identification of the one coming from heaven with the man Jesus of Nazareth whom God had raised from the dead.

ῥύεσθαι ("to save") is not as common in Paul as its synonym σῴζειν, but when it does occur, it refers to being saved or rescued *from* something (cf. Rom. 7:24; 11:26; Col. 1:13). The present tense of the participle here may indicate that the saving activity of God's son is already in progress, but since the thought of the passage is oriented to the future return of Jesus this point should not be pressed (see Zerwick, *Biblical Greek*, §372 on this passage).

Jesus' saving function is to preserve his followers "from the coming wrath (ὀργῆς)." "Wrath" is an important theological category in Paul because it is associated with God's righteous judgment against those who are evil and disobey the truth (Rom. 2:5, 8). According to Paul, God cannot judge the world with justice without inflicting wrath on evildoers (Rom. 3:5f.). God's wrath, therefore, is as necessary as God's grace and mercy. Although God's wrath against sin and those who practice it is currently being revealed (Rom. 1:18), the day of judgment will be a time of wrath for the disobedient and a day of deliverance for the people of God (cf. Rom. 5:9; 1 Thes. 5:9). Thus the coming wrath to which Paul refers in v. 10 is the wrath that will come on the day of judgment (see G. Stählin, *TDNT* V, 422-447 on wrath in the NT and in Paul).

But wrath was not merely a theological concept in Paul, it also had socio-psychological significance. It undoubtedly gave Christians a sense of ultimate power over non-Christians. Their lot might be difficult now, but they would be rewarded in the day of judgment for their sacrifice and toil (cf. 1 Thes. 5:9). Those who opposed and afflicted them or simply refused to join with them, on the other hand, would become objects of God's wrath (cf. Rom. 12:19; 2 Thes. 1:6-10). As A. Y. Collins (*Crisis and Catharsis*, 152) observes in relation to the audience addressed by the Book of Revelation, "The feeling of powerlessness due to the marginal social situation of the hearers was mitigated by the assurance that they had access to privileged information, to revealed truth of heavenly origin." At the same time, the threat of God's anger could be used to encourage proper social behavior among Christians as well (cf. 1 Thes. 4:6-8). The expectation of wrathful divine judgment, just as much as the hope of salvation, can be effective in bringing about conversion and maintaining the faithfulness and correct behavior of converts.

The implication of vv. 9f. is that the parousia expectation lay at the very heart of the Thessalonians' faith. This would appear to fit with the now widely held view that Paul's thought has an apocalyptic character to it (cf. Baumgarten, *Paulus und die Apokalyptik*; E. P. Sanders, *Paul and Palestinian Judaism*;

Beker, *Paul the Apostle*; Martyn, "Apocalyptic Antinomies"). This apocalyptic character centers on Paul's belief that in the future, at a divinely appointed time, cosmic transformation, judgment, and final salvation for the elect will occur. For this reason Longenecker ("Nature," 93) is on shaky ground in his study of eschatology in 1 and 2 Thessalonians when he asserts that "Paul's basic Christian conviction and the starting point for all his Christian theology was not apocalypticism but functional Christology." Functional christology was part of the much wider understanding that constituted Paul's apocalyptic theology or apocalyptic worldview (cf. Meeks, *First Urban Christians,* 179f.). Apocalypticism provided a symbolic construction of reality, that is, a coherent set of beliefs about the world and values by which people could live and orient their lives. Within this apocalyptic framework christology played a pivotal role because Christ was the agent of God for bringing about eschatological salvation and cosmic transformation, but Paul's christology makes no sense apart from his apocalyptic worldview.

One final point bears mentioning. The reference to the parousia in the *exordium* points forward to the only significant doctrinal issue raised in the letter, namely, the problem of the return of Jesus from heaven, which is dealt with in 4:13–5:11.

NARRATIO: 2:1–3:10

For those interested in the formal structure of the letter, chaps. 2 and 3 have proved highly problematic. Schubert (*Form and Function,* 16-27) and others (cf. O'Brien, *Introductory Thanksgivings,* 141-161) argue that the thanksgiving of 1 Thessalonians extends from 1:2 to 3:13 because of the thanksgiving formulas in 1:2; 2:13; and 3:9. But this creates a major problem for them: What is the significance of the narrative material in 2:1-12 and 2:14–3:8, which appears to have almost nothing to do with the thanksgiving formulas in the middle and at the end of the narration? Schubert (18f.) maintains that the narrative material is a digression that is somehow integral to the thanksgiving period. He even goes so far as to say that the letter has no main body since there is no doctrinal or practical section, elements normally characteristic of the main body of Paul's letters.

This view has been called in question by J. T. Sanders ("Transition," 355f.) and White (*Form and Function,* 70-72). They claim that a distinct formal break occurs between 1:10, the conclusion of the opening thanksgiving according to them, and 2:1, the beginning of the main body of the letter or "central section," as Boers ("Form-Critical Study," 145) proposes to call it. With this I am in essential agreement.

The insights of rhetorical criticism, however, now enable us to name 2:1–3:10 the *narratio.* In demonstrative rhetoric the *narratio* commonly follows the *exordium.* In parenetic letters it functions in several different ways. 1 Thessalonians 2–3 contains, for the most part, narrative of Paul's contact with and relation to the Thessalonian Christian community and the experience of the community itself.

The content of these two chapters has led Malherbe ("Exhortation in First Thessalonians") to describe them as *philophronesis,* a term drawn from ancient epistolary theory. In ancient letters an attempt was often made to overcome the distance between the writer and the recipient of a letter. According to Malherbe (241), "Such letters were regarded as substitutes for their writers' presence, and intended to be exactly what the writer's [*sic*] conversation would have been had he been present." This type of letter, Malherbe observes, sought to establish the writer's relationship with his readers. This in turn could provide a "framework for the exhortation" in a parenetic letter. Given the content of chaps. 4 and 5, there can be no doubt that Thessalonians has a parenetic or exhortative function (see Malherbe, 238f.) and therefore from Malherbe's perspective it follows that the philophronetic material of chaps. 2 and 3 paves the way for the exhortative section in the final two chapters (cf. Stowers, *Letter Writing*, 95).

Chaps. 2 and 3 also function, however, as implicit parenesis or exhortation in themselves. In ancient rhetoric and epistolography role models were given in order to provide the audience with examples of moral behavior (cf. Lyons, *Pauline Autobiography*, 189-221; Malherbe, *Moral Exhortation*, 135-138; Stowers, *Letter Writing*, 25f., 99f.). 2:1-12 in particular seems to serve this precise purpose. This is why I have argued in the Introduction that we cannot read 2:1-12 in mirror fashion. Such a method of reading results in scholars as diverse as Schmithals (*Paul and the Gnostics*, 136-155), Jewett (*Thessalonian Correspondence*, 149-157), and Kennedy (*New Testament Interpretation*, 142f.) taking the antithetical formulations of 2:1-12 as signs of an attempt by Paul to counter charges made against him by opponents. As both Stowers (*Letter Writing*, 25f., 99f.) and Lyons (*Pauline Autobiography*, 189-221) point out, this constitutes a failure to recognize the parenetic function of such narrations in moral education. This point is underscored by Malherbe ("Exhortation in First Thessalonians," 240f.; *Moral Exhortation*, 135-138), who has shown that moral examples were often delineated in antithetical fashion in the Greco-Roman world (see also R. F. Collins, "Paul," 356-358). As we will see, 2:1-12 actually functions to reconfirm the readers in the pattern of behavior that they had been taught by Paul. At the same time it provides a role model for leaders in the congregation. This model, based on Paul's missionary practices, is no less relevant for Christian ministry today than it was in Paul's day.

PAUL'S MISSIONARY STYLE AMONG THE THESSALONIANS: 2:1-12

2:1 The γάϱ of 2:1 links the *narratio* with the *exordium* of 1:2-10. This connection is based on the fact that the narration concerns both the nature of Paul's missionary visit to the Thessalonians, a theme introduced in 1:9, and the type of person he proved to be, a theme first treated in 1:5. The narrative section begins with a reference to 1:9 through the repetition of εἴσοδον ἡμῶν τὴν πϱὸς ὑμᾶς ("our entry to you"). It may be that by picking up these words 2:1 is intended to offer an explanation concerning the type of visit that Paul had with his readers. To a certain extent this is true, but the real emphasis in 2:2-12 is on the nature of Paul's ministry in Thessalonica. For this reason it is best to see 2:1 as providing the transition to the *narratio* portion of the letter by continuing the thought of the previous sentence. This simply reflects good rhetorical practice (cf. Jewett, *Thessalonian Correspondence*, 77).

Here, as in 1:5 and elsewhere in the letter, Paul calls on the knowledge of the Thessalonians (αὐτοὶ . . . οἴδατε, ἀδελφοί, "you yourselves, brothers [and sisters], know") to verify what he is about to say to them (cf. 1:5; 2:2, 5, 10, 11; 3:3f., etc.). This is typical of parenetic style that seeks to emphasize what is already known and understood (cf. comments on 1:5). In this instance he asks for confirmation that his visit "was not in vain" (οὐ κενὴ γέγονεν). This ambiguous expression may mean either that his mission to the Thessalonians was characterized by power or that it produced good results. This latter is in accord with the usual sense of οὐ κενή (and similar expressions) in Paul's letters (cf. 1 Cor. 15:10, 58; 2 Cor. 6:1; Gal. 2:2; Phil. 2:16; 1 Thes. 3:5) and is required by the parallel with 1:9-10, where the emphasis is on the result of Paul's activity among the Thessalonians. This sense also goes better with the perfect form of γέγονεν, which stresses the continuing results of his missionary activity.

2:2 The arrival of Paul and his colleagues at Thessalonica was not a triumphal entry, since they had experienced suffering and had been shamefully treated at Philippi. Paul does not make clear here or anywhere else what happened there (cf. Phil. 1:30), but his readers clearly knew, as καθὼς οἴδατε ("just as you know") reveals. According to Acts 16:19-24, 35-39 they were publicly humiliated by being beaten with rods despite their being Roman citizens and were then thrown into jail by the magistrates at Philippi. By his own admission Paul was no stranger to such treatment (2 Cor. 11:23-25), and therefore it seems entirely possible that what is described in the Acts account is what lies behind Paul's reference to "having suffered previously" (προπα-θόντες) and "having been treated shamefully" (ὑβρισθέντες) at Philippi.

While the experience at Philippi might have destroyed his own and his colleagues' sense of purpose and led them to act with far more circumspection out of fear when they came to Thessalonica, it in fact had no such effect. Quite the contrary, as Paul points out, they were emboldened by God to preach his gospel. The verb παρρησιάζεσθαι, like the noun παρρησία, from which it was derived, originally referred to speaking freely or openly but came to refer to courage or boldness in speaking. Malherbe ("'Gentle as a Nurse,'" 208; see also "Exhortation in First Thessalonians," 247-249) has shown that παρρησία was used to describe the way in which the true Cynic philosopher-cum-preacher was supposed to present his message. The Cynic used the suffering that he had experienced àt the hands of mobs to justify the harshness of his treatment of his hearers' moral shortcomings ("Exhortation in First Thessalonians," 248f.). Paul acknowledges his suffering in 2:2, but as Malherbe (249) has noted, he does not use it as an excuse for boldness. His boldness in preaching the gospel is *in spite of* suffering and humiliation. For Paul and his colleagues it was God who had emboldened them to speak his gospel.

ἐν τῷ θεῷ ἡμῶν ("in our God") is not to be interpreted by analogy with the "in Christ" formula with its symbolic mystical significance. It is rather used instrumentally. The missionaries' boldness in declaring the gospel derived from their sense of God's direction and approval of their work.

Moreover, Paul specifies that the gospel that they spoke to the Thessalonians had its source in God, as τὸ εὐαγγέλιον with the subjective genitive τοῦ θεοῦ ("of God") indicates.

The visit to Thessalonica, like the one to Philippi, was not without ordeal. Paul says that his preaching took place ἐν πολλῷ ἀγῶνι ("in the face of considerable opposition"). ἀγών, which originally concerned the exertion involved in athletic contests, has three possible senses in this context: (1) It could refer to the effort or exertion entailed in preaching the gospel (Dibelius, 6); (2) it could refer to care or anxiety arising from the persecution at Philippi (Rigaux, 405); or (3) it could allude to the missionaries' conflict with those opposed to their activity (Best, 91f.). Since 1:6 (cf. 2:13-17; Acts 17:5-9) makes it clear that the gospel was delivered in a situation of opposition in Thessalonica, it seems probable that Paul is recollecting that opposition here. By doing so he underscores how amazing his boldness was in declaring the gospel to the Thessalonians in oppressive circumstances similar to those that he experienced at Philippi. Pfitzner (*Paul*, 118) claims that Paul understood the whole of his apostolic mission as an ἀγών. It is doubtful whether we should go that far, but the evidence of 1 Thessalonians indicates that his ministry at Thessalonica was conducted in the face of considerable antagonism. Both he and the Thessalonian believers suffered duress from non-Christians.

In claiming to have preached the gospel in much ἀγών, Paul identifies himself with the best tradition among moral philosophers. Dio Chrysostom criticized those Cynic preachers who refused to become involved in the ἀγών of life (see Malherbe, " 'Gentle as a Nurse,' " 214). Paul insists in 2:2 that he and his coworkers were involved in the same struggles of life endured by their converts.

2:3   The negative and antithetical formulations of vv. 3-6 have often led scholars to maintain that Paul and his colleagues were being maligned for their behavior at Thessalonica by interlopers (cf. Schmithals, *Paul and the Gnostics*, 142-155) or by local non-Christian opponents (Holtz, 93f.). As I have suggested above, this type of assumption is unnecessary and unwarranted. The negative and antithetical formulations of vv. 3ff. have an essentially rhetorical function. Lyons (*Pauline Autobiography*, 196) maintains that the terminology in this section and the antithetical parallelisms have their background in Wisdom of Solomon, where they are used to express the abhorrence of Hellenistic Judaism for Gentile idolatry. This seems less likely than the views of a number of scholars who think that the antitheses differentiate Paul from various types of popular preachers of philosophy and religion who were notorious for their self-aggrandizing activities (cf. Malherbe, " 'Gentle as a Nurse,' " 214-217; von Dobschütz, 87; Dibelius, 8f.). Whatever the case may be in this matter, the chief intention of the antitheses is parenetic. That is, they indicate through reference to Paul's example how Christians and Christian leaders in particular should behave.

V. 3 is connected with what precedes it by γάϱ. This suggests that the assertions of the passage are intended to provide the reason why Paul had been bold to preach the gospel in the face of strong opposition. He maintains that his and his colleagues' "exhortation did not spring from error or from impurity, nor was it done with deceit" (ἡ παράκλησις ἡμῶν οὐκ ἐκ πλάνης οὐδὲ ἐξ ἀκαθαρσίας οὐδὲ ἐν δόλῳ). By implication, if it had derived from such things, Paul could not have acted with such boldness as he displayed, given the adverse circumstances encountered at Thessalonica. Preachers such as the Cynic hucksters mentioned by Dio Chrysostom (*Oration* 32.7-10; see Malherbe, " 'Gentle as a Nurse,' " 206f. for a discussion of the passage), with the negative attributes mentioned in v. 3, did not stand fast in the face of violent opposition, as Paul did.

The noun παράκλησις has a wide range of meaning, including "encouragement or exhortation," "appeal," or "comfort or consolation." Kemmler (*Faith and Human Reason,* 175-177) argues that here it means "consolation," because the gospel was preached in a situation of turmoil and offered consolation to its recipients through the hope of the parousia. He goes on to suggest that the charge of deception that he thinks Paul is trying to defend himself against arose as a result of the failure of the parousia to materialize. This view seems highly improbable since it does not give equal weight to the supposed charge of "uncleanness" and because nothing in the context relates v. 3 to the problems associated with the parousia in chaps. 4–5.

It appears much more probable that the word should be translated as "exhortation." Otto Schmitz (*TDNT* V, 795) has shown that the verb παρακαλεῖν in such passages as 2 Cor. 5:20 and 6:1 refers to "the wooing proclamation of salvation in the apostolic preaching." Clearly the context of 1 Thes. 2:3 concerns the initial delivery of the gospel to the Thessalonians (cf. vv. 2 and 4) and therefore the term παράκλησις embraces this idea by presenting Paul's original preaching as exhortation to a new faith and a new way of life (cf. Malherbe, "Exhortation in First Thessalonians," 241). It served the overall parenetic intention of the letter well to refer to "exhortation" rather than use a term for preaching, which we would have expected.

The clause constituting v. 3 does not have a verb and so the verb must be supplied from the context. The *RSV*'s "spring" is perfectly adequate since the preposition ἐκ is used with both nouns, πλάνης and ἀκαθαρσίας, to indicate that Paul's exhortation to believe in Christ did not derive or originate from either of these sources. πλάνη may mean either "error," that is, "wandering from the truth," or "deception." If the latter meaning were accepted then it would have little difference in meaning from δόλος, which follows. On the other hand, if we see it as meaning "error" it need not imply a moral aberration as does δόλος. Paul thus asserts that his understanding of the gospel and his presentation of it to the Thessalonians was not an intellectual mistake on his part. Mearns ("Early Eschatological Development," 145) uses this to claim that Paul had been charged by opponents with error because he had changed his teaching from a realized eschatology to a futuristic eschatology after leaving Thessalonica. Mearns's interpretation of this passage and the whole of 1 Thessalonians is ingenious but hardly convincing since Paul assumes that his readers hold a futuristic eschatology going back to his earlier preaching to them (cf. 1:9f.; 5:1f.).

Schmithals (*Paul and the Gnostics,* 145), seeking to prove that Paul had Gnostic opponents who followed him to Thessalonica as they did to Galatia, Philippi, and Corinth, maintains that ἀκαθαρσία, like πλάνη, refers to "lack of integrity" on Paul's part regarding his "deceitful avarice." He adduces 2 Cor. 12:16 to substantiate his claim that an accusation of financial exploitation, arising from Paul's attempt to organize the collection for Jerusalem, lies behind 1 Thes. 2:3. Nothing in the context suggests that the collection for Jerusalem is involved. In fact the epistle makes no reference to the collection anywhere. ἀκαθαρσία has been given a sexual connotation by some commentators (e.g., Rigaux, 407; Morris, 71), but the context suggests that the word implies a more general meaning, including impure motives and the attempt to flatter and please other human beings (cf. 2:4-5).

The final pejorative noun has a different preposition from the first two. Whereas it is denied that error and uncleanness were the source of the apostolic exhortation, οὐδὲ ἐν δόλῳ indicates that the apostolic exhortation was not given in an attempt to deceive the hearers. What Paul said to the Thessalonians was straightforward and had no intention of leading them astray. As Bruce (26) has put it, Paul contrasts himself with "the traveling mountebanks" of the Roman world by the three pejorative characterizations that he rejects in this verse.

2:4 Paul juxtaposes the negative formulation of the previous verse with an antithetical positive statement in this verse. The adversative conjunction ἀλλά introduces the conceptual antithesis of v. 4, which concerns the character of the apostolic delivery of the gospel. Paul begins with the assertion that he has been approved by God (δεδοκιμάσμεθα ὑπὸ τοῦ θεοῦ πιστευθῆναι τὸ εὐαγγέλιον). The perfect verb δεδοκιμάσμεθα expresses the fact that Paul has been examined and found acceptable by God to be entrusted with the gospel. He does not state on what basis he has been approved by God, though at the end of the verse he refers to God's continual testing of his heart (δοκιμάζοντι τὰς καρδίας ἡμῶν). This is a well-known theme from the OT, where God is spoken of as the one who examines people's hearts (cf. Pss. 7:9; 17:3; Je. 11:20; 12:3; 17:9). Presumably Paul's initial testing by God consisted of God examining the integrity and purity of the apostle's life and will.

God's testing and approval of Paul was directed to one purpose, namely God's intention to entrust him with the gospel (πιστευθῆναι τὸ εὐαγγέλιον). Paul uses the same expression in Gal. 2:7 of his divine commission to take the gospel to the Gentiles. Another text in Galatians, 1:16, makes it clear that it was at the time of his call to apostleship that Paul was charged with taking the message of salvation to the Gentiles. The approval that Paul has from God stands in radical contrast to the negative attributes of 2:3, which characterized the intellectual and religious hucksters of his day. At the same time it defines the way in which Paul presented his exhortation at Thessalonica. He spoke (and acted) as one approved by God for his task (οὕτως λαλοῦμεν). In the context of the letter this functions to establish Paul's authority both in the past and in the present, thereby legitimating his right to offer parenetic instruction and to use himself as a model for his converts. In effect, without direct reference to it, Paul asserts his apostolic position in this passage.

Paul proceeds to another antithetical formulation. He spoke "not as those striving to please human beings but God" (οὐχ ὡς ἀνθρώποις ἀρέσκοντες ἀλλὰ θεῷ; cf. Gal. 1:10). He consciously sought to please God with whatever he said because he was commissioned by God for his task, and God continually tested his motives (δοκιμάζοντι τὰς καρδίας ἡμῶν). Thus he could not afford to deceive his hearers, nor could he dare to seek their approval if doing so would contradict his commission from God. This does not mean that Paul was insensitive and unbending to the needs of his audiences, as 1 Cor. 9:19-23 demonstrates. To the extent that he sought to please people, it was to win them for the gospel, thereby gaining the approval of God.

The parenetic function of the letter in general and Paul's autobiographical statement in particular can clearly be seen in the reference to his effort to please not people but "God who examines our hearts." At one level Paul is obviously speaking of himself. But at another level, he intends the statement as a general theological truth designed to encourage proper moral behavior by his converts by implicitly reminding them that God also tested their hearts to determine their motives and desires. This important theological assertion thus has significant social consequences in that it encourages the readers of the letter to scrutinize their own lives to determine whether they are seeking to please God or their fellow human beings. As such it is a powerful warrant for proper Christian behavior, since the judgment would provide the final testing not only of unbelievers but also of Christians (cf. 1 Cor. 3:10-15; see also Meeks, *Moral World,* 127f.)

2:5 Whereas v. 4 provides a general statement regarding Paul's demeanor, the past tense of ἐγενήθημεν in v. 5, along with the temporal particle ποτέ, shows that he is now dealing specifically with his actions at Thessalonica. Here Paul continues the negative style of the formulations in vv. 3 and 4b through the twice repeated negative conjunction οὔτε. The two denials of v. 5 are linked with three further denials in v. 6 where οὔτε occurs three more times. (The three denials of v. 6 center on only one real issue, Paul's refusal to demand honor from people because of his divine authority.)

As γάρ indicates, v. 5 (along with v. 6) explains Paul's assertion in the second part of the previous verse that he did not speak to please people but to please God. First he denies that he had ever spoken "with flattering speech" to the Thessalonians, once again calling on their personal knowledge to verify this (for the significance of this appeal in the context of a parenetic letter see the earlier comments on 1:5). In relation to the preceding verse this denial explains how the apostle might have sought to please his prospective converts but did not. Flattery was a well-known and much-despised practice in the ancient world (Bruce, 29). Plutarch contrasted flattery with παρρησία, "boldness of speech," which according to him characterizes true friendship (*Mor.* 48E-74E; see Lyons, *Pauline Autobiography*, 197). Flattery was so common among street-corner philosophers that it was used in stereotypes of them. The true philosopher, however, repudiated such self-serving attempts to ingratiate himself to his audience (see Malherbe, " 'Gentle as a Nurse,' " 206f., 216 for references to the literature). Paul, like the Cynic philosopher Dio Chrysostom (see *Oration* 32.5f.), refused to employ flattery because it would compromise the integrity of his message and call in question his motivation in preaching the gospel (cf. 2 Cor. 2:17; 4:2).

In addition Paul maintains that he did not speak ἐν προφάσει πλεονεξίας ("with a motive of greed"). Elsewhere he condemns πλεονεξία, "greed" or "covetousness," as a form of idolatry (Col. 3:5) and includes it in a catalogue of sins that characterize the debauched nature of humankind living without recognizing God (Rom. 1:29). In these cases it may be broader than merely the desire for money. In the context of 1 Thes. 2:5, however, it probably does refer to simple monetary avarice because the motive of avarice was commonly ascribed to the wandering preachers of Paul's day.

πρόφασις has two primary meanings: "actual motive, reason" or "pretext." The latter rendering is normally preferred in this passage to emphasize the deception with which greed regularly operates (Marshall, 67). But this rendering does not suit the present context because it does not fit well with the genitive πλεονεξίας. A pretext hides the real motivation for an activity, but "nor did we act with an *ostensible motivation* of greed" (cf. Best, 98: "in a pretext of avarice") makes no sense in the context. So those who favor the meaning "pretext" must resort to paraphrasing in order to salvage any sense from ἐν προφάσει πλεονεξίας (cf. Best; *RSV*; Bruce, 30, who seems to be following the rendering of BAGD, 722). The best translation is simply to let πρόφασις have the meaning "actual motive" and then to render the clause: "We did not act with a motive of greed."

In confirmation of his assertion that he was not motivated by greed, Paul maintains that God is his witness (θεὸς μάρτυς) in this matter. On a number of other occasions Paul announces that God is a witness to the truth of what he is saying (cf. Rom. 1:9; Phil. 1:8; 1 Thes. 2:10), and on one occasion he literally appeals to God to verify what he is saying through a curse formula (cf. 2 Cor. 1:19). The practice of appealing to God as a witness has its roots in the OT (cf. Job 16:19; Ps. 89:37) and provides an asseveration formula that

Paul employs when his inner motivations are in question and can only be verified independently by God. This is how it is used in 2:5.

2:6, 7a The versification of the Greek text differs from most English versions (however, see *NIV, TEV*) in that the participial phrase δυνάμενοι ἐν βάρει εἶναι ὡς Χριστοῦ ἀπόστολοι ("being able to wield our authority as apostles of Christ") is made part of v. 7 rather than being included in v. 6. This is not of vital significance as long as the verse markings are not allowed to influence our exegetical decisions. As we will see, the thought of v. 7a (Greek text) is closely related to v. 6, and therefore the English versions are correct to put the two together in one verse.

οὔτε ("neither") at the beginning of v. 6 indicates that this is the third in the series of denials begun in v. 5 ("neither with flattering speech nor with a motive of greed") and once again concerns the character of the apostolic mission to the Thessalonians. Paul claims that in his missionary activity he was not motivated by the desire to acquire a good reputation either from his converts or from outsiders (οὔτε ζητοῦντες ἐξ ἀνθρώπων δόξαν, οὔτε ἀφ' ὑμῶν οὔτε ἀπ' ἄλλων). δόξα does not have here its usual NT meaning of glory in a religious sense, but the common nonbiblical meaning of "popular or good repute," that is, "honor" or "fame." Dio Chrysostom says that a genuine philosopher will not speak for the sake of δόξα (*Oration* 32.7-12). Like Dio's true philosopher, Paul may be contrasting his own motives with those of the popular philosophers and sophists who sought to gain honor or repute from their audiences. This is how Rigaux (415f.), Best (99), and Bruce (30), among others, understand the passage when they translate ζητοῦντες by such words as "seeking" or "desiring."

Another possibility, however, suits the context better. ζητεῖν may by extension mean "demand" or "require," and this offers a better translation in v. 6: "neither requiring honor from people, neither from you nor from any-one." This makes better sense with v. 7a where, as we shall see, Paul insists that he and his colleagues had a right to wield authority or to assert their status and v. 7b where Paul contrasts their right to act in an authoritative manner with their behavior, which was as gentle as a nurse with her own little children. The point of v. 6 then becomes the contrast between the honor or respect that might have been required of the Thessalonians by Paul and his colleagues (vv. 6, 7a) and their actual behavior (v. 7b). If, as I have suggested, one of the parenetic intentions of 2:1-12 was to provide a role model of what true leadership should be in the Christian community, then the interpretation offered here would make considerable sense.

No real distinction can be made between ἐκ and ἀπό in this verse since the two were gradually merging in meaning in Hellenistic Greek (Turner, *Syntax*, 259). But Paul stresses that he did not demand that his converts honor him: οὔτε ζητοῦντες ἐξ ἀνθρώπων δόξαν, οὔτε αφ' ὑμῶν οὔτε ἀπ' ἄλλων. This of course is not to say that Paul was not honored by them, but it does mean that he and his colleagues did not insist upon deferential treatment. They did not stand on their dignity or status as it were, but (as Paul indicates in the following verses) earned the respect of the Thessalonians by their style of life among them.

V. 7a is a concessive clause and records the grounds upon which Paul could have required the Thessalonians to honor him. The words ἐν βάρει εἶναι have generally been understood in one of two ways. Strelan ("Burden-Bearing," 267-270) has shown that βάρος and other forms of the word often relate to financial charges in the papyri. Paul may therefore be referring to the apostolic right to make financial demands of his converts (cf. 1 Cor. 9:3-18), as Bruce (30f.) maintains (cf. Holmberg, *Paul and Power*, 88). On the other hand, the word can denote dignity, authority, or influence. In the context this seems more appropriate because v. 6 is concerned with Paul's refusal to demand recognition of his dignity and status. It also suits v. 7b better. A contrast between being able to wield authority and acting as a nurse appears to make more sense than a contrast between being able to demand financial support and acting as a nurse. Furthermore, the issue of how Paul financed himself comes up in v. 9, apparently as a new idea in the discussion rather than as a continuation of an earlier statement. On the whole then it seems better to understand v. 7a as directed to the right of Paul to exercise or wield his apostolic authority (cf. Best, 100), which might include the right to be financially supported, though this idea is not in the foreground here. Paul at least consciously chose not to exercise all his apostolic rights in order not to put a stumbling block in the way of his converts (cf. 1 Cor. 9:12).

The plural form ἀπόστολοι has been the subject of much discussion since it implies that Silvanus and Timothy were both apostles in the same sense that Paul was. Best, in order to avoid this conclusion, suggests that at the time 1 Thessalonians was written Paul had not formulated his understanding of apostleship very clearly and therefore used the term in a loose way of Silvanus and Timothy. This seems highly unlikely. 1 Cor. 15:3-7 indicates that "apostle" had a fixed meaning already in the tradition received by Paul. It referred to someone who was a witness of the resurrection (cf. 1 Cor. 9:1) and, judging by Paul's experience, was commissioned to be an emissary of Christ (cf. 1 Cor. 9:2, which implies that the activity of the apostle was missionary work). 1 Cor. 15:7, incidentally, shows that in the earliest tradition "apostle" was used in a wider sense than is suggested by Acts 1:15-26, where the term seems to be limited to the twelve (see, however, Acts 14:4, 14 where the older idea is retained).

Probably Paul used the plural ἀπόστολοι simply because Silvanus was himself numbered among the apostles, as was indicated in the discussion of 1:1. This does not seem to be true of Timothy, however, since Paul does not identify him as an apostle alongside himself in such texts as 2 Cor. 1:1, Phil. 1:1, and Col. 1:1. The difference was probably that Silvanus had seen the risen Jesus, as Barnabas apparently had (cf. 1 Cor. 9:5-6), and had been commissioned by Christ as a missionary, just as Paul later was. On the other hand, Timothy, a convert of Paul himself, had not undergone this experience.

2:7b, c In vv. 5-7a Paul employs a negative formulation to stress that he was not self-serving, manipulative, or arrogant when he worked among the Thessalonians. In an age in which the Christian ministry has sometimes come into disrepute because of the reprehensible behavior of a few, Paul's self-description provides both a model for the ethical behavior of Christian ministers and leaders and a test against which to measure their behavior.

In vv. 7b-8 Paul turns to a positive statement of his behavior among them that emphasizes in deeply affective terms his friendship and love for them. We will see later that the apostle's emphasis on his intimate friendship with his converts serves an important function in the parenetic or exhortative intention of the letter.

V. 7b, c poses several exegetical conundrums that have a bearing on our interpretation of the passage. The most pressing problem concerns whether we should read νήπιοι ("infants"), which certainly has the stronger manuscript attestation (e.g., ℵ 𝔭⁶⁵ B C* cop^{sa ms, bo}), or ἤπιοι ("gentle"), which appears in a number of manuscripts (e.g., A C² Dᶜ cop^{sa, fay}). The problem is complicated by the fact that either reading can be accounted for as a scribal error: If νήπιοι were the original reading, ἤπιοι could have arisen through haplography; if ἤπιοι were the original reading νήπιοι could have come about through dittography of the "ν" of the previous word, ἐγενήθημεν.

Although better attested, νήπιοι seems less probable to many commentators because ἤπιοι suits the context better, offering an obvious contrast with the preceding expression, ἐν βάρει εἶναι, which literally refers to heaviness and metaphorically to the assertion of authority. "Gentle" also goes well with the metaphor of the caring nurse, which follows, while the word "infants" would lead to a mixed metaphor in which, on the one hand, Paul claims that he and his colleagues were like infants, and on the other, like the nurse who cares for her children. This fact alone weighs heavily against νήπιοι. To this I would add that Paul nowhere else refers to himself and his colleagues as "infants," and on the occasions when he does use νήπιοι it is almost always pejorative (cf. Rom. 2:20; 1 Cor. 3:1; 13:11; Gal. 4:1, 3). Thus in spite of the manuscript reading we should probably accept the reading ἤπιοι in preference to the printed text of *UBSGNT*. (It is worth noting that Metzger, *Textual Commentary*, 630f., along with A. Wikgren, rejects the majority decision reflected in both *UBSGNT* and Nestle-Aland²⁶.)

Punctuation raises a second problem. The *RSV* and Nestle-Aland²⁶, among others, place a full stop after ἀπόστολοι ("apostles") and a comma after ὑμῶν ("you"). The *RSV* also places a period after τέκνα ("children"), but Nestle-Aland²⁶ has a comma there. The *NEB* and the *UBSGNT*, among others, place a comma after ἀπόστολοι, a full stop after ὑμῶν, and a comma after τέκνα. This scheme of punctuating is preferable since it closely connects the contrast between vv. 6-7a and 7b, enables the ὡς . . . οὕτως ("as . . . so") correlative construction of vv. 7c and 8 to remain intact, and avoids asyndeton at the beginning of v. 8.

In v. 7b Paul sharply contrasts his own behavior with what he might have demanded if he had asserted his apostolic status and authority. The ἀλλά ("but") of v. 7b indicates this contrast and suggests that although he was entitled to wield authority and command recognition (vv. 6, 7a), Paul chose a different pattern of conduct. He acted with gentleness toward the Thessalonians, as ἤπιοι implies. As Paul told the Corinthians, he preferred to abstain from using his rights even to the point of personal deprivation, lest he do anything to hinder the communication of the gospel (1 Cor. 9:12). The "gentle" approach of Paul when he was with the Thessalonians (ἐν μέσῳ ὑμῶν) was therefore most probably part of his missionary strategy. It facilitated his personal acceptance by the Thessalonians and in turn enabled him to proclaim the gospel of God, which made serious demands on their beliefs and behavior. In adopting this strategy, Paul drew on the insights of one of the important schools of thought among the Cynics of his day, which stressed the need for gentleness toward one's audience if one were to speak with boldness as well (see Dio Chrysostom, *Oration* 77-78; Plutarch, *Mor.* ["How to Tell a Flatterer from a Friend"] 73C-74E).

In the last part of v. 7b and in the following verse Paul explains the character of his and his colleagues' gentleness. They acted like a nursing mother who lovingly cherishes her own children (τροφὸς θάλπῃ τὰ ἑαυτῆς τέκνα). The image of a woman nourishing children, the literal idea in τροφός, was essentially a positive one in the ancient world. Malherbe (" 'Gentle as a Nurse,' " 211-214) has shown that this positive image of the nurse was used among philosophers to suggest the way in which they should gently care for those whom they taught and nourished in the truth. More recently Donfried ("Cults," 238, 240) has argued for a connection between the image of the caring nurse and various figures within the mystery religions practiced at Thessalonica. Either of these two backgrounds to the term is possible, but what is important to note is that Paul uses feminine language to describe his activity because women, and in particular the maternal dimension of womanhood, were viewed in an extremely positive light in Antiquity. The image is an obvious one for expressing gentleness. It conveys more than this, however. The nurse was also responsible for protecting the children in her care. Thus Paul may have wished to evoke the image of his protective concern for his readers as well as his gentleness. From τὰ ἑαυτῆς τέκνα ("her *own* children") we may infer that Paul is alluding to the fact that a nurse who cares for other people's children cherishes her own even more. These words heighten the sense of Paul's love, concern, and feelings of tenderness toward the Thessalonians.

2:8   The image of the tender nursing mother from the previous verse is picked up by the alliterative phrase οὕτως ὁμειρόμενοι ὑμῶν ("thus feeling kindly toward you"). ὁμειρόμενος is rare in Greek writings that have survived and is employed here to express the emotional warmth felt by Paul toward the Thessalonians. This warmth, according to Paul, influenced the type of conduct that he adopted toward them. Perhaps Paul actually felt a greater sense of affection for the Thessalonians than others of his converts as a result of their having received the gospel in extremely trying circumstances. Certainly no other passage in the whole of the Pauline corpus employs such deeply affective language in describing Paul's relation with his converts.

The apostle's feeling of kindliness toward his converts resulted in more than his preaching to them: εὐδοκοῦμεν μεταδοῦναι ὑμῖν οὐ μόνον τὸ εὐαγγέλιον τοῦ θεοῦ ἀλλὰ καὶ ἑαυτῶν ψυχάς ("we were pleased to share with you not only the gospel of God but also our own lives"). εὐδοκοῦμεν ("we were pleased") must be understood as an unaugmented imperfect verb since the context refers to the apostle's attitude at the time of his mission to Thessalonica. Its use here may include the idea that Paul took delight in sharing the gospel and himself. He probably did so in reaction to the warm personal response of his converts toward him. The word ψυχή ("soul" or "life") in this clause probably goes beyond the sense of "time, energy, and health" proposed by E. Schweizer (*TDNT* IX, 648) to include the inner emotional life of Paul. He committed himself totally to the Thessalonians rather than remaining aloof and uninvolved in their struggles to come to terms with the new faith that had been declared to them. The reason Paul desired to share himself with the Thessalonians is given in the concluding causal clause of v. 8: διότι ἀγαπητοὶ ἡμῖν ἐγενήθητε ("because you became beloved to us").

The warmth of the language found in vv. 7b-8 serves the parenetic intention of the letter. For parenesis to be effective, epistolary theory dictated that the speaker have a positive relationship with those addressed (Stowers, *Letter Writing,* 95). The tenderness of the language in vv. 7b-8 is unique in Paul. But we can scarcely doubt that it functioned to create mutual love and commitment between Paul and his converts. This was intended to encourage them to listen to his exhortation with sympathetic ears. His example of love for and devotion to his converts also had other important social functions. It was designed to establish the norm for true leadership for any who aspired to lead the community. At the same time it implicitly exhorted the readers to the sense of mutuality and love that would unite them into a cohesive community, thereby strengthening them to face a hostile environment.

2:9   Paul's kindly feelings and love for the Thessalonians manifested themselves in another way: he supported himself by working with his own hands rather than burden his converts by making financial demands of them. Syntactically v. 9 explains the statement in vv. 7b-8, as the conjunction γάρ indicates. Again Paul calls on the Thessalonians' experience of him to verify his claims, but this time he uses μνημονεύετε ("you remember") instead of οἴδατε ("you know"; cf. 1:5; 2:1, 5), probably for the sake of stylistic variation.

As I have noted before, the use of such expressions is characteristic of parenetic style where a writer seeks to reinforce the behavior of his readers (see 1:5). (On the significance of ἀδελφοί see the comments on 1:4.)

What Paul asks the Thessalonians to remember is the toil and hard labor that he carried out to support himself while undertaking his preaching of the gospel to them. Paul uses the combination τὸν κόπον ἡμῶν καὶ τὸν μόχθον ("our labor and toil") here and on two other occasions in relation to his missionary activity (2 Cor. 11:27; 2 Thes. 3:8). 2 Thes. 3:8 is perhaps the model for this passage (if I am correct in maintaining the priority of 2 Thessalonians). There Paul applies the apostolic example to the Thessalonians in order to give them a paradigm for their own conduct. The same parenetic function probably exists implicitly in 1 Thes. 2:9 because here Paul lays the foundation for the exhortation in 4:11f. (see Malherbe, "Exhortation in First Thessalonians," 240 for the connection between chaps. 1–3 and the more direct exhortation in chaps. 4–5; cf. Marshall, 72), and in 2:12 he reminds the readers of the original exhortation that they had received concerning the Christian life. In 2:9 there is little to distinguish "labor and toil," but together they stress the considerable efforts to which Paul went, even to the point of hardship and deprivation, in order to avoid becoming a burden to his converts.

In the second clause of v. 9 Paul amplifies what he means by his "toil and labor": νυκτὸς καὶ ἡμέρας ἐργαζόμενοι πρὸς τὸ μὴ ἐπιβαρῆσαί τινα ὑμῶν ἐκηρύξαμεν εἰς ὑμᾶς τὸ εὐαγγέλιον τοῦ θεοῦ ("night and day working in order not to burden any of you, we preached to you the gospel of God"). He employs asyndeton to good effect, thereby placing considerable emphasis on the statement in v. 9b. He had adopted a missionary strategy that necessitated his working for his own livelihood "in order not to burden" any of his converts. Here ἐπιβαρῆσαι alludes to the apostle's physical labors and clearly denotes financial or material support such as free food and lodging. While he refused to burden those to whom he preached, once Paul had left, he was willing to receive support from churches that he had founded. In fact Phil. 4:16 indicates that the Christian community at Philippi had provided him with financial support while he was at Thessalonica, although this was presumably not of a sufficient amount to enable him to stop working altogether (cf. 2 Cor. 11:7-11).

The refusal to take, let alone demand, support from those to whom he preached was a fundamental principle for Paul as he sought to avoid putting any hindrance in the way of potential or actual converts (1 Cor. 9:12). Barrett (*First Corinthians,* 207) offers three reasons for this, two of which seem quite important in the Thessalonian situation: (1) Potential converts might have reservations about conversion if they believed that it would entail a financial commitment to the missionaries, and (2) the gospel based on love and the self-sacrifice of Jesus was incompatible with missionaries who sought their own self-interest and financial gain at the expense of their converts.

In order to avoid placing a burden on anyone at Thessalonica Paul and his coworkers worked "night and day" while they preached there. The genitive cases of νυκτός and ἡμέρας do not mean that they worked continuously but rather that they worked both at night and during the day. Paul does not mention here or anywhere else what he did, though in 1 Cor. 4:12 he says that he worked with his own hands, which suggests most probably that he was an artisan. According to Acts 18:3 he was a σκηνοποιός. This somewhat unusual word indicates that Paul was a tentmaker, and since tents were made primarily of leather we should probably accept the view of Hock (*Social Context,* 21) that Paul was essentially a leather worker, but not a tanner, which would have been an unclean trade for Jews. It has often been assumed that Paul in having a profession was merely following the practice of the rabbis who combined the study of the Torah with a trade. Because the evidence for this view comes from a later period, the assumption is questionable (Hock, 22f.). As Hock (31-37; see also "Paul's Tentmaking," 555-564) has shown, an artisan such as a leather worker generally worked from dawn to dusk, often for little more than enough money to survive on, and had very little social status. If 1 Cor. 4:11f. is anything to go by, this was certainly Paul's experience.

Given the amount of working time required by a worker to be self-sufficient, we should take the wording of v. 9b seriously: "working night and day . . . we preached the gospel of God to you." As the present participle ἐργαζόμενοι ("working") implies, their working night and day was done simultaneously with their preaching of the gospel. Paul, and presumably his colleagues, had little choice but to use the workshop as a place for communicating the gospel since so much of their time was spent there. A recent study by Stowers ("Social Status") has shown that Paul probably did not participate in street preaching and other forms of public mass appeal. Of necessity his mission work was with individuals and small groups. The workshop provided one of the recognized social contexts for this preaching (Hock, *Social Context,* 37-42; see also Hock, "Workshop," and the discussion of the character of Paul's mission in the Introduction, pp. 8f. above).

2:10 Not only did Paul and his fellow missionaries pay their own way while doing their mission work, but their behavior was beyond reproach. The thought of this verse is closely connected with the previous verse, though asyndeton is once again used for rhetorical effect. As if to heighten the impact of what he is saying Paul invokes his readers and God as witnesses (cf. 2:5). This gives the statement a solemn tone, which might suggest that Paul was concerned with criticism directed toward himself and his colleagues (so Marshall, 73). It seems more likely, however, that he is both engaging in implicit parenesis about how the Thessalonians should act based on his example and preparing for the exhortative section of the epistle where he commands his readers to provide for themselves (cf. 4:11f.; 5:14). In doing so he is approaching one of the major issues addressed in his first letter to the community, our 2 Thessalonians. The more forceful discussion of the need for everyone to earn his or her own keep in 2 Thes. 3:6-12 probably solved most of the problem, and therefore 1 Thes. 2:9, 4:11f., and 5:14 are simply intended to reinforce what had already been taught.

The clause that relates what Paul has invoked presents a somewhat unusual construction. The predicate adjectives ὅσιος, δίκαιος, and ἄμεμπτος would have gone better with the verb ἐγενήθημεν than do the adverbial forms that we have. The adverbs do, however, place the stress on the character of the missionaries' behavior rather than on the character of their persons. They behaved "in a devout and upright and blameless manner" toward the Thessalonians.

ὁσίως and δικαίως were commonly used together to indicate the keeping of divine and human law respectively (F. Hauck, *TDNT* V, 489-492). Contrary to Best (105) and Bruce (35f.), who read too much of Paul's Jewish background into the words, they probably have these senses here. This is why Paul specifies that both the Thessalonians and God are witnesses to his and his coworkers conduct. God is witness to the pious or holy way in which they had acted in their responsibility toward God. The Thessalonians are witnesses to the uprightness of their behavior toward the people with whom they had dealings. ἀμέμπτως strengthens the formulation and applies equally well to behavior in relation to God and behavior in relation to the Thessalonians: neither God nor the Thessalonians could reproach their conduct.

The dative phrase ὑμῖν τοῖς πιστεύουσιν has often caused exegetes problems. It can be taken in several different ways, the most likely of which are either "toward or to the benefit of you believers" (so Best, 105; Bruce, 36) or "among you believers" (so Rigaux, 427f.; Marshall, 73). If my understanding of "in a holy manner, uprightly, and blamelessly" is correct, then the expression must mean "among you believers."

2:11-12 These verses, which continue the discussion from vv. 9f., are best taken together because grammatically they form one continuous thought, which has led to differing divisions of the verses. *UBSGNT* separates the verses between ἑαυτοῦ ("his own") and παρακαλοῦντες ("exhorting"), while the *RSV* and most other English versions include everything up to the purpose clause beginning with εἰς τὸ περιπατεῖν ὑμᾶς . . . ("in order that you walk . . .") in v. 11.

The translation of the verses is complicated by the omission of the main verb. This leaves vv. 11f. dependent on the main clause in v. 10, "you and God are witnesses," as the parallel ὡς clauses of vv. 10 and 11 suggest. The phrase καθάπερ οἴδατε ("just as you know") repeats the idea of the main clause of v. 10 and is an expletive in the context (though see 1:5; 2:1, 2, 5 and comments). The parallelism of the ὡς clauses of vv. 10 and 11 probably led to Paul's omission of the verb, though ἐγενήθημεν is not grammatically possible with the object ἕνα ἕκαστον ὑμῶν ("each one of you"). Bruce (34) supplies "treated," and Best (106) employs "counselled." In Greek a verb like ἀνεθρέψαμεν ("we brought up" or "we trained") would be especially appropriate. ὡς ἕνα ἕκαστον ὑμῶν ὡς πατὴρ τέκνα ἑαυτοῦ should then be translated "how we brought up each one of you as a father trains his own children." The words "each one of you" have the rhetorical effect of individualizing what Paul is saying for each member of the community. It also supports our earlier assertion that Paul and his colleagues primarily preached to individuals in the social setting of their daily work.

Paul employs the father–children metaphor here and on several other occasions to express an important aspect of his relationship with his converts (cf. Gal. 4:19f.; 1 Cor. 4:14-21; 2 Cor. 6:11-13). The father in the ancient world was normally responsible for the moral instruction and behavior of his offspring (cf. 1 Cor. 4:14), and he took the leading role in socializing his children into the socio-economic and cultural way of life into which they were born. Paul of necessity took responsibility for resocializing his "children in the faith" to the sometimes radically different demands of their new social existence as Christians. Religious conversion requires resocialization to the distinctive ideas and values of the new religion if the convert is to be effectively incorporated into it (see Wilson, *Religion,* 118-120 and pp. 14f. above).

Petersen (*Rediscovering Paul,* 128-131) has pointed out that the father–children metaphors in Paul's letters imply a hierarchical relation between Paul and his converts and serve to inculcate his "loving yet superordinant position." Within this hierarchical relationship Paul expected his converts to respond like obedient children to their father when he taught and exhorted them concerning the Christian way of life. This is exactly how the metaphor is employed here to describe Paul's role in resocializing converts. Once his converts had accepted the new beliefs that he and his colleagues articulated, it was necessary for their "father in the faith" to begin exerting his authority in the process of resocializing them into a distinctively Christian way of life.

He, along with his coworkers, did this by "exhorting" (παρακαλοῦντες), "admonishing" (παραμυθούμενοι), and "testifying" (μαρτυρόμενοι) to their converts concerning the way in which they should behave. The first two participles, παρακαλοῦντες and παραμυθούμενοι, are closely related to one another semantically and in fact παραμυθέομαι and its nominal cognates are always found in Paul's letters with παρακαλεῖν or its nominal cognate, παράκλησις (cf. 5:14; 1 Cor. 14:3; Phil. 2:1). παρακαλεῖν and παράκλησις occur frequently in Paul's letters and can refer to missionary preaching, as in 1 Thes. 2:3, or to giving comfort or consolation, as in 3:7, or can serve "as a kind of formula to introduce pastoral admonition" (O. Schmitz, *TDNT* V, 799), as in 4:1. Often both admonition and comfort are meant where the verb is used, which is also true of παραμυθεῖσθαι (G. Stählin, *TDNT* V, 821).

All this makes it difficult to distinguish between the two terms in the present context. In spite of Stählin's hesitation to say that παραμυθεῖσθαι places a more pronounced emphasis on comfort in the NT and in particular in 2:12, it seems reasonable to suggest that it has this connotation for Paul, while παρακαλεῖν means "to exhort." This assumption enables us to avoid viewing παραμυθούμενοι as tautological. By using the two words together Paul brings out very clearly how he and his fellow missionaries both exhorted the Thessalonians to Christian conduct and comforted them (perhaps on account of the tribulation they experienced) with the knowledge that they would be saved in the day of judgment, as the end of v. 12 suggests. The third participle, μαρτυρόμενοι, is much stronger than the previous two terms. It indicates that the missionaries, with the authority of God, "insisted" on a certain standard of behavior from their converts.

In particular, to be a Christian meant that the converts were obligated to live lives worthy of God (περιπατεῖν ἀξίως τοῦ θεοῦ), who had called them to their new faith. The εἰς τό construction indicates that this was the aim of the "exhorting, comforting, and insisting" that Paul and his coworkers had done. Paul uses περιπατεῖν frequently to refer to "the walk of life," qualifying it with some additional word or phrase that in the context reveals that moral conduct is in view (cf. 4:1, 12; 2 Thes. 3:6, 11; Gal. 5:16; Rom. 13:13; and esp. Col. 1:10), here ἀξίως τοῦ θεοῦ. Behavior "worthy of God" reflects the character of God in terms of God's love, patience, justice, and so forth. For Paul this undoubtedly had great significance and was intended not only to demarcate or define Christian conduct over against non-Christian or pagan conduct, but also to distinguish the Christian convert from those who had not received the gospel. Failure to live up to the demands of the Christian norm, in other words failure "to walk worthy of God," could therefore lead to exclusion from the community, as Paul instructed in his previous letter (see 2 Thes. 3:6-15).

In this text a close link exists between Christian demeanor and future salvation. The conduct that Paul inculcated among the Thessalonians was required of them in order for them to live life in a manner worthy of God. Paul's understanding of grace does not allow us to speak of people earning their right to future salvation. Rather Paul understood the behavior that he demanded of his converts as a response to God's offer of salvation. This is perhaps why he adds τοῦ καλοῦντος ὑμᾶς εἰς τὴν ἑαυτοῦ βασιλείαν καὶ δόξαν ("the one calling you into his own dominion and glory"). The present participle καλοῦντες, which is used of God as "the one who calls" the Thessalonians, is in the aorist tense in some texts because Paul commonly refers to God's call in reference to the conversion experience (cf. 4:7; 2 Thes. 2:14; Gal. 1:6; 1 Cor. 1:9). The present was probably chosen by Paul here (cf. 5:24; Gal. 5:8) to reflect the fact that Christians are continually called into God's own dominion and glory, just as they must continually strive to live their lives as servants of God. In other words, a dialectic exists between call and response, which gives Christian existence a dynamic rather than static character.

Paul does not often use the term βασιλεία. (Customarily it is translated "kingdom" but "God's *dominion*" is a better approximation of the meaning of ὁ βασιλεία τοῦ θεοῦ since "dominion" can mean both "rule or power to rule" and "that which is ruled or governed.") It occurs frequently in the Gospels, where it is the hallmark of Jesus' teaching. Beker (*Paul the Apostle,* 146) suggests that its infrequent usage by Paul results from Paul's modification of the apocalyptic schema of the two ages on the basis of his belief that the new was proleptically present in the old order. This view is not altogether convincing. For Paul "dominion" usually denotes the place in which God's rule is exercised, and for the Christian this is something to be inherited in the future (2 Thes. 1:5; 1 Cor. 6:9, 10; 15:24, 50; Gal. 5:21). In 1 Thes. 2:12 this eschatological note is present, since the readers have not finally entered the dominion of God and cannot until the parousia of Jesus (cf. 1 Cor. 15:23-28; 50-57). Therefore the apocalyptic motif of the duality of this age over against the age to come is present here. This is underscored by "glory." Elsewhere Paul teaches that the Christian is to participate "physically" in the glory of God when salvation has been fully realized in the future through the resurrection of the dead and the transformation of the body (cf. Rom. 8:18-23; 1 Cor. 15:42-44; Phil. 3:20f.).

An important connection made by Paul in vv. 9-12 clearly points to the parenetic intention of the letter. In vv. 9f. Paul refers to the example that he gave to the Thessalonians both with regard to hard work and to imitating his ethical conduct. In 4:1-12 he enjoins specific types of behavior on his readers. These undoubtedly corresponded to the example he gave them earlier through his own life-style. In 2:11f. he reminds his converts about the way he had exhorted them to live lives worthy of God when he was with them. The combination of moral exhortation and personal example that Paul gave the Thessalonians while he was with them and that he now reminds them of in his absence corresponds to the best standards in moral education in the Greco-Roman world. Seneca, the Stoic philosopher who was a contemporary of Paul, recommended that people seek out for moral direction "men [*sic*] who teach us by their lives, who tell us what we ought to do and then prove it by practice, who show us what we should avoid, and then are never caught doing that which they have ordered us to avoid" (*Ep.* 52). This is precisely the approach of Paul to the resocialization of the Thessalonians into the Christian way of life according to 2:9-12.

DIGRESSION WITHIN THE *NARRATIO*: 2:13-16

The four verses of this section have been the subject of intense debate focusing on their position in the text (compilation theories) and their authenticity (interpolation theories). For details of the debate the reader is referred to the

Introduction (pp. 29-34 above); here I need only restate my conclusion that these verses are authentic and that they formed part of the original letter written by Paul to the Thessalonians. As has also been argued above, the thanksgiving statements in v. 13 and in 3:9f. are not to be explained in form-critical terms as Schubert *(Form and Function)* and O'Brien *(Introductory Thanksgivings)* attempt to do, but in terms of the rhetorical style adopted by Paul in the letter.

One of the major problems in the interpretation of 2:13-16 is its seeming lack of connection to what precedes and what follows and its disruption of the narrative flow of 2:1-12 and 2:17-3:10. Holtz (94) finds a causal connection between 2:1-12 and 2:13-16. As mentioned previously, he holds that vv. 1-12 are an apology directed against the slander of non-Christian opponents in Thessalonica. According to his reading of vv. 13-16 these same adversaries sought to pressure Paul's converts into withdrawing from the Christian community, just as the nationalistic Jews in Judea had done to their Christian compatriots—hence the connection between vv. 1-12 and vv. 13-16.

Holtz's position is an interesting attempt to link the problematic 2:13-16 to its immediate context, but it fails to carry conviction because it is based on his misunderstanding on the antithetical statements in vv. 1-12 (see the comments above on 2:3). A more promising solution to the disjunction between 2:13-16 and its context lies in the recognition that it is to be understood in terms of the rhetorical device known as digression.

Wuellner ("Greek Rhetoric") has recently pointed out the important role of digressions in Paul's letters. Digressions in the *narratio* were often intended to lay the basis for subsequent argumentation or to provide a transition to the next issue to be discussed. Like the *exordium* they were also used to solicit the favor of the audience (see Wuellner, 180f.). This admirably describes 2:13-16. In the first place, v. 13 secures the audience's favor by renewing the earlier thanksgiving for the Christians at Thessalonica with indirect praise for the manner of their acceptance of the word of God. This in effect forms a conclusion to 2:1-12 by recording the readers' response to the missionary proclamation of Paul and his colleagues, the subject of the preceding verses. In the second place, vv. 14-16 direct the recipients to their experience of persecution at the time of their conversion and the reason for the forced departure of Paul and his coworkers from Thessalonica. In doing so it creates the transition to the second stage in the narration, 2:17-3:10, where Paul recounts his relations with the church subsequent to his forced withdrawal.

At a more basic level, the digression has a parenetic function as well. It seeks to confirm the Thessalonians in their existing pattern of faithfulness regardless of the outside opposition they might experience. In order to do this, Paul attempts to show that their suffering at the hands of their compatriots was part of a wider apocalyptic pattern of the oppression of God's people. We may thus view 2:13-16 as a transition to the theme of persecution experienced by the Thessalonians. This in turn leads to Paul's explanation of how his fatherly care for his readers manifested itself in their time of distress. In speaking of the Jewish nationalist persecution of Jewish Christians in Palestine in v. 14 and of the death of the Lord and the persecution of his apostles in vv. 15-16, Paul makes a thinly veiled statement promising divine condemnation for those who persecuted the Thessalonians. By doing so Paul encourages his readers to persist in their new Christian existence.

2:13 Paul signals his shift to a new theme with the transitional phrase καὶ διὰ τοῦτο ("and for this reason"), which introduces a renewed thanksgiving to God for the readers. This transitional phrase may either refer to what has preceded in the discussion or forward to the topic to be introduced. The latter seems the better interpretation: the ὅτι ("because") clause expresses the reason for thanksgiving to God.

The second καί preceding ἡμεῖς εὐχαριστοῦμεν ("we give thanks") is difficult to interpret. Some take it with the pronoun ἡμεῖς and suggest that it indicates that Paul was responding to a communication from the Thessalonians in which they too gave thanks (Frame, 106f.; Bruce, 44). Others see it as an allusion back to 1:8f., which perhaps implies that the Macedonians and the Achaians were giving thanks concerning the Thessalonians (Marxsen, 47). Neither of these interpretations is very obvious. In the case of the former there is no evidence of such a communication, and in the latter there is no reference to the giving of thanks in 1:8f. Best (110), following Rigaux (437f.), offers a somewhat different possibility. He suggests that the καί has a weakened sense that emphasizes the ἡμεῖς: "we for our part." While this is possible, it seems better to take it with the verb εὐχαριστοῦμεν on the analogy of 3:5, where διὰ τοῦτο occurs with κἀγώ ("and I") and seems to pick up the previous discussion of 3:1. If this suggestion is correct, 2:13 returns to the theme of thanksgiving first announced in 1:2, as O'Brien (*Introductory Thanksgivings,* 153f.) maintains. Thus Paul is proposing a second reason why he and his colleagues offer thanks for the readers. (On "we give thanks to God without ceasing" see the comments on 1:2.)

The ὅτι clause may give the content of the thanksgiving or the cause of the thanksgiving. Since the prepositional phrase "for this reason" at the beginning of the verse appears to point forward to the ὅτι clause, it seems better to take this as the cause of the apostolic thanksgiving rather than its content, though obviously the two are closely connected.

Paul thanks God because of the way in which his readers received the gospel. The participle παραλαβόντες is a technical term for receiving a tradition. For example, with reference to the Eucharist, the apostle says to the Corinthians, "I received (παρέλαβον) from the Lord what I also gave to you." Similarly, in passages like 1 Cor. 15:3 and Gal. 1:12 Paul can speak of the gospel that he preached as something that he himself has received. He can also use it of the ethical instruction that his converts received from him (cf. 1 Thes. 4:1). Perhaps 1 Cor. 15:1 and Gal. 1:9 (cf. also Col. 2:6) are the closest parallels to 1 Thes. 2:13. In these texts Paul uses παραλαμβάνειν for the reception of the gospel that he preached. What is particularly interesting about each of these occurrences of the verb is the authoritative character of the message or instruction that is received, which it has because it is given by an authoritative source. This technical usage of the verb by Paul has parallels in both rabbinic tradition (see Davies, *Paul and Rabbinic Judaism,* 247-250) and Greek and Hellenistic usage (see G. Delling, *TDNT* IV, 11f.).

Paul recounts the Thessalonians' reception of the gospel in the words παραλαβόντες λόγον ἀκοῆς παρ' ἡμῶν τοῦ θεοῦ ἐδέξασθε ("receiving from us the message of God which was preached"). This is an awkward expression. It is not altogether clear what the governing noun of the genitive "of God" (θεοῦ) is, and ἀκοή may refer either to the act of hearing or to that which is heard. The most probable explanation for the striking position of "of God" is that it was an afterthought inserted into the sentence to avoid any doubt about the origin of the message that had been delivered to the Thessalonians. "From us" (παρ' ἡμῶν) is ambiguous and could be construed as meaning that the message originated from Paul and his colleagues. The insertion of "of God" into the participial phrase is actually redundant. It makes the phrase preempt the thought of the clause as a whole and detracts from the force of the contrast that Paul seeks to make in v. 13c between a message originating with human beings and the message of Paul, which stemmed from God. ἀκοή probably refers to what was heard and therefore may be rendered by a term like "preaching" (cf. Rom. 10:16f.; Gal. 3:2, 5). The point of the participial phrase as it now stands is that the word of preaching received by the Thessalonians from Paul and his colleagues was a message of divine origin.

The main verb ἐδέξασθε ("you accepted") is a synonym of παραλαβόντες but does not have the same connotation of the reception of an authoritative message. It is probably employed to emphasize the actual decision of the Thessalonians to accept the message that was declared to them. Paul points out that they accepted this message "not as a human message" (οὐ λόγον ἀνθρώπων), that is, as though it were merely a word spoken by fellow human beings, but "just as it truly is, the message of God" (καθώς ἐστιν ἀληθῶς λόγον θεοῦ); that is, they accepted it because they recognized the divine origin of the missionaries' preaching. In effect, Paul makes the implicit claim here that his and his coworkers' preaching was the very word of God. The distinction that he makes by the contrast (note the contrastive conjunction ἀλλά, "but") is of considerable importance in the context of the following verse. It implies that the suffering experienced by the Thessalonians as a result of receiving the message of the missionaries is in reality suffering on God's account. What he says gives their suffering a profound meaning and is probably intended to enable them to endure it with confidence in God.

The word of God that they received was not a meaningless idea or a doctrine to be maintained; it was a source of power in the lives of those who believed (ὃς καὶ ἐνεργεῖται ἐν ὑμῖν τοῖς πιστεύουσιν). Paul does not specify here how the gospel is effective, but undoubtedly the Thessalonians would have understood it in terms of the way in which they experienced the work of the Spirit (cf. 1:5-6), both at the time of their conversion and later in the life of their community (cf. 5:19f.).

From the perspective of Paul's rhetorical intention, v. 13 offers the readers praise for their perceptive recognition of his missionary message as the message of God. By doing so it serves the parenetic function of affirming and encouraging the Thessalonians in their Christian faith and practice. Given the adversity they had come through, this was undoubtedly an important epistolary goal from Paul's perspective. At the same time v. 13 rounds out the discussion of Paul's missionary style in 2:1-12 by validating the opening assertion of 2:1 that Paul's mission to the Thessalonians was not in vain. The success of Paul's mission was demonstrated by the conversion of the readers to the gospel of God as he had proclaimed it.

2:14 Already in 1:6 Paul had maintained that his readers had become imitators of himself and the Lord through the opposition that they had experienced at the time of their conversion. This verse extends the idea to include the fact that they had become imitators of the Jewish Christians in Judea as well. "You became imitators" (μιμηταὶ ἐγενήθητε) should not be taken in an active sense as though the Thessalonian Christians had intentionally sought to imitate the Judean Christians in suffering for their faith. Rather they had through circumstances been made imitators of the Judean Christians.

With the expression τῶν ἐκκλησιῶν τοῦ θεοῦ τῶν οὐσῶν ἐν τῇ Ἰουδαίᾳ ἐν Χριστῷ Ἰησοῦ ("the churches of God which are in Judea in Jesus Christ") Paul probably refers to the various local Christian communities not merely in the geographic area of Judea, but in what we would call Palestine, a term embracing Judea, Samaria, and Galilee. For Greek speakers ἐκκλησία required delimiting since it was not a technical term for the Christian religious assembly (see the comments on 1:1). Elsewhere Paul normally defines the Christian assemblies as those belonging to God (cf. 1 Cor. 10:32; 11:16, 22; 2 Cor. 1:1; Gal. 2:22). In the case of Judea this delimitation was not sufficient since the same might be said by Jews of their local synagogue, and therefore he defines these "churches" as those "in Christ Jesus" to make clear that it was the various local Christian communities in Palestine to which he was referring.

The ὅτι clause identifies the grounds of saying that the Thessalonians imitated the Jewish Christians of Judea: They suffered at the hands of their compatriots as the Judean Christians had at the hands of their fellow Jews (ὅτι τὰ αὐτὰ ἐπάθετε καὶ ἡμεῖς ὑπὸ τῶν ἰδίων συμφυλετῶν καθὼς καὶ αὐτοὶ ὑπὸ τῶν Ἰουδαίων). This clause poses several historical problems. First, who was responsible for causing the Thessalonians to suffer and why? Second, what does Paul allude to by his reference to the suffering of the Judean Christians? We may begin with the second problem because the experience of the

Judean Christians provided an example or type for the Thessalonians' experience. At a much earlier stage Paul himself had persecuted the Christian communities in the area of Palestine and probably Syria, though Gal. 1:22 makes it unlikely that he had done so in Judea itself. Gal. 6:12f. speaks of Christians who tried to encourage circumcision among Gentile Christians in order to avoid persecution because of the cross of Christ. The most natural understanding of this passage suggests that Jewish persecution of Jewish Christians also occurred at a period much closer to the writing of 1 Thessalonians. Jewett ("Agitators," 202-206) has convincingly argued that Jewish nationalists, or zealots as they are commonly called, probably put considerable pressure on Jewish Christians in Palestine because of the Gentile mission outside Palestine in the late forties and early fifties of the first century. Jewett is probably correct in seeing this as the fundamental cause of the Judaizer problem in Galatia. It may also account for Paul's vituperative outburst in 1 Thes. 2:15f. against those Jews responsible for the death of Jesus and for hindering the spread of the gospel. (On Jewish persecution of Christians in Palestine see also Reicke, "Judeo-Christianity," who demonstrates on the basis of the Gospel traditions that this was a widespread phenomenon.)

Obviously the persecution undergone by the Thessalonian Christians cannot be linked directly to the crisis in Judea. Rather the point of comparison, as καθώς shows, was that both groups had suffered harassment at the hands of their own compatriots (τῶν ἰδίων συμφυλετῶν). While Acts 17:5-10 indicates that Paul and his colleagues were forced to leave Thessalonica because of Jewish opposition, this does not explain fully the hostility that the largely Gentile community experienced nor would the Jews of Thessalonica necessarily be considered their συμφυλέται or compatriots.

Meeks ("Social Function," 691) believes that the exclusivism of early Christianity led to the persecution of the Thessalonians by those "with whom formerly they had shared ties of kinship and racial or local origins." Social opposition fomented by Christian exclusivism probably had something to do with the problem, but further clarification is possible.

Donfried ("Cults," 342-352), following up a suggestion of Judge ("Decrees"), has argued that Acts 17:5-9 gives the clue to the problem when it indicates that the mob charged Jason and the other Christians whom they had dragged before the city magistrates of Thessalonica with opposing the decrees of Caesar by saying that there was another king named Jesus. The message proclaimed by Paul could have been construed as being opposed to the decrees of Caesar, since it involved predictions about the future that were, to say the least, unfavorable to the continuation of rule by the emperors. Such predictions were forbidden by imperial decree. Moreover, the Lordship of Christ, as proclaimed by Paul, could have been taken as a direct challenge to the sovereignty of Caesar and as a violation of the oath of loyalty required of both Romans and non-Romans within the Empire. If Luke is correct about the charge brought against the Thessalonian Christians, then they were viewed as a potential political threat for their refusal to participate in the powerful civil religion of the imperial cult. By espousing a religious alternative to the dominant political ideology they became competitors with the civil religion of Thessalonica. This led to their being persecuted by their own compatriots (see Jewett, *Thessalonian Correspondence*, 123-125).

This also points to an important social fact. The willingness of the Thessalonians to convert to Christianity and to remain Christians in the face of strong coercion from their society indicates an acute sense of dissatisfaction with that society and their position in it. Undoubtedly they found in Paul's apocalyptic worldview an alternative symbolic world that made greater sense of their lives than the symbolic world that they implicitly rejected in withdrawing from Roman civil religion and rejecting Roman social and political hegemony (see pp. 5f., 14-16 above for a discussion of symbolic world and its significance; cf. Meeks, *Moral World*, 13-15).

2:15-16 The reference to the Jews as persecutors in v. 14 is continued in vv. 15f. by a series of four participial phrases and one adjectival phrase. Together, along with the latter part of v. 16, these phrases appear to constitute a vitriolic piece of anti-Judaism (a term more accurate in this context than the more common "anti-Semitism," which would imply racial hatred on Paul's part). This has led many to deny that Paul could have written these verses because of his supposedly positive stance toward the people of Israel in Romans 9–11. As we will see, the differences between 2:15f. and Romans 9–11 can be overplayed, even if Paul is not saying precisely the same thing in the two places. But there is another factor involved that has largely been overlooked by commentators. To the extent that the Thessalonians had become imitators of the Judean Christians through suffering at the hands of their fellow citizens at Thessalonica, the attack on the Jewish people is also indirectly an attack on those who oppressed the recipients of the letter. This point becomes even more poignant if Acts 17:5 is correct in maintaining that the trouble at Thessalonica was fomented by members of the Jewish community. 1 Thes. 2:15f. certainly gives considerable credence to this possibility.

To begin with, Paul accuses the Jews of being responsible for the death of "the Lord Jesus and the prophets." The participial construction τῶν καὶ τὸν κύριον ἀποκτεινάντων Ἰησοῦν καὶ τοὺς προφήτας, like those that follow (as well as the one adjectival phrase), is best rendered in English as a relative clause: "who killed. . . ." The charge that the Jewish people were responsible for the death of the prophets is certainly not novel in the NT (cf. Mt. 23:29-37 par. Lk. 11:47-51 and 13:34; Acts 7:52) nor in Jewish literature from the period (cf. *Mart. Is.* 5:1-14). In fact the charge goes back to the OT itself, as 1 Ki. 19:10-14, a passage quoted by Paul in Rom. 11:3, shows (cf. 2 Ch. 36:15f.). The polemical accusation that the Jews were responsible for the death of Jesus is characteristic of the Gospel of John (cf. Jn. 5:18; 7:1; 8:59;

11:45-53; 18:14, 31) and is implied by Acts (cf. Acts 2:36; 3:13), but is nowhere else leveled by Paul, unless Rom. 11:11f. contains an allusion to it (see Cranfield, *Romans* II, 556). This indictment implies that Paul saw a continuity in the pattern of Jewish rejection of God's agents from OT times to his own.

This pattern continued in the Jewish response to the Christian mission, as ἡμᾶς ἐκδιωξάντων ("who persecuted us") reveals. Whether ἡμᾶς ("us") refers to Christians in general or to Paul and his fellow missionaries in particular is uncertain. In favor of a general reference is the fact that the fourth participial phrase (κωλυόντων ἡμᾶς τοῖς ἔθνεσιν λαλῆσαι, "who hinder our speaking to the Gentiles," v. 16a) alludes specifically to the Pauline mission, and therefore the words "who persecuted us" might include the wider opposition to the Christian movement. On the other hand, Paul was no stranger to hostility from fellow Jews, as both Gal. 5:11 and 2 Cor. 11:24-26 demonstrate. If ἐκδιωξάντων is taken literally as meaning "who drove out," this favors limiting ἡμᾶς to Paul and his colleagues. This view accords with the past tense of the participle since the phrase then probably refers to the way in which some Jews were involved in forcing the missionaries to leave Thessalonica (cf. Acts 17:5-10; Malherbe, *Paul and the Thessalonians*, 62).

Paul's charge in the next phrase that the Jews were displeasing to God (θεῷ μὴ ἀρεσκόντων) probably stems from the fact that they had not accepted Jesus as the agent of God for bringing about their salvation, as well as the fact that they were impeding God's will through their disruption of the Christian mission and their persecution of Jewish Christians.

The following words, πᾶσιν ἀνθρώποις ἐναντίων ("opposing everyone"), reflect the general anti-Judaism of the Greco-Roman world, where Jews were seen as opposed to their fellow human beings on account of Jewish ethnic and religious exclusivism. Josephus, for example, claims that Apion falsely maintained that Jews swore to God to "show goodwill to no foreigner, especially Greeks" (*Ap.* 2.121), and Tacitus, the Roman historian, says disparagingly of the Jews, "among themselves there is unswerving loyalty, ready compassion, but hostility and hatred toward all others" (*Ann.* 5.5.2; both quotations are from Whittaker, *Jews and Christians*, who has brought together a number of quotes from Antiquity on attitudes toward the Jewish people in general including statements of anti-Judaism).

But for Paul, unlike Gentile polemicists, the Jews' ultimate antagonism toward non-Jews had to do with their hindering of his mission to the Gentiles whom he sought to lead to salvation. The participial phrase κωλυόντων ἡμᾶς τοῖς ἔθνεσιν λαλῆσαι ἵνα σωθῶσιν ("hindering our speaking to the Gentiles . . .") is parallel to the four preceding phrases, but is nonetheless intended to explain the last one, the adjectival phrase at the end of v. 15, since it is not joined with a coordinating conjunction to what precedes. Acts has numerous references to Jews hindering of the Pauline mission to the Gentiles (cf.

13:45-50; 14:2, 19; 17:5-9, 13; 18:12), and such activity probably forms the background to 2 Cor. 11:24, where Paul speaks of the numerous beatings he had received at the hands of the Jews. The ἵνα clause in 1 Thes. 2:16a may well express both the purpose and the result of Jewish attempts to prevent Paul from speaking the gospel to Gentiles (Best, 118). Here, as frequently in Paul, the verb σῴζειν denotes the goal of the redemptive process without specifying its content. The image, however, calls to mind the two sides of redemption, namely "being saved from" divine wrath (cf. 1:10; Rom. 5:9) and "being saved to" the future life of glory (cf. 2:12; Rom. 8:18-24).

Paul appears to have understood the continuing opposition of the Jews to the Christian mission and therefore to the will of God in terms of his apocalyptic framework, as v. 16b, c shows (see Bammel, "Judenverfolgung," 301). V. 16b suggests the image of a scale weighing up the sins of the Jewish people until the fixed amount is achieved that will lead to their judgment (Marshall, 80). The infinitive construction εἰς τὸ ἀναπληρῶσαι αὐτῶν τὰς ἁμαρτίας πάντοτε ("in order to fill up the measure of their sins at all times") probably embraces the thought of vv. 15 and 16a since πάντοτε ("at all times") suggests an ongoing process that cannot be restricted temporally to the time of the Gentile mission but includes the history of the Jewish people stretching back to the prophetic period of the OT. The infinitive ἀναπληρῶσαι, when taken with πάντοτε, does pose some problems, however. The latter implies a continuous action while the former indicates a punctiliar action. Frame (113) is probably correct in seeing this as a reference to a series of actions viewed collectively. The infinitive phrase with εἰς τό may express either purpose or result. The former seems more likely here on the basis of normal Pauline usage (BDF §402.2; Turner, *Syntax*, 143) and would imply that the Jews' filling up of their sins was according to the purpose of God, an idea that has parallels in Romans 11 (cf. 11:7-10, 28, 32). The theme of "filling up the measure of sins" is found in several places, including Gn. 15:16; Dn. 8:23; and 2 Macc. 6:14.

Mt. 23:31-36 is particularly interesting because a number of the themes of 1 Thes. 2:15f. are juxtaposed there. The scribes and Pharisees are said to be the sons of those who murdered the prophets (cf. 2:15a), and they are accused of filling up the measure of their fathers' deeds (cf. 2:16b), which will lead in the judgment to their condemnation to hell (cf. 2:16c). What makes the similarity between Mt. 23:31-36 and 1 Thes. 2:15f. most striking is that both refer to the Jewish opposition to the Christian mission. This may well indicate that Paul has taken over a traditional set of ideas in vv. 15f. (see Orchard, "Thessalonians and the Synoptic Gospels," 19-42 and more recently Schippers, "Pre-Synoptic Tradition," 223-234; Davies, "Paul and the People of Israel," 7f. compares 2:15f. with Mk. 12:1-9; see also Wenham, "Paul and the Synoptic Apocalypse," 361f.), though naturally this does not mean that either Paul or Matthew is dependent on the other.

The final clause of v. 16 has been the greatest source of difficulty in interpreting these two verses. What "wrath" has "come upon" the Jews (note the aorist form of ἔφθασεν), and how should εἰς τέλος be understood? We may note first that in the context of the letter ὀργή with the definite article refers back to the eschatological wrath, mentioned in 1:10, that Paul associates with divine judgment (cf. 5:9).

Scholars like Pearson ("1 Thessalonians 2:13-16," 81-84) who take 2:13-16 to be an interpolation maintain that v. 16c is a reference to the fall of Jerusalem because they insist on a literal interpretation of the aorist verb ἔφθασεν. Alternative views have been suggested that allow for a literal interpretation of the aorist but do not associate it with the destruction of Jerusalem. For example, Bammel ("Judenverfolgung," 300f.) connects this text with the expulsion of the Jews from Rome by Claudius, while Jewett ("Agitators," 205 n. 5) favors a massacre in Jerusalem in AD 49 that may have resulted from the violence of Jewish nationalists according to a report by Josephus (*War* 2.224-227; for other possibilities see Best, 119f.)

The apocalyptic character of the statement, however, warns against insisting that an actual event lies behind the verb. As J. J. Collins (*Apocalyptic Imagination*, 214) has noted, apocalyptic language is not "descriptive, referential newspaper language, but the *expressive* language of poetry, which uses symbols and imagery to articulate a sense or feeling about the world." Best (120) and Marshall (80f.) may be correct in taking the verb to mean that divine wrath had in Paul's view "drawn near" to the Jews, so near that it was inevitably about to manifest itself (cf. the use of the aorist form ἔφθασεν in Mt. 12:28 par. Lk. 11:20) when the measure of their sins was completely filled up (v. 16b). It may be, however, that Paul had given his readers the keys with which to interpret the eschatological events that were unfolding. Thus what is enigmatic for us may have been clearly understood by the original readers of the letter.

Regardless of this, what Paul may be expressing here is a belief that because of the "filling up of the measure of their sins" God's eschatological wrath has overtaken the unbelieving and disobedient Jews in that they have been hardened by God and no longer experience God's grace. That they had not believed the gospel would have been proof enough of this for Paul.

Εἰς τέλος may be interpreted in several different ways. Best (121) correctly recognizes that the parallel between v. 16c and v. 16b, with its temporal use of πάντοτε, requires a temporal sense for εἰς τέλος. This tends to exclude the possible sense of "completely, totally" (German *gänzlich*), which Holtz (110) prefers. Best translates εἰς τέλος as "in the end, finally," though he acknowledges that the sense "forever," found on a number of occasions in the Septuagint (Pss. 76:8; 78:5; 102:9 LXX), is also possible. Both of these translations create problems in light of Rom. 11:25-32 and 1 Cor. 9:20 because they tend to absolutize the divine wrath coming upon unbelieving Jews into a final rejection (cf. Holtz, 109f.). For this reason it is better to interpret εἰς τέλος to mean that divine wrath will rest upon those unbelieving and disobedient Jews until the end of the age comes, when Christ will return (cf. the use of ἕως τέλους, "until the end," in 1 Cor. 1:8 and 2 Cor. 1:13).

Unlike Romans 9–11, with its somewhat tortured explanation of how God is using the Gentiles to stir up the jealousy of Israel in order to bring about Israel's salvation, 1 Thes. 2:16 does not say what will happen to disobedient Israel. As Davies ("Paul and the People of Israel," 8f.) suggests, Paul probably had not formulated his final understanding about the position of Israel in the divine scheme when he wrote 1 Thessalonians. What was clear to him, however, was that the majority of the Jewish people had not accepted their own messiah and that they positively were hindering the spread of the gospel of God to non-Jews. This would account for the strong sense of frustration and antagonism found in 2:15f., without closing the door to the sort of further reflection found in Romans 9–11.

One final point needs to be made about vv. 14-16 as a whole. The type of vitriolic attack that we find in this passage directed against the Jews was a stock feature of ancient rhetoric called *vituperatio*. It functioned in the context of social conflict between individuals or groups with competing interests and claims (see Freyne, "Vilifying the Other," 118f.). A. Y. Collins ("Vilification," 314) observes that the vilification of the Jews in Rev. 2:9 and 3:9 served an important social function from the Christian perspective of the period. In a situation in which Jews and Christians found themselves competing for everything from social status to adherents, vilification of the Jews in the Book of Revelation "expresses and reinforces a consciousness of a difference in values, in symbolic universes," which in turn helps "to demarcate and define a new group" while "casting doubt on the legitimacy of the rival group."

A similar phenomenon is at work in Paul's vituperation in 1 Thes. 2:14-16. His attack on the Jewish people who had refused to accept Jesus as their messiah strengthens the distinction between unbelieving Jews and believing Christians, whether Jews or Gentiles. The passage also calls into question the legitimacy of the traditional claim of the Jewish people to be the people of God (they do not please God and fill up their sins, vv. 15c and 16b), and this in turn serves to affirm for Paul's converts their own relationship with God and the validity of the religion they had adopted as their own.

While this understanding of the passage does not do away with the anti-Judaism of the text, it has the virtue of placing the vituperation in proper perspective. The statements in 2:14-16 reflect the beginnings of the struggle of first-century Christianity for a separate identity from its parent, Judaism. Paul and the other writers of the NT who engaged in this struggle for a separate identity, using vituperation directed at the Jewish people as a tool in the struggle (see especially the Gospels of Matthew and John and the Book of Revelation), never dreamed of the consequences of their statements on subsequent generations. Their anti-Jewish statements, based on a situation of competition with the mother religion when they felt the very survival of their faith was endangered by the dominant position of Judaism, have been used for justifying everything from the pogroms against Jews in the Middle Ages and the inquisitions of the early modern period to the Holocaust itself. Such vituperation lost its rationale once Christianity became an equal competitor with Judaism and later became the more dominant of the two religions (cf. Collins, "Vilification," 320). That many Christians persisted in anti-Judaism on theological grounds and still persist in it today can only be a cause for shame and repentance on the part of contemporary Christians.

PAUL'S CONTINUING RELATION WITH HIS PERSECUTED CONVERTS AT THESSALONICA: 2:17–3:10

This section of the letter deals with Paul's continuing concern for the church after his untimely departure and sets out how he maintained contact with his converts over the period prior to the writing of 1 Thessalonians. Funk ("Apostolic *Parousia*," 250) identifies this section in terms of both form and content as pertaining to Paul's apostolic parousia. According to Funk (249), Paul normally has a more or less discrete section in his letters in which he indicates "his reason for or disposition in writing, his intention or hope to dispatch an emissary, and his intention or hope to pay the congregation a personal visit" (cf. Rom. 15:14-33; 1 Cor. 4:14-21; Phil. 2:19-24; Phm. 21f.). Letters, emissaries, and personal presence represented three different ways in which Paul asserted his apostolic authority in his churches and therefore were forms of his apostolic parousia (on the use of the term parousia in this sense see such passages as 2 Cor. 10:10; Phil. 1:26; 2:12). Funk is clearly correct that these three factors come together in 2:17–3:10 and were media used by Paul to maintain his authority and control over the congregations that he had established.

Funk's form-critical observations do not, however, explain the rhetorical nature and goals of the continuation of the *narratio*. As with 2:1-12 Paul's essentially parenetic intention is served through the narration of his ongoing relation with his converts. The theme of friendship, a common one in ancient letters, dominates 2:17–3:10, and leads to the deep pathos with which Paul writes regarding his relationship with the Thessalonians (see Kennedy, *New Testament Interpretation*, 143). According to the epistolary theory handed down in the name of Demetrius of Phalerum, letters of friendship need not be written by peers. A superior could write a letter of friendship in order to lay the basis for making a request of an inferior (see Stowers, *Letter Writing*, 58f. and the quotation there from Demetrius's *On Style*). The theme of friendship in 2:17–3:10 may be understood as preparing the way for the explicit parenesis

119

of chaps. 4 and 5. This seems to follow the advice of Plutarch in *Mor*. 73C-74E ("How to Tell a Flatterer from a Friend"). He recommends that true friends should pay close attention to their friends. If the need for reproof arises, one should first commend the behavior of a friend in an effort to create a situation in which frankness can be used to correct the friend's behavior. Praise of the Thessalonians, especially in 3:6-10, functions rhetorically to create a situation in which Paul may exhort his readers to maintain their Christian behavior and beliefs, as he does in 4:1–5:22.

The material in 2:17–3:10 divides neatly into three sections on the basis of the subjects treated: (1) In 2:17-20 Paul explains his desire to see the Thessalonians and his attempts to revisit them; (2) in 3:1-5 he discusses his motivation for sending Timothy to them; and (3) in 3:6-10 he describes his reaction to the return of Timothy and the favorable report that he brought.

His Desire to See the Thessalonians and Attempts to Revisit Them: 2:17-20

2:17 Expressing his deep affection for his converts at Thessalonica (cf. 2:7f., 11f.), Paul turns to the theme of his untimely separation from his converts, a theme prepared for by the digression in 2:13-16. ἡμεῖς δέ ("now we") at the beginning of v. 17 is resumptive of the narrative concerning Paul's relation with the church. Here, as on other occasions in the letter when Paul begins a new topic, he addresses his readers directly with ἀδελφοί ("brothers [and sisters]"; cf. 2:1; 4:1, 13; 5:1, 12). The strong attachment that Paul felt for the Thessalonians is revealed by the phrase ἀπορφανισθέντες ἀφ' ὑμῶν ("being torn away from you"). ἀπορφανίζεσθαι was frequently used either of children who had been orphaned or of parents bereaved of their children. Since the passive form of the participle would require Paul to be portraying himself as an orphaned child, it seems better to understand the participle in a metaphorical sense as referring to the sudden and violent loss of the Thessalonians, which the apostle had experienced as a result of Jewish intervention (see 2:15f.). At the same time the temporal phrase, which is a combination of πρὸς καιρόν ("for a time") and ὥρας ("of an hour"), emphasizes that the separation was for a limited time rather than an indefinite or permanent time. For Paul, at the time of writing, this separation was over because the sending of Timothy (3:1-5) had renewed his own contact and relationship with the church. In this sense Timothy served as his representative and therefore as an agent of Paul's apostolic parousia. Using a traditional theme from friendship letters (see Stowers, *Letter Writing*, 59f.) Paul maintains that he was absent προσώπῳ οὐ καρδίᾳ ("in face not in heart"; cf. 2 Cor. 5:3; Col. 2:5).

The enforced separation created a powerful desire on Paul's part to return to the Thessalonians. Paul stresses this point in the main clause of v. 17, where he employs both the adverb περισσοτέρως ("excessively") and the prepositional phrase ἐν πολλῇ ἐπιθυμίᾳ (with great desire") to modify the verb ἐσπουδάσαμεν ("we were anxious"). σπουδάζειν indicates more than mere desire; it denotes actual effort on Paul's part to fulfill his desire, as v. 18 is intended to demonstrate. ἐπιθυμία, which normally refers to evil desires, has a positive sense here as in Phil. 1:23.

Exegetes debate whether περισσοτέρως has a comparative force here or is elative. The context supplies no obvious point from which a comparison is made and therefore several different suggestions have been made. Marshall (85), for example, mentions the possibility that Paul "was more eager to return than he would have been if he had not been forced to leave Thessalonica against his will and earlier than he had intended" (see Frame, 119 for other possibilities). Although Best (125) argues that Paul often uses περισσοτέρως comparatively without any indication of the point of comparison, two of his three examples (2 Cor. 2:4; 7:15) are ambiguous and may be explained as having an elative sense (so BAGD, 651). With Frame (119) and Morris (94) the elative sense of "excessively" fits the context best and clearly underscores Paul's effort "to see" the Thessalonians "face to face."

2:18 The causal conjunction διότι indicates that v. 18 is subordinate to the previous verse and implies that the reason for Paul's keen desire to revisit the Thessalonians is about to be given. In fact the apparent reason is only fully offered in vv. 19f., whereas the clause that follows the causal conjunction (ἠθελήσαμεν ἐλθεῖν πρὸς ὑμᾶς, "we resolved to come to you") does little more than reiterate what was said in v. 17. The verb θέλειν refers to more than a wish or desire here; it has the connotation of a wish made with resolve to fulfill it, a point Paul stresses by his personal interjection that he tried to come to the Thessalonians on more than one occasion but was prevented from doing so. This interjection, ἐγὼ μὲν Παῦλος καὶ ἅπαξ καὶ δίς ("I, Paul, once and twice"), indicates that he is the real composer of the letter. Undoubtedly both Silvanus and Timothy agreed with the contents of the letter, but this verse, along with 3:5 and 5:27, provides the basis for discussing the letter primarily as a production of Paul rather than of the three missionaries.

Some doubt exists as to how to take καὶ ἅπαξ καὶ δίς. It could mean "not only once but twice," or as Morris ("Καὶ ῞Απαξ," 205-208), following Frame, urges, it may be an idiom that means "more than once." Morris bases this on the four occurrences of ἅπαξ καὶ δίς in the LXX (Dt. 9:13; 1 Kgdms. 17:39; Ne. 13:20; 1 Macc. 3:30), where it has the meaning "more than once." If this is correct then the first καί is ascensive, and the whole phrase should be translated "and that more than once." In the end there is little difference in meaning since either way Paul is saying that at least twice he resolved to come to them.

In the final part of the verse Paul returns to the first person plural. Making use of the dualistic thought of the apocalyptic tradition, he claims that it was Satan who "hindered" (ἐνέκοψεν) them from returning. The idea of

Satan as a personal figure only began to emerge in the late OT tradition, where Satan was portrayed as an adversary (see Job 1:6–2:7; 1 Ch. 21:1; Zc. 3:1-2). The idea probably came from the cosmic dualism of Zoroastrianism in the Persian period, taken over by Judaism to explain the existence of evil and sin in the world without compromising the goodness and sovereignty of God. (On the development of Satanology in the post-OT period see W. Foerster, *TDNT* VII, 151-156.)

Paul appears to have believed in a personal evil power who was God's enemy (Rom. 16:20), who sought to tempt the followers of Christ (3:5; 1 Cor. 7:5), and who could even cause physical illness in Paul himself (2 Cor. 12:7). More importantly, Paul maintained that Satan worked against the interests of the Christian community in a variety of ways (cf. 3:5; 2 Cor. 2:11; 11:13-15). The last mentioned passage is particularly interesting because Paul "Satanizes" his "Christian" rivals and opponents in Corinth: He castigates Jewish Christian missionaries who were interlopers at Corinth and who claimed to be apostles by identifying them as servants of Satan seeking to disguise themselves as "servants of righteousness," just as Satan "disguises himself as an angel of light." The apocalyptic character of Paul's understanding is brought out clearly by 2 Thes. 2:8-12 where Paul depicts the "lawless one" who must appear before and in conjunction with the parousia of Christ (cf. Rom. 16:20, which probably refers to Satan's defeat at the parousia) as the agent of Satan who will work for the destruction of those refusing the gospel.

As important as what Paul says about Satan is, what he does not say is more important. Conzelmann (*Theology,* 18) correctly points out that "Paul outlines man's position before God, the nature of sin, judgment and salvation without using the idea of Satan." In other words Paul does not offer a systematic understanding of Satan or even a clearly developed doctrine of Satan in which Satan is used to explain either death or sin.

In 1 Thes. 2:18 Paul attributes his inability to return to Thessalonica to the interference of Satan, who opposes God at every opportunity. (Although v. 18c returns to the first person plural with the ἡμᾶς, it seems probable that Paul stands behind it, in the light of 3:1, where Paul almost certainly uses the first person plural to refer to himself.) By this means Paul avoids personal responsibility for his failure to revisit his readers, attributing his failure to the malevolent activity of Satan's supernatural powers. This was perhaps intended to allay doubts about his commitment to the Thessalonians and his reasons for not coming back to them himself. If Paul is referring to his own inability to return, as seems likely, then Marshall (86) may be correct in using the "thorn in the flesh, the messenger of Satan" from 2 Cor. 12:7 to suggest that it was physical illness that was responsible for Paul's inability to return. Undoubtedly Timothy, or whoever delivered the letter to the Thessalonians, explained the meaning of Paul's remark about Satan's hindering his return.

This verse raises an important theological point for us in the modern world. To what extent is it helpful or even legitimate to think of Satan as a personal force able to interfere in human existence? Without wishing to deny the existence of a personal evil power, I believe that we should take Best (127) seriously when he warns against the danger of too easily using Satan as an explanation for evil and human failure. Such a practice often leads people to obscure the real causes of evil and results in their failing to deal with those causes.

2:19 The connective γάρ ("for") of this verse takes up the thought of the previous two verses where Paul expresses his desire to visit the Thessalonians again. In this verse he offers his reason for wanting to see them again in terms of their significance for him personally within the eschatological context of his ministry. Paul asks rhetorically: "For who is our hope and joy and crown of pride?" (τίς γὰρ ἡμῶν ἐλπὶς ἢ χαρὰ ἢ στέφανος καυχήσεως). ἢ ("or") is used here almost as a copulative conjunction with little sense of disjunction (see BDF §446) as Paul successively supplements "hope" with "joy" and "joy" with "crown of boasting." The Thessalonians are Paul's "hope, joy, and crown of boasting" at the public manifestation of Christ because they are the fruit of his ministry as an apostle of Christ. They thus demonstrate his faithfulness in carrying out the mission given to him by the risen Christ (cf. 1 Cor. 9:2 where Paul describes the Corinthians as the seal [σφραγίς] of his apostleship).

Paul feared that in the face of the adverse situation that they were experiencing the Thessalonians might be tempted to abandon their new faith. If they were to do so it would render his labor among them useless (3:5). They were therefore the object of Paul's "hope." Their failure to remain faithful would directly diminish his own sense of achievement and confidence at the coming of Christ. But for the very reason that they had continued in the faith in spite of considerable opposition they were a source of "joy" for Paul and would be so at the coming of Jesus. χαρά ("joy") was for him the opposite of λύπη ("grief" or "sadness") and was one of the important hallmarks of the Christian experience. The joy of the early Christians was based on their certainty of future salvation regardless of what happened to them in the present (see the comments on 1:6 and cf. Gal. 5:22; Rom. 14:17; 15:13 and the use of the verb χαίρειν in Rom. 12:12, 15; Phil. 4:4). In 1 Thes. 2:19, as in Phil. 4:1, χαρά is used of Paul's converts as the persons who cause his joy. In the context of 1 Thessalonians 2, the image of the parent who speaks of his or her child as "my joy" is perhaps suggested (Best, 128), but the point of what Paul says concerns the positive pride and pleasure that the Thessalonians will give to him at the return of Jesus. The pathos of Paul's language in 1 Thessalonians 2, which is unique in his letters, perhaps suggests that the Thessalonians were particularly dear to Paul. If this is correct the affection may have been due to the adversities they had endured without wavering in their faith.

Although στέφανος καυχήσεως ("crown of pride") occurs in the LXX in

Ezk. 16:12; 23:42; and Pr. 16:31 these texts have no bearing on its application here. Instead Paul uses it here in the sense of a "crown of pride" like the victory wreath placed on the heads of victorious military commanders or the winners of athletic contests to signify their achievement. For Paul the Thessalonians were like a victory wreath of which he could be proud at the coming of Christ. They were a proof of his toil and achievement for Christ as a missionary to the Gentiles (cf. 2 Cor. 1:14; Phil. 2:16). Even this triumph, however, Paul saw as a demonstration of God's grace (1 Cor. 15:10) since he repudiates human boasting (1 Cor. 1:29). Nevertheless, Paul was aware that his work would be judged to determine the reward that he would receive for his missionary work (cf. 1 Cor. 3:10-15). Although many commentators appear reluctant to attribute motives of self-interest to Paul, W. Grundmann (*TDNT* VII, 630) is almost certainly correct when he writes:

> Paul realises that he and all believers are definitively saved by the Lord. But in the judgment the fruits of his life will be measured and judged, cf. 1 C[or]. 15:10; also 3:11-15; 4:1-5; 5:5; 9:5-18; 2 C[or]. 5:10 etc. Paul does not merely want to be saved personally. He wants a reward and praise for the results of his life because they prove to be enduring. The fact that they endure finds expression in the churches as his crown and joy and hope and glory on the day of the *parousia.*

The structure of the sentence is broken by Paul's answering his own rhetorical question parenthetically before completing the sentence. "Is it not indeed you?" (ἢ οὐχὶ καὶ ὑμεῖς) indicates that it is Paul's readers, the Thessalonians, who are his "hope, joy, and crown of pride." Frame (122) and Dibelius (12) among others, followed by Best (129), take καὶ ὑμεῖς in the sense of "you *as well as others.*" Bruce (53) makes the interesting suggestion that ἦ, a synonym for ἄρα, should be read instead of ἤ, so that the question does not indicate an alternative between the Thessalonians and others, as ἤ would imply. The interrogative clause may then be translated with Bruce as "is it not indeed you?" This approach seems preferable since it does not introduce another otherwise unidentified group into the text and avoids the problems that ἤ causes by implying an alternative.

The final part of the interrupted initial question has already been mentioned. ἔμπροσθεν τοῦ κυρίου ἡμῶν Ἰησοῦ ἐν τῇ αὐτοῦ παρουσίᾳ ("before our Lord Jesus at his appearing") qualifies "who is our hope, joy, and crown of pride" by indicating that Paul is concerned with the end of the age when Jesus will return. The phrase gives clear expression to Paul's apocalyptic eschatology and indicates his own personal belief that his apostolic ministry has its context in and takes its meaning from the imminent events of the *eschaton* or end of the age.

The key word is "parousia," which is used six times in 1 and 2 Thessalonians for the return of Jesus and only once elsewhere in Paul for this

(1 Cor. 15:23). The word is probably drawn from the earliest layers of the Christian tradition, as it is a technical term for the coming of Jesus as sovereign Lord in a number of the NT documents (cf. Mt. 24:3, 27, 37, 39 [the latter three refer to the parousia of the Son of Man]; Jas. 5:7, 8; 2 Pet. 1:16; 3:4; 1 Jn. 2:28), though its earliest extant occurrence is in 1 and 2 Thessalonians. A. Oepke (*TDNT* V, 865) insists that it never has the sense of "return" in the early Christian tradition. The reason is that the life of the earthly Jesus was not a parousia in the technical sense of the term. Its technical meaning in the Hellenistic world concerned the visit of a human ruler or a high official to a city, with appropriate ceremonies being held and honors being bestowed, or of the visit of a god to an individual or to cultic followers. For the early Christians who viewed the human existence of Jesus as a life of suffering and humiliation even to the extent of being crucified (see Phil. 2:6-9), Jesus would only come as the divine sovereign when he came to bring judgment and condemnation for godless sinners and final salvation for the elect; this would be his parousia when all would be required to give to him honor (cf. Phil. 2:10f. and 1 Cor. 15:23-28).

In this sense the parousia of Jesus is connected especially with such OT ideas as the day of the Lord (Is. 2:10-12; Am. 5:17-18), God's visiting of Israel and particularly the rulers of Israel for judgment (Je. 5:9; Ho. 2:13 [Hebrew 2:15]; Zc. 10:3, where the *RSV* has "punish" for Hebrew *paqad,* which has the root meaning "visit" or "inspect"), and the day of salvation when God would come to rule over Israel (Is. 52:6-10). (See A. Oepke, *TDNT* V, 858-871; Best, 349-354; G. Braumann and C. Brown, *DNTT* II, 898-935 for detailed discussions of the word "parousia.")

But the formerly pagan Thessalonians probably understood the parousia of Christ in terms of the visits of the imperial rulers of Rome. These rulers were increasingly being thought of as the manifestations of deities who required elaborate ceremonies and honors when they visited the various cities of the Empire. When Christ came even the rulers of this world would have to give him his rightful honor and would be subject to divine judgment. While Paul does not make the point here explicit, the Thessalonians' belief that their Lord would return to bring judgment would have given them a sense of power over their oppressors. As the followers and servants of the Lord they would be honored participants in the public manifestation of Christ while their enemies would experience the fearful judgment of the Lord. Thus the current social relations between oppressors and oppressed would be reversed. Such a belief provides a sense of power enabling an oppressed group like the small Christian community at Thessalonica to endure with hope.

2:20 In this verse Paul formally answers his rhetorical question from the previous verse by indicating that the Thessalonians are in fact his glory and joy and by implication that they will be so at the public manifestation of Christ if they remain faithful. Their significance to Paul is stressed by the emphatic position of ὑμεῖς ("you"). δόξα ("glory") is essentially parallel to στέφανος καυχήσεως ("crown of pride") in the previous verse and refers to the Thessalonians as those in whom Paul takes deep pride (cf. the use of δόξα in 1 Cor. 11:7). Obviously χαρά ("joy") is simply repeated from the previous verse.

What Paul actually accomplishes in these two verses is the linkage of his own confidence and feelings of pride and joy in the face of the imminent appearance of Christ to his converts' faithful adherence to the gospel that he had preached to them. As he makes clear in 3:5, their failure to remain steadfast would have meant the failure of his toil among them. The effect of such language is to encourage the Thessalonians to remain faithful to Christ and to his apostle, Paul, regardless of the hardships and opposition that they encounter. Thus the parenetic intention of the letter lies just below the surface here.

The Sending of Timothy: 3:1-5

In this paragraph Paul discusses his sending of Timothy to the Thessalonians when he himself was unable to visit them and explains why he sent Timothy as an agent of his own apostolic parousia. The return of Timothy to Thessalonica renewed the personal contact of the missionaries with their converts after a period of enforced separation. If I am correct in my analysis of the relation between 1 and 2 Thessalonians it was for this occasion that 2 Thessalonians, Paul's first letter to the church, was written.

3:1 Feeling exceedingly anxious as to whether the Thessalonians would be able to withstand the considerable pressures on them to abandon their new faith, Paul decided to send Timothy to them when it became clear that he himself would not be able to return to Thessalonica, at least for the time being. The inferential conjunction διό ("therefore") picks up the thought of 2:17f. and indicates that what follows explains how Paul dealt with his concern for the Thessalonian community and his own inability to return to them. The crisis for Paul came when he could no longer endure (μηκέτι στέγοντες) the separation from the Thessalonians that prevented him from effectively establishing them in the faith and encouraging them to remain faithful (3:2). It left him ignorant of how his converts were weathering the troubles that they experienced in the wake of their conversion (3:5).

The plural form of the verb εὐδοκήσαμεν ("we resolved") stands in logical tension with the expression καταλειφθῆναι . . . μόνοι ("to be left alone"). In what sense was Paul really left alone in Athens if the plural verb refers to himself and Silvanus? The language seems a bit too strong if Paul and Silvanus made a mutual decision to remain in Athens while sending Timothy back to Thessalonica. Could this then be an example of an epistolary plural? Most commentators argue against this possibility in favor of a genuine plural (e.g., Frame, 125; Best, 131; Marxsen, 54; Bruce, 60), but in v. 5, where Paul mentions sending Timothy to Thessalonica, he slips into the first person singular. This should warn us against assuming too hastily that the plural of 3:1 is genuine (see Dibelius, 12 and with qualification Marshall, 89f.).

Although Acts reports Paul's stay in Athens it is of no help since it does not indicate that Timothy or Silvanus (Silas) was ever in Athens with Paul. According to Acts 17:15 Paul went to Athens alone but sent word back to Timothy and Silvanus in Macedonia to join him there. Acts 18:5 suggests, however, that they only rejoined Paul after he had moved on to Corinth. Thus at this point the narrative of Acts exhibits either a lack of knowledge concerning the precise details of the missionaries' movements in Greece or a tendency to condense the narrative, thereby sacrificing an exact account in the process. Clearly, 1 Thes. 3:1 must be taken as historically correct over against the Acts narrative at this point, though I favor the view that the plurals of 3:1-4 should be taken as epistolary rather than genuine and thus that Paul was left alone in Athens. Unfortunately information is not available to indicate the whereabouts of Silvanus if he was not with Paul. Perhaps he had remained at Beroea. This possibility would have some credibility if (1) Silvanus was sent with Paul to missionize among Jews as the representative of Jerusalem and (2) the Acts report is accurate in indicating a positive response to the mission work among the Jewish community at Beroea (Acts 17:10-11).

3:2 Paul sent (ἐπέμψαμεν) Timothy back to Thessalonica as his official representative, and therefore Timothy was authorized to act in his place in dealing with the community. While Paul does not use the term here since it might have proved confusing, Timothy functioned as his "apostle" (cf. Phil. 2:25, where Paul calls Epaphroditus the "apostle" of the church at Philippi; see the material on the Jewish concept of the *šalîaḥ* in Borgen, "God's Agent"; Barrett, "Shaliah"). This was but the first of many occasions on which Timothy served as Paul's agent when Paul was unable to pay a personal visit to one of the churches that he had established (see 1 Cor. 4:17; 16:10; Phil. 2:19).

The long phrase τὸν ἀδελφὸν ἡμῶν καὶ συνεργὸν τοῦ θεοῦ ἐν τῷ εὐαγγελίῳ τοῦ Χριστοῦ ("our brother and coworker of God in the gospel of Christ") states Timothy's credentials that entitle him to act as Paul's representative. In context they may be intended to reassure the Thessalonians that Timothy had Paul's complete confidence when he visited them by himself. But the phrase may also have been intended to prepare the way for Timothy to take them the letter in which the phrase appears, when that letter was completed.

"Our brother" may imply more than simply that Timothy was a fellow Christian or even a close friend of Paul's. Ellis (*Prophecy and Hermeneutic*, 13-22) has suggested that "brother" was used not only in a general sense of all believers but also in a restricted sense of Paul's coworkers (see 1 Cor. 16:19-20 and Phil. 4:21-22, where the "brothers" seem to be distinguished from the church at large). Whether the term has such a technical meaning, and Marshall (90) for one doubts that it does, it clearly designates Timothy as Paul's coworker in this passage (cf. 1 Cor. 1:1; 16:12; 2 Cor. 1:1; 2:13; 8:18; Phil. 2:25, etc.).

But Paul goes even further when he identifies Timothy as the συνεργὸν τοῦ θεοῦ ("coworker of God"), a reading attested in D* 33 it[d, e, mon]* Ambrosiaster Pelagius Ps.-Jerome. The textual tradition, however, shows considerable disruption at this point. When various conflated texts are discounted as obviously secondary, two other possible wordings emerge besides συνεργὸν τοῦ θεοῦ. These are καὶ διάκονον τοῦ θεοῦ ("and servant of God"), which has the strongest external attestation (ℵ A Ψ 81 629* 1739 it[61] vg syr[h] cop[sa, bo, fay]), and the simple συνεργόν ("coworker," i.e., of Paul: B 1962). The most likely explanation for the variant readings is that scribes found the expression συνεργὸν τοῦ θεοῦ, when applied to Timothy, too bold and altered the original reading by either substituting διάκονον for συνεργόν or dropping the reference to God, leaving Timothy the coworker of Paul on the basis of the ἡμῶν occurring with ἀδελφόν (see Metzger, *Text of the New Testament*, 240-242). Although the statement is bold, Paul describes himself and Apollos as "coworkers (συνεργοί) of God" in 1 Cor. 3:9, and in his classic statement concerning his ministry in 2 Cor. 5:16–6:2 he seems to speak of working with God in his exhortation to the Corinthians to receive the grace of God (for this interpretation see Barrett, *Second Corinthians*, 183 on 2 Cor. 6:1). Paul apparently understood the missionary vocation as a form of cooperation with God in bringing people to faith in Christ. By designating Timothy as his own brother and "God's coworker in the gospel of Christ" ("in the gospel of Christ" goes with both "brother" and "coworker of God"), Paul attributed considerable status to Timothy in order to confirm his past work among the Thessalonians on Paul's behalf and to prepare for his possible return to them.

It is probably best to take Χριστοῦ as an objective genitive expressing the content of the gospel that Paul proclaimed, since the gospel has its origin (subjective genitive) not in Christ but in God. As Paul indicates in the carefully formulated prescript of Romans, he was appointed "to the gospel of God," which has as its content God's son (Rom. 1:1-4).

On his previous visit, Timothy's role had been to confirm (στηρίξαι) the Thessalonians in their new convictions (cf. the use of στηρίξαι in Rom. 16:25) and to encourage (παρακαλέσαι) them for the benefit (ὑπέρ) of their faith, so that their faith might increase. Paul was particularly concerned that this pastoral function should take place, given the pressures that the Thessalonians had been put under by their fellow citizens after their conversion. Quite apart from the external pressure mentioned in v. 3, however, Paul was aware of the pressing need to continue the process of resocialization to the new Christian way of life and to further inculcate the new beliefs and values the Thessalonians had received when they accepted the gospel of Christ. Failure to do so could result in his work among them being in vain (see 2:18). If in fact Timothy was to return to the Thessalonians yet again, this would undoubtedly be his continuing task.

2 Thes. 2:17, in which both παρακαλέσαι and στηρίξαι occur, indicates that when 2 Thessalonians was written Paul was concerned that the Thessalonians receive consolation or encouragement and that their Christian way of life become established. Since Paul's prayer request for the Thessalonians in 2 Thes. 2:17 corresponds to the role Timothy was assigned when he returned to the church on Paul's behalf as indicated in v. 3, this lends support to the view that Timothy carried our 2 Thessalonians with him on that occasion (see pp. 37-46 above on the sequence of the letters).

3:3 Timothy's work of confirming and encouraging the Thessalonians in their new faith had an important purpose, namely, helping them to face and endure the oppression that they experienced as a result of their conversion to the Christian faith. In his concern that not one of his converts be lost Paul had sent Timothy back to Thessalonica. This point is made by the infinitive clause in v. 3a, which is final in character.

The meaning of σαίνεσθαι ("to disturb"), however, is somewhat problematic. The verb occurs only here in the Greek Bible. The term originally was used of the wagging of a dog's tail and then metaphorically of fawning or cringing by humans. Earlier commentators took the passive form of the verb to mean "be beguiled" in this passage (e.g., Frame, 128). In contrast to this interpretation, all of the ancient versions as well as the Greek interpreters of the passage without exception understood the verb to mean "move, disturb, or agitate" (BAGD, 740; F. Lang, *TDNT* VII, 55f.). This meaning fits well with the context and lexicographers have been able to adduce several other instances where σαίνειν seems to have this sense (see Lang; Bammel, "Preparation"). In one, taken from a papyrus text that reports a discussion between Origen and Bishop Heraclides, Origen states, "τὰ μὲν περὶ πίστεως ὅσα ἔσηνεν ἡμᾶς συνεξετάσθη" ("all questions of faith that unsettled us have been tested"; the text is quoted by Bruce, 62). In another instance it is reported of a crowd after Pythagoras's reputed account of his journey to Hades that οἱ σαινόμενοι τοῖς λεγομένοις ἐδάκρυον ("those who were agitated cried at the things that were being spoken"; Diog. Laert. 8, 41, quoted by BAGD, 740).

Using this last text as a point of departure Bammel ("Preparation," 91-100) argues that σαίνεσθαι is the reaction of people faced with an extreme situation. He then proceeds to argue that one finds a striking similarity between στηρίξαι, σαίνεσθαι, and θλῖψις in 1 Thes. 3:2f. and the language employed in Jewish apocalyptic texts for extreme situations and experiences. From this he deduces that σαίνεσθαι in 3:3 has its place in the eschatological perspective of the whole letter and that Paul was worried about the possibility that the Thessalonians would be disturbed in the eschatological situation of tribulation preceding the return of Christ. According to Bammel, Paul sought

129

to establish (στηρίξαι) his converts as a precaution against the possibility of any of them being disturbed by the tribulations of the end—the so-called "messianic woes" of Jewish apocalyptic writings. Bammel's thesis merits consideration. It highlights the eschatological character of the situation as perceived by Paul and makes clear that the Thessalonians' sufferings were part of the necessary experience of the Christian before the coming of Christ.

What few commentators seem to have noticed is the correlation between the concern that led Paul to send Timothy back to the church, namely his fear that his converts might be disturbed or shaken by their ordeal of persecution, and the situation that led to the writing of 2 Thessalonians. In 2 Thes. 2:1-2 Paul speaks of his concern that his converts might be quickly shaken (ταχέως σαλευθῆναι) with regard to the parousia of the Lord Jesus Christ. Since 2 Thessalonians 1 makes it clear that Paul's anxiety had arisen in the context of the Thessalonians' experience of persecution and since σαλευθῆναι (2 Thes. 2:2) and σαίνεσθαι (1 Thes. 3:2) are synonyms in the two passages, this provides further evidence for my claim that 2 Thessalonians was delivered by Timothy when he revisited Thessalonica for the first time after he and Paul had departed from the city.

In the second part of v. 3, which together with v. 4 is a digression, Paul goes on to say that the Thessalonians themselves are already aware of what he is speaking of. He is merely reminding his readers of what he taught them when he was with them and, if 2 Thessalonians was his first letter, what he had written to them previously (cf. 2 Thes. 1:3-12). He seeks to reassure his readers that the tribulations suffered at the hands of their fellow citizens were neither arbitrary nor isolated happenings but part of their God-appointed destiny (κείμεθα). Paul writes in the first person plural at this point in order to indicate that they were part and parcel of the same sufferings that he and all other Christians (for example, those in Judea, mentioned in 2:14) had to face and endure. God had destined Christians for affliction as part of the process that leads to their salvation.

Therefore suffering of affliction is actually a proof of divine election and of the imminence of redemption for the people of God. This idea was taken over from Jewish apocalyptic thought, where it was maintained that the righteous were destined to undergo affliction or tribulation before the emergence of the new age (see Dn. 12:1; *Jub.* 23:13f.; *2 Bar.* 70:2-10; 2 Esdr. 5:1-12; 13:30f.; 14:16f.), and it became part of the earliest Christian tradition, as Mk. 13:7f. shows. In the context of 1 Thessalonians Paul's reminder serves the parenetic function of encouraging the recipients of the letter to persevere in their new Christian way of life.

3:4 Paul reminds the Thessalonians that while he was still with them (ὅτε πρὸς ὑμᾶς ἦμεν) he forewarned them about the inevitability of their suffering as Christians. The imperfect verb προελέγομεν indicates that Paul had told them about the ineluctability of their suffering on a number of occasions, and thus the verb should be translated "we used to tell you beforehand." The choice of the words μέλλομεν θλίβεσθαι is significant. The verb μέλλειν with the present infinitive is frequently used in the NT to indicate an event or action resulting from a divine decree (BAGD, 501; for other examples of this usage in Paul see Rom. 4:24; 8:13). In other words, μέλλομεν θλίβεσθαι reiterates what was said in the previous verse with κείμεθα, and refers to the eschatological suffering preceding the end of the present age.

Thus Paul interpreted the suffering experienced by the Thessalonians as part of the eschatological tribulation and taught them to regard it as such while he was still with them. For this reason he can write that they know (οἴδατε), probably in the sense that they both know that he told them about their imminent suffering and know its meaning in terms of God's eschatological plans. Meeks ("Social Function," 692) notes that the fulfillment of Paul's earlier prediction regarding persecution strongly reinforced the new, separate identity of the converts over against the larger society of which they had been a part. Perhaps more importantly it also strengthened their commitment to their new Christian beliefs and values since one of the cardinal beliefs associated with the imminent parousia of Christ, namely, the suffering of the people of God before the coming of their Lord, was being fulfilled in their own experience and indicated that the end of the age was at hand.

3:5 Having digressed in vv. 3b-4 from his explanation of why he had sent Timothy to his readers, Paul returns in v. 5 to this theme in preparation for vv. 6-10 where he discusses his reaction to the return of Timothy after his visit to Thessalonica. While διὰ τοῦτο ("on account of this") refers back to the immediately preceding verses, where Paul speaks of the oppression that the Thessalonians had suffered as the primary reason that he sent Timothy back to them, it also resumes what was said in vv. 1f. This is shown by the fact that the idea of vv. 1-2a is virtually repeated in κἀγὼ μηκέτι στέγων ἔπεμψα ("and when I could no longer endure, I sent"). But this time Paul employs the first person singular (see 3:1 on the significance of the singular).

The reason for sending Timothy is amplified in v. 5. Although Paul's primary purpose was to confirm and encourage the Thessalonians in their faith during their time of tribulation (vv. 2-3a), he also wanted to learn how they were weathering the storm. Thus the infinitive clause εἰς τὸ γνῶναι τὴν πίστιν ὑμῶν ("in order to learn about your faith") expresses the secondary purpose for Paul's sending Timothy back to his converts in Thessalonica. πίστις has the sense of "faithfulness" here though it can hardly be dissociated from the actual confidence or faith of the Thessalonians in God and in the promise of Christ's coming in power. Behind Timothy's mission was Paul's deep-seated concern that the Thessalonians either as a group or in significant numbers might abandon the new beliefs and values that they had accepted at their conversion. Undoubtedly this is the sort of anxiety he refers to in 2 Cor. 11:28 as being constantly with him.

μὴ πως, also written as one word, μήπως, is dependent on the verb ἔπεμψα and expresses the genuine mood of apprehension felt by Paul when he sent Timothy back to Thessalonica (see BDF §370.2). As was suggested in the Introduction, this may to some degree explain the character of 2 Thessalonians if it is the letter Paul sent in his anxiety. His concern was that "the tempter might have tempted" the Thessalonian Christians," so that his and his co-workers' work would be "in vain" (ἐπείρασεν ὑμᾶς ὁ πειράζων καὶ εἰς κενὸν γένηται ὁ κόπος ἡμῶν). That is, in the difficult situation the Thessalonians had faced without their spiritual mentors, they might have renounced their Christian beliefs and way of life. According to 1 Cor. 7:5 Satan is the one who tempts Christians, and this is who Paul has in mind here as well (cf. 2:18). The aorist ἐπείρασεν is written from the perspective of Paul before Timothy went back to Thessalonica. His apprehension had been that his readers might already have succumbed to Satan's testing of them before Timothy was able to return to strengthen and encourage them. If this had happened, then the missionaries' hard labors among the Thessalonians (cf. 2:9) would have proved useless or to no purpose (εἰς κενόν).

The imagery of Satan as the tempter of Christians was derived from Paul's apocalyptic framework in which Satan was viewed as the arch-adversary of God (see Beker, *Paul the Apostle*, 188 and the comments above on 2:18). Paul went so far as to call him "the god of this age" who "has blinded the minds of unbelievers" in order to prevent them from accepting the gospel of Christ (2 Cor. 4:4; cf. 2 Thes. 2:9-12). Within his apocalyptic under-standing of the two ages, Paul saw Satan as the one who has "usurped God's authority" to become the ruler of the present age but who will be overthrown when God establishes his dominion in the age to come (Barrett, *Second Corinthians*, 130).

It is no wonder then that Paul also portrayed Satan as seeking to destroy the fruits of the Christian mission (cf. 1 Cor. 7:5; 2 Cor. 2:10f.; 11:13-15; 1 Thes. 2:18). In the context of 1 Thes. 3:5, Paul implicitly demonizes those who afflict the Thessalonians because they are by implication the agents of Satan's temptation. This certainly must have had the effect of heightening the separation between the new and struggling Christian community at Thessalonica and the social world from which its members had removed themselves. This in turn fits in with his parenetic intention throughout the letter because it strengthens the identity of his readers as Christians.

Timothy's Return: 3:6-10

Paul no doubt waited expectantly for the return of Timothy, who would be able to give him a firsthand report on the situation in Thessalonica and especially on the state of the Christian community there. As 3:6-10 reveals, 1 Thessalonians was written after the return of Timothy, who reported that the community had weathered the departure of the missionaries and the oppressive conditions that they had experienced without a significant loss in numbers or in commitment to their new religious faith. They still thought highly of Paul and Silvanus and wished that they might return. The relief of Paul at this news is clearly indicated by 3:6-10 as well as his affection for the Thessalonians and his own longing to return to them in order to complete more fully his work of "Christianizing" them. The rhetorical function of this section resides in its philophronetic intention. Paul seeks to overcome his distance in both time and place from his readers by taking up traditional themes associated with friendship in the ancient world (cf. Stowers, *Letter Writing*, 60). By doing so he lays the basis for his direct ethical exhortation in chaps. 4–5 in good rhetorical fashion (on philophronesis see Malherbe, "Exhortation in First Thessalonians," 241).

3:6 The words ἄρτι δὲ ἐλθόντος Τιμοθέου πρὸς ἡμᾶς ἀφ' ὑμῶν ("and now that Timothy has returned to us from you") suggest that 1 Thessalonians was composed almost immediately after Timothy had returned to Paul. Certainly Paul wished to communicate this impression to the Thessalonians as a demonstration both of his concern and the warm affection that he felt for them. Whether Silvanus was with Paul when Timothy came back is uncertain. πρὸς ἡμᾶς ("to us") implies that he was, but as on several other occasions the first person plural may be no more than a so-called epistolary plural. Acts 18:5 seems to suggest that Timothy, as well as Silvanus, had been in Macedonia and that they rejoined Paul together in Corinth, but Paul neither indicates where he was at the time nor where Silvanus was, unless the plural is a genuine plural.

From Paul's perspective the important thing was that when Timothy returned he was able to report that the Thessalonians were coping and even progressing in their faith. Curiously Paul employs the participle εὐαγ-γελισαμένου ("proclaiming good news") to describe Timothy's report. While the verb originally denoted any announcement of good news and may have no more than this meaning here, the very choice of the word probably was intended by Paul as a play on the word used by himself and other early Christians as the word par excellence for communication of the Christian message (1 Cor. 15:1f.; Gal. 1:8, 11, 16). Marshall (94), who follows Masson (41) and Best (139f.), reads too much into the word when he claims that it may denote the proclamation of the gospel in the normal technical sense here. He has succumbed to the ever present temptation to "over-theologize" a word.

The good news Timothy announced to Paul concerned at least two facts. First, the Thessalonians had not wavered in their new beliefs and behavior patterns. This seems to be the idea conveyed by the report concerning τὴν πίστιν καὶ τὴν ἀγάπην ("the faith and love") of the Thessalonians. πίστις should probably be understood in terms of their confidence in God, which was severely tested by their suffering. Paul was relieved to hear that their new

133

beliefs had not been shaken with a concomitant turning away from the Christian religion. At the same time Paul was undoubtedly pleased to learn that their Christian conduct, which he characterizes as "love," had endured. In Paul's understanding, love was not a mere human emotion but revealed itself in action (Rom. 13:9-10). As he says elsewhere, "What has power or meaning in Christ Jesus is faith working through love" (Gal. 5:6). For Paul belief in God and his saving purposes should lead to a response of active love manifested particularly in the way Christians behave toward one another (see 1 Thes. 4:9). It is this understanding of faith and love that probably lies behind what Paul says in 3:6.

Second, the Thessalonians held Paul in high regard and longed to see him, as the words ἔχετε μνείαν ἡμῶν ἀγαθὴν πάντοτε ("you always think of us affectionately") reveal. The apostle gives the impression that he was especially pleased to learn the Thessalonians had a "kind or affectionate remembrance" (μνείαν ἀγαθήν) of him and his colleagues. This perhaps implies that he was concerned about how the Thessalonians viewed him after his departure. Several possibilities exist for the basis of his concern. It might have resulted from the manner in which he left, especially if he had been forced to leave unexpectedly. Acts 17:5-10 portrays his and Silvanus's departure as so hasty that they were unable to prepare the community properly for it. Another possibility is that the Thessalonians might have resented the situation of oppression in which they found themselves when they discovered that the supposed good news Paul had announced to them was in reality "bad news" in that it led directly to their suffering (Bruce, 66). A third possibility is that Paul feared the Thessalonians would be disappointed in him and perhaps even reject him for not having himself returned to them already. 2:17f. provides strong support for this understanding since in those verses, as we have seen, Paul insists that he had longed to see them and had even planned to visit them on several occasions, only to be prevented from doing so by the arch-enemy, Satan. This looks like an apology for his failure to return and may imply apprehension over the reaction of the Thessalonians in this matter. For this reason Paul was pleased to learn of their continuing affection and their desire to see him again. Paul responded to their desire to see him (ἐπιποθοῦντες ἡμᾶς ἰδεῖν) by indicating through the elliptical expression καθάπερ καὶ ἡμεῖς ὑμᾶς ("just as we also you") that his readers' desire was reciprocated by his own desire to see them. Such reciprocity in affection was intended to demonstrate Paul's true friendship with his readers. In effect Paul here reiterates what he said in 2:17. Along with the verses that follow it prepares for Paul's exhortation in chaps. 4–5 through its philophronetic impact.

3:7 The grammatical structure of vv. 6 and 7 is broken because Paul failed to complete the sentence begun in v. 6. The anacoluthon results from the inclusion of the causal phrase, διὰ τοῦτο ("for this reason") at the beginning of v. 7, in the midst of the temporal clause begun in v. 6. Paul may have commenced with a sentence like the following in mind: "But now since Timothy has come to us from you and told us the good news concerning your faith and love and that you always have a kind remembrance of us, desiring to see us, just as we long to see you, *we are encouraged*, brothers (and sisters), etc." In waiting too long to put the main verb into the sentence, the structure of the sentence was forgotten and anacoluthon resulted. Best (141) suggests that the broken sentence came about when Paul decided in mid-thought to add something concerning his own reaction to Timothy's return before going on to the thanksgiving in v. 9, which was originally to be the main clause of the sentence. This is possible, but what I have suggested here has the advantage of being simpler.

Whatever may be the cause of the broken sentence structure in vv. 6f., Paul describes the positive impact of Timothy's report in vv. 7f. On account of the news Timothy brought, Paul himself was encouraged (παρεκλήθημεν). The first ἐπί following παρεκλήθημεν has a causal sense and, with the pronoun ὑμῖν, offers the basis on which Paul was encouraged ("because of you"). He singles out their faith in the phrase διὰ τῆς ὑμῶν πίστεως, where διά is used instrumentally, as the real source of his encouragement.

Paul identifies his own situation ἐπὶ πάσῃ τῇ ἀνάγκῃ καὶ θλίψει ἡμῶν ("in all our distress and tribulation") as the context in which the report concerning the Thessalonians proved to be so encouraging. ἀνάγκη and θλίψις are occasionally used together in the LXX (Job 15:24; Pss. 24:17 [25:17]; 118:143 [119:143]; Zp. 1:15) and elsewhere by Paul in 2 Cor. 6:4, but there is no real difference in their meanings. In 1 Cor. 7:26 Paul appears to employ ἀνάγκη of the eschatological distress preceding the parousia of Christ, and a few verses later in 7:28 he uses θλίψις of the special tribulation that those who marry may experience in the crisis period. In light of Zp. 1:15, an OT eschatological passage, and Paul's own usage in 1 Cor. 7:26 and 28, Best (141) is probably correct in saying that the two terms formed "a word-pair denoting the persecutions, sufferings and distresses of the End."

We do not have any information from either Paul or Acts that the apostle underwent affliction and tribulation from external sources in the period immediately after he left Thessalonica. This leads Bruce (67; cf. Malherbe, *Paul and the Thessalonians*, 65 n. 10) to claim that the distress and affliction may have been primarily psychological in nature. This, however, seems to be a modern interpretation of the word-pair since in Paul they can be shown to denote almost always external or physical deprivation and/or oppression (see Rom. 5:3; 1 Cor. 7:26, 28; 2 Cor. 1:8; 6:4; 12:10; 1 Thes. 1:6; 3:3). Certainly Paul experienced considerable distress and affliction, as passages such as 2 Cor. 6:4 and 11:23-28 reveal, but given the eschatological character of the time, Paul would have understood whatever hardships he experienced as part of the final distress and affliction preceding the return of Christ. For this reason it is unnecessary to look for some specific reference, given our paucity of knowledge concerning the day-to-day life of Paul.

135

What is clear is that Paul wished to identify with the feelings and experiences of the Thessalonians in order to indicate to them that they were not the only ones suffering for the sake of the gospel of Christ and thereby to encourage them to continue in the Christian life. In doing so he emphasizes the reciprocity of his relationship with his readers, a common theme in letters of friendship in Antiquity, as mentioned above. He sent Timothy to encourage (παρακαλέσαι) his readers in their affliction (3:2) and he in turn was encouraged (παρεκλήθημεν) by them in his affliction.

3:8 The thought of v. 8 is subordinated by ὅτι to v. 7, but the causal translation "because," which both Best (138) and Bruce (67) favor, seems too strong for the context. It is better to translate it "for," which indicates the close relation between vv. 7 and 8 without stressing the existence of a causal relationship. νῦν ("now") suggests that Paul's statement "we live" (ζῶμεν) was his direct response to the news that the Thessalonian Christians were withstanding the various adversities that they had suffered.

ζῶμεν is obviously metaphorical here since Paul's physical existence was not threatened by the possibility that the Thessalonians would abandon their new faith. It implies that Paul derived a sense of strength from the endurance of his converts that enabled him to continue his missionary work in the face of opposition and oppression. If the Thessalonians had renounced their faith, Paul appears to imply, this would have called into question his "life's work," as his own personal sacrifices in bringing the gospel of Christ to the Gentiles derived meaning from the existence of his converts as faithful followers of Christ.

This point is made clear by the conditional clause ἐὰν ὑμεῖς στήκετε ἐν κυρίῳ ("if you stand firm in the Lord"). The use of ἐάν with the present indicative is somewhat unusual in the NT but in the context alludes to the fact that Paul's sense of well-being would continue as long as the Thessalonians continued to remain faithful. W. Grundmann (*TDNT* VII, 637) is certainly correct when he maintains that the conditional clause has a "hidden hortatory meaning." Paul sought to encourage the Thessalonians through linking their "perseverance" or "standing firm" (στήκετε) "in the Lord" to his own life and work (cf. Phil. 4:1 where the expression στήκετε ἐν κυρίῳ is imperative). "In the Lord" is used in the same way as the more common "in Christ" formula to denote that the Christian's existence is determined by the Lord. But there may be something in Moule's claim (*Origin of Christology,* 58-60) that a difference does sometimes exist between "in the Lord" and "in Christ." He maintains that "Lord" is employed "when it is a matter of exhortation or commands, in the subjunctive or the imperative." This appears to be true of v. 8, and fits with the general parenetic intention of the narrative section of the letter.

3:9 In this verse Paul poses a rhetorical question concerning what thanksgiving he should offer to God for the sense of joy he felt at learning of the Thessalonians' continuance in faith and love (3:6f.) in spite of serious adversity. This and the following verses are of considerable interest because they offer us some insight into Paul's personal prayer life. From v. 9 it is apparent that both thanksgiving and rejoicing were characteristic features of the apostle's prayers.

Schubert *(Form and Function)*, O'Brien *(Introductory Thanksgivings)*, and others, as we have seen, maintain that vv. 9-13 form the conclusion to the longest thanksgiving period in any of Paul's letters. This form-critical observation, however, as we have previously noted, is not altogether satisfactory. It confuses a formal structure in Paul's letters, the thanksgiving period, with a rhetorical genre in which thanksgiving to God is used to remind the congregation "of the pattern of praiseworthy and blameworthy behavior suitable to the new age in which they have become participants" (Jewett, *Thessalonian Correspondence*, 72). The *narratio* section of the letter, which contains a great deal of implicit parenesis, as I have shown, serves to prepare the reader for the explicit parenesis in the following chapters.

γάρ links vv. 9f. to what precedes it as an inference in the form of a question (τίνα γὰρ εὐχαριστίαν δυνάμεθα τῷ θεῷ ἀνταποδοῦναι περὶ ὑμῶν, "for what thanksgiving are we able to return to God concerning you?"). Two things are implicit in this question. First, Paul was profoundly thankful for the continuing faithfulness of the Thessalonians. Frame (134) suggests that ἀνταποδοῦναι ("return"), which may be used either in a negative sense (cf. 2 Thes. 1:6; Rom. 12:19) or in a positive sense, as it is here (cf. Rom. 11:35), is stronger than ἀποδιδόναι. Following Milligan he argues that it has the nuance of "complete return." With τίνα ("what") it suggests that Paul felt unable to give sufficient thanks to God for the tremendous sense of relief and joy he experienced at hearing the good news concerning his converts at Thessalonica. Second, that Paul wished to give thanks to God for the Thessalonians suggests that the apostle had a powerful awareness of God's working in and among his converts to enable them to remain true to their new beliefs and behavior patterns as Christians.

While the phrase περὶ ὑμῶν ("concerning you") shows that Paul's feeling of thankfulness was based on his readers' steadfastness in the gospel, the phrase ἐπὶ πάσῃ τῇ χαρᾷ ᾗ χαίρομεν δι' ὑμᾶς ("for all the joy with which we rejoice on account of you") designates the immediate cause of his desire to give thanks to God. Best (144) claims that ἐπὶ πάσῃ τῇ χαρᾷ ("for all the joy") was intended as a deliberate balancing of ἐπὶ πάσῃ τῇ ἀνάγκῃ καὶ θλίψει ("in all our distress and tribulation") in v. 7. For this reason he translates ἐπί in both cases as "in." Apparently Best understands ἐπί in v. 9 in the sense of "manner," so that the prepositional phrase explains the manner of Paul's thanksgiving. This, however, obscures the fact that εὐχαριστίαν ἀνταποδοῦναι ("to return thanksgiving") is the semantic equivalent of εὐχαριστεῖν ("to give thanks") and therefore that ἐπί is dependent on it and expresses the basis for the action contained in the verbal idea "to return thanksgiving." For this reason ἐπί should be translated by a preposition like "for" or even "on account of" to indicate Paul's motivation for rendering thanks, which is the tremendous joy he experienced because of the Thessalonians' continuing faith. The reason for this joy and the ensuing thanksgiving can be seen if we look back at 2:19f., where Paul tells the readers that they are his "glory and joy" before the Lord Jesus at his coming, but this of course depended upon their remaining faithful. Thus when Paul discovered that they had continued in their commitment to Christ as Lord it was a source of tremendous joy for him, as well as a source of encouragement (3:7), and led to his desire to express in an adequate way his sense of thankfulness to God. The fact that "the joy with which we rejoiced" was ἔμπροσθεν τοῦ θεοῦ ("before God") implies that his rejoicing was done in the context of prayer.

3:10 The previous verse presents two aspects of Paul's prayer life: rejoicing before God and the rendering of thanksgiving to God. This verse offers another component: petitioning or making specific requests of God. Wiles (*Intercessory Prayer Passages,* 175-229) has argued that one of the important functions of prayer reports like 3:10, which are common in Paul's letters (cf. 1:2f.; Rom. 1:9f.; Phil. 1:4, 9-11), is that they "announce either the central message or the precise occasion of the letter, and anticipate its main paraenetic thrust" (229). This is certainly true of 3:10, as we shall see.

Paul indicates the constancy of his prayer requests for the Thessalonians in the words νυκτὸς καὶ ἡμέρας ὑπερεκπερισσοῦ δεόμενοι ("night and day praying earnestly"). The unusual adverb ὑπερεκπερισσοῦ communicates the intensity of Paul's prayer as well as the intensity of the desire that lies behind his prayer request. As Bruce (68) notes, "Paul is fond of compounds expressing superlativeness" (cf. ὑπερπερισσεύειν in Rom. 5:20; 2 Cor. 7:4; ὑπεραυξάνειν in 2 Thes. 1:3; ὑπερεκπερισσοῦ in 1 Thes. 5:13; ὑπερλίαν in 2 Cor. 11:5; 12:11, etc.). ὑπερεκπερισσοῦ δεόμενοι literally means something like "making requests quite beyond all measure."

Paul mentions two things concerning which he petitioned God. First, he reports to his readers that he prayed εἰς τὸ ἰδεῖν ὑμῶν τὸ πρόσωπον ("to see you face to face"). He had already told them that he desired to do this (2:17f.; 3:7), and by mentioning it here as a part of his regular prayer life he reiterates his genuine commitment to return to the Thessalonians. This seems to reflect very clearly the occasion of the letter. Paul seeks to keep open the possibility of his own return to Thessalonica while reassuring his readers of his continuing concern for them.

Second, he explains why he wished to return. Because his departure from the Thessalonians was apparently abrupt, he tells his converts that he wants to return καταρτίσαι τὰ ὑστερήματα τῆς πίστεως ὑμῶν ("to complete the deficiencies of your faith"). Paul has in mind the opportunities that a visit would afford for giving his converts further personal instruction and exhortation, the very thing that his letters were intended to do in his absence (cf.

Lyons, *Pauline Autobiography,* 218). The neuter plural τὰ ὑστερήματα ("deficiencies") when taken with the genitive τῆς πίστεως ὑμῶν ("of your faith")
indicates a concern not for a lack of faith on the part of his readers but for the
need to deepen their understanding and encourage their Christian behavior.
Timothy had been sent to begin this task (3:2), but Paul informs his readers
that he still wishes to come to them and personally continue their instruction
in the faith. Paul shows here a profound awareness of the need to continue the
process of resocializing the Thessalonians into the Christian way of life (see
comments on 2:11f.). Although he desired to do this in person, his letter to
the Thessalonians was intended to serve as a substitute for his presence, just
as Timothy had substituted for him when he had visited them. In the light of
this, we may understand 4:1–5:22 as an attempt by Paul to make good the
deficiencies in his converts' understanding of their new faith and its requirements with respect to their ethical conduct. Thus 3:10 helps to prepare for the
parenetic material in chaps. 4–5.

One further point needs to be made regarding the resocialization process
alluded to in v. 10. Living in a culture shaped by the beliefs and values of the
Christian tradition, contemporary Christians are prone to forget or ignore the
magnitude of the change in beliefs and values undergone by Paul's pagan
converts in becoming Christians. This problem was compounded by the lack
of any NT to document for them the Christian way of thinking and acting.
Hence the primary burden rested upon Paul and his colleagues to "Christian-
ize" their pagan converts, and to a lesser degree their Jewish converts. Paul
fully understood this and devoted his ministry to the dual task of converting
and resocializing people to be Christians.

Contemporary Christians can learn from Paul's missionary practice by
recognizing that meaningful evangelism must aim for more than acceptance
of Christian beliefs by converts. Evangelical Christianity needs to strive to
create a social context or community in which converts may be resocialized
into a new and distinctively Christian pattern of behavior and practice.
Without this, conversion is not complete and has little chance of being
genuinely transformative in the long term.

TRANSITUS FROM *NARRATIO* TO *PROBATIO*: 3:11-13

Boers ("Form-Critical Study," 152f.), using what may be called epistolary analysis, follows the lead of Funk ("Apostolic *Parousia*") in relating 3:11 to 2:17–3:10. Together this material forms what he describes as a section dealing with Paul's apostolic parousia and concludes the philophronetic or friendship portion of the letter before moving on to the parenetic or advice section of the letter in 4:1–5:22.

From the perspective of rhetorical analysis it is much more appropriate to refer to 3:11-13 as a *transitus*, as Jewett (*Thessalonian Correspondence*, 77f.) points out. A *transitus*, which is the usual way of concluding a *narratio*, summarizes the themes of the *narratio* while introducing the themes of the following section.

3:11-13 takes the form of what Wiles (*Intercessory Prayer Passages*, 22-107) describes as an intercessory wish-prayer. Wiles traces the origin and development of the intercessory wish-prayer to the OT (see esp. Ps. 20:1-5, 9 and 1 Ki. 8:57-61), where direct liturgical prayers were transformed into wish-prayers when written down, as well as to the Jewish epistolary tradition (see 2 Macc. 1:2-6), which drew on pagan-Hellenistic antecedents.

The wish-prayer in 1 Thes. 3:11-13 contains three petitions that serve to draw the first main section of the letter to a conclusion. They reiterate: (1) Paul's desire to visit the Thessalonians (v. 11; cf. 2:17–3:10, esp. 2:17f.; 3:6, 10); (2) his hope that their Christian love would increase and abound as his love for them abounds (v. 12; cf. 2:1-12, where Paul gives his own behavior as a model for his converts, and 3:6); and (3) his concern that they should persevere until the parousia or coming of Christ (v. 13; cf. 3:1-5). The implicit parenetic character of the last two petitions serves as a transition to the main parenetic section of the letter by introducing the themes of that section: holiness or Christian ethical behavior (4:1-12; 5:13-22) and the parousia (4:13–5:11).

But quite apart from the functional role it plays in the letter, the wish-prayer in vv. 11-13 offers us a further window into Paul's personal prayer life, in which intercessory prayer played a vital role (see also 5:23f.; 2 Thes. 2:1f.; 3:5, 16; Rom. 15:5f., 13, 33; 1 Cor. 1:8f.; Phil. 4:19).

3:11   The first request of Paul's wish-prayer concerns his desire to return to the Thessalonians. In v. 11 both God the father and the Lord Jesus are invoked: αὐτὸς δὲ θεὸς καὶ πατὴρ ἡμῶν καὶ ὁ κύριος ἡμῶν Ἰησοῦς ("Now, [may] our God and father himself and our Lord Jesus"). This, along with 2 Thes. 2:16-17, is the earliest documented evidence of the profound change in prayer language that took place in Christianity as the early Christian community moved away from traditional Jewish prayers, where God alone was addressed or invoked, to the address and invocation of both God and Jesus Christ. Now both God and Jesus Christ are addressed or invoked. Sir. 23:4 is especially illuminating. It is one of the earliest extant examples of Jewish petitionary prayer addressed to God as father, but the full form of address is "O Lord, father and God of my life" (cf. Sir. 23:1). Within this formula appears the terminology—"Lord" and "father"—used by Paul to distinguish between God and Jesus. This suggests that the early Christian prayer address in texts like 1 Thes. 3:11 was based on assigning traditional Jewish appellations directed exclusively toward God to both God and Jesus.

The choice of πατήρ ("father") to go with θεός ("God") reflects the preeminence of God within Christian thought, while the pronoun ἡμῶν ("our"), occurring with it, implies a relationship between God and the Christian that may be described metaphorically as a parent-child relationship. This in turn means that Christians have a relationship with one another as metaphorical brothers and sisters, with the love and commitment this entails. Thus "God our father" actually prepares for the exhortation regarding love in chap. 4 and for the second petition of the wish-prayer. (See Petersen, *Rediscovering Paul*, 206-217 for an important discussion of the parent-child kinship system in Paul's letters as it applies to the parent-children metaphor.) The invocation formula αὐτὸς ὁ θεός ("God himself"), found here and in 5:23, was probably "taken over from conventional liturgical language to which the apostle and his readers were accustomed through both their Jewish and their Hellenistic background" (Wiles, *Intercessory Prayer Passages,* 30). The intention was to give a liturgical fullness to the invocation and to emphasize the majesty of the one addressed.

Use of κύριος ("Lord") with Jesus ascribes sovereignty to him whom the early Christians believed to be God's son and agent in salvation (cf. the traditional piece in 1 Cor. 8:6). The qualifying ἡμῶν implies a metaphorical master-servant relation between Jesus and the believer (cf. Rom. 6:16-19, 22; 1 Cor. 7:22; Gal. 1:10). Interestingly, in 2 Thes. 2:16 Paul places the appellation αὐτὸς ὁ κύριος ἡμῶν Ἰησοῦς Χριστός ("Our Lord Jesus Christ himself") before the appellation "God our father." This suggests that the order was not fixed and that Christ was placed on the same honorific plane as God.

Paul employs the optative mood (κατευθύναι) in his prayer to indicate his wish, as was common in the period (cf. 3:12; 5:23; 2 Thes. 2:17; 3:5, 16; Rom. 15:5, 13). Some have argued that the singular form of the verb with the twin subjects God and Christ has important theological significance, demonstrating that Paul held to the oneness of God and the Lord Jesus (Neil, 71) or the full deity of Jesus (Morris, 111). Hewett ("1 Thessalonians 3.13," 54), following A. T. Robertson, has shown that compound subjects occur regularly with singular verbs in the NT (see, e.g., Jas. 5:3; Mt. 5:18; Mk. 4:41) without this sort of implication. He quite correctly maintains that the articles occurring with each of the subjects (ὁ θεός . . . ὁ κύριος) indicate that God and the Lord Jesus were viewed as two separate personalities by Paul. The singular verb, however, reveals that Paul understood them as having a close relation. Thus although 1 Thes. 3:11 does not constitute evidence for a trinitarian theology in Paul, the basis for it was already being laid in the earliest Church through the identification of Jesus as the son of God who ruled in the place of God (see 1 Cor. 15:23-28; Phil. 2:6-11) and of the Spirit as the agent of God and Christ (Rom. 8:9-11).

κατευθύναι with the words τὴν ὁδὸν ἡμῶν πρὸς ὑμᾶς refers to Paul's desire for God either to direct his way to the Thessalonians in the sense of leading him to return to them or to smooth his way in the sense of overcoming whatever obstacles might prevent him from returning (cf. 2:18). This prayer petition thus serves to reiterate Paul's deep desire to revisit the Thessalonians in order to further strengthen their faith, and thereby it draws to a conclusion the main theme of Paul's apostolic parousia in the second part of the *narratio* (2:17–3:10). This desire was only fulfilled much later when Paul returned to Corinth from Ephesus via Macedonia (cf. 1 Cor. 16:5; 2 Cor. 2:13; Acts 19:21; 20:1f.).

3:12 Paul's second petition is directed specifically to "the Lord," whom we must understand as "the Lord Jesus" from the previous verse. Paul expresses his wish-prayer for his converts with the words ὑμᾶς δὲ ὁ κύριος πλεονάσαι καὶ περισσεύσαι τῇ ἀγάπῃ εἰς ἀλλήλους καὶ εἰς πάντας ("and may the Lord cause you to increase and abound in love for one another and for everyone"). The two optative verbs πλεονάσαι and περισσεύσαι are synonyms and lend an emphatic tone to Paul's desire that the love of the Thessalonians should be richly increased. While the apostle can pray for this to happen, he also enjoins his readers to strive for greater love in 4:9f. This reveals an awareness on his part that Christians are responsible for their own behavior in cooperation with God who works through his Spirit in their lives.

The love that Paul desires his readers to have is to be εἰς ἀλλήλους καὶ εἰς πάντας ("for one another and for everyone"). There can be no question but that Paul was concerned with inculcating the need for love among his converts at Thessalonica, as everywhere else. A profoundly important social reason existed for him to do so. Paul had converted individuals and household units to the faith, but if 1 Corinthians is anything to go by, his converts came from varying social and economic strata within the community and therefore did not necessarily have a great deal in common, if anything at all (see Theissen,

Social Setting, 69-119 for a study of the social stratification at Corinth and Meeks, *First Urban Christians,* 51-73 for a somewhat more general study). This meant that Paul and his fellow missionaries had to create a sense of shared identity and community where none had previously existed. Theissen (107f.) argues with considerable cogency that this was done through what he calls "love-patriarchalism." The socially superior were required to exercise "love and respect" while the socially inferior were to practice "subordination, fidelity, and esteem." That this was true in Thessalonica can be seen from 1 Thes. 5:12-15. In this context, mutual love, which was to be demonstrated by people's behavior toward one another, functioned to pull together individuals and households from differing socio-economic backgrounds into a new community and then to keep them together.

With the additional words καὶ εἰς πάντας ("and for everyone") Paul prays for the love of the Thessalonians to extend to those outside the community of faith. While this is not a common theme in Paul, it expresses the same thing as Gal. 6:10, which reads "Let us do good to everyone, but especially to those who are of the household of faith." Just as the basis for Christians' loving one another was essentially practical, so also was the reason for their loving those outside the community (cf. Rom. 12:17). By demonstrating love as a way of life, Paul hoped that the Thessalonians would avoid giving offense to outsiders (cf. 4:12) and draw them into the community of faith.

The parenetic quality of the prayer becomes obvious in the words καθάπερ καὶ ἡμεῖς εἰς ὑμᾶς ("just as we for you"). The clause is elliptical but the context requires that it be understood as "just as we *abound in love* for you." Paul thus cites his own unselfish love toward the Thessalonians as a clear example of what he means by loving one another and those outside the community (cf. Wiles, *Intercessory Prayer Passages,* 59). He had shared himself with the Thessalonians, who themselves had originally been outsiders, because they had become dear to him (2:8). This had led him to labor night and day in order to avoid placing any burden on them while he was preaching the gospel to them (2:9). Only his love for them could account for such self-sacrifice. Thus Paul says in 2:10f. that he treated them like a father treats his own children (cf. 2:7). Similarly his present concern for them in their suffering and his attempts to revisit them, as well as his sending Timothy to them, were manifestations of his love for them. By alluding to his love for them as an example, he interrupts the wish-prayer and implicitly exhorts them to love and act toward one another as he loved and acted toward them. In this way v. 12 points forward to 4:1-12 and 5:12-22, where Paul lays out some of the implications of loving one another.

3:13 This verse does not offer a formal petition. The phrase εἰς τὸ στηρίξαι ὑμῶν τὰς καρδίας ἀμέμπτους ("to establish your hearts as blameless") is an infinitival purpose clause dependent upon the main clause of v. 12 instead of a prayer-wish with an optative verb as in the previous two wishes.

Nevertheless, the thought of v. 13 constitutes an additional wish on the part of Paul for his readers. He desires that his converts be blameless when they stand in the presence of God at the judgment. Paul's hope that his readers would love one another as well as those outside their community has as its intention that their hearts should be established as blameless ἐν ἁγιωσύνῃ ("in holiness"). The verb στηρίξαι suggests that the Thessalonians will feel secure on the day of judgment if they love as Paul wants them to (cf. Findlay, 76f.).

The connection between vv. 11 and 12 implies that the apostle elevated love to the level of the highest norm in Christian behavior in very much the same sense that Jesus did for his followers in the great diad on love, in which the whole of the law was expressed in terms of the commands to love God and one's neighbor (Mt. 22:29-34). In Rom. 13:8 Paul instructs the Christians at Rome, "Owe no one anything except to love one another; for the one who loves the other has fulfilled the law." Similarly he writes to the Galatians, "For the whole law has been fulfilled in the one command, 'Love your neighbor as yourself'" (Gal. 5:14). (Both Rom. 13:8 and Gal. 5:14 probably allude to the Jesus tradition. See Käsemann, *Romans*, 361.)

These texts explain why the apostle can link his wish that his readers "increase and abound in love for one another" to the establishment of their hearts as "blameless in holiness before God." To love one's fellow Christians in particular, in the sense of behaving in a loving manner (see 1 Corinthians 13 for the type of behavior envisaged), fulfilled the ultimate ethical norm against which Christians were to be judged. Therefore to love as Paul desired his converts to love would result in their living sanctified lives, placing them beyond any opprobrium at the judgment.

καρδία ("heart") here, as in 2:4, refers to the thinking, willing, and feeling dimension of human existence, in modern terms the human personality. ἀμέμπτους in the context connotes a condition of blamelessness in which the individual is found to have done nothing deserving condemnation by God, who tests and tries the hearts of people (cf. 2:4). Although ἁγιωσύνη ("holiness") is almost synonymous with ἀμέμπτους in this verse (cf. 2 Cor. 7:1), its different semantic field adds an important connotation. Holiness is one of the primary characteristics of God in the biblical tradition (cf. Pss. 71:22; 89:18; Is. 1:4; Je. 50:9; Ezk. 39:7; 1 Pet. 1:15f.; Jn. 17:11; Rev. 4:8; see K. G. Kuhn and O. Procksch, *TDNT* I, 89-101). Therefore, if the Thessalonians are to be established "without blame in holiness," this implies their moral conformity to the very character of God. That this was of fundamental importance for Paul can be seen in 4:3, where sanctification or holiness (ἁγιασμός) is said to be the will of God for the Thessalonians.

This verse, as well as 1:9f. and 5:2-10, reveals Paul's imminent expectation of the parousia or coming of Christ at the time when the letter was written by stressing the need for readiness on the part of the recipients. The formulaic expression ἔμπροσθεν τοῦ θεοῦ καὶ πατρὸς ἡμῶν ἐν τῇ παρουσίᾳ τοῦ κυρίου ἡμῶν Ἰησοῦ ("before our God and father at the coming of our Lord Jesus") repeats, on the one hand, the invocation of v. 11 and, on the other, clearly refers to the coming judgment by God at Christ's parousia. The theme of eschatological judgment seen here had an important social function in the writings of Paul. It reinforced the community-oriented social behavior required by Paul from the Thessalonians. The significance of this becomes clear when we recall that Paul's converts came from different social groups and included individuals who had no previous social contact, let alone commitment to one another (see comments on v. 12). In order to maintain the disparate individuals and the pre-existing social groups represented in the Christian community as one body Paul inculcated a common identity based on shared ethical values and a common social behavior (for another example of this in Paul's letters see Rom. 14:1-12).

The phrase μετὰ πάντων τῶν ἁγίων αὐτοῦ ("with all his holy ones") has been interpreted in various ways. Findlay (77) thinks that it refers to the saints or holy ones who are Christ's human followers. This understanding conforms to the normal meaning of ἅγιος in Paul's letters (cf. Rom. 1:7; 8:27; 1 Cor. 1:2; 14:33; 2 Cor. 1:1; 8:4; Phil. 1:1, etc.). Frame (136, 139), Best (152f.), and Marshall (102f.), among others, claim that it refers to the angels of God, who were called the "holy ones" in the OT and the apocalyptic tradition of Judaism (Job 5:1; 15:15; Ps. 89:7-8; Dn. 4:34; 7:18; 8:13; and esp. Zc. 14:5, which may be the source of Paul's thought; *1 Enoch* 1:9; Tob. 11:14; 12:15). Some, like Rigaux (492) and Morris (115), argue that both groups are included. Paul specifically states that the angels will come with Christ in 2 Thes. 1:7 (cf. 1 Thes. 4:16). The Christian saints, however, will not come with Christ at his parousia. Rather they will rise to meet him in the air according to 1 Thes. 4:15-18. In light of this it seems likely that the ἅγιοι of 3:13 are the angels, though this cannot be maintained dogmatically, as apocalyptic language is intended to be evocative rather than purely descriptive or literal.

The ἀμήν in square brackets in the *UBSGNT* at the end of v. 13 is textually uncertain. The evidence for and against its inclusion is fairly evenly balanced. Its inclusion by later copyists could easily have come about because of the wish-prayer and the liturgical character of the language in vv. 11-13. On the other hand its exclusion can be explained on the grounds that copyists considered "amen" in the text of an epistle inappropriate (Metzger, *Textual Commentary*, 631). In either case the meaning of the passage is not affected.

V. 13 directs the readers' attention to the themes of parenesis (v. 13a) and the coming of the Lord Jesus at the end of the age (v. 13b). These form the dominant concerns of 4:1-5:22. In this way the verse provides the transition to the *probatio* portion of the letter.

PROBATIO: 4:1–5:22

The *probatio* is the second main division of the letter. The first main division, 2:1–3:10, as I have shown, is a *narratio* with the philophronetic intention of reestablishing Paul's relationship with his converts. His friendship with his readers then becomes the basis for his exhortation in 4:1–5:22. Nevertheless, the first main section has a considerable amount of implicit parenesis, as has been noted.

The *probatio* section, 4:1–5:22, is a set of proofs demonstrating the contention in 4:1f. that as the Thessalonians know how to behave and to please God so they must continue to live as they have been instructed by Paul, but with renewed fervor. This gives the section its parenetic or exhortative quality (cf. Bjerkelund, *Parakalô,* 128-135; Boers, "Form-Critical Study," 154-158; Malherbe, "Exhortation in First Thessalonians"). That Paul does not call for changes in behavior but affirms his readers' current practices indicates that the parenesis is rhetorically epideictic or demonstrative, not deliberative in character (see the section on rhetoric in the Introduction, pp. 46-48 above). Not only does Paul wish to give advice to his converts about their behavior, he also seeks to comfort them regarding one of the fundamental beliefs of their Christian symbolic world, namely, belief in the coming of the Lord Jesus Christ from heaven (4:13-18). The claim by Koester ("I Thessalonians," 38-40) that the material in 4:1–5:11 is of a general character and therefore does not reflect any of the specifics of the situation at Thessalonica seems unlikely (cf. Boers, "Form-Critical Study," 154; Malherbe, *Moral Exhortation,* 76f.).

The *probatio* divides into four main subsections that together constitute Paul's proof. 4:1-12 contains exhortative material directed toward the ethical conduct of the Thessalonians. A clear division occurs between vv. 8 and 9, so that Jewett (*Thessalonian Correspondence,* 75) may be correct in seeing two separate proofs in this section. 4:13-18 constitutes a proof that the dead in Christ will share in his parousia and the assumption of believers to heaven. This functions as an exhortation to maintain Christain hope even in the face of death. 5:1-11 comprises a proof regarding the need for readiness for the parousia of the Lord. This subsection has a decidedly parenetic intention. The final section, 5:12-22, which precedes the conclusion of the letter, has a rather general character and is a proof directed toward the proper functioning of the Christian community at Thessalonica.

The transition to the *probatio* with its parenesis is signaled by the words λοιπὸν οὖν in 4:1. λοιπόν can best be translated "finally," indicating the transition to the last main section of the letter (cf. 2 Cor. 13:11; Phil. 3:1; 4:8). (Boers, "Form-Critical Study," 156 maintains that 4:1–5:11 constitutes the main body of the letter. This, however, represents a failure to fully appreciate the importance of the *narratio* section of the letter as implicit parenesis through philophronesis.) The inferential conjunction οὖν probably embraces the whole of 2:1–3:13 rather than merely the *transitus,* since what Paul says in this part of the letter is what he would have liked to tell the Thessalonians if he could have been present with them.

ETHICAL EXHORTATION: 4:1-12

This subsection contains three distinct units: 4:1-2, 4:3-8, and 4:9-12. The first contains general parenesis articulating the proposition to be demonstrated in the *probatio,* namely, that the readers know how to conduct themeselves in order to please God. The second and third subsections address issues arising in the community. The social function of this material is twofold: it helps to define the boundaries of the community (that is, what it means to be a Christian) over against the dominant pagan society, while at the same time it helps to develop what Meeks (*First Urban Christians,* 100) describes as "internal cohesion" within the community.

Exhortation to Continue in Current Behavior: 4:1-2

4:1 Paul's direct address of his readers through the term ἀδελφοί ("brothers [and sisters]"), along with the expression λοιπὸν οὖν ("finally therefore"), marks what follows as a new section (cf. 2:1; 5:1, 13). Paul's use of ἀδελφοί here is important from a theological and sociological point of view. It reflects the new metaphorical relationship entered into by Christians with one another. Although use of ἀδελφοί was not unknown in clubs and pagan cults, Paul undoubtedly borrowed it from his Jewish background. It was used both in the OT (e.g., Ex. 2:11; Dt. 3:18) and in intertestamental writings like 2 Macc. 1:1, where it occurs in the address of a letter. Quite apart from the background of the term, however, it was an important linguistic tool, an organizing metaphor (see Petersen, *Rediscovering Paul,* 206) that portrays the community as a family. It served to link together people who often had no previous contact with one another (see Meeks, *First Urban Christians,* 87-89). The use of familial language was probably justified by the symbolic understanding of God as the father of the members of the community (see the comments on 3:11, above). As the metaphorical children of the one father Christians were themselves brothers and sisters who were to behave toward one another as family members.

147

Such metaphorical language clearly aided in creating community cohesion among people who had no prior social involvement or commitment to one another (cf. Meeks, *Moral World,* 129 and the comments on 3:12, above).

Paul exhorts his brothers and sisters to continue living according to the behavioral patterns that they had received from him. ἐρωτῶμεν ("we implore") and παρακαλοῦμεν ("we exhort") are virtually synonymous here and together emphasize that Paul required his converts to behave in a manner appropriate for followers of Christ. Bjerkelund (*Parakalô,* 109f.) has shown that Paul is following a common Hellenistic Greek formula used in both private letters and official correspondence for requesting or commanding that some action take place. The formula consisted of παρακαλεῖν ("exhort") or one of its synonyms in the first person (here ἐρωτῶμεν καὶ παρακαλοῦμεν) with the vocative address (here ἀδελφοί). Normally with more official letters a prepositional phrase was also included (here ἐν κυρίῳ Ἰησοῦ ["in the Lord Jesus"]). The request or command was usually then expressed by an infinitive or a ἵνα clause (here ἵνα περισσεύητε μᾶλλον ["that you abound the more"]). Bjerkelund has demonstrated that this pattern recurs in Paul's letters at a number of points (e.g., Rom. 12:1f.; 15:30-32; 16:17; 1 Cor. 1:10; 4:16; 16:15f.; 2 Cor. 10:1f.; 1 Thes. 4:10b-12; 5:14) and conforms most closely to the pattern used by a ruler to his subjects.

Here the formula and the sentence as a whole are disrupted by the two καθώς clauses following immediately after the first ἵνα. The formula is only completed when ἵνα is repeated (technically it was unnecessary to repeat it) with a clause stating Paul's actual request that his readers progress more and more (περισσεύητε μᾶλλον). The Thessalonians were to abound in the type of behavior taught by Paul and practiced in his absence according to the two καθώς clauses.

The prepositional phrase ἐν κυρίῳ Ἰησοῦ ("in the Lord Jesus") serves to emphasize Paul's position as an authoritative representative of Jesus (contra Best, 156) and to remind the Thessalonians that their lives as Christians were under Jesus' control. Therefore they were responsible to him for their conduct and in particular for carrying out the instructions given by Paul, a point that the next verse makes explicit.

The words καθὼς παρελάβετε παρ' ἡμῶν τὸ πῶς δεῖ ὑμᾶς περιπατεῖν καὶ ἀρέσκειν θεῷ ("just as you received from us how it is necessary for you to behave and to please God") refer to the ethical norms and patterns inculcated by Paul (the verb παραλαμβάνω is often a technical term for the reception of authoritative tradition) among the Thessalonians at the time of their conversion to Christ. These norms and patterns were based on traditional OT and Jewish behavioral codes and practices as well as on some drawn from Hellenistic philosophies (Holmberg, *Paul and Power,* 71). Taken together they constituted the distinctive Christian way of life that Paul required of his converts, as the words "how it is necessary for you to behave and to please

God" indicate. The patterns of conduct Paul enjoined on his converts were intended to separate them from the pagan social world out of which they had come and to facilitate harmony and a common identity among the members of the newly formed community (see Meeks, *First Urban Christians*, 97-103). The second καθώς clause, καθὼς καὶ παριπατεῖτε ("just as also you do behave"), stresses that Paul wished his readers to continue doing what they were already doing in their Christian lives.

This leads to the very general request ἵνα περισσεύητε ("that you progress more and more") at the conclusion of the sentence. Had he not already indirectly exhorted them through the two καθώς clauses ("just as you received from us how it is necessary to behave and to please God, just as you do behave"), the actual exhortation would undoubtedly have been more specific. But as the sentence now stands the request that they "progress more and more" derives its meaning from the καθώς clauses. Paul clearly is pleased with the general moral development of his converts and simply wants them to continue in their current ways with renewed commitment and effort. This is a standard theme in parenetic letters where authors assume their readers are living and acting as they should and wish to encourage them to continue putting into practice what they know (Stowers, *Letter Writing*, 103).

4:2 In this verse Paul points out to his readers that what he is about to say merely reiterates what he had previously taught them concerning the way they should conduct themselves as Christians. The sentence is linked with the preceding statement by an explanatory γάρ. Here, as on a number of occasions in the letter, Paul calls on the knowledge of his readers with οἴδατε ("you know") to confirm what he is saying (cf. 1:5; 2:1, 5, 11; 3:3f.; 5:2).

He wants his readers to remember τίνας παραγγελίας ἐδώκαμεν ὑμῖν ("what commands/instructions we gave to you") because these were the organizing principles for their Christian lives. The noun παραγγελία occurs only in this verse in the undisputed Pauline letters, but the verb παραγγέλλειν appears several times (1 Cor. 7:10; 11:17; 1 Thes. 4:11; 2 Thes. 3:4, 6, 12). The passages in which Paul uses either the verb or the noun "have the character of authoritative apostolic ordinances, behind which stands the full authorisation of Christ Himself" (O. Schmitz, *TDNT* V, 764). This is particularly clear here, as the phrase διὰ τοῦ κυρίου Ἰησοῦ ("through the Lord Jesus") reveals. Although the prepositional phrase has been interpreted in various ways (see Best, 157f. and Marshall, 105f.), διά with the genitive of the person frequently indicates the originator of an action. Here it probably goes with the verbal idea implicit in the noun παραγγελία, referring thereby to the authoritative instructions that Paul had given to the Thessalonians. Thus the thought, but not the grammar, is very similar to 1 Cor. 7:10, where Paul writes, "To those who are married I command (παραγγέλλω), not I but the Lord. . . ." Paul may have given the instructions or commands, but they were from Christ and therefore carried the authority of Christ as Lord (cf. Frame, 144).

The Reinforcement of Sexual Norms: 4:3-8

In all probability Timothy had brought word to Paul that a problem existed in Thessalonica regarding the stringent sexual code that the missionaries had taught their converts as part of the necessary life-style for those who would please God. This and the problems associated with the parousia treated later in the letter may have been the specific reasons why almost immediately after Timothy's return from Thessalonica the apostle wrote the letter. In this paragraph Paul reinforces the sexual morality that he had originally given his readers by introducing strong sanctions against deviation and by linking the morality he had taught them to their very identity as Christians.

4:3 Paul begins and concludes this paragraph on sexual morality with a reference to the divine sanction for the behavior pattern that he had given to his readers. While the sense of the words τοῦτο γὰρ ἐστιν θέλημα τοῦ θεοῦ, ὁ ἁγιασμὸς ὑμῶν ("this is the will of God—your sanctification") is relatively clear, the best way to construe them is not so apparent. Should τοῦτο ("this") or θέλημα ("will") be viewed as the subject of the copulative verb? Why is θέλημα anarthrous? How is ὁ ἁγιασμὸς ὑμῶν related to the previous words?

The sentence as it stands is explanatory of the previous sentence (v. 2), as the γάρ shows. That τοῦτο should be taken as the subject of the sentence and θέλημα θεοῦ as the predicate is suggested by 5:18, where the sentence (with ἐστιν understood) occurs again and where τοῦτο must be the subject and θέλημα θεοῦ the predicate. That θέλημα is anarthrous in both 4:3 and 5:18 suggests that the article was omitted because "the will of God" was a well-known formula for Paul and his readers (see BDF §252; Bruce, 81f.). Paul defines "the will of God" for the Thessalonians by the additional words ὁ ἁγιασμὸς ὑμῶν, which stand in apposition to τοῦτο (Frame, 146).

While Paul is said to be the apostle of the "law-free gospel," this can only accurately refer to his rejection of the Jewish law and in particular the cultic and ritual law as a means of salvation (see E. P. Sanders, *Paul and Palestinian Judaism*, 474-511). Paul maintained the ethical law of Judaism as normative for Christians because, as far as he was concerned, it remained the will of God. The reason for this is contained in the expression "your sanctification." Paul understood God to be the holy God of the OT who was set apart from every form of sin and impurity and who demanded similar holiness from the people of Israel through separation (Lv. 11:44f.; 19:2; 21:8). God had not changed, so the same requirement was laid on the new people of God, the Christians.

ἁγιασμός may denote either the process whereby the Thessalonians would become sanctified or consecrated to God through their separation from immorality (cf. v. 7) or the outcome of that process. Given that Paul is spelling out one aspect of the process of sanctification in his discussion of Christian sexual morality, the former sense may be more appropriate. Whichever is the correct understanding, separation from sinful existence, that is sanctification, was a fundamental part of Paul's understanding of Christian existence (cf. Rom. 6:19, 22). According to Rom. 6:22 the goal of sanctification is nothing less than eternal life. This explains why Paul can say it is the will of God for the Thessalonians.

The infinitival subordinate clause ἀπέχεσθαι ὑμᾶς ἀπὸ τῆς πορνείας ("that you abstain from sexual immorality") is implicitly imperatival because it represents a requirement made by God. Jewish literature from the period reveals an abhorrence of πορνεία (cf. *Jub.* 20:3-6; 39:6; Sir. 23:16-27; Philo, *Spec. Leg.* 3.51) understood as any type of unlawful sexual activity from prostitution to adultery or fornication (see Jensen, *"Porneia,"* 161-184). The reason for this abhorrence was twofold. First, for the Jew, participation in any form of sexual immorality was tantamount to forsaking the holy God, who demanded separation from all forms of sexual immorality and impurity (cf. Ex. 20:14; Lv. 20:10-23, 26; *Jub.* 20:3-6; 39:6). Closely associated with this was the persistent belief that non-Jews were guilty of sexual immorality and that this was the direct result of their idolatry (cf. Wis. 14:12-31; Philo, *Leg. All.* 3.8; see also *Jub.* 25:1; Rom. 1:24-27). Both of these factors may well lie behind Paul's call to the Thessalonians. In fairness to the ethical norms of the wider Greco-Roman society it should be said, however, that the standard demanded by Paul was also the accepted standard for decency among morally sensitive pagans (see Musonius Rufus, *Fragment* 12; cf. Meeks, *Moral World,* 128f.; Malherbe, "Exhortation in First Thessalonians," 250). The infinitive ἀπέχεσθαι in the middle voice means "to keep away" or "abstain." Thus Paul plays on the noun ἁγιασμός that precedes, since sanctification or consecration is a form of separation.

What Paul now reiterates in the letter is the call, which accompanied his original preaching to the Thessalonians, to "keep away from sexual immorality." Not only is such separation the "will of God," but it constitutes a fundamental change from the readers' pagan past, where sexual morality had perhaps played little or no role (cf. Malherbe, *Paul and the Thessalonians,* 51). Paul has made traditional Jewish sexual behavior a part of the boundary between his converts and the pagan world they formerly inhabited. Here he seeks to reinforce this morality (cf. 1 Cor. 6:12-20), which is not only important as a group boundary, but is also crucial for maintaining harmony and cohesion within the community, as the following verses demonstrate.

4:4 Vv. 4f. form the second infinitive construction dependent on the main clause in v. 3. V. 4 poses difficult problems for interpreters because the meaning of the key words σκεῦος (literally "vessel" or "implement") and κτᾶσθαι (literally "gain" or "acquire") is uncertain. The context, vv. 3b and 5, makes it clear that the verse is directed to the sexual mores of the community at Thessalonica, but what they are being instructed to do in order to avoid πορνεία is less clear. What is it that they are to know how "to acquire in holiness and honor"?

The meaning of σκεῦος has been in question since the patristic period. Some like Theodore of Mopsuestia and Augustine understood it to mean "wife" with the resultant translation, "that each one of you know how to take a wife for yourself in holiness and honor" (cf. *RSV*). Others like Tertullian and John Chrysostom believed that it denoted "body," which led them to interpret the clause as "that each one of you know how to keep your own body in holiness and honor" (cf. *NEB*; *NIV*). (For patristic references see C. Maurer, *TDNT* VII, 365 nn. 48f.)

That σκεῦος means "wife" has been argued in the twentieth century by such scholars as Frame (149f.), Maurer (*op. cit.,* 365-367), Best (161-164), Friedrich (237f.), and Holtz (157f.). This view rests on the figurative use in Rabbinic writings of Hebrew *keˡlî,* which corresponds to Greek σκεῦος, of women and, as Maurer (361f.) has shown, euphemistically of sexual intercourse with a woman with verbs like "use" and "make." Maurer also maintains that Paul probably translated the technical Hebrew expression from the OT *bāˁ al ˀišâ,* meaning "possess a woman sexually," by the Greek phrase κτᾶσθαι γυναῖκα and then simply substituted σκεῦος for γυνή. This implies that the wife is merely a sexual object who is possessed by her husband.

Quite apart from the low view of women that it predicates of Paul, this interpretation presents several problems. The Thessalonians did not know Hebrew and therefore Paul could not rely on them to make the kind of connections made by Maurer and others in arriving at this interpretation. Moreover, it leaves unexplained why Paul used an ambiguous and even obscure expression when he could have made his point with the normal Greek word for woman/wife, γυνή. Maurer's appeal to 1 Pet. 3:7, where ὡς ἀσθενεστέρῳ σκεύει τῷ γυναικείῳ ("the woman as the weaker vessel") occurs, actually works against his understanding, as σκεῦος there refers to the woman's body. It also implies that men are also "vessels," so that σκεῦος is not synonymous with "wife" in 1 Pet. 3:7 at all. A final point against the interpretation of σκεῦος as "wife" is that this understanding does not suit the context in 1 Thes. 4:3b and 5, where illicit and undesirable sexual behavior is proscribed. A command to keep or possess a wife in holiness and honor (Maurer, *op. cit.,* 366 and Best, 162 argue that κτᾶσθαι has a durative force here rather than its normal sense of "to acquire" or "to gain") would seem to have little to do with concern about illicit sex (v. 3b) or uncontrolled sexual desire (v. 5).

Given the problems attached to understanding v. 4 as referring to the proper attitude of husbands toward their wives, it seems better to understand σκεῦος as connoting the human body in its sexual aspect, that is, as a euphemism for the genitalia. This view has been maintained by such contemporary scholars as Rigaux (504-506), Morris (123f.), Marxsen (60f.), Bruce (83), and Marshall (108f.) and is the most natural interpretation of σκεῦος. σκεῦος meant not only "vessel" but also "tool" or "implement" and is used of

152

the human body in 2 Cor. 4:7 and 1 Pet. 3:7. It was also a recognized euphemism for the genital organs in Greek (see LSJ, 1607). It is perhaps worth noting that the Hebrew root *k^elî* is used of the male sexual organ in 1 Sa. 21:5f., where the Septuagint (1 Kgdms. 21:5f.) translates it with σκεῦος, although this distorts the meaning of the original Hebrew, perhaps intentionally.

κτᾶσθαι probably has the sense "to gain control or mastery" here, and even though the pronouns are masculine the instruction to gain mastery over the desires associated with the genital organs would apply equally to women. Thus Paul exhorts the members of the Thessalonian Christian community to avoid sexual immorality of any sort (v. 3b) and to exercise control over their own sexual drives ἐν ἁγιασμῷ καὶ τιμῇ ("in holiness and honor").

ἁγιασμός is repeated from v. 3 and applied here explicitly to Christian sexual practices. V. 4 thus stresses that human sexuality among the followers of Christ must be characterized by holiness (here the emphasis of ἁγιασμός appears to be on the outcome of the process of sanctification) if the Thessalonians are to attain to divine sanctification. τιμή suggests that their conduct must be honorable toward others. The sexual promiscuity of an individual always has consequences for the self and for others because it dishonors both participants, and therefore Paul requires that sexual control be exercised out of respect for oneself and other people. For the Christian there is another aspect to honor in sexual conduct. Paul says that the body is both a member of Christ and a temple for the Holy Spirit of God (1 Cor. 6:15, 19). Thus to use the body dishonorably and to cause another Christian to do so is to dishonor both God and Christ. That a thought similar to 1 Cor. 6:12-20 is present here in 1 Thessalonians is suggested by 4:7-8, where Paul warns his readers that God did not call them to impurity but in holiness and that to reject this is to reject God who gives his Holy Spirit to them.

4:5 The thought of v. 4 is continued in this verse by a negative observation concerning the Gentiles or, as they must be understood in this text, non-Christian and non-Jewish people: μὴ ἐν πάθει ἐπιθυμίας καθάπερ καὶ τὰ ἔθνη τὰ εἰδότα τὸν θεόν ("not in the passion of desire like pagans who do not know God"). Both πάθος ("passion") and ἐπιθυμία ("desire") can have pejorative connotations. For example, in Gal. 5:24 Paul speaks of those who belong to Christ as having crucified the flesh with its passions (τοῖς παθήμασιν) and desires (ταῖς ἐπιθυμίαις; cf. Col. 3:5). Although this may refer to something broader than sexual passions and desires, it undoubtedly includes them. In 1 Thes. 4:5 the context demands an allusion to unwholesome sexual passion driven by a desire for what is forbidden.

Such behavior was from the Jewish standpoint typical of pagan existence and connected with Gentile idolatry (see comments on 4:3). Paul takes up this stereotypical representation from Jewish literature with "like pagans who do not know God," attributing the sexual immorality of the pagans to their ignorance of God (cf. Rom. 1:24-27). He does this to provide a clearly

153

negative contrast to the proper Christian sexual conduct set forth in v. 4. At the same time it emphasizes the separation of Christians from their pagan neighbors.

This verse is of interest for another reason unrelated to its principal thought. From the Jewish point of view humanity was divided into two groups: Jews and Gentiles (τὰ ἔθνη). Here Paul differentiates between his converts at Thessalonica and the pagan Gentiles. While he could refer to Gentiles as offspring of Abraham by virtue of their faith (cf. Gal. 3:6-9, 28f.), he nowhere speaks of them as "Jews," since this was an ethnic distinction. By the time of Ignatius of Antioch early in the second century Christians were speaking of three races instead of two: Jews, Gentiles, and Christians. Already this distinction is implied here with Paul's distinction between his converts at Thessalonica and the Gentiles. The majority of the Christians at Thessalonica had come from the ranks of the Gentiles, but their conversion gave them a new identity. They had not, however, become Jews, and therefore they represented a distinctively new grouping of humanity from Paul's perspective (cf. Gal. 3:28; Col. 3:11).

4:6 Some commentators have argued that this verse introduces a new topic, that of business dealings among the members of the community, rather than continuing the discussion of sexual morality (cf. Beauvery, "Πλεονεκτεῖν," 78-85; Holtz, 161f.). They base their view on the use of the article with the infinitive in τὸ μὴ ὑπερβαίνειν ("let no one transgress"), which, so it is said, indicates a new subject. It is also argued that the infinitives ὑπερβαίνειν and πλεονεκτεῖν ("take advantage") make better sense if business ethics rather than sexual ethics are under discussion, and Holtz (162) maintains that sexual immorality is often associated with avarice in Jewish writings. Furthermore, according to this view, it is not clear how a brother or sister could be taken advantage of or defrauded if v. 4 refers to sexual relations within marriage.

Several factors militate against this interpretation. In the first place the τὸ μή construction is uncertain in meaning (Frame, 151f.). That a new subject is being introduced seems unlikely since a transition to business ethics would be abrupt in the context, and v. 7 seems to refer to sexual aberrations, the theme of vv. 3-5. The prepositional phrase ἐν τῷ πράγματι cannot be taken to mean "in business affairs," as Beauvery and Holtz suggest, because the noun has never been shown to have a peculiarly commercial connotation (Frame, 153; C. Maurer, *TDNT* VI, 639) and the singular form of τῷ πράγματι does not suit a general reference. The most natural meaning of ἐν τῷ πράγματι is "in *this* matter," referring back to the theme of sexual immorality introduced in v. 3. If this interpretation is correct it confirms the view that τὸ μή is resumptive in force.

The argument that the infinitives ὑπερβαίνειν and πλεονεκτεῖν best fit a commercial context is also specious. The former denotes an overstepping of something or, figuratively, transgression of some law or command, and therefore lacks any specific commercial connotations. The latter refers to desire to claim more than one's fair share or to taking advantage of someone. While this could have an economic connotation, it need not, since it is equally possible to take advantage of someone or to "desire" what one has no right to in sexual matters. That v. 6a does not make any sense in connection with the marriage relation discussed in v. 4 is based on a faulty interpretation. In all probability v. 4 refers to premarital and extramarital sexual affairs, not to a husband's attitude toward his own wife, as was shown above.

Dibelius (17) has attempted to overcome the weaknesses inherent in understanding v. 6a in terms of business ethics by suggesting that it might refer to a legal proceeding or lawsuit. Baltensweiler ("Erwägungen") has developed Dibelius's idea by relating v. 6 to legal problems surrounding the laws of inheritance in some Greek cities. When there were no direct male heirs, a female heir was forced to marry her next-of-kin to keep the inheritance in the family. Lawsuits often ensued because several relatives might seek to marry a woman in order to take advantage of the situation. This interpretation can then be linked to the problem of sexual immorality for Christians. An existing marriage by a female heir could be annulled, and she could be forced into a marriage relationship proscribed by Jewish marriage regulations, thus forcing her into a technical situation of immorality. This view is ingenious. The text, however, does not offer sufficient evidence that so specific and complex a problem lies behind v. 6. Also, unlike 1 Cor. 6:1, where πρᾶγμα clearly refers to a legal action, as Dibelius points out, there is nothing in the context of 1 Thes. 4:6 to suggest that a lawsuit is involved.

So Paul was very probably concerned that no Christian should overstep the mark or take advantage of his or her fellow Christians in sexual matters. Not that he would have said the matter was unimportant vis-à-vis non-Christians (cf. 1 Cor. 6:12-20), but a different issue was at stake if one Christian wronged another by his or her sexual activity. That a brother, in particular, might be wronged reflects the nature of the largely patriarchal model of family and household structures existing in the period. If a Christian used his familiarity and friendship to gain sexual favors from a member of a Christian brother's family or extended household, then he had overstepped the mark by taking advantage of or defrauding τὸν ἀδελφὸν αὐτοῦ ("his brother") in Christ. This theme is not unique to Paul, as Malherbe ("Exhortation in First Thessalonians," 250) has shown. The Hellenistic moral philosopher Musonius Rufus speaks of "the adulterer who wrongs the husband of the woman he corrupts" (*Fragment* 12 quoted from Malherbe, *Moral Exhortation*, 153).

Undoubtedly Paul's concern was more than just a matter of morality. The sort of action proscribed in v. 6 could threaten the very existence of the community in at least two ways: (1) It could lead to the breakdown of the ethical discipline that served as part of the group boundary separating Chris-

155

tians from paganism, and (2) it could destroy the carefully cultivated sense of kinship among members of the community. This understanding best explains the strong language in the second part of the verse that places a severe sanction against deviation from acceptable Christian behavior in the matter of sexual morality.

διότι in v. 6b is causal and indicates that what follows is the reason that a follower of Christ must not wrong a fellow believer in the matter of sexual conduct, though περὶ πάντων τούτων ("concerning all of these things") shows that the instructions in vv. 3b-5 fall under the sanction as well. The actual sanction that Paul employs is the most powerful one available to him. He threatens his readers with the fact that the Lord is an avenger or punisher (ἔκδικος κύριος) in all the matters just mentioned by him. The language is drawn from the OT (see esp. Ps. 94:1, which Paul may be quoting). But he probably has in mind here an apocalyptic image of the Lord Jesus as the coming avenger or agent of God's wrath who will inflict severe punishment on wrongdoers who violate the demands of the gospel. This understanding fits with the sense of imminent expectation and the apocalyptic imagery found in 1 and 2 Thessalonians (cf. 1:10; 5:1-11; 2 Thes. 1:7-10; cf. Rom. 12:19; Col. 3:23-25).

The warning made here was not a new one. Paul employed the same type of threat when he was at Thessalonica trying to inculcate the new Christian life-style necessitated by conversion. He reminds his readers of this with the words καθὼς καὶ προείπαμεν ὑμῖν καὶ διεμαρτυράμεθα ("as indeed we warned you and solemnly testified to you"). The thought of the two verbs is essentially parallel and is intended to emphasize the seriousness of what Paul is saying. The past tense of the verbs alludes to the period when Paul was still present in Thessalonica. While προειπεῖν might mean "telling about something before it happens" as Marshall (112) maintains, it seems more likely that here, as in Gal. 5:21, Paul refers to the warning that he gave to his readers in sanctioning proper Christian behavior. The verb διαμαρτύρεσθαι can mean "to warn" or "to testify solemnly" and strengthens the seriousness and ominous nature of Paul's threat.

4:7 Having expressed a negative reason that his readers should not indulge in any form of sexual immorality, and in particular that they dare not take advantage of a fellow Christian, Paul now offers positive warrant for ethical conduct among Christians. He reminds the Thessalonians of an important aspect of their call by God to salvation in Jesus Christ with the words οὐ γὰρ ἐκάλεσεν ἡμᾶς ὁ θεὸς ἐπὶ ἀκαθαρσίᾳ ἀλλ᾽ ἐν ἁγιασμῷ ("for God did not call us for uncleanness but in holiness").

ἡμᾶς embraces both the readers and the writer together as the ones called by God (on God as the one who calls see the comments on 2:12). Put negatively, God did not call them ἐπὶ ἀκαθαρσίᾳ ("for uncleanness"). This expression can indicate either the purpose of their call or the grounds or condition of their call by God (see Frame, 155). While it is difficult to decide between these two, the former seems more likely in the context because Paul has shown himself to be concerned with problems related to possible sexual impurity among Christians in vv. 3-6. V. 6, in fact, raises the possibility that a Christian might even use his or her status as one called by God for immoral purposes. Paul states emphatically that they were not called for the purpose of indulging in impure or immoral sexual acts (see 2 Cor. 12:21 for a similar use of ἀκαθαρσία; cf. Gal. 5:19; Rom. 1:24; Col. 3:5). This was precisely what they had been called to separate themselves from at the time of their conversion.

The negative view of their call, expressed in the words "God did not call us to uncleanness," is contrasted with a positive understanding in the words ἀλλ' ἐν ἁγιασμῷ ("in holiness"). The change to the preposition ἐν serves to stress the contrast between the negative understanding of the call and its positive dimension. ἐν can be used in place of εἰς with the verb καλεῖν ("to call"; see 1 Cor. 7:15), but as Turner (*Syntax*, 263) notes, this may well be a pregnant construction of Paul's that should be interpreted similarly to the "in Christ" formula. If this is correct, the meaning is that the Thessalonians were called "into the sphere where God's sanctification takes place." This picks up the theme of 4:3. The emphasis, however, is not on the readers' need to strive for sanctification but rather on the fact that Christian existence is to be lived in the sphere of God's holiness.

4:8 The last clause of this subsection contains an implied threat intended to reinforce the reasons given in the previous two verses for the Thessalonians to conform to the sexual norms laid down in 4:3-6. The unusual particle τοιγαροῦν ("for that very reason") occurs in the NT only here and in Heb. 12:1. It is a strengthened form of τοιγάρ indicating a logical inference from what has preceded: if God has called Christians to live in holiness (ἁγιασμός), it follows that to live in sexual debauchery (ἀκαθαρσία) constitutes a rejection of God's call.

The main clause of v. 8, τοιγαροῦν ὁ ἀθετῶν οὐκ ἄνθρωπον ἀθετεῖ ἀλλ' τὸν θεόν ("for that very reason the one who rejects [these things] does not reject humanity but God") is a negative statement closely related to a tradition found in somewhat different forms several places in the Gospels (see Mk. 9:37 par.; Mt. 10:40; Lk. 10:16; Jn. 12:44; 13:20). Its antecedents occur in the OT, as 1 Sa. 8:7 shows. The closest of the Gospel parallels is Lk. 10:16: ὁ ἀκούων ὑμῶν ἐμοῦ ἀκούει, καὶ ὁ ἀθετῶν ὑμᾶς ἐμὲ ἀθετεῖ ("the one hearing you hears me, the one rejecting you rejects me"). Whether Paul knew this particular form of the tradition and modeled v. 8 on it cannot be determined because he might well have based his saying on the principle that lies behind Lk. 10:16 without knowing Jesus' saying.

The principle involved concerns the Jewish idea of the šālîaḥ, who was the appointed representative of another. According to the rules of conduct associated with šālîaḥs, the representative of a person could act in his place with full legal rights. To receive or to reject such a representative was to receive or reject the sender. (For studies on the *šālîaḥ* principle see K. H. Rengstorf, *TDNT* I, 413-420; Borgen, "God's Agent"; Barrett, "Shaliaḥ"). This is particularly relevant because the idea of apostleship in early Christianity had its roots in the *šālîaḥ* tradition of Jewish thought (Rengstorf, 421).

The participial construction ὁ ἀθετῶν, best translated as "the one who rejects," does not have an expressed object, but from the context it is clear that the implied object is the regulations concerning sexual conduct in vv. 3-6. The anarthrous noun ἄνθρωπος is not indefinite, as Best (169) maintains, but is a paraphrasis for Paul himself as the one who has given the regulations, which are nothing less than the will of God (v. 3). The omission of the article underscores the qualitative aspect of the noun, namely, the "humanness" of the one giving the instructions. The noun is negated by the οὐκ and indicates that the instructions given by Paul were not his own but God's. Therefore to repudiate them was to reject or disregard not Paul but God. Behind this lies the thought that Paul was the *šālîaḥ* or representative of God in his task of explicating the will of God concerning sexual behavior.

God is identified as τὸν θεὸν τὸν [καὶ] διδόντα τὸ πνεῦμα αὐτοῦ τὸ ἅγιον εἰς ὑμᾶς ("the one who gives his Holy Spirit to you"). This participial phrase is closely parallel to Ezk. 36:27 and 37:14, though that need not be intentional since the idea was certainly well-known in Jewish thought and became foundational for the early Christians. The present tense of the participle διδόντα ("giving") probably means no more than that God was the bestower of the Spirit, though some manuscripts have the aorist participle to avoid the idea that God was continuously granting the Spirit to the Thessalonians. The words τὸ πνεῦμα αὐτοῦ τὸ ἅγιον ("his Holy Spirit") underscore that the Spirit is God's Spirit, while the word order emphasizes that the Spirit is characterized by being Holy.

Although it is not clear precisely why Paul includes a reference to the giving of the Spirit here, it serves at least two functions in the context: (1) The phrase heightens the seriousness of the strong sanction for the behavior being inculcated, and (2) it appears to imply that if anyone repudiated the instructions given in the preceding verses their action was tantamount to a rejection of the Spirit who was a gift from God to bring holiness into the lives of believers (cf. Gal. 5:22f. on the Spirit as the source of holiness in the lives of Christians and 1 Cor. 6:15-20 for the mention of the Spirit in a sanction against sexual immorality).

While Paul deals with sexual immorality in other letters, most notably 1 Cor. 6:12-20, nowhere does he employ such coercive language to enforce proper Christian conduct. The serious and even threatening tone of vv. 6-8 suggests very strongly that Paul was dealing with a problem that had actually emerged in the community at Thessalonica and that he viewed with considerable concern. The instructions in vv. 3-6 and, especially, the sanctions of vv. 6 and 8 were undoubtedly intended to compel proper behavior among the readers in all sexual matters. The specific situation envisaged by vv. 5f. lends support to my contention that Paul is not merely concerned with general parenetic instruction in vv. 3-8, but a specific problem in the life of the community. At the same time the passage emphasizes the separation of converts to Christianity from the immorality characteristic of the pagan world abandoned by them. In this way it works both to encourage people in their new Christian identity and to enforce Christian behavioral norms in sexual matters.

Familial Love and the Quiet Life: 4:9-12

The words περὶ δέ ("now concerning") at the beginning of v. 9 indicate a transition from the previous subject to a new one. A number of scholars in the past (e.g., Milligan, 126; Frame, 140, 157; Faw, "Writing," 221) have held that the phrase is a formula that discloses that Paul was responding to a letter from the Thessalonians. They base this view on the use of the expression in such texts as 1 Cor. 7:1, 25; 8:1; 12:1. But unlike 1 Cor. 7:1, where there is a specific reference to issues raised in a letter sent by the Corinthians, Paul mentions nothing about having received a letter from the Thessalonians anywhere in his own letter.

It is possible, however, that he is responding either to an oral question asked through Timothy or to Timothy's report regarding the situation at Thessalonica. If the former is the case it is just possible (contra Bruce, 89) that the Thessalonians had raised a question about the limits of their responsibility to love their Christian brothers and sisters. If so Paul urges them to maintain their current practices and perhaps extend them (v. 10b). On the other hand, Paul may simply be praising their mutual love in order to encourage it even more.

Vv. 11f. are grammatically connected to vv. 9-10a by v. 10b and add the thought that Paul's readers are to live quiet and self-sufficient lives. At first sight this does not appear to have much to do with familial love in the Christian community, but when read in light of 2 Thes. 3:6-15, the connection becomes clear, as I will show.

4:9 Although Paul writes to the Thessalonians περὶ δὲ τῆς φιλαδελφίας οὐ χρείαν ἔχετε γράφειν ὑμῖν ("now concerning sisterly and brotherly love you have no need [for us] to write to you"), that he mentions it is itself indicative of the importance that he attaches to it (cf. 3:12). This statement represents a use of paralipsis (cf. 5:1 and 2 Cor. 9:1), a rhetorical device whereby writers mention something that they pretend they are going to pass over (see BDF §495). Such statements are typical of parenesis in ancient moral exhortation (Malherbe, *Moral Exhortation,* 125) and are found in parenetic letters where parenesis was used to confirm people in their good conduct (Stowers, *Letter Writing,* 103).

159

In Greek and Jewish writings, with the exception perhaps of 2 Macc. 15:14, the word group φιλαδελφία/φιλάδελφος was used almost exclusively of love for blood brothers and sisters (cf. 4 Macc. 13:23, 26; 14:1). In Christian usage it came to have a metaphorical meaning (cf. Rom. 12:10; Heb. 13:1; 1 Pet. 1:22; 3:8; 2 Pet. 1:7), as it has here. Paul's metaphorical application reflects the way in which he sought to encourage a genuine feeling of kinship among his converts in order to provide a basis for their sense of community (cf. Best, 172 and see the comments on 4:1). It is interesting to note that φιλαδελφία, unlike ἀδελφοί, constitutes an example of ancient inclusive language, since it was applied to both brotherly and sisterly love.

The reason that Paul had no need to write instructions about brotherly and sisterly love to his readers was that God was teaching them to love one another: αὐτοὶ γὰρ ὑμεῖς θεοδίδακτοί ἐστε εἰς τὸ ἀγαπᾶν ἀλλήλους ("you yourselves are taught by God to love one another"). γάρ indicates that v. 9b gives the reason for or basis of the statement in v. 9a. The subject of the subordinate clause, αὐτοὶ ὑμεῖς ("you yourselves"), in v. 9b is emphatic.

θεοδίδακτος ("taught by God") appears to be a Pauline coinage since there are no known instances of the term prior to Paul, and outside Christian circles there are virtually none after him (Koester, "I Thessalonians," 39 n. 14). The LXX text of Is. 54:13 juxtaposes the words διδακτοὺς θεοῦ ("taught of God") and is quoted in Jn. 6:45. Although it would be impossible to demonstrate that Paul thought of Is. 54:13 as he coined the word, the theme of the passage is not without interest. Isaiah 54 is an OT eschatological text that looks forward to an age of salvation when the children of Zion will be taught by the Lord God, who will reign over them (cf. Pss. Sol. 17:32 LXX). For Paul the age of salvation had begun with Christ's resurrection from the dead, and therefore he may have equated this with the age of salvation described in Isaiah 54. For Christians to be taught by God was then a sign of their participation in the age of salvation. Whether Paul had a specific experience in mind or simply referred to his converts' general Christian experience is at first glance not altogether clear.

The purpose of God's teaching the Thessalonians is expressed in the infinitive phrase εἰς τὸ ἀγαπᾶν ἀλλήλους ("to love one another"). This well-known biblical theme can be traced back to the command in Lv. 19:18, "You shall love your neighbor as yourself" and was an important theme in Jesus' teaching (Mk. 12:29-32). As was suggested above (see the discussion of 3:12), Paul's emphasis on mutual love for fellow Christians was intended to create a new sense of identity and commitment among people who had no basis for a mutual relation prior to their conversion to Christ. Perhaps, then, in this verse the apostle has in mind the fact that, because his readers do indeed love as their brothers and sisters those who formerly were not even acquaintances, this can only mean that God has led them or taught them to do so. In other words, Paul begins with the fact of his converts' love for one another and concludes that its existence can only be explained by virtue of their having "learned" to do so from God. By putting the matter in this way Paul actually introduced the highest possible warrant for mutual love among the Thessalonians, namely, that it was God-ordained. Thus the expression "you yourselves are taught by God" has the same function as the words "this is the will of God" in 4:3.

Koester ("I Thessalonians," 39) misses the point of Paul's language when he argues that " 'taught by God' emphasizes that the recipients are not dependent upon the writer's instructions." In the very next verse, as elsewhere in the letter, Paul "exhorts" them on the basis of his own authority, clearly indicating that he was aware of his right as an apostle of Christ to instruct his converts in the ways of God.

If we could ask Paul to explain how God's people are taught to love, undoubtedly he would say it is done through the Spirit whom God gives to them (cf. v. 8 and see also 1 Cor. 2:13; Gal. 5:22). Clearly v. 9 is intended to affirm the recipients of the letter in their current practices, and in doing so implicitly praises their behavior. This is then carried over into v. 10 and reflects a standard feature of ancient parenesis whereby writers used an essentially positive approach to encourage their readers in good moral practices.

4:10   Paul offers a second reason (the γάρ of this verse is parallel with the γάρ of the preceding verse) why he has no need to write to the readers regarding familial love: καὶ γὰρ ποιεῖτε αὐτὸ εἰς πάντας τοὺς ἀδελφοὺς [τοὺς] ἐν ὅλῃ τῇ Μακεδονίᾳ ("for indeed you do this for all the brothers [and sisters] in the whole of Macedonia"). One feature of Paul's missionary activity was to link his various missionary churches together on a regional basis so that they would provide mutual support (see 1 Cor. 16:1, 19; 2 Cor. 1:1; Gal. 1:2), not primarily of a material character, but of a psychological nature. In socio-psychological terms the more people who believe something, the truer it seems, with the result that they are more likely to hold on to the belief (cf. Festinger, Riecken, and Schachter, *When Prophecy Fails,* 28). Because Paul linked his congregations together in this way they provided precisely this kind of encouragement for one another in an otherwise hostile environment.

At a more practical level it meant that Christians traveling between cities could obtain hospitality from their brothers and sisters in places where they knew no one. This is exactly what Paul asks of the Roman Christians for Phoebe, a sister and servant of the church at Cenchreae in Achaia (Rom. 16:1f.). In all probability then the Thessalonians had demonstrated their love for their Christian brothers and sisters in Macedonia by providing hospitality for them when they visited Thessalonica, a major port and commercial center as well as the seat of Roman administration for the province.

The second part of v. 10 could be taken with what follows, suggesting that a new theme is being introduced. On the whole, however, it seems more likely that when Paul says παρακαλοῦμεν δὲ ὑμᾶς, ἀδελφοί, περισσεύειν μᾶλλον ("and we exhort you to abound [in love] more and more"), he is referring back to their love for the family of God. Nevertheless, the infinitive περισσεύειν ("to abound") is the first in a series of four infinitive constructions dependent upon the main verb παρακαλοῦμεν ("we exhort"). This clearly indicates that what follows in vv. 10b-11 continues the theme of familial love begun in vv. 9-10a.

According to v. 10b, the recipients of the letter already demonstrate their love by the way in which they act toward one another as genuine brothers and sisters. Paul urges them to *increase* their feelings and expressions of love for their brothers and sisters, since Christian love should never become complacent, as though a certain level of love were sufficient to please God.

4:11 The exhortation to love the family of God in v. 10 is followed by three infinitive phrases (in addition to the one in v. 10b) dependent on the verb παρακαλοῦμεν in the previous verse. They carry the force of commands, as the words καθὼς ὑμῖν παρηγγείλαμεν ("just as we instructed you") at the end of v. 11 indicate. The sentiments of this verse and v. 12 have close parallels in the ethical exhortation of ancient moralists, according to Hock (*Social Context*, 42-47, see esp. 46) and Malherbe ("Exhortation in First Thessalonians," 251). This is important to bear in mind as there has been considerable debate about the precise reasons for the exhortation of v. 11.

Schmithals (*Paul and the Gnostics,* 158-160), for example, believes that Gnostic enthusiasts were disturbing the congregation and stirring up pneumatic excitement. This seems improbable. Unlike 1 Corinthians, where Paul discusses the Spirit in great detail, there is almost nothing in 1 and 2 Thessalonians about the Spirit. If Paul were concerned about spiritual enthusiasm, he would almost certainly have offered corrective teaching.

Most recent commentators favor a different view. 2 Thes. 3:6-13 reveals that some of Paul's converts were refusing to work to earn their own keep. This is then connected with the eschatological expectation of the community, to suggest that some had stopped working because they believed that the coming of Jesus was so near at hand that there was no reason to work (cf. Frame, 159f.; Rigaux, 519-521; Best, 175f.; Bruce, 90f.). Against this view, however, is the fact that Paul does not himself make this connection in any explicit way. It also leaves unanswered the relation between the exhortations to familial love and to the quiet, self-sufficient life. A clearer picture of the situation at Thessalonica will emerge if we pay attention to the insights of Hock and Malherbe.

The first exhortation in v. 11 (the second in the series begun in v. 10) consists of two infinitival phrases. Paul exhorts the Thessalonians φιλοτιμεῖσθαι ἡσυχάζειν καὶ πράσσειν τὰ ἴδια ("to aspire to live quietly and to tend to your own affairs"). The expressions "to live quietly" and "to tend to one's own affairs" go together and have unmistakable political connotations (Hock, *Social Context*, 46f.). To say, as Frame (161) does, that they could not have

162

this public sense in our text because the Christians were not philosophers but workers ignores one of the vital pieces of data in the letter. When Paul's readers had converted to Christianity, as has previously been observed, a public outcry arose and resulted in oppressive measures against them (cf. 1:6; 2:14; 3:3f.). Whether willingly or unwillingly, they had come into public view and had suffered for their faith. Thus Paul's exhortation to them "to aspire to live quietly and to mind your own affairs" was an eminently practical piece of advice. He hoped that by maintaining a low profile they would avoid further trouble for themselves. The likelihood of this suggestion receives support from v. 12, as we shall see.

Paul's final entreaty in the series is for his readers ἐργάζεσθαι ταῖς [ἰδίαις] χερσὶν ὑμῶν ("to work with your [own] hands"). This too was a common theme among moralists, as Dio Chrysostom, *Euboicus* 7:103-153 reveals (see Hock, *Social Context,* 44-45 for a discussion of this material). Hock argues that Paul was not concerned about the problem of idleness engendered by the imminent expectation of the parousia; rather he was offering general advice to avoid unacceptable occupations, or he may simply have been suggesting as a general rule that Christians should engage in manual labor. Because he rejects the Pauline authorship of 2 Thessalonians, a questionable presupposition as I have shown in the Introduction, Hock ignores 2 Thes. 3:6-12. But even without the evidence of 2 Thes. 3:6-12, 1 Thes. 5:14 makes specific reference to the need to admonish the idle, suggesting that some were lazy and failing to take responsibility for maintaining themselves. Quite apart from this, however, Hock also incorrectly assumes that parallel language must be used for similar purposes. Given that we have evidence of a problem with idleness (5:14 and 2 Thes. 3:6-10) it seems more reasonable to believe that Paul was addressing an actual situation in the community at Thessalonica.

The problem directly concerned Christian love and responsibility. People who were essentially poor and did not work every day with their own hands, either as artisans or day laborers, of necessity must have been economically dependent on others. In all probability the somewhat better-off members of the community felt obliged to support such people, out of their sense of Christian obligation, engendered by Paul's exhortation to love co-religionists as though they were family members. Thus, while on the one hand Paul sought to encourage familial love and responsibility among his converts, on the other he did not wish to allow his instructions regarding familial love to be exploited by anyone. This interpretation is to some extent confirmed by the second part of v. 12.

καθὼς ὑμῖν παρηγγείλαμεν ("just as we commanded you") goes with the whole series of infinitive expressions in vv. 10b-11. In the case of the last infinitival phrase we know that Paul did command the Thessalonians to be self-sufficient through working with their own hands when he was with them, as 2 Thes. 3:10 evinces, and the discussion in 2 Thes. 3:6-12 is directed to the same point. What is clear from 2 Thes. 3:6-12 is that Paul thought the issue of self-sufficiency was a major source of discord in the community when he wrote 2 Thessalonians. For this reason he lays out disciplinary measures to be followed if members of the community fail to comply with his command (cf. 2 Thes. 3:14f.). If, as I contend, 2 Thessalonians was written first, then Paul's command in v. 11 that his converts should work with their own hands to support themselves reiterates his teaching from that earlier letter.

4:12 The purpose of the ethical exhortation of the previous two verses is twofold according to v. 12. The second purpose, ἵνα . . . μηδενὸς χρείαν ἔχητε ("that you have need of nothing"—or "no one" if μηδενός is taken as masculine rather than neuter) is linked most closely with the requirement that the readers "work with their own hands." By doing this they would provide for themselves sufficiently well to avoid needing material assistance from their fellow Christians. It is improbable that idle Christians would find any support outside the church. Therefore it seems reasonable to see ἵνα περιπατῆτε εὐσχημόνως πρὸς τοὺς ἔξω ("that you live becomingly toward outsiders") as providing the purpose of "aspiring to a quiet life" and "minding their own affairs." Paul's hope was that no new wave of oppression would break out in Thessalonica if his converts acted with circumspection toward their non-Christian neighbors (τοὺς ἔξω), thereby giving them no reason to react against the Christians. The phrase "those outside" derives from the fact that Paul had erected a group boundary for his converts and wished to preserve it in order to maintain their sense of identity and separation from the pagan society of which they had formerly been a part (cf. 1 Cor. 5:12f. and Col. 4:5; see Meeks, *First Urban Christians,* 84-107 on group boundaries in Pauline Christianity).

INSTRUCTION CONCERNING THE PAROUSIA AND ASSUMPTION: 4:13-18

The material in this subsection of the *probatio* is concerned with a problem that appears to have arisen in the community at Thessalonica regarding the dead and their participation in the coming of Christ from heaven. The passage raises several extremely difficult questions for the interpreter. Perhaps the most problematic, why did the Thessalonians grieve over their brothers and sisters who had died? Marshall (120-122) has isolated five different types of solutions to this vexing question. All five have varying degrees of plausibility, but none of them is completely satisfactory.

In recent years the view receiving the greatest support has claimed that Paul's belief in the imminent return of Christ meant that he had given no systematic instruction about the resurrection. As a result, when Christians began to die this raised a question about their fate. Most people holding this view maintain that a shift occurred in Paul's thought between 1 Thessalonians and 1 Corinthians. This shift, they believe, led to Paul's full-fledged understanding of the resurrection as expressed in 1 Corinthians 15. (For recent proponents of this view see Marxsen, "Auslegung," 23-37 and especially Lüdemann, *Paul: Apostle to the Gentiles,* 212-238. Lüdemann uses the "early" character of the parousia/resurrection teaching in 1 Thessalonians to support his thesis for radically redating Paul's missionary activity and letters. Cf. also Mearns, "Early Eschatological Development.")

This explanation fails to carry conviction for several reasons. In the first place, even if 1 Thessalonians were written much earlier than is normally thought, it is unlikely that Paul had failed to encountered Christians who had experienced the death of fellow believers. If such bereaved people had no concept of the resurrection, they presumably would have had the same problem as the Thessalonians are reputed to have had, thus leading to a solution before Paul ever began his mission in Thessalonica. Second, Paul clearly taught the resurrection of Jesus himself as a part of the tradition, as 1 Cor. 15:3-8 shows, and this was associated with the parousia expectation at Thessalonica (1:10). Third, as a person with a Pharisaic Jewish background (Phil. 3:5), Paul almost certainly believed in the general resurrection of the dead. If 1 Cor. 15:20 is anything to go by, he simply incorporated Christ's resurrection into his previous thought concerning the general resurrection by making Christ the "first fruits of those who had died." Thus belief in the resurrection of Christians was implicit in Paul's Jewish beliefs and his understanding of the resurrection of Jesus. It certainly did not require the crisis at Thessalonica to precipitate such a conclusion. Finally, 1 Thes. 4:16, which makes specific reference to the resurrection of the dead, is a traditional piece of material going back to the earliest days of the Christian movement (see below) and therefore is clear evidence that the resurrection of dead Christians was not an afterthought for Paul.

The claims by Schmithals (*Paul and the Gnostics,* 160-164) and Harnisch (*Eschatologische Existenz,* 16-51) that Gnostic interlopers had created doubts concerning the resurrection with their spiritualizing interpretation of it find little support in the text. Paul does not seem to be involved in a polemical debate with gnosticizing opponents. Moreover, as Peel ("Gnostic Eschatology," 141-165) has demonstrated, Gnostic groups did not necessarily reject the resurrection. (See also the discussion of Schmithals's position in the Introduction, pp. 53f.)

Hyldahl ("Auferstehung," 119-135) suggests that the real problem was a loss of confidence in the parousia itself when some Christians died in Thessalonica before it had taken place. But this runs up against the fact that Paul nowhere in the letter seeks to reassure, let alone prove, that the parousia would take place.

Marshall (120-122) accepts what may be described as the traditional view, which is that while the Thessalonians had received instruction from Paul regarding the resurrection of the dead, they had not fully appreciated it. But if the Thessalonians had absorbed Paul's teaching regarding the return of Christ from heaven, it seems hard to believe that they would have found it difficult to accept his normal teaching concerning the resurrection. As I will show, it was not the resurrection as such that proved problematic, but concern about the connection between the resurrection and the parousia.

Perhaps the most convincing explanation to date comes from Plevnik ("Taking Up," 274-283; see also "Parousia as Implication," 199-272), who takes up the work of Lohfink *(Himmelfahrt Jesu)* and applies it to 1 Thes. 4:13-18. Lohfink has shown that in the OT and Jewish apocalyptic literature those who are assumed (i.e., taken up into heaven) are always alive, and in fact it is axiomatic that those who are dead cannot be assumed into heaven. From this Plevnik concludes that the issue at Thessalonica was not whether dead Christians would share in the resurrection but the fear that they would be disadvantaged by not being able to participate in the assumption to heaven.

The origin of this problem may lie in Paul's denial that the day of the Lord has come in 2 Thes. 2:1-12, if I am correct that 2 Thessalonians was the first letter of Paul to the community (see the discussion on the sequence of the Thessalonian correspondence in the Introduction). The precise nature of the problem is not clear, but the possibility of a connection between the belief that the day of the Lord had in some senses come (assuming that Paul was accurately informed about the situation when he wrote 2 Thessalonians) and anxiety about those who had died seems to make considerable sense out of an otherwise enigmatic situation (see the discussion of 2 Thes. 2:1f.).

In 4:13-18 Paul attempts to provide comfort for his converts at a time when they were apparently mourning the death of some of their Christian sisters and brothers and worrying about the implications of their deaths. The apostle seeks to console his readers through instruction regarding the relationship between the resurrection and the parousia of Christ. Stowers *(Letter Writing,* 145) notes that Paul's discussion parallels a theme in other complicated parenetic letters from Antiquity, which often have consolation as part of their purpose. Interestingly, he mentions that writers of letters of consolation often encouraged their readers to use their words of comfort to exhort themselves. This is precisely what Paul does in v. 18. (For examples of letters of consolation from antiquity see Stowers, 145-151).

4:13   The transition from v. 12 to v. 13 is somewhat abrupt. The words οὐ θέλομεν δὲ ὑμᾶς ἀγνοεῖν, ἀδελφοί, περὶ τῶν κοιμωμένων ("Now, we do not wish you to be ignorant, brothers [and sisters], concerning those who are asleep") show that a new subject is being introduced (cf. the use of "we do not wish you to be ignorant" in Rom. 11:25; 1 Cor. 10:1; 12:1: in each case it is a transitional phrase). The construction δέ . . . περὶ τῶν κοιμωμένων ("now . . . concerning those who are asleep"; cf. 4:9) suggests that the matter discussed in 4:13-18 was either raised in a communication from the Thessalonians or more probably by Timothy's report regarding the situation that prevailed in Thessalonica. Paul has a didactic intention in this section, as the introductory clause clearly reveals (cf. R. F. Collins, "Tradition," 325). The information, though, need not be completely new. Rather Paul employs traditional material to comfort his readers by overcoming their grief through his teaching concerning Christian hope. Malherbe ("Exhortation in First Thessalonians," 254-256) finds precedent for this feature of the letter in the epistolographic handbooks from the period, which treat consolation under the heading of parenesis.

Terms for sleep were widely used in Antiquity as euphemisms for death both in Greek writings from earliest times (cf. Homer, *Il.* 11.241; Sophocles, *El.* 509) and in Jewish and Christian writings (see Gn. 47:30; Dt. 31:16; 1 Ki. 2:10; Job 14:12f.; Ps. 13:3; Je. 51:39f.; 2 Macc. 12:45; Jn. 11:11-13; Acts 13:36; 1 Cor. 11:30). This is how the participle τῶν κοιμωμένων is employed here. In both Greek writings and throughout the OT, with the exception of the Book of Daniel, the metaphor of sleep for death was used by those who had no real concept of afterlife. Although Paul uses κοιμᾶσθαι in relation to those who die prior to the resurrection in v. 13 (cf. 1 Cor. 15:20f.; Dn. 12:2 served as a precedent for connecting the sleep of death with the resurrection), it is precarious to make any deductions regarding Paul's understanding of an intermediate state between physical life and the resurrection.

The ἵνα ("in order that") clause presents the problem to be overcome among the Thessalonians. Paul explains his purpose in the words μὴ λυπῆσθε ("[that] you may not grieve"). The reason that they should not grieve, however, is only stated explicitly in the next verse. Nevertheless, Paul does say that he does not want his readers to be καθὼς καὶ οἱ λοιποὶ οἱ μὴ ἔχοντες ἐλπίδα ("like the rest of humanity, who have no hope") for life beyond death. καθώς indicates that what follows is a comparison between the readers and those outside the Christian community, who are designated by the expression οἱ λοιποί ("the rest of humanity"; cf. 5:6) and who are οἱ μὴ ἔχοντες ἐλπίδα ("those who have no hope").

If Paul meant that those who were not part of the Christian community had no sense of afterlife and thus no hope for their dead, he overstates the case to some extent. Among the Greek philosophers, at least from the time of Plato onward, there were always those who maintained that the soul was immortal and would therefore survive death. But they were usually vague about the nature of this existence. The mystery religions sought to insure their initiates of afterlife. But such ideas were not well-defined and appear not to have been held widely at a popular level (see Frame, 167f.; Best, 185f.). Paul accepted a further reason for the hopelessness of pagans: they had rejected God and acted disobediently in terms of his decrees; they would thus be subject to his wrath in the judgment (cf. Rom. 1:18-32; 1 Thes. 1:10; 5:9).

According to v. 14 another aspect of Christian hope versus non-Christian hopelessness concerned Paul and is the basis for the comparison between why Christians should not grieve for their dead while pagans will inevitably grieve for theirs.

4:14 The cause of the Thessalonians' sadness begins to emerge in this verse and becomes clearer in the succeeding verses as Paul explains why they should not be filled with sadness. γάϱ connects this verse with the previous verse, so that v. 14 offers the reason that Christians should not grieve. This reason is couched in a conditional sentence, the protasis of which concerns belief in the death and resurrection of Jesus and the apodosis of which concerns the assurance this gives regarding those who have died: εἰ γὰϱ πιστεύομεν ὅτι Ἰησοῦς ἀπέθανεν καὶ ἀνέστη, οὕτως καὶ ὁ θεὸς τοὺς κοιμηθέντας διὰ τοῦ Ἰησοῦ ἄξει σὺν αὐτῷ ("for if we believe that Jesus died and was raised, thus also [we may believe that] God will bring those who have fallen asleep through Jesus with him").

The phrase πιστεύομεν ὅτι ("we believe that") is a typical introduction to a credal formula according to Havener ("Pre-Pauline Formulae," 111; cf. Rom. 10:9) and probably introduces one here. It is disputed, however, whether Paul cites the full creed or not. The words "we believe" link his faith with that of his readers while the words "Jesus died and was raised" present the foundational belief distinguishing followers of Christ from the "rest of humanity," mentioned in the previous verse. "Jesus died and was raised" may be a short summary of the more extensive version of the same information found in 1 Cor. 15:3f. But it seems unlikely that Paul is responsible for the summary here because he seldom uses the verb ἀνίστημι ("to raise") for the resurrection. With the exception of 1 Thes. 4:16, which may be under the influence of 4:14 or part of a traditional formulation, it only occurs in quotations (cf. Rom. 15:12 and 1 Cor. 10:7, the only other occurrences in Paul unless Eph. 5:14 is Pauline). The apostle normally employs ἐγείϱειν (37 times) for the resurrection, whether Christ's or his followers. This verb is almost always found with an indication that it was God who raised Jesus and will raise his followers (cf. Rom. 6:4, 9; 8:11; 10:9; 1 Cor. 15:12, 20; Gal. 1:1). The designation "Jesus" in the formula without any titular qualifications is atypical of Paul and may go back to a stage before other christological titles were associated with Jesus (Havener, 111f.). If this is the case the formula is indeed very early and reflects the basic data from which all subsequent christology developed, namely, the death and resurrection of Jesus.

It seems unlikely, however, that a credal formula would not have gone on to express the purpose of Jesus' death. For this reason it is possible that Paul truncated the original formula, which contained a ὑπὲϱ/πεϱὶ ἡμῶν ("for us") phrase (cf. 5:10), in order to apply it directly to the situation being addressed. (The argument of Havener, 112 against this view is precarious because his examples from the Gospels are not credal formulas at all, and the

supposedly parallel instance in Rom. 14:9 shows clear signs of being re-
worked in order to fit the context.)

οὕτως καί marks the inference to be drawn from what precedes and
presupposes the words "we may believe that." Belief in the death and
resurrection of Jesus should lead to belief that God will bring those who have
died with Jesus at his coming. This raises a very important question. If Paul's
concern in this paragraph were the resurrection of dead Christians as such,
why did he not repeat the verb ἀνέστη in the future ("will raise") instead of
using ἄξει ("will lead")? While the second part of the sentence, "God will
bring with him those who sleep through Jesus," obviously presupposes the
resurrection of those who have died in Christ, Paul directs the focus of
attention to the coming of Jesus from heaven, as vv. 15-17 demonstrate. This
very strongly suggests that the problem addressed by Paul was not about the   ✓
resurrection as such, but concerned the relationship of dead Christians to the
parousia, as Luz (Geschichtsverständnis, 318-331) has argued, and more
particularly the relationship of the dead in Christ to the assumption to heaven
of those who remain alive, as Plevnik ("Taking Up") has shown. This
interpretation will be confirmed by my exegesis of v. 15.

Two other minor problems remain to be cleared up concerning v. 14.
The prepositional phrase διὰ τοῦ ᾿Ιησοῦ ("through Jesus") could go with the
verb ἄξει ("will lead"). In this case it would denote that Jesus was the agent
of God in bringing "those who sleep." Alternatively, it may go with the
participle κοιμηθέντας ("those who have fallen asleep"), though commentators
debate what it might mean if construed this way (see Best, 188f. for the full
range of suggestions). If σὺν αὐτῷ ("with him") did not follow immediately
after the verb "will lead," the first possibility would be the more attractive one
without doubt, but the doubling up of the predicate complements before and
after the verb renders that option dubious on grammatical grounds. It has often
been missed that Paul changes from the present participle κοιμωμένων in v. 13
to the aorist participle κοιμηθέντας in v. 14. This means that v. 14 refers to the
moment of their dying (cf. Bruce, 98), when the issue of whether they
belonged to Christ or not was of central importance for their future salvation.
God will not bring with Christ all those who sleep but only those who died
while in relationship to him. διά with the genitive is certainly an unusual way
to express this idea (cf. Rom. 1:5; 5:9, 17f.; 8:37; 2 Cor. 1:20), as though Jesus
were the agent responsible for their dying, but it probably means little different
from Paul's "in Christ" formula (cf. 1 Cor. 15:18).

The other problem relates to where God is intending to lead them.
According to Marshall (124f.), it is unlikely that Paul meant that the dead
would be led to heaven with Christ. Marshall maintains that for Paul the
parousia consisted of Christ coming to earth to a new world freed from
corruption. This interpretation ignores the following verses, where Paul
speaks of the living and the dead in Christ being caught up into the clouds

bringing Jesus at his parousia. Wherever the ultimate dwelling place of the people of God may be, the imagery of vv. 16f. is that of an assumption to heaven. To the extent that the place of Christ is with God in heaven, the people of God are to be brought to the place of God, namely, heaven. Thus ἄξει ("will bring") does not refer to the resurrection of the dead in Christ but to their being brought to heaven at the parousia of the Lord. They will be assumed to heaven like those who remain alive until the coming of Jesus.

4:15 Vv. 15-17 pose several important but difficult questions. What is Paul alluding to when he asserts that he is speaking ἐν λόγῳ κυρίου ("by word of the Lord")? If Paul is quoting a source, how much of the material is to be understood as included in the "word of the Lord"? To what extent is the material in vv. 15-17 traditional in origin and what is its provenance? These questions have been so much the focus of attention that little thought has been given to another important issue: What is the *function* of the material, especially the words τοῦτο γὰρ ὑμῖν λέγομεν ἐν λόγῳ κυρίου ("for this we tell you by word of the Lord")?

The γάρ of v. 15 indicates that v. 14 is to be explained and confirmed by what follows (Frame, 170). τοῦτο ("this") refers forward to the explanation regarding the relation of living and dead Christians to one another and the coming of Christ from heaven. Two basic views have been put forward concerning the meaning of "this we tell you by word of the Lord."

The *first* has two variations. (a) Paul may be quoting what he believes to be an actual statement of Jesus. Against this view is the fact that the Gospels contain no saying that may be directly equated with the statements in vv. 15b-17. This has led some (e.g., Frame, 171; Morris, 141; Jeremias, *Unknown Sayings*, 80-83) to claim that Paul is quoting or paraphrasing an *agraphon*, that is, an otherwise unknown saying of Jesus not preserved in any written sources. 1 Cor. 7:10 and 9:14 as well as 11:23 are examples (the only other ones in fact) in which Paul specifies that he is speaking a word originating from Jesus. In these three cases, however, definite references in the Gospels are identifiable.

(b) Since the *agraphon* view by its very nature can never be proven, some have claimed that Paul is alluding more loosely to what he understood to be the teaching of Jesus on the subject without citing or paraphrasing a specific saying (see, e.g., Rigaux, 539; Hartman, *Prophecy Interpreted*, 187-190, 246; Hyldahl, "Auferstehung," 130). This interpretation finds in Mark 13 and Matthew 24 the traditional material Paul drew upon and recognizes that the term λόγος does not refer to a saying of the Lord but may denote a discourse or instruction.

The *second* possibility is that Paul employed a saying uttered in the name of the risen Lord by an early Christian prophet or perhaps even one originating with Paul himself (e.g., Harnisch, *Eschatologische Existenz*, 39-41; R. F. Collins, "Tradition," 331-333; Mearns, "Early Eschatological Development," 140f.; Lüdemann, *Paul: Apostle to the Gentiles*, 231).

170

The problem of interpretation is further complicated by the difficulty in deciding whether v. 15b or vv. 16f. constitute the "word of the Lord" to which Paul refers. V. 15b may be Paul's summary of the "word of the Lord" with vv. 16-17 containing the saying in a more complete form. If so, Paul may have derived this material from an apocalyptic discourse ascribed to Jesus that has left its marks on the "apocalyptic discourse" of Mark 13, Matthew 24, and Luke 17.

While certainty is not possible, I am inclined to agree with Hartmann (*Prophecy Interpreted,* 247) who notes that "the form of the parenetic 'midrash' [in 1 Thes. 4:15-17] is that of a teacher and not that of a community, nor of an inspired prophet, who, as it is sometimes assumed, was interpreted as being the mouthpiece of the risen Lord." Since, as Hartman (187-190) has shown, 4:15-17 is midrashic in character, and almost everyone agrees it goes back to a time before Paul's writing, it seems plausible that the basic content of the verses, but not their present wording, stems from an apocalyptic discourse by Jesus concerning the end of the age. The similarities between Mt. 24:29-31, 40f. in particular, and the images and language used in vv. 16f. suggest that Paul was utilizing what he took to be the teaching of the Lord regarding the end of the age.

According to Holtz (194) we cannot assume that a more didactic approach to the parousia would have carried less weight than an instruction from the Lord. He believes that Paul chose to use the word of the Lord because of the significance of its content for the situation. This view underestimates the intrinsic authority of the word of the Lord for Paul and his converts.

The choice of the expression "we say to you by word of the Lord" has an important function in the argument independent of any particular provenance for vv. 15b-17. V. 18 makes it clear that Paul intended to comfort his readers through his elaboration of details regarding the parousia of Jesus. By placing his assurance that the living would not have precedence over the dead at the coming of the Lord under the rubric "a word of the Lord," Paul attributed the highest possible authority to his assertion in v. 15b. In doing so he undoubtedly hoped to give his readers certitude regarding the participation of dead Christians in the assumption to heaven with their Lord, thereby consoling the living and in fact overcoming the reason for sadness among them. On this interpretation v. 15b represents the conclusion drawn by Paul himself from the apocalyptic discourse tradition going back to Jesus. Vv. 15b-17 may well constitute his own midrash on the tradition.

One important feature of Paul's eschatological understanding, at least at the time that he wrote 1 Thessalonians, becomes evident from v. 15b. He believed that he and many of his contemporaries would still be alive at the time of the Lord's coming, as the phrase ἡμεῖς οἱ ζῶντες οἱ περιλειπόμενοι εἰς τὴν παρουσίαν τοῦ κυρίου ("we who are living, who remain until the coming of the Lord") demonstrates. Marshall (127) is unconvincing when he tries to

171

smooth over this implication. Paul could have used the indefinite third person had he not wished to include himself among those who would probably survive to the parousia. Instead he uses the somewhat emphatic first person plural construction ἡμεῖς . . . οὐ μὴ φθάσωμεν ("we . . . shall certainly not precede" or "have an advantage"). That Paul believed the coming of Christ to be imminent is shown by the way in which his parenetic instruction in 1 Cor. 7:25-31 is determined by his belief that the adult generation at the time of his writing was the last generation before the end. As Bruce (99; cf. Beker, *Paul the Apostle,* 178) points out, in the course of time Paul may have come to recognize that he might not survive to the parousia of the Lord (cf. 2 Cor. 1:8f.; 5:8; Phil. 1:21-24).

The words οὐ μὴ φθάσωμεν τοὺς κοιμηθέντας ("we shall certainly have no advantage over those who have fallen asleep") are of particular importance for determining the problem addressed by Paul in 4:13-17. οὐ μή with the aorist subjunctive verb is an expression of emphatic future negation (cf. Frame, 173). Marshall (127) maintains that the verb φθάσωμεν has the sense of "doing something before someone else and so of gaining an advantage over him [*sic*]." From this clause we can see that the Thessalonians feared that their dead would lose out on the chance to be assumed to heaven at the time of the parousia. Plevnik ("Taking Up," 281) provides a highly plausible explanation of the situation. According to him, the Thessalonians were troubled about their dead because they believed that to be assumed to heaven with Christ at his parousia one had to be alive. What then of the resurrection? The apocalyptic tradition sometimes separated the resurrection of the dead from events comparable to the parousia of Christ, as 2 Esdr. 7:25-44; *2 Bar.* 29–30; and Rev. 20:4-6 demonstrate. 2 Esdr. 13:24 is particularly interesting because it maintains that those who survive to the end are more blessed than those who have died. This clearly supports the possibility of the interpretation presented here.

4:16 Using apocalyptic imagery Paul depicts the events of the parousia in this and the following verse in order to support his dictum in v. 15b that the living will have no advantage over the dead in attaining salvation (cf. 1 Cor. 15:51-53 for a similar presentation of the end but with an added feature involving the transformation of the living). Marshall (128) offers a helpful discussion on the need to understand that this description of the end is in symbolic terms since the imagery and symbolic presentation "if pressed literally, lead to antinomies and contradictions." What J. J. Collins (*Apocalyptic Imagination,* 214) has written concerning the language of apocalypses (which I quoted earlier in connection with 2:16) is equally true of the wider phenomenon of apocalyptic language as found in 4:16f. and again in 2 Thessalonians 2:

> The language of the apocalypses is not descriptive, referential newspaper language, but the *expressive* language of poetry, which uses symbols and

imagery to articulate a sense or feeling about the world. Their abiding value does not lie in the pseudoinformation they provide about cosmology or future history, but in their affirmation of a transcendent world.

Whether Paul understood the apocalyptic language he employed as symbolic or not is more difficult to answer. While a literal realization of Paul's symbolic depiction of the coming of Christ seems implausible for many people today, the distinction between the message of a symbolic presentation and its potential objective reality would not have been easy to make for someone at home with an apocalyptic worldview. In all probability Paul did believe in some type of historical realization of his description of the end since he had received it from the Jesus tradition and it formed part of his hope in the parousia (cf. Holtz, 206f., who makes a somewhat similar point).

At first sight v. 16 speaks of three audible acts associated with the coming of the Lord from heaven. Paul says that αὐτὸς ὁ κύριος ἐν κελεύσματι, ἐν φωνῇ ἀρχαγγέλου καὶ ἐν σάλπιγγι θεοῦ, καταβήσεται ἀπ' οὐρανοῦ ("the Lord himself will descend from heaven with a cry of command, with the voice of the archangel, and with the trumpet of God"). The three prepositional phrases could be temporal and could indicate the moment at which Christ's descent will occur. It is better, however, to take them in the sense of circumstances attendant with the Lord's descent from heaven, since all three are probably to be connected with the resurrection of those who sleep.

The "cry of command" may come from the archangel. If this is correct the καί connecting ἐν φωνῇ ἀρχαγγέλου ("with the voice of an archangel") to ἐν σάλπιγγι θεοῦ ("with the trumpet of God") implies that the last two prepositional phrases should possibly be taken together as epexegetical to the first. If so, they express the means by which the command is issued (so Frame, 174; L. Schmid, *TDNT* III, 658). Another possibility is perhaps more likely. The juxtaposition of κελεύσματι ("cry of command") with the phrase αὐτὸς ὁ κύριος ("the Lord himself") suggests that Christ's cry of command is directed to the dead, whom he calls to the resurrection by means of the voice of the archangel and the trumpet of God. This interpretation is perhaps supported by the statement in Jn. 5:25-29 that the dead will hear the voice of the Son of God and will come forth to the resurrection and the judgment. This is probably a pre-Johannine tradition, perhaps originally about the Son of Man. As part of the apocalyptic component of the Jesus tradition it may have been known to Paul.

The "trumpet of God" is an image occurring frequently in the OT in contexts of theophany and eschatological judgment (cf. Ex. 19:16, 19; Is. 27:13; Joel 2:1; Zp. 1:14-16; Zc. 9:14) as well as in both Jewish and Christian apocalyptic traditions (cf. *Pss. Sol.* 11:1; 2 Esdr. 6:17-24; *Apoc. Mos.* 22, 37–38; Mt. 24:31; Rev. 8:2, 6, 13; 9:14). (For a good discussion of the eschatological significance of the trumpet-sound see G. Friedrich, *TDNT* VII, 80, 84, 86-88.)

The Greek Bible has the designation ἀρχαγγέλος only here in 1 Thes. 4:16 and in Jude 9. The idea of principal angels, however, goes back to Dn. 10:13 (cf. 12:1), where the angel Michael is described as εἷς τῶν ἀρχόντων ("one of the princes"), and was part of the apocalyptic tradition of Judaism (cf. 2 Esdr. 4:36f.). Angels were frequently connected with the end of the age (cf. *1 Enoch* 1:9; 2 Thes. 1:7; Mk. 8:38; Mt. 24:31; Rev. 15:1), though the association of an archangel's voice with the end is an unparalleled image. In all probability the voice of the archangel and the trumpet of God belonged together originally as "the sound of the trumpet," but because φωνή could also mean "voice" the expression was separated into two parts.

According to Mt. 24:31 a "great trumpet call" will precede the gathering of the elect, but in 1 Cor. 15:51f. the trumpet blast seems to call the dead to their resurrection. In 1 Thes. 4:16 it would appear that the cry of command by Christ and the voice of the archangel and the trumpet of God, which carry out the command, are all intended to call those who sleep to the resurrection.

When this happens the Lord καταβήσεται ἀπ' οὐρανοῦ ("will descend from heaven"), and οἱ νεκροὶ ἐν Χριστῷ ἀναστήσονται πρῶτον ("the dead in Christ will rise first"). The "in Christ" formula simply means that those who will rise are those who belong to Christ at the time of their deaths. L. Schmid (*TDNT* III, 658f.) is incorrect in maintaining that the πρῶτον–ἔπειτα ("first-then") of vv. 16f. "has a qualitative rather than a chronological significance." In terms of the word of comfort Paul wished to impart, the πρῶτον must be understood temporally. It was intended to assure the Thessalonians that the dead in Christ would be raised before the assumption to heaven and therefore that they would take part fully in the parousia of Christ and the assumption to heaven (cf. Rev. 11:3-13, where the two murdered witnesses are first brought back to life or physically raised from the dead before being assumed to heaven).

4:17 Having said that the coming of the Lord from heaven would include a summons to the dead in Christ to rise first, Paul now proceeds to connect those who are resurrected with those who belong to Christ and remain alive at the time of his coming. The sequence of events is emphasized again by ἔπειτα ("then") at the beginning of v. 17. The living are drawn into the unfolding events only after the resurrection of the dead has occurred first (v. 16). As I have mentioned, Paul may well have utilized an already existing tradition regarding the coming of the Son of Man in vv. 16f. If so, he probably repeated the phrase ἡμεῖς οἱ ζῶντες οἱ περιλειπόμενοι ("we who are living, who remain") from v. 15 to make his interpretation clearer (cf. Holtz, "Traditionen," 65). This should warn us against seeing vv. 16f. as a pre-formed *logion* or saying, as Best (196) appears to hold.

Those who survive until the coming of the Lord from heaven will be brought together with those who have been summoned to the resurrection: ἅμα σὺν αὐτοῖς ἁρπαγησόμεθα ἐν νεφέλαις εἰς ἀπάντησιν τοῦ κυρίου εἰς ἀέρα ("together with them we will be caught up on clouds to meet the Lord in the air"). From the time of the OT the clouds of the heavens were associated with theophanies (cf. Ex. 16:10; 19:16), and in such texts as Is. 19:1 and the vision of Ezk. 1:4-28 a cloud becomes the celestial vehicle of God. It was probably owing to this influence that the writer of Dn. 7:13f. employed clouds to transport the "one like a son of man" into the presence of God, and from here the clouds passed into the stock of apocalyptic images. The description of the Son of Man coming to earth at the end of the age on the clouds in Mk. 13:26 (par. Mt. 24:30) was based on Dn. 7:13. But the Danielic vision has been interpreted so that "one like a son of man" becomes "the Son of Man," and whereas the clouds originally took the figure to God, the movement is reversed in that they now bring him to earth. Paul has drawn on this traditional imagery derived from the teaching of Jesus regarding his epiphany from heaven, but he may also draw on the tradition found in Acts 1:9, which portrays Jesus himself as ascending by means of a cloud.

The verb ἁρπάζειν is used in Gn. 5:24 (LXX) for the taking up of Enoch to heaven and by Paul in 2 Cor. 12:2 and 4 to refer to his own ascent into the third heaven. In these instances, as in v. 17, it implies that the ascent is brought about by a force outside the individual.

The expression εἰς ἀπάντησιν was a technical expression in Hellenistic Greek for the departure from a city of a delegation of citizens to meet an arriving dignitary in order to accord the person proper respect and honor by escorting the dignitary back to the city. Whether this technical application should then be taken in a literal sense in v. 17 to suggest that the Lord and those with him will return to earth, as Marshall (131) conjectures, seems unlikely. Those who meet the Lord in the air (the space between the earth and the heavens in Jewish cosmology) are caught up in a heavenly ascent by the clouds without any indication that they then return to earth. Apart from the possible connotation that ἀπάντησις might have for a return to earth, the rest of the imagery (the clouds and being caught up to the Lord) are indicative of an assumption to heaven of the people who belong to Christ. That Paul adds his own definitive statement concerning the significance of this meeting in the clause καὶ οὕτως πάντοτε σὺν κυρίῳ ἐσόμεθα ("and thus we will always be with the Lord") suggests that both dead and living Christians will return to heaven with the Lord, not only to enjoy continuous fellowship with him, but also, in terms of 1:10, to be saved from the coming wrath of God. The idea of a return to heaven is also supported by 1 Cor. 15:23f. According to this text the dead will be raised at the coming of Christ, and then will come the end when he will deliver his dominion to God after he has destroyed all rule, authority, and power. While it is always dangerous to press apocalyptic imagery and accounts too literally, this does imply that the return to heaven is necessary for Christ to render up his rule to God. That 1 Thes. 4:16f. has an assumption in mind is also confirmed by the statement in v. 14 that "God will lead those who sleep in Jesus with him." Since they are to be taken up into the air to meet Jesus this can only refer to their being led to heaven with Jesus.

Although an attempt has been made here to organize the details of vv. 16f. into a reasonably coherent picture of the events of the end, it must be acknowledged that Paul was probably not interested in giving us a literal description. His goal was to reassure the Thessalonians that their fellow Christians who had died would participate on equal terms with them in the salvation experience accompanying the parousia of the Lord. This is why he does not mention what will become of godless pagans, why he does not discuss the transformation of the living, as in 1 Cor. 15:51-57, and why he does not describe the final state of salvation into which the living and the dead in Christ will enter.

4:18 Paul's own intention in describing the events that he believed would take place when Christ came from heaven to gather his followers becomes clear in the words ὥστε παρακαλεῖτε ἀλλήλους ἐν τοῖς λόγοις τούτοις ("so then comfort one another with these words"). He wished his readers to comfort one another as a result of what he had told them (ὥστε signifies that v. 18 is a result clause), thereby overcoming their sadness about those who had died or would die before the coming of the Lord. The basis of the consolation was to be Paul's assurance, based on a word from the Lord, that the living and the dead, who will be raised, will be assumed to heaven together with the Lord Jesus when he comes at his parousia.

1 Thes. 4:13-18 fits very clearly into the parenetic intention of the letter as a whole by offering consolation to those who grieved because "consolation was conceived of as belonging to paraenesis" (Malherbe, "Exhortation in First Thessalonians," 254). At the same time this section of the letter was directed to clearing up a problem in the belief structure or symbolic world inhabited by the Thessalonians. That they had not understood Paul's eschatological teaching completely should come as no surprise. To the extent that most of them had been pagans rather than Jews, they were forced to assimilate an entirely new understanding of the world when they became Christians. The sort of changes being made to their symbolic world required time to absorb. In this respect vv. 13-18 were intended to clarify and reinforce Paul's eschatological teaching in such a way as to remove a major problem with it for the Thessalonians.

ESCHATOLOGICAL EXPECTATION AND PARENESIS: 5:1-11

The theme of the parousia is still very much the topic of discussion in 5:1-11, but the focus shifts to parenesis concerning the need for constant vigilance and readiness for the arrival of the parousia. Rigaux ("Tradition et Rédaction,"

176

320-335) has examined 5:1-11 in terms of clearly evident traditional material embedded in the passage and Paul's redaction of the material. He has detected three themes in 5:1-11 that are marked out in the structure of the passage and that he regards as helpful in understanding the passage's development of thought. Vv. 1-3 deal with the day of the Lord; vv. 4-8a treat the need for vigilance on the part of the Thessalonians in view of the coming of that day; vv. 8b-10 concern Christian existence. V. 11, which repeats the basic idea of 4:18, functions as a general conclusion to 4:13–5:10. Although this outline is interesting, it is not without problems. Grammatically v. 8 cannot be split into two parts, and in fact the second part extends the exhortative idea of the first part of the verse.

Meeks (*First Urban Christians,* 175) contends that vv. 1-8 contain two separate pieces of tradition having an apocalyptic character. One tradition spoke of the day of the Lord coming like a thief in the night, and the other involved a "dualistic admonition" to remain alert directed to the "children of light" in contradistinction to the "children of darkness." Meeks is undoubtedly correct about this but is wrong in trying to link the material in 5:1-11 directly to 4:13-18. It is difficult to see how 5:1-11 addresses the concerns of the community at Thessalonica for their dead brothers and sisters.

Rather, if I am correct that 2 Thessalonians was Paul's first letter to the community, then 5:1-11 functions to re-instill a sense of the imminence of the parousia of Christ. Paul may have felt this was necessary in order to compensate for the possible false impression that 2 Thes. 2:1-12 might have created regarding an extended warning time before the parousia. As I show in the discussion of 2 Thes. 2:1-12, the intention of that passage was not to argue for the delay of the parousia, as is often maintained, but to demonstrate that the day of the Lord could not possibly have come. For early Christians there was no necessary contradiction between signs of the impending parousia of Christ and its sudden occurrence, as I shall show.

5:1 Here for the third time in the parenetic section of the letter Paul introduces a change of topic with a περὶ δέ ("now concerning") construction (cf. 4:9, 13). But here the topic is closely related to what immediately precedes it. The change of subject is also signaled by the direct address of the readers as ἀδελφοί ("brothers [and sisters]"), a device occurring frequently in Paul's letters by which he marks a change of topic (cf. 2:1, 17; 4:1, 13; 5:12), and by οὐ χρείαν ἔχετε ὑμῖν γράφεσθαι ("you have no need to be written to"; cf. 4:9). The latter expression, as noted previously, implies that Paul is simply reiterating previous instruction, a common feature of parenetic style. The περὶ δέ formulation here, as in 4:9 and 13, may indicate that Paul is addressing himself to an issue raised by the Thessalonians with Timothy when he visited them or perceived by Timothy to be a problem while he was in Thessalonica.

Although 4:13-18 involves the salvation to be brought about at the parousia, few scholars seem to have noticed that 5:1-10 views the subject from

177

the perspective of impending judgment and the possible threat that this might pose to Christians. The attempts of commentators like Findlay (107) and Morris (149f.) to distinguish between χρόνων ("times") as the duration of the periods before the coming of Christ and καιρῶν ("dates") as the quality of the times are unconvincing. The terms had by the NT period come to be synonymous (cf. Sir. 29:5; Acts 3:19-21) and were frequently used in collocation with one another in a stereotyped fashion (cf. Dn. 2:21; 7:12; Wis. 8:8; Acts 1:7). In 5:1 they allude to the parousia as a time of judgment. This suggestion is based on several considerations. The use of "the time(s)" as a cipher for the period (often the endtime) when divine intervention and judgment would occur can be found in the OT, particularly in Jeremiah and Daniel (Je. 6:15; 10:15; 18:23; 50:31; Dn. 8:17; 11:35; 12:1, 4, 9), in intertestamental Jewish writings (2 Bar. 14:1; 20:6; 1QS 9:13-15; 1QpHab 2:9-10; 2 Esdr 7:73f.), and in the NT (Mk. 13:33; Mt. 8:9; Lk. 21:8; Acts 3:19-21; Rev. 1:3). Paul himself uses the word καιρός ("time") to refer to the judgment in 1 Cor. 4:5. In addition the expression "the times and dates" is parallel to the expression ἡμέρα κυρίου ("the day of the Lord") in v. 2. This clearly alludes to the day of judgment.

The words "you have no need to be written to" (cf. 4:9) suggests that the timing of the parousia was a subject about which Paul had already instructed his readers. Undoubtedly he did so at the time of his mission to Thessalonica, but also in his previous letter to the community (cf. 2 Thes. 2:1-12). This is confirmed by 5:2. Nevertheless, mention of the parousia here and the discussion of at least one important aspect of its occurrence, namely, its suddenness and unexpectedness, reveals that Paul felt obliged to restate what he had told them or to give further instructions about it. This is not surprising since millenarian movements such as the apocalyptic Christian movement Paul established at Thessalonica inevitably develop tensions over the time of fulfillment when the expectations of the participants are finally to be realized. In what follows Paul does not give an answer to the question of when, perhaps because he recognized that it was dangerous for the movement to develop too specific an idea about when the end of the age would happen. The failure of the eschatological events to materialize would ineluctably lead to doubts about the Christian belief system and disaffection from Christianity. Paul deflects attention away from possible eschatological scenarios and agendas by stressing that his readers must always be prepared for the coming of their Lord. While this has given some modern scholars the impression that 5:1-11 contradicts 2 Thes. 2:1-12, first-century Christians clearly had no trouble holding together the idea of the imminence of the coming of Christ with a series of events portending its coming, as Mark 13 shows.

5:2 Paul explains in this verse why the Thessalonians have no need to be written to regarding "the times and the dates," as the connective γάρ shows. The subject of the clause αὐτοὶ . . . οἴδατε ("you yourselves know") is emphatic. Paul asserts that his readers "know quite well" (ἀκριβῶς οἴδατε) what is to be known about the parousia. Findlay (108) has suggested that ἀκριβῶς, found only here in the undisputed Pauline letters (however, cf. Eph. 5:15), may have been taken by Paul from a letter sent by the Thessalonians. This is possible but not necessary to account for the word's presence in the text. It is a literary device: As Best (205) has noted, this verse contains an element of irony. Paul reminds his readers that they themselves are quite well aware of the unpredictability of the day of the Lord because it comes ὡς κλέπτης ἐν νυκτὶ οὕτως ἔρχεται ("like a thief in the night"), that is, when no one expects it.

ἡμέρα κυρίου ("the day of the Lord") appears to be a fixed phrase already known well enough among Paul's readers not to require the article (BDF §259.1). It is parallel to the phrase "times and dates" from the previous verse and refers to the parousia in terms of divine judgment (cf. Nebe, *"Hoffnung,"* 96-98). It is derived from Hebrew *yôm Yahweh*, which the LXX translated as ἡμέρα κυρίου since in Hebrew *'ādôn* ("Lord") was read wherever the written Hebrew text had *Yahweh*. This made it easy for early Christians to transfer the OT "day of the Lord" to Christ, whom they identified as their "Lord" (see Phil. 1:10; 2:16: "the day of Christ"; Phil. 1:6: "the day of Jesus Christ"; 1 Cor. 1:8: "the day of our Lord Jesus Christ"; 2 Cor. 1:14: "the day of our Lord Jesus"; or, as in 1 Thes. 5:2; 2 Thes. 2:2; 1 Cor. 5:5: "the day of the Lord"). In the OT "the day of the Lord" is associated with the time of divine judgment against God's opponents (cf. Am. 5:18-20; Ob. 15; Joel 1:15; 2:1f.; Zp. 1:14-16), but for the people of God the time of judgment can also be a time of deliverance (cf. Joel 2:31-32; Zc. 14:1-21). The same twofold significance can be found running through the Pauline passages mentioned above.

In 1 Thes. 5:2, however, the emphasis is on the "day of the Lord" as a threatening time of judgment. This is implied by the two principal images Paul utilizes to describe it in vv. 2 and 3. First he says it ὡς κλέπτης ἐν νυκτὶ οὕτως ἔρχεται ("comes like a thief in the night"). This metaphor is found in the Q parable of Mt. 24:43 and Lk. 12:39, which compares the unexpected coming of the Son of Man to the unexpected coming of a thief in the night. Harnisch (*Eschatologische Existenz,* 94) believes that the image is derived from an otherwise unknown Jewish apocalyptic tradition. But Rigaux ("Tradition et Rédaction, 324) has rightly pointed out that Harnisch follows in this way a counsel of despair. The image of the parousia of the Lord, found in both Paul and the Q material, may just as easily go back to Jesus (Rigaux's view) or to an early Christian prophet who passed it into the traditions associated with Jesus (cf. 2 Pet. 3:10; Rev. 3:3; 16:15, which contain a simile based on this tradition). Whatever its origin, Paul chose this traditional metaphor in order to emphasize that the day of the Lord would come both at an unexpected point in time and that it would be a threat to those unprepared for its arrival.

5:3 The ominous character of the parousia, or day of the Lord, is heightened by the imagery of this verse: ὅταν λέγωσιν, Εἰρήνη καὶ ἀσφάλεια, τότε αἰφνίδιος αὐτοῖς ἐφίσταται ὄλεθρος ὥσπερ ἡ ὠδὶν τῇ ἐν γαστρὶ ἐχούσῃ, καὶ οὐ μὴ ἐκφύγωσιν ("when they say, 'Peace and security,' then sudden destruction approaches like labor [coming on] a pregnant woman, and they will not escape"). The statement has been recognized as having a proverbial quality about it (e.g., Best, 207; R. F. Collins, "Tradition," 336). The contents suggest that it may have arisen in an apocalyptic milieu (Rigaux, "Tradition et Rédaction," 325). Certainly the formulation is not typical of Paul. The words ἀσφάλεια ("security"), αἰφνίδιος ("suddenly"), and ἐφίσταται ("approach") are all *hapax legomena* in his writings. In addition εἰρήνη ("peace"), which usually has a religious significance in Paul, is parallel to "security" and has a nonreligious sense in this verse. Also unusual for Paul is the impersonal use of λέγωσιν ("they say"). This latter point leads Rigaux (*op. cit.*, 325) to conclude that 5:3 is apocalyptic in origin because the impersonal verb is characteristic of apocalyptic style (cf. Lk. 17:26f. par. Mt. 24:37-39). He further observes a correspondence between the suddenness of the coming of Christ and the need to flee what is to happen in both 5:3 and the apocalyptic material of Lk. 21:34-36.

The conception of the false cry of peace, while not strictly apocalyptic, goes back to the OT prophets, where it is associated with the false prophets who proclaim a time of peace when the destructive force of divine judgment is about to be unleashed on them and their society (Je. 6:14f.; Ezk. 13:10-16). The same idea is present here. Paul declares that when people speak of a time of peace and security as though everything were fine, "then sudden destruction comes upon them," and he adds in emphatic fashion that "they will not escape" from it.

The metaphor describing the suddenness of the day of the Lord, "like labor (coming upon) a women who is pregnant," was a natural one to apply in an eschatological context concerned with judgment. It occurs frequently in the OT prophets, where it is almost always used of the distress experienced in the face of divine judgment (cf. Is. 13:6-8; 26:16-19; Je. 6:22-26; 22:20-23; 50:41-43; Mi. 4:9f.), and from there it entered into the apocalyptic tradition, where it was used in the same way (cf. *1 Enoch* 62:1-5). Paul uses it here with a different connotation from the one found in the OT. He uses it primarily to illustrate the abrupt way in which the day of the Lord will occur, as its connection to what precedes shows. But it also serves to illustrate the inescapable trauma of the day of the Lord as the words "and they shall not escape," indicate.

Thus the metaphor of v. 2, amplified by the proverb and the metaphor of v. 3, stresses the unexpectedness of the day of the Lord and its ineluctability and destructive potential for those unprepared for its arrival. Paul has used these traditional eschatological and apocalyptic images, perhaps all of them already part of the Jesus tradition, for his own parenetic ends (cf. Meeks, *First Urban*

180

Christians, 175). As R. F. Collins ("Tradition," 337) has observed, "Paul has adapted and structured some pre-Pauline apocalyptic themes *in order to create an apocalyptic scenario which will impart a note of urgency to the paraenesis which will follow*" (emphasis added).

5:4 Here Paul begins the actual parenesis, building on the foundation of the motivational material regarding the day of the Lord in vv. 2f. In this and the subsequent verses he contrasts darkness and night with light and day (vv. 4f.), those who sleep with those who remain watchful (vv. 6-7a), and drunkenness with sobriety (vv. 7b-8a). Such antithetical pairs are characteristic of the dualism of apocalyptic writings (see especially the various Qumran documents) and serve to divide humanity and even the cosmos itself into simplistic categories. At the same time they strengthen group identity and the group boundaries of those who employ the antitheses to create their own positive self-image (cf. Meeks, *First Urban Christians,* 94-96).

In v. 4 Paul poignantly directs his readers to the point of what he was saying in the previous verses, as the somewhat emphatic form of address, ὑμεῖς δέ, ἀδελφοί ("but you, brothers [and sisters]"), reveals. The connective δέ ("but") contrasts them with those in the previous verse whose destruction will occur suddenly when they least expect it.

The words οὐκ ἐστὲ ἐν σκότει ("you are not in darkness") also take up the thought of the previous verse and imply a contrast between Paul's readers and those who live ἐν σκότει ("in darkness") outside their group. The phrase "in darkness" can have two possible senses here. (1) It may mean that those spoken of in the previous verse are distant from and even opposed to God. The use of language regarding light to symbolize God and darkness to symbolize alienation from and opposition to God goes back to the OT (cf. Job 22:9-11; Pss. 27:1; 74:20; 82:5; 112:4; Is. 2:5; 9:2; 60:19f.; Pr. 4:18f.). It also played a significant role at Qumran (cf. 1QS 3:13-4:26; 1QM). Paul himself uses the imagery of light and darkness in a similar fashion on several occasions (cf. Rom. 13:12; 2 Cor. 4:6; 6:14; 11:14; Col. 1:12f.). (2) Paul may be using the phrase "in darkness" figuratively of ignorance (cf. Rom. 1:21; 2:19; 1 Cor. 4:5). This understanding would go well with the following result clause ἵνα ἡ ἡμέρα ὑμᾶς ὡς κλέπτης καταλάβῃ ("so that the day [of the Lord] does not overtake you as a thief"). Understood in this way v. 4 emphasizes that Christians differ from outsiders in that they are *aware* of the imminence of the day of the Lord, while the day will overtake those who are ignorant about its coming like a thief. On the other hand, the light and darkness antithesis of v. 5 suggests that Paul has in mind darkness as that which is alien and opposed to God. If we accept this interpretation the second possibility mentioned above is implicit in any case since those who live in the darkness of their pagan ways also live in ignorance of the coming day of judgment.

ἡ ἡμέρα ("the day") refers back to the day of the Lord in v. 2 just as ὡς κλέπτης ("like a thief") picks up the thief metaphor from v. 2. (Those Alexandrian texts having κλέπτης in the accusative plural represent a secondary reading by scribes who applied the simile to the subject of v. 2, "you yourselves," instead of to ἡμέρα, with the resultant sense of "you are not in the darkness so that the day overtakes you like [it overtakes] thieves in the night.") The threatening nature of the day of the Lord is probably implied by the verb καταλάβῃ, which is often used in relation to something hostile or frightening (BAGD, 413). Clearly the day of the Lord will be just such a time for those who are unprepared for its arrival.

5:5   The reason why the Thessalonians are not in darkness and therefore unprepared for the coming time of judgment is given in v. 5: πάντες γὰρ ὑμεῖς υἱοὶ φωτός ἐστε καὶ υἱοὶ ἡμέρας ("for you are all children [literally: sons] of the light and children [literally: sons] of the day"). They have come out of darkness, out of their pagan past (1:9f.), and have entered into what Paul elsewhere calls the light of the gospel of the glory of Christ (2 Cor. 4:4). For this reason he applies to them the designation "children of light."

The combination of "son of" used in a figurative sense with a descriptive or possessive genitive is a Hebraism (see BDF §162.6; Turner, *Syntax,* 207f.) reflective of a patriarchal society. It occurs regularly in the OT (e.g., 1 Sa. 2:12; Ps. 89:22; Is. 14:12; 19:11; 49:15; 61:5; 62:8—note that some of these are rendered very differently from the original Hebrew in modern English translations), and is also found in the NT (cf. Mk. 3:17; Mt. 9:15 [Greek]; Lk. 10:6; 16:8; Jn. 17:12; Eph. 2:2). The precise formulation "sons of light" (τοὺς υἱοὺς τοῦ φωτός) appears in Lk. 16:8 (cf. Jn. 12:36). But it is best known for its frequent usage in the Qumran documents, where the sons of light, that is, the members of the community who share in eschatological salvation available only in the community, are opposed by the sons of darkness, that is, anyone outside the community (cf. 1QS 1:9-10; 3:13, 24-25; 1QM 1:1, 3).

The "son of light" terminology plays a similar role here in 1 Thes. 5:5. It clearly distinguishes those who belong to the community of faith from those outside, who are part of the darkness to be judged and condemned when the Lord Jesus comes (cf. 2 Cor. 6:14-18 for use of the motifs of light and darkness to symbolize and reinforce the separation of members of the community belonging to Christ from outsiders who are said to belong to Belial; however, whether this passage is authentically Pauline or not is a hotly debated matter [see Furnish, *II Corinthians,* 371-383]).

The formulation υἱοὶ ἡμέρας "sons of the day" is not attested anywhere else and so may have been a Pauline neologism (R. F. Collins, "Tradition," 338). The association of light with day makes the connection of the two in v. 5 a natural one, but the metaphor "sons of the day" in the context cannot be divorced from the theme of the passage, the day of the Lord. To be a "son of the day" is to be one who awaits with expectancy the day of the Lord. Expressions such as "sons of the day" and "sons of light" reflect the patriarchal society in which they emerged (ancient Israel) and the one in which they were taken up (the Greco-Roman world). Today they should probably be translated inclusively (cf. v. 8). The "children of the day" are simply those women and men who belong to the day, and the "children of light" are those women and men who belong to the light.

By way of contrast and to emphasize the distinctiveness of Christian existence Paul adds an asyndetic sentence, οὐκ ἐσμὲν νυκτὸς οὐδὲ σκότους ("we are not of the night nor of darkness"). When it is taken together with the previous clause an antithetical chiastic structure is formed:

A You are all children of light
   B and children of the day.
   B' We are not of the night
A' nor of darkness.

This structure may not have been intentional since Paul does not include "children" with the two genitives "night" and "darkness" in their second appearances.

Nevertheless, he does make clear the difference between the Thessalonians and those outside, οἱ λοιποί of v. 6. While v. 5a defines the difference in positive terms, v. 5b does so in negative terms. His readers are not to be accounted as belonging to either night or darkness, that is, to the realm where God is neither present nor acknowledged. The antithetical language of v. 5 functions to reinforce the separation between those who follow Christ and everyone else who is viewed as an outsider belonging to the realm of darkness. Those who read this for the first time very probably gained a sense of power over their neighbors and particularly any who opposed them (see 2:13–3:6). As Christians they had "inside" information that would enable them to be saved from the coming wrath of God (cf. 5:9f.), whereas the rest of humanity who opposed them remained ignorant of the fate that awaited unbelievers. To the extent that the phrase "children of the day" refers to the coming day of the Lord, it is possible to see an allusion to the coming judgment in the word "darkness" because in the OT the day of the Lord is associated with darkness. It is an oppressive and threatening time of divine retribution (cf. Joel 2:2; 3:31; Am. 5:18-20).

The change to the first person plural subject in v. 5b (ἐσμέν ["we are"]) is noteworthy. It prepares the way for the exhortative material in vv. 6-8 where Paul uses the hortatory subjunctive to call his converts to participate with him in being ready for the coming day of the Lord.

5:6 Having described his readers as belonging to the light and to the day, not to night or darkness, Paul turns to draw a parenetic conclusion from this. As is typical of Paul, the passage moves from the indicative in v. 5 to the imperative in vv. 6-8. The transition is indicated by the words ἄρα οὖν ("therefore"). Paul frequently uses this combination (especially in Romans) when drawing conclusions from what has preceded (cf. Rom. 5:18; 7:3; 8:1,

12; Gal. 6:10; 2 Thes. 2:15). The latter three references are particularly relevant since in them Paul pronounces ethical conclusions from what precedes.

Paul uses the hortatory subjunctive four times in vv. 6 and 8 to call his readers to participate with him in vigilance for the coming of the parousia. The first exhortation uses the verb καθεύδωμεν ("let us sleep") figuratively of those who are unconscious of the coming day of the Lord and of the urgency of religious and moral preparation for its arrival. Undoubtedly this metaphor was suggested by the contrast in the previous verse between those of the day and the light and those of the night and darkness. Those outside the community (οἱ λοιποί; cf. 4:13), who remain in the darkness of paganism and ignorance concerning the intentions of God, as well as of moral turpitude, are like sleepers who know nothing of what goes on around them. Christians, Paul exhorts, must not behave as though they are part of the sleeping mass of those outside the faith upon whom God's wrath will come.

To put the matter positively, Paul admonishes his readers by saying ἀλλὰ γρηγορῶμεν καὶ νήφωμεν ("but let us be vigilant and self-controlled"). γρηγορεῖν means literally "keep awake" and therefore offers a literal contrast with καθεύδειν ("to sleep"), but it also has the metaphorical sense of "be watchful" or "be vigilant," thus contrasting also with the metaphorical use of καθεύδωμεν in the first part of the verse. It is associated with apocalyptic eschatology in the early Christian tradition. In Mk. 13:34-37 it occurs three times in the conclusion of the apocalyptic discourse as the disciples are exhorted to be vigilant for the return of Jesus. It is also found twice in Mt. 24:42-44, where watchfulness is demanded in relation to the coming of the Son of Man (cf. the closely related tradition in Lk. 12:37). It is perhaps no accident that Mt. 24:42f. includes the parable of the householder who would have watched more carefully if he or she had known when the thief was coming in the night (see also Mt. 25:13). This may indicate that Paul drew on this specific tradition or one similar to it in writing 1 Thes. 5:2-8.

To the exhortation to be watchful, Paul adds the demand that his readers be self-controlled. The only instances of νήφειν in the undisputed Pauline letters are here and in v. 8 (cf. 2 Tim. 4:5). It literally refers to being sober (as opposed to drunk). In 1 Thessalonians 5, however, it is used metaphorically of the need for ethical restraint among those who wait expectantly for the day of the Lord (see 1 Pet. 5:8 where both νήφειν and γρηγορεῖν appear in a section of ethical exhortation). Watchfulness without such self-control would prove fruitless since readiness for the day of the Lord means moral and religious readiness for the judgment of God.

5:7 Paul appears to interrupt the thought begun in v. 6 (see comments on v. 8) by introducing a truism, namely, that οἱ γὰρ καθεύδοντες νυκτὸς καθεύδουσιν, καὶ οἱ μεθυσκόμενοι νυκτὸς μεθύουσιν ("those who sleep, sleep at night and those who get drunk, get drunk at night"). He probably hoped it would clarify and drive home the point of v. 6. Bruce (112) interprets the truism only as a factual statement. But in the light of v. 6 and the repetition of "night" from v. 5, where it stands in contrast with "children of the day," there can be little doubt that Paul intended v. 7 as a figurative underscoring of the exhortation in v. 6. What is true at the level of everyday human experience applies on the religious and ethical plane. Those who are unaware of the coming judgment of God, either because they have not heard or refuse to listen to the gospel, are "asleep" with regard to the danger of their situation. They see no need for vigilance. Similarly those who show no ethical self-control are "drunk" and in danger of divine wrath. Implicit in v. 7 then is the fact that Christians belong to the day and therefore their behavior must conform to the standards of the day and not to the standards of the night, where God is ignored, or worse, disobeyed.

5:8   The first part of v. 8 confirms the interpretation suggested above for the underlying thought of v. 7. The conjunction δέ has its normal adversative function in this verse so that ἡμεῖς δὲ ἡμέρας ὄντες νήφωμεν ("but let us who are of the day be self-controlled") contrasts sharply with the clause "those who get drunk get drunk at night" in v. 7. V. 8a adds nothing new to the exhortation found in v. 6, but it does make clear the link in Paul's mind between vigilant, self-controlled behavior and belonging to the day rather than to the night. V. 8a reasserts the last point of the exhortation in v. 6 and is probably intended as a summary of v. 6. This and the lack of any logical connection between "let us be self-controlled" (v. 8) and the participle ἐνδυσάμενοι ("having put on") that is dependent on it suggest that v. 7 is a parenthetical remark that disrupted the train of Paul's thought. (It should not be forgotten that Paul in all likelihood dictated his letters [cf. Rom. 16:22] and such breaks in thought are common in dictation.) If this is correct v. 8 is a somewhat ineffectual attempt to get back on course so that Paul can introduce a third item in his exhortation, namely, the need to put on Christian armor as a protection against the possible dangers of darkness (cf. Rom. 13:12, where Paul calls on his readers to put on the armor of light as a defense against the deeds of darkness).

The aorist tense of the participial phrase ἐνδυσάμενοι θώρακα πίστεως καὶ ἀγάπης καὶ περικεφαλαίαν ἐλπίδα σωτηρίας ("having put on a breastplate of faith and love and as a helmet the hope of salvation") presupposes an action antecedent to the main verb and thus renders difficult the interpretation of Marshall (138), who claims that the action was "coincident with the adoption of a sober attitude." Presumably, if Lightfoot, whom Frame (187) quotes, is correct that Paul moved from vigilance to the idea of the sentry equipped and on guard duty (Marshall agrees with this picture, which he takes over from Best), then logically putting on equipment would occur before taking up the post requiring vigilance. Whether we should understand the participle "having put on" as referring back to the time of conversion is not altogether clear, and in fact the time when it is done is not particularly relevant to the imagery in the present context.

θώραξ ("breastplate") and περικεφαλαία ("helmet") as a combination almost certainly go back to Is. 59:17, where God is said to "put on righteousness as a breastplate and a helmet of salvation." This is probably why Paul does not add a third item of armor to his formulation even though he uses the triad of faith, love, and hope, which would have fit more neatly with three items of armor (cf. Eph. 6:14-17, which develops the theme of Is. 59:17 more explicitly as other items of equipment are added to the original two; each item is then correlated with a particular Christian virtue or concept). Paul has only used Is. 59:17 as a point of departure, applying an image used exclusively of God in that text to himself and his readers. He does so by modifying the characteristics associated with the two pieces of armor to conform to the Christian triad of faith, love, and hope. The original connection of salvation with the helmet of God in Is. 59:17 may have suggested to Paul the possibility of using the imagery of armor in this context in the first place.

The expression "hope of salvation" is of considerable importance in understanding Paul's views regarding salvation at the time that he wrote the letter. He believed that salvation for the Christian still lay in the future when Christ would come from heaven for his people (cf. 1:3; 4:16f.; 5:9f.), and therefore it was the object of Christian hope in the present. This sense of expectancy is considerably diminished in some of the later letters of the Pauline corpus, for example in Ephesians, where salvation has already been achieved, and thus a strongly realized eschatology is present (see Eph. 2:1-10). The striking difference between the "hope of salvation" in 1 Thes. 5:8 (cf. Rom. 13:11) and the "realized" salvation of Ephesians 2 is one of the principal reasons why many scholars find the Pauline authorship of Ephesians a major difficulty.

Paul has introduced the triad of faith, love, and hope into the parenetic section of 1 Thessalonians to remind his readers of the need to maintain these Christian virtues. Maximum preparedness is required of the readers because the time of their salvation is potentially close at hand.

5:9-10 In the causal clause of vv. 9f. Paul offers a motivation for the Christian behavior enjoined on the Thessalonians in vv. 6 and 8. The reason he and his readers must be vigilant and self-controlled is expressed in the words ὅτι οὐκ ἔθετο ἡμᾶς ὁ θεὸς εἰς ὀργὴν ἀλλὰ εἰς περιποίησιν σωτηρίας ("God did not appoint us for wrath, but for obtaining salvation"). In this clause Paul continues the contrast between Christians who belong to the light and the day and the rest of humanity who live in darkness, but now the contrast focuses on the diametrically opposite destinies of the two groups. This tends to reinforce both the motive of self-interest in being a Christian and the sense of ultimate well-being in spite of present circumstances.

In 1:4 Paul referred to the election of his readers with the words τὴν ἐκλογὴν ὑμῶν ("your election"). Here he employs the verb τιθέναι to denote God's role in predestining people to wrath or salvation. The fact that τιθέναι with the double accusative occurs in quotations from the OT (cf. Rom. 4:17 citing Gn. 17:5; Rom. 9:33 citing Is. 28:16; outside Paul see Acts 13:7 citing Is. 49:7) has led Rigaux ("Tradition et Rédaction," 333) to view it as a Hebraism. As it is perfectly good Greek, however, this seems to read too much into the expression. On the other hand those like Harnisch (*Eschatologische Existenz*, 121-125), Plevnik ("Parousia as Implication," 85-87), and Havener ("Pre-Pauline Formulae," 115-121) who believe that Paul may be using a modified form of a pre-existing formula regarding election or calling may be closer to the truth, although there is no agreement about the exact nature of the formula. The suggestion that it had a baptismal connection is little more than an overworked assumption, as baptism is used as a catch-all *Sitz im Leben* for traditional material (cf. Best, 215f. on 5:4-8 and Havener, "Pre-Pauline Formulae," 120f., who seems ambivalent about the matter with regard to vv. 9f. but offers important words of caution about attempts to isolate baptismal traditions). If Paul is in fact making use of already existing material, Havener is probably correct that he has put together a tradition about divine calling or election containing the stereotyped expression εἰς περιποίησιν ("for obtaining"; cf. 2 Thes. 2:14; Eph. 1:11-14; 1 Pet. 2:9; Heb. 10:39) with a well-known credal formula concerning Christ's death "for us."

The contrast in v. 9 between wrath and salvation is significant. The wrath of God played an important role in the thought of Paul and the Thessalonians, as 2:16 and especially 1:10 show (cf. Rom. 1:18; 2:5; 5:9). The idea derives from the OT, where the day of the Lord is presented as a time when the wrath of God will be manifested against all disobedience (Zp. 1:15; 2:2; Joel 1:15; Ob. 15). The reference to the wrath of God in v. 9 had a double function for the original readers. On the one hand it defined Christian identity negatively in terms of those not destined to wrath. On the other hand it served to comfort and reassure the readers of the letter that their efforts at vigilance and ethical propriety would not go unrewarded. God had appointed them "for obtaining salvation." This phrase picks up σωτηρία ("salvation") from the previous verse, where it specifies the content of Christian hope. Here it indicates that their hope will be realized because this is their divinely appointed destiny. Paul does not specify the content of salvation in v. 9 except negatively as the avoidance of divine wrath and later in v. 10 as continued existence with Christ beyond the day of judgment.

περιποίησιν with the objective genitive σωτηρίας has the active sense of acquiring or obtaining (cf. 2 Thes. 2:14). This is important for our overall understanding of the passage. Koester ("I Thessalonians," 43f.) claims that Paul has "de-eschatologized" the apocalyptic thrust of the original material used in 5:1-10 in order to undermine eschatological expectation through an emphasis on participation in a present eschatological reality (cf. Harnisch,

Eschatologische Existenz, 136f.). This kind of interpretation ignores the significance of 5:1-3 for determining the meaning of the whole paragraph. As Nebe (*"Hoffnung,"* 109) maintains, the whole of 5:1-11 emphasizes the character of eschatological salvation as a process. That salvation is something to be obtained, that it is an object of hope for Paul and his readers (v. 8), warns against minimizing the future orientation of 5:1-10.

In vv. 9b and 10a Paul grounds the hope for salvation in christology and more particularly in Christ's death. The phrase διὰ τοῦ κυρίου ἡμῶν Ἰησοῦ Χριστοῦ, τοῦ ἀποθανόντος ὑπὲρ ἡμῶν ("through our Lord Jesus Christ, who died for us") is grammatically to be taken with the verbal idea present in the noun περιποίησιν ("obtaining") rather than the verb ἔθεντο ("appointed"). Thus Christ mediates salvation itself and not the divine appointment to it. This fits with Pauline usage elsewhere. Paul utilizes the seemingly fixed phrase "through our Lord Jesus Christ" in several texts to emphasize that Christ is God's agent in bringing about salvation for the believer (cf. Rom. 5:1, 11; 1 Cor. 15:57). The participial clause τοῦ ἀποθανόντος ὑπὲρ ἡμῶν ("who died for us") is a traditional christological formulation going back to the earliest stages of christological reflection (see Wengst, *Christologische Formeln und Lieder,* 78f.; cf. Rom. 5:6; 8:3; 14:15; 1 Cor. 15:3). It is inserted here to explain why salvation is to be obtained through the Lord Jesus Christ. Without his death "for us" the believer's destiny, like that of the unbeliever, would be the wrath of God. It would be going too far to read a full-fledged doctrine of substitutionary atonement into this one phrase, but there can be little doubt that Paul taught that Christ's death was somehow to the benefit of his followers.

In the next clause Paul stresses the particular purpose of Christ's death: ἵνα εἴτε γρηγορῶμεν εἴτε καθεύδωμεν ἅμα σὺν αὐτῷ ζήσωμεν ("in order that whether we are awake or asleep we shall live together with him"). The connection of this purpose clause to what precedes it explains "salvation" in v. 9 as living together with Christ. Because of what God has accomplished through Christ and because of who Christ is, Paul does not need to elucidate the meaning of salvation further to his readers. The expression "we shall live together with him" is intended to invoke the same sense of security and well-being previously invoked by 4:17, where Paul told his readers that with the parousia they would meet Christ in the air, ascend to heaven, and remain in his presence forever. Implicit in this is the assumption that death, the ultimate limiting factor of human experience, will be overcome once and for all. Paul makes this point by alluding back to his discussion in 4:13-17, where he sought to demonstrate that both the living and the dead in Christ would share together in the salvation event inaugurated by the coming of the Lord.

The terms employed by Paul to make this point, γρηγορῶμεν ("we are awake") and καθεύδωμεν ("we sleep"), are drawn from the more immediate context of 5:6f., but there they have a very different meaning than they do here. In vv. 6f. they are used antithetically to differentiate those who are Christians and therefore keep alert for the coming of their Lord from those who are outside the community and are therefore oblivious to the approach of God's judgment. In v. 10 the distinction between those who are asleep and those who are awake does not pertain to preparedness for salvation. That Paul has reapplied the terminology of vv. 6f. to the problem discussed in 4:13-17 concerning "those who sleep" (κοιμᾶν in 4:13-17 is a synonym of καθεύδειν here) and "those who remain" (γρηγορῶμεν here corresponds to οἱ περιλειπόμενοι in 4:15-17) is confirmed by ἅμα σὺν αὐτῷ ζήσωμεν ("we shall live together with him"), which repeats the idea contained in the words σὺν κυρίῳ ἐσόμεθα ("we will be with the Lord") in 4:17. By thus referring back to 4:13-17 Paul pulls the eschatological parenesis of the letter together and ends it on a powerful note of hope for future salvation for both the living and the dead in Christ based on his redemptive death (cf. Holtz, 182f.).

The behavior of the Thessalonian Christians must distinguish them from the rest of humanity who have no hope of salvation and therefore no reason to be prepared for what is to come. Because Christians have been appointed to salvation, they must behave in an appropriate manner, that is, with vigilance and self-control, as befits those who belong to the light and to the day rather than to the night and to darkness. In other words, Paul uses the notion of election to salvation, only to be actualized on the day of judgment, as a motivation to encourage proper religious and ethical conduct among his converts in the present.

　　5:11 Paul concludes his parenesis regarding the parousia of Christ and the need for readiness by urging his readers to exhort and build up one another in faith. The conjunction διό is inferential, but v. 11 is certainly not a necessary or even obviously logical inference from what immediately precedes it. Paul's thought appears to return to his earlier assertion that the day of the Lord will come as a thief in the night, and therefore Christians must be constantly vigilant and behave as people belonging to God. It is from this that Paul's inference springs.

　　παρακαλεῖτε ἀλλήλους ("exhort one another") repeats the wording of the summary in 4:18, though here the emphasis of the verb is more on mutual exhortation or encouragement than on comfort as in 4:18. This interpretation is evinced by the words καὶ οἰκοδομεῖτε εἷς τὸν ἕνα ("and strengthen one another"), which clarifies and amplifies the exhortative connotation given to παρακαλεῖτε. Metaphorical use of οἰκοδομεῖν ("strengthen" or "build up") can be traced back to the LXX, especially to Jeremiah, where the prophet promises that God will "build up" Israel (Je. 24:6; 31[38]:4; 33[40]:7; 42[49]:10) and even Israel's neighbors if they call upon God (Je. 12:16). But Jeremiah also views his own role as one of rebuilding the community after the destruction of the evil nation (Je. 1:10). The idea of building up either the community or

189

the individuals who form it is found frequently in 1 and 2 Corinthians, where both the verb and its cognate noun οἰκοδομή ("edification" or "instruction") function to express this idea. In 2 Cor. 10:8; 12:19; and 13:10 Paul describes his own apostolic role as one of building up the Corinthians rather than tearing them down. The connection with the call of Jeremiah seems unmistakable (cf. Je. 1:10). But the apostle also speaks of the need for members of the community to build one another up (1 Cor. 8:1; 14:4, 17). Paul reveals the close relationship exhortation and building up or edification have in his mind in 1 Cor. 14:3, where he uses οἰκοδομή with παράκλησις ("exhortation" or "encouragement"), the cognate noun of παρακαλεῖν, to describe the function of prophecy within the life of the community (see O. Michel, *TDNT* V, 136-147 for a helpful treatment).

Paul's particular concern in 1 Thes. 5:11 lies with the mutual responsibility of members of the community to aid one another in inculcating and carrying out the ethical demands of the faith and in communicating the theological concepts supporting those demands. In the context of this verse the most obvious theological structure undergirding the ethical requirements of the faith is the promise/threat of the parousia of Christ. Christ's coming will be a glorious public manifestation of the Lord for his obedient followers, but the day of judgment for unbelievers and the disobedient. Thus the eschatological instruction of Paul served to encourage acceptable behavior among his converts with its promise/threat.

The most important factor, however, in ensuring that the norms of behavior taught by Paul were maintained was the sense of community fostered by the apostle among his converts. Group control and pressure are generally decisive in regulating the behavior of members of a group. Paul's implicit recognition of this has much to do with the relative success of his missionary activity as a whole and for the continuing success of Christianity at Thessalonica. In v. 11 Paul merely seeks to affirm the Thessalonians in their practice of mutual exhortation and edification, as the final words of the verse, καθὼς καὶ ποιεῖτε ("just as you also are doing"), demonstrate.

GENERAL EXHORTATIONS: 5:12-22

The penultimate part of the letter is parenetic in character, as was the previous subsection of the *probatio,* but the exhortation covers a number of different themes in vv. 12-22. Five basic areas of concern are recognizable: (1) recognition and respect for leaders (vv. 12-13); (2) exhortation of those who require it (v. 14); (3) basic instruction for personal relationships (v. 15); (4) requirements for Christian religious life (vv. 16-18); and (5) living with and in the Spirit (vv. 19-22). This series of injunctions has as its primary goal the ordering of community life and relations within it (cf. Laub, *Eschatologische*

Verkündigung, 69f.). Given its proximity to the statement in v. 11 that the Thessalonians should exhort and build one another up, Paul probably intends the exhortations of vv. 12-22 to perform that same function for the community.

To what extent Paul directed his admonitions to specific problems in the Thessalonian community is difficult to evaluate. He did, as we have seen, have considerable information about the state of the community from Timothy, but the very brevity of each individual item suggests that he was not dealing with issues that were crises.

Moreover, in Romans 12, part of a letter addressed to a non-Pauline community, Paul exhorts his readers in a way highly redolent of 1 Thes. 5:12-22. The following parallels are noteworthy:

1 Thes. 5:13b	Rom. 12:18
5:15	12:17a
5:16	12:12a
5:17	12:12c
5:19	12:11b
5:21b-22	12:11b

These similarities have led Best (241f.) to conclude that Paul was probably using traditional parenetic material of Jewish-Christian provenance. This may well be true, but Marshall (146) is almost certainly correct in saying that Paul has shaped this material in light of his knowledge of the situation at Thessalonica. In particular vv. 12-13a, for which there is no parallel in Romans 12 (Marshall's suggestion of Rom. 12:3-8 as a parallel is not convincing), may reflect concern on Paul's part regarding an undercurrent in the life of the community that, as I shall intimate below, may have had a social basis. This may be true of other parts of the exhortation as well, but we do not have enough information about the community to give us any certainty. On the whole the information in 5:12-22 has greater value for determining general characteristics of community life and personal relations within the Pauline mission than the specific situation prevailing at Thessalonica.

5:12 Paul continues his parenesis by addressing a new theme, as the direct address of the readers with the term ἀδελφοί ("brothers [and sisters]") shows (cf. 2:1, 17; 4:1, 13; 5:1, 14). The new topic is the proper recognition and deference to be accorded to leaders of the community. The verb ἐρωτῶμεν ("we implore"), while less forceful, is essentially synonymous with παρακαλεῖν ("exhort"), which Paul uses more frequently, and in fact they are used in parallel in 4:1, the opening verse of the parenetic section.

Paul's request is for the Thessalonians εἰδέναι τοὺς κοπιῶντας ἐν ὑμῖν καὶ προϊσταμένους ὑμῶν ἐν κυρίῳ καὶ νουθετοῦντας ὑμᾶς ("to recognize those who toil among you, and are concerned for you in the Lord, and admonish you"). The infinitive εἰδέναι is not easy to translate in this passage. More is meant than the usual "to know," "to understand," or "to recognize." Best (224) and Marshall (146f.) favor "to respect" on the basis of the meaning of ἐπιγινώσκετε in 1 Cor. 16:18 and, in the case of Best, on Ignatius of Antioch's use of εἰδέναι in *Smy.* 9:1. A better rendering takes εἰδέναι in the sense of "to acknowledge," a recognized meaning for the verb (see LSJ, 483) and the usual translation in 1 Cor. 16:18. If εἰδέναι were taken as "to respect" then ἡγεῖσθαι in v. 13 would be tautological. Furthermore, as I shall show, the meaning "to acknowledge" is decisive for a proper understanding of the verse.

Paul calls on the Thessalonians to acknowledge those who toil among them, care for them, and admonish them. The three participles, κοπιῶντας, προϊσταμένους, and νουθετοῦντας, are connected into a series by the repetition of καί, and the article with κοπιῶντας governs all three of them. This means that Paul is talking about one group of individuals in terms of three aspects of their activity.

κοπιᾶν is used generally of physical labor (2 Thes. 3:8; 1 Cor. 4:12) but more commonly in Paul's letters of his own activity in spreading the gospel (1 Cor. 15:10; Gal. 4:11; Phil. 2:16; Col. 1:29) or the efforts of others on behalf of the gospel (1 Cor. 16:16; Rom. 16:6, 12). 1 Cor. 16:16 is especially interesting because the verse requires obedience to those who toil among the Corinthians. I will come back to the significance of this later. The verb undoubtedly has the sense of toiling for the needs of the church in 1 Thes. 5:12, as it is coupled with the words "among you." Paul does not give any indication of what this "toiling" consisted. Presumably the Thessalonians knew to what and to whom Paul alluded.

The next term is amenable to several different interpretations. προϊσταμένους may mean "those who rule you," "those who are concerned about you," or "those who stand before you as protectors" (see B. Reicke, *TDNT* VI, 700f.). Rigaux (576-579) prefers the first meaning because he views it as better attested, and it seems to fit better with his understanding of the beginnings of a hierarchical differentiation within local congregations (cf. 1 Tim. 3:4, 12; 5:17). In Rom. 12:8, however, the participle occurs in a context enumerating various gifts necessary for the well-being of the community and is placed between ὁ μεταδιδοὺς ἐν ἁπλότητι ("the one sharing in liberality") and ὁ ἐλεῶν ἐν ἱλαρότητι ("the one showing mercy with cheerfulness"). There it is probable that ὁ προϊστάμενος is "the one who cares for others" materially. Best (223f.) interprets it in 1 Thes. 5:12 in a similar way, arguing that προϊσταμένους explains the more general term κοπιῶντας and that in this situation a transition to the idea of authority would be out of place. If Paul had intended the participle to refer to "presiding," it would have been more natural to have put it first rather than in the middle of the series. This argument is persuasive against the idea that the term should refer to those who presided over the church, and in fact apart from the problematic text of Phil. 1:1 we have no reference in the undisputed letters of Paul to those who could be said to "preside" in a formal sense.

The third possibility, "those who stand before you as protectors," is supported by Meeks (*First Urban Christians,* 134), who recognizes that the second sense is inherent in the third. As he points out, the letters to the Corinthians suggest that figures of relatively greater wealth and status naturally served as patrons or protectors of the community. (For a valuable treatment of the social position and function of the leadership group of the Corinthian church see Theissen, *Social Setting,* 83-99.) This understanding is confirmed by Rom. 16:1f. where the feminine cognate noun προστάτις ("patron") describes the role of Phoebe toward the church and toward Paul himself. The meaning "president," which the noun could have, is not possible in the context because Paul acknowledges that Phoebe served as a προστάτις to him as well. As Schüssler Fiorenza (*In Memory,* 181f.) has argued, this can only mean that Paul stood in a client relation to Phoebe.

Once we recognize that προϊσταμένους refers to those functioning as patrons of the community at Thessalonica then a further observation of Meeks may be introduced: "a position of authority grows out of the benefits that persons of relatively higher wealth and status could confer on the community" (*loc. cit.*; cf. Schüssler Fiorenza, 181f.). This is why those who were patrons at Thessalonica had an authoritative function as νουθετοῦντας, as "those who admonished" the church. Paul uses νουθετεῖν both for mutual admonition among Christians (Rom. 15:14; Col. 3:16; 2 Thes. 3:15) and for his own work among his converts (1 Cor. 4:14f.; Col. 1:28). In 1 Cor. 4:14f. Paul connects his admonition of the Corinthians to his role as their "spiritual father." To the extent that 1 Thes. 5:12 envisages a group of people responsible for admonishing the rest of the community in proper ethical behavior, their role is somewhat analogous to that of Paul in 1 Cor. 4:14f.

We can now come back to Paul's use of εἰδέναι. From what has been said regarding the three participles in v. 12 we can conclude that Paul had in mind the leaders who had emerged in the church on the basis of their functions within the community. He makes no appeal to persons appointed by himself, and thus it cannot be assumed that at this stage in the Pauline mission organized offices within the local church existed. Rather, as in v. 12, Paul calls on the community to recognize as their leaders precisely those people who functioned in such a way as to toil for them, to protect and care for them physically and materially, and to direct them ethically. Malherbe (*Paul and the Thessalonians,* 88f.) claims that Paul does not have a specific group in mind, but the grammar clearly suggests otherwise. As previously noted, the article τούς governs all three participles, which refer, therefore, to three functions exercised by one group of people. In light of 1 Corinthians 16 this group must be those who were in effect the patrons of the community (cf. Holmberg, *Paul and Power,* 99). What is implied here is that the rest of the church should be subject to them just as Paul explicitly tells the Corinthians to be subject to their patron Stephanas and his household (1 Cor. 16:15-16).

That we should understand 1 Thes. 5:12 this way is established by the fact that the command ἐπιγινώσκετε οὖν τοὺς τοιούτους ("therefore acknowledge such people") in 1 Cor. 16:18 is parallel to the exhortation ὑμεῖς ὑποτάσσησθε τοῖς τοιούτοις ("be subject to such people") in 16:16. In both cases reference is made to Stephanas and others associated with him.

Though Paul does not explicitly call for obedience to those who toil at Thessalonica, the request that certain people be recognized in the community probably implies such obedience. Paul seems to have in mind the need for the community to acknowledge as leaders certain of its members because they carry out important functions in its life. On the basis of our knowledge of Stephanas and his role as patron of the church at Corinth, it may be assumed that the leaders at Thessalonica were those who had sufficient status and wealth to act as patrons to the community. Such a non-egalitarian form of leadership should not surprise us as this is precisely the way leadership in the Diaspora synagogues emerged and it reflects the hierarchical character of Greco-Roman society. (For a brief overview of the development of local leadership in the Pauline churches see Holmberg, *op. cit.*, 112-116.)

5:13 Paul not only requests recognition for those who function as leaders of the community, but he also urges the Thessalonians ἡγεῖσθαι αὐτοὺς ὑπερεκπερισσοῦ ἐν ἀγάπῃ διὰ τὸ ἔργον αὐτῶν ("to esteem them highly in love on account of their work"). This whole infinitival construction is dependent upon the main verb "we implore" in v. 12 and is therefore parallel to the one in v. 12.

The verb ἡγεῖσθαι creates problems for the interpreter. The context seems to require the sense "to esteem," but this meaning is nowhere else attested for the word (see Rigaux, 579f.). Another possibility is to take it with ἐν ἀγάπῃ, resulting in the sense "to consider in love" or simply "to love" (see Findlay, 122f.). The usual arguments offered against this possibility are that "in love" is too distant in the grammatical structure from the infinitive to be taken with it and that the infinitive does not require a qualifying prepositional phrase. A third view is that the adverb ὑπερεκπερισσοῦ gives the infinitive the meaning "esteem" because "to consider exceedingly highly" is paraphrastic for this sense. Although there are no other known instances of ὑπερεκπερισσοῦ being used with ἡγεῖσθαι in this way, other adverbial modifiers are used in a similar way (see Hdt. 2.115 and Thucydides, *Hist.* 2.89). For this reason I prefer this third explanation, but whichever is chosen the meaning remains more or less the same.

In the phrase διὰ τὸ ἔργον αὐτῶν ("on account of their work") Paul explains why the Thessalonians should respect those described in the three participles of v. 12: their work is done for the sake of the community and its members. Therefore Paul urges that they be treated with the deference due to them.

In commenting on this verse Marshall (148f.) claims, "In the NT church honor is not given to people because of any qualities that they may possess due to birth or social status or natural gifts but only on the basis of the spiritual task to which they are called." This is a theological statement articulating an important principle, but it bears little correlation with the actual situation prevailing in the Pauline churches based on the evidence available in the apostle's writings. Theissen (*Social Setting*, 96) concludes after a careful survey of the evidence for Corinth that "in all probability the most active and important members of the congregation belonged to the οὐ πολλοὶ σοφοί, δυνατοί, and εὐγενεῖς [cf. 1 Cor. 1:26]." The few who were wise, powerful, and well-born were, according to the evidence from 1 Corinthians and Romans 16, those who exercised real influence in the community. Meeks (*First Urban Christians*, 51-73), who refines and extends the approach of Theissen, comes to essentially the same conclusions from a study of the whole of the Pauline corpus and relevant sections of Acts (cf. Holmberg, *Paul and Power*, 99-102).

If my interpretation of προϊσταμένους in the previous verse is correct, then the situation that prevailed at Corinth and elsewhere also existed at Thessalonica. It was the relatively better off and those with relatively higher social status who could afford to toil and care for the community at their own expense, serving as its patrons and protectors (cf. the implied social position and function of Stephanas in 1 Cor. 16:15-18 and of Philemon in the letter written to him). Theissen (*Social Setting*, 107f.), borrowing an idea from E. Troeltsch, maintains that already in Paul's writings a type of Christian "love-patriarchalism" can be observed. According to Theissen (*op. cit.*, 107),

> This love-patriarchalism takes social differences for granted but ameliorates them through an obligation of respect and love, an obligation imposed upon those who are socially stronger. From the weaker are required subordination, fidelity, and esteem.

The better off often manifested their love by accepting responsibility for helping the less well off in their material needs. Vv. 12f. seem to evince just such a social relation within the church at Thessalonica since Paul distinguishes between those who toil, care for, and admonish the community on the one hand and those who are to esteem the former highly in love on account of what they do.

The command at the end of v. 13, εἰρηνεύετε ἐν ἑαυτοῖς ("be at peace among yourselves"), is to be taken with what precedes since v. 14 introduces a new topic. It is asyndetic, giving it added force and emphasis within the structure of vv. 12f. Some important texts ($\mathfrak{p}^{30}$ ℵ D) have a variant reading, αυτοῖς with or without a rough breathing mark, for ἑαυτοῖς, which is the equivalent of ἀλλήλοις here. If the rough breathing mark is accepted then the meaning would be the same as ἑαυτοῖς; if, however, we accept the smooth breathing, then the rendering would be "be at peace with them," that is, with "those who toil." On the whole it is perhaps better to read ἑαυτοῖς since, as Rigaux (578) notes, it is easier to explain the transition from ἑαυτοῖς to αὐτοῖς in the textual transmission than the other way around. Also, as Frame (195f.) has observed on the basis of Rom. 12:18, μετὰ αὐτόν would be a more natural way of putting what ἐν αὐτοῖς would have to mean (cf. 1 Thes. 5:28).

Paul also urges that his readers be at peace in Rom. 12:18 and 2 Cor. 13:11. Outside Paul's letters similar injunctions are found in Mk. 9:50 and Heb. 12:14. From this we can infer that it was a piece of common early Christian parenesis. This poses the question whether its appearance in 1 Thes. 5:13 has any significance for the situation at Thessalonica. Frame (195) thinks that Paul sought to end friction between the leaders and the idle mentioned in 4:11, 5:14, and 2 Thes. 3:15. This is nothing more than a guess. Nevertheless the connection of this command (note the imperative mood of the verb) with the request that the members of the community acknowledge and esteem their leaders does give credence to the possibility that some tension did exist in the church centering on the de facto leadership role of the socially and economically more prominent members of the church. Perhaps, and this is only a suggestion, the reality of love-patriarchalism may have caused some to react with hostility toward the emerging class of leaders because they were excluded from that class. Taken together with the request for recognition and esteem of the de facto leadership, the command that the Thessalonian Christians be at peace among themselves was probably intended to support the existing social structure of the community against any who had more radical ideas.

5:14 The introductory formula "we exhort you, brothers [and sisters]" marks v. 14 as introducing a new topic. The formula is reproduced from v. 12 except that the synonymous term παρακαλοῦμεν is substituted for ἐρωτῶμεν. With Findlay (124) and others, it is tempting to see v. 14 as addressed to the leaders of the community because νουθετεῖν ("to admonish") was used in v. 12 of the leadership function and in this verse Paul instructs those who are addressed to "admonish." Against this is the fact that nothing in the text itself hints that any particular group is being spoken to (cf. Best, 229). As Holmberg (*Paul and Power,* 117f.) recognizes, although the whole church is addressed in v. 14 (cf. 4:18; 5:11), Paul does differentiate functions within the community, as 5:12f. and 1 Cor. 16:15f. show, and therefore some were more responsible than others for the sorts of actions Paul calls for in v. 14.

First Paul urges his readers: νουθετεῖτε τοὺς ἀτάκτους ("admonish the idle"). ἀτάκτους has two possible meanings, either of which is appropriate to the context. The original denotation of the word concerned undisciplined or disorderly actions or persons, but in papyri from the Hellenistic period it is used of idle or lazy individuals as well. If we accept the Pauline authorship of 2 Thessalonians, then the latter meaning is the more likely here. The verb ἠτακτήσαμεν ("we were not idle") occurs in 2 Thes. 3:7 and the adverb ἀτάκτως

196

appears in 3:6 and 11. While both meanings might fit for 2 Thes. 3:6, in 3:7 and 11 the concern is clearly idle behavior, and it can be assumed that the same is true of 3:6 as well. When this is coupled with the reminder in 1 Thes. 4:11 that the Thessalonians should work with their own hands, a strong case appears for understanding ἀτάκτους in 1 Thes. 5:14 as those who were idle or lazy. Nevertheless, the close connection between laziness and disorderly behavior should not be ignored. In 4:11 not only does Paul call for people to work with their hands, but he also exhorts them to aspire to live quietly and mind their own business. The same point applies in 2 Thes. 3:11, where Paul says, "For we hear some among you are living idly, not working, but being busybodies." He goes on to order such people to work quietly (μετὰ ἡσυχίας), an obvious verbal link with the exhortation in 1 Thes. 4:11 "to aspire to live quietly" (φιλοτιμεῖσθαι ἡσυχάζειν).

The connection between the exhortation to admonish the idle in v. 14 and 2 Thes. 3:6-15 has significance in another important way. The instruction to admonish the idle in 1 Thes. 5:14 reads like a reminder to do something the community has previously been instructed to do (see 4:11). In 2 Thes. 3:10f., on the other hand, it looks as though Paul has only just heard of the problem of the idle, and in fact it would appear that the emerging problem of indolence was one of the main reasons why 2 Thessalonians was written in the first place. The apparent relation between 2 Thes. 3:6-15, which treats the problem of the idle as a new one, and 1 Thes. 5:14, which treats it as an existing problem, favors my view that 2 Thessalonians was written before 1 Thessalonians.

Paul also urges his readers in v. 14: παραμυθεῖσθε τοὺς ὀλιγοψύχους ("encourage the faint-hearted"). The verb παραμυθεῖσθε can be used in the general sense of "to encourage" (cf. 2:12) or in the more specific sense of "to console" or "to comfort" in the face of death or a tragic event. The adjective ὀλιγοψύχους is rather indefinite in meaning and could apply to worry, fear, or discouragement, according to Best (230). Paul could have in mind those who were shaken by the persecutions experienced by the community (cf. 2:14) or those who had doubts and anxiety regarding various aspects of the parousia (cf. 4:13–5:10). Obviously, Paul was concerned for any who struggled with worry or doubt regarding their new faith, or feared rejection or persecution because of it. Such people, Paul recognized, needed encouragement from the stronger and more confident members of the community to enable them to persevere.

The same sort of imprecision also characterizes the next exhortation. Paul summons his readers to a third task: ἀντέχεσθε τῶν ἀσθενῶν ("help the weak"). Best (230f.) suggests that "the weak" are to be understood as Christians who sought guidelines on how to indicate their rejection of paganism. He bases his view on such texts as 1 Corinthians 8 and 10 and Rom. 14:1–15:6. Marshall (151) argues that Paul has in mind those who are susceptible to temptation and sin, on the strength of passages like Rom. 4:19; 5:6; 8:3, 26;

1 Cor. 2:3; and 2 Cor. 12:5, 9f. Linguistically it could also refer to the physically weak or to the economically needy. This latter deserves some consideration since προϊσταμένους ("those who care for") from v. 12 might allude to caring for the needy. Perhaps Paul left these exhortations intentionally vague knowing that his readers would recognize whom he was speaking about and then try to meet whatever their particular needs were, a view Best (231f.) appears to have some sympathy for. If this is what Paul was attempting to do, he sought to give the whole community a sense of pastoral responsibility.

The final charge, μακροθυμεῖτε πρὸς πάντας ("be patient toward everyone"), is probably intended to enjoin patience on those who admonish, encourage, and help fellow Christians. Patience is an important virtue for the Christian according to Paul (Gal. 5:22) and is in fact a manifestation of love (1 Cor. 13:4). The need for patience in dealing with the sorts of people Paul has in mind in v. 14 is obvious since such people often become irritating and burdensome to those who seek to care for them.

5:15 A tendency exists among commentators to link the negative and positive statements of this verse with the general injunction at the end of v. 14 calling for patience toward everyone (cf. Frame, 198f.; Best, 233; Marshall, 152). This is unnecessary. Paul is merely presenting a series of exhortations loosely connected by the fact that they prescribe (or in v. 15a, proscribe) certain types of conduct among members of the community. These exhortations are intended to encourage the cohesion of the community. Only within a stable community could the plausibility of people's faith and commitment be maintained. As Berger (*Social Reality,* 55) has pointed out, "The reality of the Christian world depends upon the presence of social structures within which this reality is taken for granted. . . ." By his exhortations in 1 Thessalonians Paul sought to shape the Christian community into a stable environment in order to ensure that Christianity would remain real to his converts.

In v. 15 the exhortation takes the form of an aphorism with general applicability for regulating relations both inside and outside the community, as εἰς ἀλλήλους καὶ εἰς πάντας ("toward one another and toward everyone") at the end of the verse demonstrates. The whole sentence, ὁρᾶτε μή τις κακὸν ἀντὶ κακοῦ τινι ἀποδῷ, ἀλλὰ πάντοτε τὸ ἀγαθὸν διώκετε [καὶ] εἰς ἀλλήλους καὶ εἰς πάντας ("See that no one returns evil for evil, but always pursue what is good toward one another and toward everyone"), contains several unusual features. First, it is the only instance of Paul using ὁρᾶτε ("see") as a parenetic verb. Second, a shift occurs from second person ὁρᾶτε to the indefinite pronoun τις, the subject of the negated aorist subjunctive verb ἀποδῷ ("returns"), which itself has the force of an imperative. The indefiniteness of the subject in the negative statement after the definiteness of the second person plural ὁρᾶτε and the shift back to the second person plural in the second half of the verse suggest that Paul is quoting an aphorism.

The proscription of retaliation has its roots in the sapiential tradition of Judaism that rejected the *lex talionis* of Israelite religion (cf. Pr. 20:22; Sir. 28:1-7). But Paul does not merely forbid any form of retaliation, he goes on by way of contrast to say, "but pursue what is good toward one another and everyone." This further imperative gives the impression that Paul believed in and inculcated an unqualified selflessness on the part of Christians. Such an impression stands in tension with other statements in Paul where an underlying motive is mentioned that undermines the high moral tone of v. 15b. In Rom. 12:17-21 Paul expresses the same thought as in 1 Thes. 5:15 when he urges: "Repay no one evil for evil, but have regard for what is noble in the eyes of everyone." He then motivates this on the grounds that God's wrath will exact retribution in the judgment so that it is unnecessary for Christians to avenge themselves in the here and now. The same idea of God's judgment as revenge is to be found in 2 Thes. 1:6, where Paul declares that God will afflict in turn those who afflict the Thessalonians at the time of the judgment.

While Christianity was a tremendous force for what we today would call the humanizing of its world and the humanizing of relations between people, its roots in the apocalyptic tradition of Judaism also carried with it the seeds of a "loveless Christianity" toward those who were outsiders. Paul himself, whether consciously or unconsciously, reflects that tension, and when 1 Thes. 5:15 is read alongside 2:14-16 and 2 Thessalonians 1 it is clear that the tension existed in his teaching to the Thessalonians. Nevertheless, in 1 Thes. 5:15 the apostle demands an unqualified concern on the part of all his readers for the well-being of both those within and outside the community without offering either negative or positive motivation. For this reason it seems likely that Paul is reiterating here what he had previously taught the Thessalonians. Whatever may have been his explicit motivation, the underlying motives probably reflect his desire to foster solidarity in the community and to encourage the sort of behavior toward those outside that might lead to their conversion and inclusion in it, even among those who had been responsible for afflicting the community at an earlier stage.

5:16 So far in this section Paul's exhortation has been directed to matters of responsible behavior in interpersonal relations inside and even outside the community. In vv. 16-22 he turns to the readers' religious duties. Each of the three actions that he commands in vv. 16-18 either has its source in God, as in the case of the first one, or is directed toward God, as in the case of the last two.

He first instructs his readers, πάντοτε χαίρετε ("rejoice always"). This is an integral part of Christian living, as other Pauline texts such as Gal. 5:22 and Phil. 4:4 reveal. The subject of joy or rejoicing has come up in 1 Thessalonians several times already. In 1:6 we read how the Thessalonians "received the word in much tribulation with the joy of the Holy Spirit." There the Spirit is portrayed as the source of their joy, and as I suggested in my discussion of that verse, their joy was closely associated with their confidence in future salvation and vindication as part of the community of God's people. In 3:9 Paul asks the rhetorical question, "What thanks are we able to give to God concerning you for all the joy with which we rejoice on account of you before our God" (cf. 2:20). Paul's rejoicing is grounded in his knowledge of God's working among the Thessalonians and is directed toward God. Although Paul does not spell out the source or basis of Christian joy in 5:16, the instruction to "rejoice always" derives its meaning from the earlier passages in the letter. To rejoice always is to see the hand of God in whatever is happening and to remain certain of God's future salvation. Without such conviction joy would not be possible in the face of affliction, suffering, and death.

5:17 Not surprisingly Paul wished his converts to be people of prayer. He himself was devoted to prayer as a fundamental activity in his life (cf. 1:2f.; 2 Thes. 1:11; Rom. 1:10; Col. 1:3, 9). In several of his letters he instructs his readers to devote themselves to prayer (cf. 5:25; 2 Thes. 3:1; Rom. 12:12; Phil. 4:6; Col. 4:2, 3). Undoubtedly he believed it was the Christian's duty to engage in prayer regularly. Since the next injunction concerns giving thanks, which is an integral part of Christian prayer (cf. 1:2f.), when Paul writes ἀδιαλείπτως προσεύχεσθε ("pray without ceasing"), he may well have in mind intercessory prayer (cf. 5:25), though the term is actually a general one for prayer. Obviously he does not mean this to be taken literally, but he does expect his converts to remember continually to pray for their own needs and the needs of others. This was presumably to be done both privately and in the corporate prayers of the church.

5:18 Paul's third injunction, ἐν παντὶ εὐχαριστεῖτε ("give thanks . . ."), requires the interpreter to decide whether ἐν παντί is temporal ("at all times") or expresses the circumstance ("in every situation") in which thanksgiving should be made to God. In favor of the former is that temporal adverbs qualify the previous two instructions and that in 1:2 and 2:13 Paul employs temporal adverbs with εὐχαριστοῦμεν ("we give thanks"). Against it is that temporal use of ἐν παντί does not seem to occur elsewhere in Paul (Best, 236). While the temporal understanding is to be favored slightly, the sense of what Paul is saying is not appreciably affected. To thank God at all times is to see God working in every situation to bring about the divine saving will. This is not to say that God causes suffering and affliction, but to acknowledge, as Paul does in Rom. 8:28, that God works for the good of the elect through every situation. For this reason the Christian is obliged to give thanks to God at all times.

Paul concludes the three commands of vv. 16-18 with the motivational observation, τοῦτο γὰρ θέλημα θεοῦ ἐν Χριστῷ Ἰησοῦ εἰς ὑμᾶς ("for this is the will of God in Christ Jesus for you"). There is no good reason for limiting this statement to only the last of the three injunctions. The parallel imperatival form of all three indicates an equal stress on each one. It would be indeed peculiar if Paul thought only giving thanks was the will of God, but not rejoicing and especially praying. Somewhat surprisingly Paul almost never grounds either ethical or what we might call spiritual behavior in the will of God (cf. 4:3, the only other instance). That he does so here places a very strong warrant on the behavior commanded by him. This in turn indicates how much importance he places on it for his converts. For Paul praise, intercession, and thanksgiving were not optional for the Christian, but were required just as much as proper ethical conduct.

The Unity and Purpose of 5:19-22

The terse style of directives used in vv. 16-18 is continued in vv. 19-22 as Paul moves from the spiritual activities of rejoicing, praying, and giving thanks to the issue of the Spirit in the life of the individual and the community. Although it is possible that the command in v. 21a and the clarifying imperatives of vv. 21b and 22 could be taken independently of the directives concerning charismatic gifts and manifestations in vv. 19f., it seems much more probable that the conjunction δέ in v. 21 has its normal adversative function and therefore that a close link exists between the thought of vv. 20 and 21. This observation will be supported in what follows.

Some scholars, in particular Schmithals (*Paul and the Gnostics,* 172-175), see the instructions of vv. 19-22 as aimed at a very specific and problematic situation in the life of the Thessalonian church. Schmithals claims that Paul was trying to defend himself against an anticharismatic backlash precipitated by a group of Gnostic pneumatics similar to those who agitated within the community at Corinth and elsewhere. Schmithals's views are not convincing because he assumes his conclusion and then interprets the evidence to fit it. According to Schmithals, if Paul directs his criticism toward the over-zealous use of charismatic gifts, then he is attacking Gnostic pneumatics. If, on the other hand, as in 1 Thes. 5:19-22, Paul argues that spiritual gifts must not be rejected, then he is fighting a backlash against Gnostic pneumaticism within the community. In 1 Thessalonians the evidence is totally lacking to prove that a pneumatic problem of any sort was a serious factor. If anything 5:19-22 looks like support for Gnostic pneumatics, though it seems unlikely that such a group played any role at Thessalonica during the period when 1 and 2 Thessalonians were written. (See pp. 53f. above for further criticism of Schmithals.)

The most likely possibility for understanding the injunctions of vv. 19-22 is that Paul wished to encourage pneumatic activity as a sign of the eschatological times in which the Thessalonians found themselves (vv. 19f.). At the same time he sought to place restraints on such manifestations to prevent them from getting out of hand. From the present tense of the prohibitions in vv. 19 and 20 we may infer that some disruption of pneumatic activity was reported to Paul by Timothy and that he seeks here to prevent excesses. The nature of the problem will be discussed further below.

5:19 Paul first instructs the Thessalonians: τὸ πνεῦμα μὴ σβέννυτε ("do not quench the Spirit"). Clearly this prohibition involves the manifestations of the Spirit in the lives of individuals and the community. The succeeding verse shows that Paul is not primarily concerned with the role of the Spirit in ethical reorientation, as in Gal. 5:22-24. Rather he is concerned about charismatic signs, so-called *charismata* or gifts of the Spirit. These included not only prophecy (see v. 20) and speaking in tongues (cf. 1 Cor. 14:1-19), but also utterances of wisdom and knowledge, great faith, the power to perform miracles and healings, and to interpret manifestations of the Spirit (1 Cor. 12:7-11). Elsewhere Paul describes Christians as possessing "the first fruits of the Spirit" (Rom. 8:23) and as having received the Spirit as "a down payment" (2 Cor. 1:22). Apparently Paul understood the Spirit as a sign or proof that God's final salvation was to be given to the Christian community. Both speaking in tongues and prophetic utterance had a role to play in this. The former was a sign to unbelievers and the latter to believers (cf. 1 Cor. 14:22-25). To quench the Spirit was to suppress or restrain the Spirit from manifesting itself in charismatic activities like speaking in tongues and uttering prophecy within the life of the community (see F. Lang, *TDNT* VII, 168). This was tantamount to hindering the role of the Spirit as a guarantor of God's final salvation.

5:20 In this verse Paul offers a specific example of the way in which the Spirit should not be thwarted. Following the negative format of the previous directive, he tells his readers, προφητείας μὴ ἐξουθενεῖτε ("do not despise prophecy"). The noun προφητεία may refer either specifically to the gift of prophecy or to the utterances of a person prophesying. The accusative plural form of the noun here and the lack of an article favor the latter. From 1 Cor. 14:1 it is apparent that Paul placed a high value on prophecy in the life of the Church. The revelation given to a person who prophesied was primarily intended for the "edification, exhortation, and encouragement" of the Christian community (1 Cor. 14:3, 31). To treat prophetic utterances as of no account was to refuse to listen to God's word and God's will for the community. Paul qualifies his directive not to despise prophecy in vv. 21f. to prevent any possible abuse of prophecy in the church assembly.

The present imperatives of vv. 19f. do suggest some hindrance to or disruption of what Paul considered normal Spirit-inspired activity. To the extent that any group within the community stood to gain from suppressing the manifestations of the Spirit, it would most likely be the emerging leadership. They may have sought to control spiritual gifts like prophecy and interpretation of tongues. Because it is difficult to challenge what is uttered or done in the name of the Spirit, so-called spiritual gifts are open to abuse by those who wish to manipulate others. Spiritual gifts also give authority and status to those outside the ranks of traditional leadership. Thus, in order to prevent competitors, the patrons and leaders spoken about in 5:12f. sought to suppress spiritual gifts.

Jewett (*Thessalonian Correspondence,* 175f.), who holds a somewhat similar position, goes beyond the evidence, however, in finding an organized "charismatic" opposition to the community leaders and patrons. If problems were as serious as Jewett suggests, it is unlikely that Paul would have provided the "charismatics" with the support for their position offered by 5:19f. Jewett appears to be reading the Corinthian situation into the Thessalonian correspondence. If 2 Thessalonians was written prior to 1 Thessalonians, Paul himself may have been partly responsible for the suppression of prophecy because of his statement in 2 Thes. 2:2 that the Thessalonians should not be troubled by pneumatic utterances. But Paul immediately moves in vv. 21f. to put limitations on claims made in the name of the Spirit and deeds done in the Spirit. He does this so that excesses can be curtailed if they go beyond the norms of proper Christian demeanor.

5:21-22 Important as spiritual gifts were, Paul recognized that they could be abused and cause disorder in the church, as 2 Thes. 2:2 and especially 1 Corinthians 12–14 demonstrate. For this reason he balances his demands that the manifestations of the Spirit not be thwarted or disdained by calling on his readers to test them.

He charges the Thessalonians: πάντα δὲ δοκιμάζετε ("test everything"). The contrastive conjunction δέ is missing from some important manuscripts and witnesses, but was probably original. It may have been lost either by assimilation to the δ of δοκιμάζετε or because a scribe failed to see the connection with the previous verses (Best, 240). In the context the πάντα almost certainly refers to manifestations of the Spirit in the words and deeds of the members of the church. People were capable of abusing the gifts of the Spirit in various ways, such as making unchristian pronouncements (cf. 1 Cor. 12:3; 1 Jn. 4:1-3) or even self-aggrandizing statements (cf. Did. 11:12) in the name of the Spirit. Thus Paul exhorts the community to evaluate what is said or done in the name of the Spirit or under the supposed influence of the Spirit (cf. 1 Cor. 14:29). He does not specify what criteria should be used in determining whether something is good or evil, but presumably he expected his readers to weigh supposed Spirit-inspired words and deeds against the doctrinal and ethical norms they had received from him. While Paul does not say so here, it is the Spirit who enables a person to determine the genuineness of a word or deed done in the Spirit (cf. 1 Cor. 12:10).

The command τὸ καλὸν κατέχετε ("hold fast to what is good") explains what is to be done positively with those deeds and words tested and found acceptable and beneficial for the lives of individuals and the community. They are to be accepted and made normative for Christian self-understanding and behavior. On the other hand, in case anything should fall outside Christian norms, Paul instructs his readers in v. 22: ἀπὸ παντὸς εἴδους πονηροῦ ἀπέχετε ("keep away [or abstain] from every kind of evil"). Although the three imperatives of vv. 21f. go specifically with the statements regarding the Spirit and its manifestations in vv. 19f., Paul's readers would almost certainly not have limited their applicability to this alone. The need to test everything and then either accept or reject it on the basis of whether it was good or evil had general relevance to every aspect of Christian thought and behavior.

PERORATIO AND EPISTOLARY CLOSING: 5:23-28

Doty (*Letters*, 43), who practices form-critical analysis of Paul's epistles, calls this section the letter closing. The letter closings of Paul's letters vary to some extent, but each of them contains a benediction and normally a greeting, as well as a doxology (see Doty, 43 for a helpful chart on this). According to Doty v. 26 constitutes the greetings, v. 23 the doxology, and v. 28 the benediction. In the case of the greetings and the benediction there can be little doubt about the correctness of his view, but it is difficult to take v. 23 as a doxology. Vv. 23f., while couched in the form of a wish-prayer, recapitulate the major theme of the letter. Nothing else is remotely similar to a doxology.

This has led Jewett (*Thessalonian Correspondence*, 76) to designate vv. 23-28 with the rhetorical term *peroratio*. A *peroratio* is the concluding part of a speech or written discourse in which a summary of the major theme or themes is presented. This description seems to fit in an admirable way the content of vv. 23-24, but obscures the character of vv. 25-28. These latter verses form part of the epistolary framework into which the rhetorical structure is set.

5:23 Paul begins his letter conclusion with a wish-prayer invoking God with the words αὐτὸς δὲ ὁ θεὸς τῆς εἰρήνης ἁγιάσαι ὑμᾶς ὁλοτελεῖς ("now may the God of peace himself sanctify you completely"). δέ is transitional, while αὐτός has the effect of making the invocation majestic (Wiles, *Intercessory Prayer Passages,* 30f.). The description of God as the God of peace occurs on several other occasions in what Wiles defines as wish-prayers (cf. Rom. 15:33; 16:20a) and also in declarations of God's presence with his people (cf. 2 Cor. 13:11; Phil. 4:9). In each of these instances "peace" means more than that God is not a God of disorder. For Paul divine peace ultimately refers to eschatological salvation, as is indicated by such passages as Rom. 2:10; 5:1; 8:6; 14:17; Phil. 4:7. To describe God as the God of peace as 1 Thes. 5:23 does is to view God as the source of all well-being for the people of God, an idea originating in the OT understanding of šālôm (see G. von Rad and W. Foerster, *TDNT* II, 402-408).

Paul's first wish for his readers is for God to ἁγιάσαι ὑμᾶς ὁλοτελεῖς ("sanctify you completely"). The sanctification of the Thessalonians was already the last main theme in the earlier wish-prayer of 3:11-13, which, when taken with the present wish-prayer, thus forms a bracket around the parenetic material in 4:1–5:22, which has as one of its principal goals that of aiding the Thessalonians in the process of sanctification. In fact the thought of v. 23 is clearly modeled on 3:13. 5:23 recognizes that only God can bring about complete sanctification (with Frame, 210 I understand the predicate adjective ὁλοτελεῖς, which I have translated as though it were an adverb, quantitatively not qualitatively). This is God's will for the Thessalonians according to 4:3, but as this text suggests they are involved in the process of sanctification by virtue of what they do or do not do. For this reason we must interpret the aorist optative ἁγιάσαι as embracing the whole process. Aorists used this way are common in prayers (see BDF §337.4). The living of sanctified or holy lives is directed toward the coming of Christ and the day of God's judgment when believers will stand before God (3:13).

The second wish of the prayer repeats and expands on the first: καὶ ὁλόκληρον ὑμῶν τὸ πνεῦμα καὶ ἡ ψυχὴ καὶ τὸ σῶμα ἀμέμπτως ἐν τῇ παρουσίᾳ τοῦ κυρίου ἡμῶν Ἰησοῦ Χριστοῦ τηρηθείη ("and may your spirit and soul and body be kept complete, without blame, at the parousia of our Lord Jesus Christ"). The wording of this clause is problematic. The aorist passive optative verb τηρηθείη ("may it be kept") has both a predicate adjective, ὁλόκληρον ("complete"), virtually identical in meaning with ὁλοτελής of the previous clause, and a predicate adverb, ἀμέμπτως ("without blame"), which has to be translated as though it were a predicate adjective. The meaning of the verb and the predicate words is not in doubt. Paul clearly wants his converts to be found complete and without fault in every aspect of their existence at the time of the public manifestation of their Lord.

The most debated problem of the verse involves the juxtaposition of "spirit and soul and body," which appears to presuppose a tripartite view of human nature not found elsewhere in Paul, or for that matter in the rest of the NT. Jewett (*Paul's Anthropological Terms*, 175-183; see also *Thessalonian Correspondence*, 107f.) argues that this trichotomy derived from Gnostic or Gnostic-like anthropology, taken up by enthusiasts who sought to distinguish between the divinely given spirit and the corrupt human body and soul. He further claims that Paul sought to correct this understanding by his emphasis on wholeness or unity in the human being. Several objections may be made to this view. To begin with we have no evidence for a developed Gnostic anthropology this early. More significantly, if Paul had faced the difficulty envisioned by Jewett, it seems doubtful that a wish-prayer was either an appropriate or an adequate place to attempt to correct such a problem.

E. Schweizer (*TDNT* VI, 435) suggests that Paul is merely reflecting popular Hellenistic anthropology in the trichotomy of spirit, soul, and body and, given the liturgical setting of the statement, agrees with Dibelius (24) that this should not be taken as a precise description of the constitutive parts of human nature. This explanation, which Best (243f.) also adopts, seems to suit the passage adequately without involving us in speculative attempts to assign different aspects of human nature to each term. Paul's intention was not to offer an anthropological definition. Rather he sought to emphasize his desire that God would preserve his readers as complete human beings, blameless in the impending judgment of the day of the Lord or parousia (cf. 3:13).

In another essay Jewett ("Form and Function," 18-34) has argued that benedictions or wish-prayers like v. 23 function as summaries of the preceding section or letters. This is clearly the case with v. 23. It sums up the dominant theme of the whole letter, parenesis for Christian living. In effect Paul calls on God to aid the readers in their moral and spiritual progress. This would have the effect of reassuring the Thessalonians that they were under the protection of God, whatever circumstances they might experience. At the same time, the prayer takes up the theme of the parousia, which plays a major role in 4:13–5:11. Paul points forward to the coming of the Lord Jesus Christ as the consummation of the process leading to his readers' salvation. It is to this goal that the parenesis of the letter is directed.

5:24 Those Thessalonians aware of their own human limitations might well have wondered how they could be kept blameless until the coming of Christ. In order to avoid raising any doubts in their minds about their prospects at the judgment Paul reassures them by immediately adding, πιστὸς ὁ καλῶν ὑμᾶς, ὃς καὶ ποιήσει ("the one calling you is faithful, who will indeed do [this]"). The present tense of the participle καλῶν ("the one calling") stresses that God does not merely call Christians once and then leave them on their own. Instead God continues to call the followers of Christ to salvation. Mention of God's faithfulness by Paul is intended to assure the Thessalonians that God will not reject them or withdraw the call directed to them (cf. 1 Cor. 1:8f. where God's faithfulness is associated both with the day of judgment and God's call to Christians). Paul seems to have had in mind the fact that God would completely sanctify the Thessalonians, enabling them to be preserved blamelessly at the coming of Christ when all humankind would be judged. Paul did not have to add that his readers were required to pursue their own sanctification by living lives of obedience. The parenetic thrust of the entire letter made this amply clear.

5:25 Paul requests his readers, ἀδελφοί, προσεύχεσθε [καὶ] περὶ ἡμῶν ("brothers [and sisters], pray for us also"). This was a common request by Paul in his letters (cf. 2 Thes. 3:1-2; Rom. 15:30-32; 2 Cor. 1:11; Col. 4:3-4). Just as Paul and his fellow missionaries interceded on behalf of their converts, they asked to be remembered in prayer by them. This formed a bond of mutual intercession. If καί is accepted as part of the original reading, and the textual evidence is fairly evenly balanced on this, the point becomes all the stronger. Since v. 23 was a wish-prayer on behalf of the Thessalonians, Paul may well be alluding directly to it as an example of his prayer for the community that he would like the Thessalonians to reciprocate.

5:26 At the conclusion of three of Paul's other letters he asks his readers to greet one another with a holy kiss (cf. Rom. 16:16; 1 Cor. 16:20; 2 Cor. 13:12). In each of those cases he uses ἀλλήλους, but here he writes, ἀσπάσασθε τοὺς ἀδελφοὺς πάντας ἐν φιλήματι ἁγίῳ ("greet all the brothers [and sisters] with a holy kiss"). Masson (79) has claimed that the letter was addressed to the leaders of the community, and therefore Paul was instructing them to greet the other members of the church with a kiss. This goes beyond the evidence to a considerable degree since the letter was addressed to the whole church (cf. 1:1), not to a particular group.

The kiss in the ancient world had a variety of functions both within the family and outside it. Kisses were used to indicate love, respect, reconciliation, even the striking of a contract. They also played various roles in pagan cults (see G. Stählin, *TDNT* IX, 119-127). That Paul speaks of kissing all the brothers (probably kissing of the opposite sex was not encouraged—see *Apostolic Constitutions* 2.57.17 for evidence from the fourth century that probably reflects the practice from a much earlier time) suggests that the act had a family connotation for him. The community was part of the one family of God.

That the kiss was to be ἁγίος ("holy") indicates that it was of religious significance and may point to a setting in the liturgical life of the community (Stählin, *op. cit.*, 139f.), possibly the Eucharist, as Bruce (133f.) suggests. Bruce points out that Justin Martyr (ca. AD 150) speaks of the exchange of a kiss during the eucharistic part of the service. He also borrows from Marshall (145) to show that 1 Cor. 16:20-22 seems to presuppose that a kiss was given as a holy greeting at the time of the Eucharist in the Pauline churches. On the strength of this he suggests that Paul may have intended the letter to be read at the eucharistic meal of the community. Although our knowledge concerning the liturgical practices of the Pauline communities is not extensive, Bruce's suggestion is plausible, especially because Paul insisted that the letter be read to all the members of the church (v. 27), and the eucharistic service was probably one of the best opportunities for this to happen. Whatever may be the case with this suggestion, the holy kiss served to symbolize the unity of the community as the family of God.

5:27 The shift to the first person singular in the verb ἐνορκίζω ("I adjure") is unexpected, but probably means that Paul took over writing the letter from the amanuensis to whom he had been dictating or who was writing the letter on Paul's behalf. This corresponds to 2 Thes. 3:17, where Paul tells his readers that it is his practice to write the final greetings in his own hand as a sign of authenticity. The original readers would of course have immediately noted the change in handwriting, if this suggestion is correct, and would presumably have recognized it as Paul's since elsewhere the apostle seems to imply that his script was unusual (Gal. 6:11).

The exhortation ἐνορκίζω ὑμᾶς τὸν κύριον ἀναγνωσθῆναι τὴν ἐπιστολὴν πᾶσιν τοῖς ἀδελφοῖς ("I adjure you by the Lord that this letter be read aloud to all the brothers [and sisters]"), is stated quite strongly. ἐνορκίζω takes a double accusative and has a causal sense denoting that the speaker or writer wishes to extract an oath from the addressee(s). The second accusative, in this case τὸν κύριον ("the Lord"), indicates the thing or person by whom the addressees were to swear. The forcefulness of this statement is highly unusual, and in fact it is the only instance in Paul's letters where such a charge is laid on the recipients of one of his letters. Why he should employ such forceful language regarding the reading of this letter and none of the others is not altogether certain. To state the obvious, he wanted to make sure that everyone heard the letter because he felt its contents were of particular importance to the whole community. In the context no evidence is available to enable us to specify the part or parts he was especially concerned should be read to everyone. In the light of 2 Thes. 2:2 Paul's intention may have been to ensure that every member of the community was made aware of what he had said so that no further confusion would arise. ἀναγνωσθῆναι almost certainly means that the letter was to be read aloud to the assembled community. This would prevent it from being controlled by a small section of the community and used selectively. On the whole it seems unlikely that the textual variant ἁγίοις ἀδελφοῖς is original because the expression does not occur in any other Pauline writing and in any case is slightly less well attested.

5:28 In characteristic fashion Paul concludes this letter with a benediction. With the exception of 2 Corinthians, which has a more elaborate threefold benediction (cf. 2 Cor. 13:13), and Colossians, which has an attenuated one (Col. 4:18), the benedictions of Pauline letters show only slight variations. Variations occur in how Paul refers to Jesus ("our Lord Jesus" occurs in Rom. 16:20; 1 Cor. 16:23; and "our Lord Jesus Christ" in Gal. 6:18; Phil. 4:23; 2 Thes. 3:18; Phm. 25) and to the recipients of the benediction (the simple form "with you" occurs in Rom. 16:20; 1 Cor. 16:23; "with your spirit" in Phil. 4:23; Phm. 25; the more liturgical expression "with your spirit, brothers [and sisters]; amen" in Gal. 6:18; and "with all of you" in 2 Thes. 3:18).

The benediction here, ἡ χάρις τοῦ κύριου ἡμῶν Ἰησοῦ Χριστοῦ μεθ᾽ ὑμῶν ("the grace of our Lord Jesus Christ be with you"), is identical to that of Rom. 16:20 and 1 Cor. 16:23. The relatively fixed form probably derives from the liturgical language used by Paul and in the Pauline churches, but it reflects the profound theological conception of the early Church that Jesus Christ was the source of divine grace, that is, "the totality of salvation" (H. Conzelmann, *TDNT* IX, 394), for those who confessed him as Lord.

COMMENTARY ON
2 THESSALONIANS

EPISTOLARY PRESCRIPT: 1:1-2

The prescript of 2 Thessalonians is quite similar to that of 1 Thessalonians. The same three senders are identified; the recipients are the same; and the greeting again includes the words "grace and peace." The prescript of 2 Thessalonians, however, is longer. Because I have already treated the prescript of 1 Thessalonians in detail, I will only comment on those features peculiar to 2 Thessalonians.

1:1-2 The first difference between the salutation of 2 Thessalonians and that of the other letter addressed to the church at Thessalonica is to be found in the qualification of God as πατρὶ ἡμῶν ("our father"). The appellation of God as "our father" is common in the salutations of Paul's letters and in fact is only lacking in 1 Thessalonians (cf. Rom. 1:7; 1 Cor. 1:3; 2 Cor. 1:2; Gal. 1:3; Phil. 1:2; Col. 1:2; Phm. 3). It reflects Paul's conception of Christians as forming the family of God in a metaphorical sense and is to be seen alongside those texts where believers are called the children of God (cf. Rom. 8:14-23; Gal. 3:26; 4:4-7).

The greeting of this letter is fuller than that in 1 Thessalonians. But it corresponds to those of every other letter of Paul except Colossians (and possibly Galatians, depending on how the textual evidence is assessed), if ἡμῶν ("our") in ἀπὸ θεοῦ πατρὸς ἡμῶν καὶ κυρίου Ἰησοῦ Χριστοῦ ("from God our Father and the Lord Jesus Christ") is part of the original text. The textual evidence is divided fairly evenly on this. Both the presence and the absence of the "our" are explicable in terms of normal rules of textual criticism. A copyist might have added it to conform to the standard greeting of the Pauline letters or omitted it for stylistic reasons since the same wording occurred in the preceding verse. Therefore the precise formula of the original text cannot be decided on with certainty. In any case this is not a significant factor since God has been described already as "our father" in the previous verse.

Trilling (35), who maintains that Paul did not write 2 Thessalonians, claims that the prescript itself provides evidence for his position. He argues that the prescripts of 2 Thessalonians and 1 Thessalonians are more alike than those of any other two Pauline letters and that certain peculiarities of 1 Thessalonians have been preserved in 2 Thessalonians. The unusual features include the naming of three senders (two of whom play no further part in the letter), the naming of the addressees as "the church of the Thessalonians" not

213

"the church in Thessalonica," the direct connection of the recipients with God and Christ, and the absence of Paul's apostolic title. All this for him is a sign of inauthenticity as it reflects borrowing from the first letter in an attempt to create the impression of authenticity. He also believes that the expanded greeting in 2 Thessalonians (v. 2) is awkward because of the mention of "God our father and the Lord Jesus Christ" in v. 1. According to Trilling this may show an awareness of the standard greeting of later Pauline letters.

These arguments are questionable. The unusual details of 1 Thes. 1:1 might equally be used to argue for the inauthenticity of the whole of 1 Thessalonians. Moreover, the supposedly striking differences are not as striking as Trilling thinks. In both 1 Cor. 1:1 and Phil. 1:1 Paul associates others with himself in the writing of those letters. In the case of the former, Sosthenes, who is a co-sender with Paul, plays no further role in the letter, and in the case of the latter, Paul does not refer to his apostolic title, perhaps out of deference to his inclusion of Timothy as an sender of the letter. If Paul could address 1 Thessalonians to "the church of the Thessalonians," there is no reason why he could not have done it a second time. With regard to the supposedly expanded greeting of v. 2, it is just as possible that the greeting of 1 Thessalonians should be viewed as attenuated over against the normal one employed by Paul in 2 Thes. 1:2 and most of his other letters. To the extent that the repetition of "God our father and the Lord Jesus Christ" is otiose and awkward in the prescript it would have been so as much for an imitator as for Paul himself, and so this proves very little.

Trilling's treatment of the prescript must be rejected as an unconvincing attempt at substantiating his thesis regarding the inauthentic nature of 2 Thessalonians. If 2 Thessalonians is inauthentic, the prescript does not provide serious evidence for the thesis.

EXORDIUM: 1:3-12

Those scholars who practice epistolary analysis find in vv. 3-12 a typical opening thanksgiving segment expressing the apostle's thanks for the community and its progress in the faith. The limit of the thanksgiving section is set by 2:1, where the beginning of a new section is indicated by the introductory formula ἐρωτῶμεν δὲ ὑμᾶς, ἀδελφοί ("now we beg you brothers [and sisters]"; cf. 1 Thes. 5:12). As O'Brien (*Introductory Thanksgivings,* 168) has observed regarding this opening thanksgiving, it "has an epistolary, didactic and paraenetic function as well as giving evidence of Paul's pastoral concern."

While there is nothing exceptionable about the views of O'Brien and others practicing epistolary analysis, rhetorical analysis offers considerably more clarity about the function of vv. 3-12 in the overall structure of the letter. In rhetorical terms vv. 3-12 constitute the *exordium.* As I have discussed in relation to 1 Thes. 1:2-10, the *exordium* has two primary functions. First, it seeks to make the audience, or in the case of a letter, the readers, "well-disposed, attentive, and tractable" toward the person addressing them. Second, it should announce the main theme(s) of the communication. The material in vv. 3-12 fulfills both these functions. Paul compliments his readers on their progress in the faith in spite of persecution (vv. 3-4) and reminds them of the reward that awaits them as well as the punishment in store for their oppressors (vv. 5-10). This material helps create the mood for what follows in the letter. At the same time vv. 5-10 clearly introduce the theme of the day of the Lord and the fact that it still remains in the future. This is the problem to which Paul's argument is directed in 2:1-12. God's election of the Thessalonians, mentioned in v. 11, points forward to the theme of 2:13-17 and to the parenesis found in 3:1-15.

The *exordium* contains only two sentences in Greek, with the first running from v. 3 through v. 10 and the second comprising vv. 11 and 12. The first sentence is long and complex. The author moves from the actual statement of thanksgiving in vv. 3f. to a word of teaching and encouragement in vv. 5-10 centered on the impending righteous judgment of God when the Thessalonians will be vindicated for their suffering for the sake of the dominion of God. The *exordium* concludes in vv. 11f. with Paul's customary report of intercessory prayer for the recipients.

1:3 The *exordium* begins with a thanksgiving section, a feature found in all Paul's letters except Galatians. The thanksgiving actually serves as a form of praise regarding the readers' progress in the faith. This in turn works to establish *pathos* or a positive emotional response in the readers.

Here the thanksgiving is introduced with two expressions not appearing in any other letters in the Pauline corpus. The first is εὐχαριστεῖν ὀφείλομεν τῷ θεῷ πάντοτε περὶ ὑμῶν, ἀδελφοί ("we are obliged to give thanks always for you to God, brothers [and sisters]"). This formulation occurs again in 2:13, a second thanksgiving section in the letter, but nowhere else in Paul's letters. This statement is strengthened by καθὼς ἄξιόν ἐστιν ("just as is fitting"), which is also without parallel in Paul. Together these two clauses give the impression that it was a duty rather than a joy to give thanks for the readers.

The combination of these two unusual expressions in introducing the thanksgiving section has led scholars to ask why this deviation from Paul's normal mode of expression occurs here. Frame (221) suggested that the Thessalonians, in a letter sent to Paul with Timothy, had protested at Paul's effusive praise of them in his first letter by claiming that they were unworthy of it (cf. Bruce, 144, who takes the same position). This view remains at best hypothetical. But if I am correct that 2 Thessalonians was the first letter, not the second, it has no validity whatsoever. Aus ("Liturgical Background," 422-438), following the lead of Harnack, has argued that the language about "the necessity and propriety of giving thanks" may have a liturgical setting in Judaism and early Christianity. Even if this is so it fails to answer the question why this influence is seen in 2 Thes. 1:3, but not in the introductions to other Pauline thanksgivings. Others like Trilling (43f., see esp. n. 83) maintain that the uniqueness of the introduction with its supposedly cool tone is indicative of the non-Pauline authorship of this letter. Against this assertion is that the ὅτι clause that follows is full of warmth and positive reinforcement for the behavior of the readers. Marxsen (63-65) claims that vv. 3f. were intended as instruction for post-Pauline communities about how they should pray for one another and emulate communities experiencing persecution in order to share in the praise of Paul for the Thessalonians. Marxsen's position is methodologically interesting. He applies a redaction-critical method to his analysis of 2 Thessalonians because he believes it was written for the post-Pauline church. But his views, like most redaction-critical results, are by their very nature incapable of proof and in any case excessively subtle.

The most probable explanation for the language of obligation in v. 3 is that it indicates the compulsion Paul felt to give thanks on account of the continued faithfulness and progress of his converts. The obligation was not felt toward the Thessalonians but toward God who had worked among them. Thus the language should not be understood as distant or cool; vv. 3b-4 makes this clear. Quite the contrary, Paul's deep sense of gratitude for the readers *demanded* that thanksgiving be given to God for them. πάντοτε ("always"), a common feature in Paul's introductory thanksgivings (cf. 1 Thes. 1:2; 1 Cor. 1:4), should probably be taken with εὐχαριστεῖν ("to give thanks").

216

The ὅτι clause in the second part of the verse provides two reasons that Paul and his colleagues feel duty-bound to offer thanks for the Thessalonians. In the first place, he tells them it is ὅτι ὑπεραυξάνει ἡ πίστις ὑμῶν ("because your faith is increasing beyond measure"). The verb ὑπεραυξάνει is noteworthy in two respects. First, it is well-known that Paul is fond of compounds with ὑπέρ that intensify the meaning of the word. This is the only occurrence of this word in the NT. As Best (250) has noted, this is not the kind of linguistic usage that an imitator of Paul would have been likely to have noticed and used. Second, the verb is in the present tense, implying that the increase of the readers' faith is an ongoing process rather than an accomplished fact.

Trilling (47) tries to read πίστις ("faith") in v. 3 against the usage in the Pastorals, though he does not say so explicitly. This is unnecessary. A parallel understanding of faith as something that increases and leads to greater commitment to the beliefs and practices of the Christian religion occurs in 2 Cor. 10:15 where the simple form of αὐξάνειν ("to increase") is found. This is a very different understanding of faith from the dominant one in the later Pastoral Epistles. In the Pastorals faith is frequently viewed as a fixed set of beliefs to which Christians must adhere (cf. 1 Tim. 2:19; 5:8; 2 Tim. 1:5). On the basis of 1 Thes. 1:3, we can be certain that Paul had in mind an increase of faith manifesting itself in the deeds of the Thessalonians and especially in the way they had withstood opposition and persecution, as 2 Thes. 1:4 demonstrates.

Paul offers a second reason for feeling compelled to thank God for his readers: πλεονάζει ἡ ἀγάπη ἑνὸς ἑκάστου πάντων ὑμῶν εἰς ἀλλήλους ("the love of each one of all of you is growing for one another"). The wording is somewhat awkward but ἑνὸς ἑκάστου πάντων ὑμῶν ("each one of all of you") stresses that Paul was thinking of the readers as individuals whose love for one another was growing (πλεονάζει like ὑπεραυξάνει is in the present tense), just as their faith was increasing. This of course is another way of saying that their sense of community was developing as their sense of commitment to one another grew and revealed itself in deeds of love done for one another.

By mentioning their increasing faith and love Paul undoubtedly wished to further encourage these traits among his readers. Those who would argue that the writer of 2 Thessalonians is merely taking up the existing language and ideas of 1 Thes. 1:3 and 3:12 must explain why no mention is made here of hope, which would have formed a triad similar to the one found in 1 Thes. 1:3, and why nothing is said about increasing love for those outside the faith as in 1 Thes. 3:12.

1:4 The growing faith and love of the Thessalonians was not only a matter for thanksgiving to God, but Paul also praised them in other churches. By doing so he sought to provide other communities with a model of Christian commitment under adverse conditions. ὥστε ("so that") with the infinitive ἐγκαυχᾶσθαι ("to boast") indicates that the boasting done by Paul in other churches was a result of his readers' ever-increasing faith and love.

αὐτοὺς ἡμᾶς ("we ourselves") is the subject of the infinitival result clause and is normally said to imply a contrast because of the intensifying effect of αὐτούς. But commentators find it difficult to decide with whom or what the contrast is being made. Frame (224), for example, thinks Paul is contrasting the missionaries' willingness to boast with the deference of the Thessalonians themselves, but this is based on his questionable explanation of v. 3 (see above). Others have suggested that boasting was out of keeping with Paul's normal practice, but he felt obliged to do so in the case of the Thessalonians, or that Paul considered boasting sinful except in the Lord but made an exception with respect to the Thessalonians (cf. Rigaux, 615). 2 Cor. 9:1-5, however, seems to refute both of these ideas. Another possibility is that a contrast is intended with those mentioned in 1 Thes. 1:9 who reported so favorably concerning the Thessalonians, but an implied contrast with something mentioned in another letter appears too remote and subtle. Paul probably wished to say no more than that the Thessalonians' behavior had led to his taking the unusual (but not unique) step of boasting about their endurance and faith to other churches.

ἐν ταῖς ἐκκλησίαις τοῦ θεοῦ ("in the churches of God") is uncharacteristic of Paul. On every other occasion where the plural form of ἐκκλησία is employed it is given a geographic limitation. By contrast the singular is normally used for the wider church community. Here Paul simply means to suggest that he has boasted to various churches with which he has been in contact without limiting the reference to a precise geographic area (cf. 1 Thes. 1:8, where Paul speaks hyperbolically of a report sounding forth about the Thessalonians "in Macedonia, Achaia, and *in every place*"). This tells us something very important about the experience of the early communities founded by Paul: persecution was probably the exception rather than the rule for them, and therefore the perseverance of the Thessalonians in adversity was exemplary for other churches that might face similar hostility in the future.

Although Paul's boasting about his readers resulted from their increasing faith and love, he presents a more precise reason for it in the words ὑπὲρ τῆς ὑπομονῆς ὑμῶν καὶ πίστεως ἐν πᾶσιν τοῖς διωγμοῖς ὑμῶν καὶ ταῖς θλίψεσιν αἷς ἀνέχεσθε ("concerning your endurance and faith in all your persecutions and the afflictions that you are enduring"). Some have seen in ὑπομονῆς ("endurance," "steadfastness," "perseverance") a reference to Christian hope, thus completing the triad of faith, love, and hope begun in the previous verse. While it is true that Paul associates "endurance" with hope in 1 Thes. 1:3, the context here does not provide any real basis for interpreting the word as meaning "patient expectation," the sense it would have to have if the word were to substitute for ἐλπίς, the normal term for "hope."

The Thessalonians' endurance arose out of their refusal to renounce their new Christian faith in spite of intense local opposition to them. Paul brings together "endurance" and πίστις in this context. Here the latter has the sense of both "faith" in the new beliefs concerning God and Christ and "faithfulness" in maintaining the new beliefs and practices inculcated by Paul. In effect the Thessalonians' faith constituted the measuring stick for determining both their endurance and the basis of that endurance. In the next verse one of the central pillars of their faith becomes clear as Paul mentions the dominion of God for which they suffered. The Thessalonians faithfully endured intense opposition because of their hope in the future order to be revealed with the parousia of Christ (cf. v. 7). For this reason to say, as Trilling (47) does, that hope has become mere endurance devoid of "the characteristic dimension of hope" found in Paul is unsubstantiated. Faith and endurance are oriented toward future salvation at the coming of the Lord Jesus from heaven. It is unfortunate that Paul does not specify more clearly the nature of the persecution and oppression (διωγμός and θλῖψις are virtually synonymous, cf. Rom. 8:35) his readers experienced, though from 1 Thes. 2:14 we know that it was inflicted by the Thessalonians' fellow citizens (see the comments on 1 Thes. 2:14 for possible suggestions regarding reasons for the opposition).

When 2 Thessalonians was written, persecution and affliction were still part of the readers' continuing experience, as the present tense of ἀνέχεσθε ("you are enduring") shows. This is striking because in 1 Thes. 2:14 the aorist tense is used of the opposition they had suffered (ἐπάθετε), indicating that it was in the past. The oppression of the Thessalonians went back to the very earliest period of Paul's missionary work among them, as 1 Thes. 1:6 demonstrates. This implies, as I have suggested in the Introduction, that 2 Thessalonians was written during the initial period of persecution associated with the conversion of the Thessalonians, whereas 1 Thessalonians was written at a later time when the persecutions were a thing of the past.

Bruce (146), recognizing the significance of this for determining the order of the two letters, maintains that the aorist ἐπάθετε in 1 Thes. 2:14 does not prove that the afflictions mentioned in 1 Thessalonians belonged to the recent past as opposed to the present suffering mentioned in 2 Thessalonians. His only evidence for this assertion would appear to be 1 Thes. 3:3. This passage provides evidence that oppression had not ceased, at least as far as Paul was aware, when he sent Timothy to Thessalonica the first time. But this is no proof at all because a period of time passed between the first mission of Timothy to Thessalonica and the writing of 1 Thessalonians upon his return to Paul. There is no reason why the open opposition to the Thessalonian Christians may not have ended during this time, or even before Timothy was sent to Thessalonica for the first time, since Paul would not have received daily news about the state of affairs in Thessalonica.

Although it is thus possible that persecutions may have stopped for a time and then restarted, nothing in either 1 or 2 Thessalonians suggests that this happened. All the above considerations point to the conclusion that 2 Thessalonians was written by Paul for Timothy to take with him upon the occasion of his first return to Thessalonica, and that at that time Paul believed his converts were still undergoing affliction. The subsequent discussion in 2 Thessalonians 1 supports this conclusion. The strong statement concerning the impending affliction of those who afflicted the Thessalonians (v. 6) would have been more appropriate in providing comfort in the period of initial persecution than after opposition had largely subsided. The view of Best (254) that persecution was endemic in the early Church has no basis in the evidence available in the Pauline letters. Therefore it is likely that once matters had settled down at Thessalonica they remained stable.

One further point in v. 4 bearing on the order of the letters should be mentioned. Paul says that he boasts in the churches of God about the patient endurance of oppression by his converts in Thessalonica. According to 1 Thes. 1:6-8 the report of the Thessalonians' faithful reception of the gospel amid persecution is widely discussed among the churches of Macedonia, Achaia, and everywhere else. The relation of these two reports, one in which Paul reports of his own boasting to the churches (2 Thes. 1:4) and the other in which he reports that the Christians in various places speak so freely about the unique experience of the Thessalonians that he has no need to say anything (1 Thes. 1:6-8), is best understood if 2 Thessalonians was written first. Undoubtedly Paul and his missionary colleagues were among the first to carry the reports of what happened at Thessalonica to other groups of Christians. Once Paul had boasted of the Thessalonians, it became unnecessary for him to continue praising them because other Christians did so. Thus the change in circumstance reflected in the letters to the Thessalonians favors the priority of 2 Thessalonians.

1:5 The interpretation of this verse is pivotal for a proper understanding of the whole letter. Unfortunately it resists easy explanation. Uncertainty exists concerning the connection of ἔνδειγμα τῆς δικαίας κρίσεως τοῦ θεοῦ ("evidence of the righteous judgment of God") with its immediate context and the significance of the term ἔνδειγμα ("evidence" or "sign"). Since ἔνδειγμα can be either nominative or accusative, we must either supply ὅ ἐστιν or take ἔνδειγμα as an accusative in apposition. In either case the question arises as to what constitutes the evidence of God's righteous judgment. There are three possible answers: (1) It is the Thessalonian Christians' endurance and faith; (2) it is the persecution and affliction that they experience; or (3) it is their endurance and faith in the face of persecution and affliction.

The most common explanation among English-language commentators views the "evidence" as the perseverance of the Thessalonians in spite of persecution and affliction (see, e.g., Frame, 226; Morris, 198; Bruce, 149; Best, 254f. pushes this interpretation further by claiming that even Paul's boasting is included in the sign). Common to this understanding of the "evidence" is the belief that Phil. 1:28, where ἔνδειγμα ("sign" or "proof") occurs, offers a basis for explaining 2 Thes. 1:5. According to Phil. 1:28 the fact that the Philippians were not intimidated by those who opposed them was a sign (ἔνδειγμα) of destruction to their opponents but for them it was a sign of their salvation from God. Thus for the Thessalonians the evidence of the righteous judgment of God consisted in their endurance of oppression. Their perseverance would not have been possible without God's help. Best (255), along with most others holding this view, sees a reference to the eschatological judgment of God, but Marshall (173) urges that the judgment in mind was a process taking place at the time the letter was written.

This whole line of explanation, whether the judgment is seen as a present process or a future one, fails on two scores. First, the grammar does not require us to assume that the "evidence" is the endurance and faithfulness of the Thessalonians in their persecution and affliction. In fact it is more natural to relate it to the words "in all your persecution and the affliction that you suffer" because of the word order in the sentence. The validity of this observation is confirmed by v. 5's focus only on the suffering of the Thessalonians, not on their perseverance; furthermore, in vv. 6f. the righteous judgment of God is based on the application of the *lex talionis* to the oppressors, while those who are afflicted are granted relief without emphasis on their endurance (see von Dobschütz, 242). (I shall explore the way in which the suffering of the Thessalonians is understood as evidence for the righteous judgment of God in a moment.)

Second, reference to Phil. 1:28 is of dubious value since the meaning of the sign differs between that text and 2 Thes. 1:5. In the former the sign is proof of salvation for Christians and destruction for their adversaries, while in 2 Thes. 1:5 the sign concerns the righteous judgment of God. Bassler ("Enigmatic Sign," 499) rightly points out that the righteous judgment of God is not nearly so obviously connected with the endurance of the Thessalonians in the face of persecution as is the Philippians' salvation with their fearless adherence to the faith. Put slightly differently, it is difficult to conceive in what way the Thessalonians' perseverance presages the righteous judgment of God without introducing extraneous ideas into the text such as the notion that God has granted the Thessalonians the ability to persevere and remain faithful (see Rigaux, 620).

This observation effectively rules out the first and third possibilities described above for the identification of the "evidence" of God's righteous judgment. It also points to the second, namely, that the persecution and affliction that the Thessalonians experienced was the evidence referred to by Paul.

The view that the evidence involved the actual persecution and the affliction of the Thessalonians has the support of a number of scholars (e.g., von Dobschütz, 242; Dibelius, 26; Rigaux, 620; Marxsen, 68; Bassler, "Enigmatic Sign," 500f.). But generally this position has suffered from the inability of those who hold it to explain how tribulation and suffering provide direct evidence for the righteous judgment of God any better than those maintaining the third position described above.

Bassler (*op. cit.*, 501-506), building on the work of Wichmann *(Leidenstheologie)*, has convincingly shown that v. 5 should be understood in terms of a theology of suffering that began to emerge prior to and during the first century AD (cf. Aus, *Comfort,* 71-75). Four elements played an important role in the theology of suffering, as such texts as *Ps. Sol.* 13:9-10, 2 Macc. 6:12-16, and *2 Bar.* 13:3-10; 78:5 (see also 48:48-50 and 52:5-7) demonstrate (cf. Heb. 12:3-11, which also has strong affinities with a theology of suffering). First, a powerful sense of God's retributive justice existed; second, present suffering by the pious was explained as chastisement (or atonement) that would make them worthy of future glory; third, the present untroubled position of the godless and their future affliction by God were seen as the reverse of the experience of the pious; and fourth, the present suffering of the elect was accepted as evidence of God's election and justice. The affinities of 2 Thes. 1:5 and its context with the primary features of the emerging theology of suffering are striking, as Bassler has pointed out. First, vv. 6 and 8f. emphasize the retributive justice of God; second, v. 5 stresses that the suffering of the Thessalonians was intended to make them worthy of the future blessing described as the dominion of God; third, vv. 6f. present a reversal of fortunes when those who afflict others will themselves be repaid by God with affliction and those who are currently afflicted will be granted rest; and fourth, vv. 3f. reveal that the evidence for the righteous judgment of God is the actual suffering of the Thessalonians that has the effect of making them worthy of God's dominion (cf. Heb. 12:3-11).

Bassler ("Enigmatic Sign," 507-509) demonstrates that this interpretation has an important consequence for our understanding of the relation between 1:5-12 and 2:1-12. Taking up a suggestion of R. Aus (*Comfort,* 36), she maintains that 1:5-12 "deal[s] directly with the issue [of persecution] that raised the Day-of-the-Lord question" in 2:1-12 (508). Bassler reconstructs the connection in the following manner. For some reason the community assumed that the day of the Lord had come (or the author thought that they did; 2:2), but their experience of persecution directly contradicted this, calling into question God's justice since the oppression of the elect should not have persisted after the day of the Lord had arrived. The author of the letter used ideas drawn from the theology of suffering to argue that the persecution of the readers was actually evidence for God's justice in that it was making them worthy to share in the dominion of God in the future and at the same time he maintained that those who oppressed them would be subject to divine retribution at the time of the parousia (1:6, 8f.; 2:9-12).

Although Bassler's views concerning the day of the Lord require refinement (see my comments on 2:1), the strength of her interpretation is that it makes better sense of 1:4f. than any other explanation of these problematic verses, and attempts to clarify the inner connection between the affliction of the Thessalonians and the problem created by various claims among them that the day of the Lord had arrived. Thus, as suggested above, the correct understanding of vv. 4f. enables us to interpret more precisely the main thrust of the letter.

The evidence spoken of by Paul involves τῆς δικαίας κρίσεως τοῦ θεοῦ ("the righteous judgment of God"). This can only be a reference to future judgment associated with the day of the Lord. Paul does not bring the judgment into the present on account of his belief in the imminence of the parousia of Christ (cf. 1 Cor. 4:5). The mention of the future retributive justice of God in v. 6 and the compensatory justice of God in v. 7 confirms this interpretation. The prospect of the righteous judgment of God in the near future was integral in maintaining the faith and commitment of new Christians when they encountered opposition from those around them and in the face of the behavioral demands of their new religion.

The clause εἰς τὸ καταξιωθῆναι ὑμᾶς τῆς βασιλείας τοῦ θεοῦ ("that you may be considered worthy of the dominion of God" [on the use of "dominion" for βασιλεία see comments on 1 Thes. 2:12]) may express either purpose or result. Best (255) relates it directly to the preceding phrase "the righteous judgment of God." It seems much more probable, however, that it refers back to the persecution and affliction mentioned in v. 4. The idea of being considered worthy of the dominion of God is difficult to understand either as the purpose of the righteous judgment of God or as its result without reference to the behavior or experience of the Thessalonians (cf. 1 Thes. 2:12). Also the phrase "the dominion of God" is qualified by the words ὑπὲρ ἧς καὶ πάσχετε ("for which also you suffer"). This directs the reader back to the words "in all your persecutions and afflictions that you bear." If the εἰς τό clause refers back to the persecution and affliction mentioned in v. 4, then it should be taken as a result clause. It was not necessary for the readers to suffer in order to be considered worthy of God's dominion, but the writer certainly wished to comfort them with the fact that as a result of their experience of affliction they were considered worthy of it by God (cf. Aus, *Comfort,* 60).

"The dominion of God" here, as is generally the case in Paul's letters, alludes to the sphere in which the future salvation of God will be experienced, and, as on a number of occasions, its use is connected with the behavioral or experiential side of the Christian faith (cf. 1 Thes. 2:12; 1 Cor. 6:9f.; Gal. 5:21). The Thessalonians' suffering resulted from their desire to share in the dominion of God, and hence Paul seeks to reassure them that their suffering will be rewarded (v. 7), while those who inflict suffering on them will in turn suffer (vv. 6, 8f.).

1:6 The righteous judgment of God (v. 5) has both negative and positive dimensions vis-à-vis the experience of the community at Thessalonica. First Paul expresses the negative aspect. εἴπερ is a conditional particle, but here no hint of doubt is intended so it may be rendered "since," with what follows an assumed fact. δίκαιον παρὰ θεῷ ("it is just in the sight of God") takes up τῆς δικαίας κρίσεως τοῦ θεοῦ from v. 5 and underscores that both the negative and the positive components of God's judgment mentioned in vv. 6 and 7a are fair because they represent a just or right judgment by God. The infinitive ἀνταποδοῦναι ("to repay") expresses God's decision with regard to both those who afflict the Thessalonians (τοῖς θλίβουσιν) and the Thessalonians themselves as those who are afflicted (v. 7). ἀνταποδοῦναι τοῖς θλίβουσιν ὑμᾶς θλῖψιν ("to repay with affliction those who afflict you") state the principle of retribution, the *lex talionis* associated with the day of the Lord in such OT texts as Is. 66:6 where recompense is promised to the enemies of God (cf. Ob. 14). In 2 Thes. 1 the enemies of the people of God are portrayed as the enemies of God as well, and their just recompense is said to be their affliction by God on the day of judgment. V. 9 gives a glimpse of what their affliction will be when it speaks of the destruction and eternal exclusion from the presence of God awaiting those not knowing God and those who refuse to obey the gospel. For those suffering for their faith in Christ the prospect of obtaining justice against their oppressors on the day of the Lord was probably intended to provide them with a sense of power over their foes. Their enemies might oppress them for the time being, but in the end the roles of the oppressed and their oppressors would be dramatically reversed.

1:7 If those who have persecuted the Thessalonian Christians are to experience the retributive justice of God, the Thessalonians themselves are to receive recompense from God on the day of judgment for their suffering. The positive dimension of God's just decision for Paul's converts is ἀνταποδοῦναι ... ὑμῖν τοῖς θλιβομένοις ἄνεσιν μεθ' ἡμῶν ("to repay to you who are afflicted rest with us"). Several features of this statement are noteworthy.

First, the present form of the participle θλιβομένοις confirms that the Thessalonians' experience of affliction was taking place as the letter was being written. Paul goes on to relate this to the parousia of Christ in the second part of the verse. This strongly suggests that he may have had in mind the concept of the "messianic woes." Aus ("Relevance," 260-265) provides ample evidence to demonstrate the existence in the first century of the belief that the coming of the messiah would be preceded by a period of intense distress for the faithful (e.g., 1QH 3:2-18; Mark 13; Revelation 8, 9, 11). He also shows that Isaiah 66, a text with connections to the previous verse, was interpreted as referring to the "messianic woes." This has considerable bearing on the problem addressed in chap. 2, as Aus (263f.) recognizes. The Thessalonians may have connected their suffering with the "messianic woes" (cf. 1 Thes. 3:3f.), and this may have contributed to their belief that the events of the day of the Lord were already unfolding in their experience. From this perspective 2:1-12 can be viewed as an attempt to put a brake on their "over-realized" expectations.

Second, v. 7a seems to presuppose that God was to reward the Thessalonians on account of their experience of suffering. This might be construed by some as undermining Paul's teaching on grace, but a persistent aspect in the apostle's writings concerns the notion that in the judgment God will consider the deeds of people in determining their retribution or recompense (cf. Rom. 2:5-11; 1 Cor. 3:12-15; 4:5; 2 Cor. 5:10). On account of their having suffered affliction from their opponents the Thessalonian Christians will be granted ἄνεσις ("rest") by God. What exactly is meant by this term is not clear, though it is obviously intended as a positive reward to compensate the readers for their experience of affliction.

A third important feature in v. 7a is the phrase μεθ᾿ ἡμῶν ("with us"). Paul understood his own vocation as inevitably requiring that he undergo various types of suffering and affliction (cf. 1 Cor. 4:8-13; 2 Cor. 6:4-10; 11:21-29). By adding the words "with us" in v. 7 he indicates that the Thessalonians will share the same reward as that given to him and to his fellow missionaries for their suffering for the sake of the gospel of Christ.

Trilling (52f.), reacting to the claim of Dobschütz that the identification of the author with his readers was a mark of authenticity that an imitator would not have introduced, maintains that it would equally well suit the post-Pauline period where a tendency existed to connect the experience of the apostle and the apostolic community together. In point of fact, however, neither authenticity nor inauthenticity can be demonstrated from this, and, more importantly, this debate obscures the function of the identification between the apostle and the community. The identification is designed to give added meaning to the readers' affliction by identifying their troubles with those undergone by their "father in the faith" as an apostle of Christ. This in turn locates their persecution in a wider context of meaning, namely, the struggle for the truth of the gospel against the forces of unbelief arrayed against it. In other words, this passage implies the dualistic structure of the apocalyptic worldview around which the Thessalonians' faith and hope were oriented.

The apocalyptic significance of v. 7a is confirmed by v. 7b. It depicts the end of the existing order at the appearing of the Lord Jesus on the day of judgment. God's decisive act of repaying the enemies of Christ's people with affliction and rewarding the faithful for their endurance of affliction will occur ἐν τῇ ἀποκαλύψει τοῦ κυρίου Ἰησοῦ ἀπ᾿ οὐρανοῦ μετ᾿ ἀγγέλων δυνάμεως αὐτοῦ (v. 7b) ἐν πυρὶ φλογός (v. 8a) ("at the revealing of the Lord Jesus from heaven with the angels of his power [or might] in flaming fire").

The character of this event as an ἀποκάλυψις ("revelation") is mentioned elsewhere in 1 Cor. 1:7 (cf. Rom. 2:5; 8:18f.; 1 Cor. 3:13, all of which involve aspects of revelation in conjunction with the day of judgment). The parousia or coming of Christ is revelatory in that the Lord Jesus is currently hidden in heaven, and therefore those who persecute the readers are in (willful) ignorance about him (cf. v. 9). As a result they have no idea about the danger

225

confronting them in the impending judgment (see vv. 9f.). The parousia of the Lord Jesus will come as an unexpected and frightening turn of events for them. On the other hand, for the oppressed it will vindicate their steadfastness. Paul's intention may have been to provide his readers with the power to withstand their oppressors through esoteric knowledge of the coming reversal. Aus (*Comfort*; "Relevance") has provided ample evidence to demonstrate that in doing so Paul drew on traditional Jewish themes and images associated with divine theophany and with an agent of God (either the angel Michael, the Son of Man, the messiah, or Melchizedek) who would come to bring judgment against the enemies of God and comfort to the oppressed people of God. In particular he shows that the description of the Lord Jesus' coming as a "revelation" may well be derived from the Targumic tradition of Is. 66:7. This tradition interpreted the passage in terms of the king or messiah being revealed on the day of judgment (see "Relevance," 267).

The connection of angels with divine theophanies is another traditional Jewish image employed both here and in 1 Thes. 3:13 (cf. Ex. 19:13, 16, 19; Ps. 68:18 [Hebrew]; Zc. 14:5; *1 Enoch* 1:9; Mk. 13:26f.). It was intended to heighten the drama and importance associated with the events signifying the end of the age. The actual expression μετ' ἀγγέλων δυνάμεως αὐτοῦ in 2 Thes. 1:7 is capable of several different renderings. It might mean "his powerful angels," a Hebraism, with δυνάμεως being taken as a genitive of quality (so Bruce, 150). Frame (230) thinks the phrase refers to a specific class of angels, namely, "his angels of power." Another possibility is to take it as "the angels through whom he exercises his power," or as "the angels of his army" on the basis of a Hebrew play on words (see Aus, *Comfort*, 77f.). However, since the passage concerns the revelation of the Lord from heaven, it is best to render the phrase as "the angels of his power" in order to emphasize the character of the coming Lord, rather than the quality or nature of the angels who will accompany him.

1:8 ἐν πυρὶ φλογός ("in flaming fire") poses several problems. In the first place there is a well-supported textual variant, ἐν φλογὶ πυρός ("in flames of fire," B D F G), that provides a more felicitous reading and corresponds to such LXX texts as Is. 29:6; 66:15; Dn. 7:9; Ps. 28 (29):7. On the other hand some LXX texts have πῦρ φλογός, sometimes as a variant in the textual tradition (cf. Ex. 3:2; Sir. 8:10; 45:19). In terms of the normal rules of textual criticism the reading ἐν πυρὶ φλογός should probably be preferred as the more difficult reading, but it makes no difference to the interpretation which reading is chosen.

The second problem is more difficult. Does the phrase go with what precedes or what follows? Commentators are divided on this issue (e.g., Best, 259 favoring the former and Marshall, 177 the latter). Given the way in which 2 Thessalonians 1 appears to draw on Isaiah 66 (see Aus, "Relevance," 263-268), we should probably take "in flaming fire" with διδόντος ἐκδίκησιν since this looks like a paraphrase of Is. 66:15 (LXX), a text depicting the Lord coming ἀποδοῦναι ἐν θυμῷ ἐκδίκησιν καὶ ἀποσκορακισμὸν ἐν φλογὶ πυρός ("to give out vengeance in wrath and damning in flames of fire"; cf. Is. 66:16, which describes the Lord as judging all the earth in fire). (It is curious that both Best, 259 and Aus, "Relevance," 266, who recognize the connection between v. 8 and Is. 66:15, prefer to relate the "flaming fire" to what precedes on the grounds of similarity to OT theophanic traditions such as Ex. 3:2 [Best] or Dn. 7:9 [Aus] rather than to what follows in conformity to the thought of Is. 66:15f.)

The author of 2 Thes. 1:8 uses the image of the flaming fire to portray the frightening experience awaiting the enemies of God when God inflicts vengeance on the Thessalonians' oppressors. ἐκδίκησις could be translated simply as "punishment," but the context makes it clear that it connotes retributory punishment or vengeance directed toward those afflicting the Thessalonians (cf. v. 7; see Rom. 12:19 for another example of ἐκδίκησις in the sense of vengeance).

Not only the persecutors of the Thessalonians will be subject to divine vengeance at the day of judgment. They belong to a much larger group that will be punished. Thus Paul warns that τοῖς μὴ εἰδόσιν θεὸν καὶ τοῖς μὴ ὑπακούουσιν τῷ εὐαγγελίῳ τοῦ κυρίου ἡμῶν Ἰησοῦ ("those not knowing God and not obeying the gospel of our Lord Jesus") will receive divine retribution.

Some, like Frame (233) and Marshall (177f.), believe that the Greek construction refers to Jews and Gentiles as distinct groups. They correctly take the phrase "those not knowing God" as modeled on OT texts such as Je. 10:25 and Ps. 79:6 (LXX 78:6 S†; these two texts reflect literary dependence or a common tradition) that describe the Gentiles (τὰ ἔθνη) as those not knowing God (τὰ μὴ εἴδοτα; cf. Is. 55:5). They then see an allusion to the Jewish people in the words "those not obeying the gospel," which is probably derived from Is. 66:4 (LXX), where οὐχ ὑπήκουσάν μου ("they did not obey me [God]") is found (cf. Rom. 10:16).

This interpretation has a major problem. For Paul the second phrase applies equally to Gentiles and Jews, as Rom. 11:30-32 demonstrates. Moreover, the Jewish people are frequently described in the OT (cf. Je. 4:22; 9:3, 6; Ho. 5:4) as not knowing God. For this reason it is unwise to distinguish between allusion to Jews and Gentiles. Besides it is questionable whether the Thessalonians, who as Gentiles lacked in-depth knowledge of the OT, could have correctly interpreted such an allusion in the first place.

In all probability Aus (*Comfort,* 88) and Trilling (56) are correct when they claim that "those not knowing God" and "those not obeying the gospel of our Lord Jesus" form a synonymous parallelism (cf. 1:9f.). Trilling's further assertion that this is a characteristic of the author of 2 Thessalonians but atypical of Paul is misleading. As I will show later, vv. 7b-10 were a pre-formed unit (see comments of v. 10).

While the expression "those not knowing God" may be related to the idea in Rom. 1:18-32 that humankind has generally refused to acknowledge God (v. 28) and therefore can be said not to know God, the language of 2 Thes. 1:8, like so much of Paul's language, cannot be reduced to mere theological propositions. The language of v. 8 is that of social exclusion by virtue of contrast with the implied condition of the readers, who are those knowing God and obeying the gospel of the Lord Jesus. Not to be part of the community that knows God and obeys the Lord is to be excluded from salvation itself and condemned to divine retribution (cf. Meeks, "Social Function," 689). Neither the writer nor the readers were worried about the absoluteness and possible unfairness of such an assertion because they perceived reality in terms of the dualistic world of apocalypticism.

One other dimension of the language should be mentioned. Not only did it demarcate the difference between the elect and those who were outsiders, especially those who persecuted the elect, but it also functioned as a veiled threat to those within the community. To leave the community, even if under strong duress, was to join the ranks of the condemned on whom God would inflict divine vengeance. The danger of exclusion from the people of God is vividly depicted in the next verse. Also 3:6 and 12 pose the question of obedience to the Lord directly for the members of the Thessalonian Christian community. To fail to obey Paul's command regarding the idle, given in the name of the Lord Jesus Christ, was to risk exclusion from future salvation. As Meeks ("Social Function," 689) recognizes, eschatological beliefs are used in 2 Thessalonians for the purpose of social control within the community.

1:9 The apocalyptic orientation of much of the imagery of 2 Thessalonians warns against overly literalistic attempts at interpreting what is said because the power of apocalyptic results from its imaginative or symbolic presentation. Paul seeks to portray the frightening punishment awaiting those outside the community and especially the enemies of the community.

οἵτινες ("such people") is used qualitatively and is resumptive of the two τοῖς constructions of the previous verse, just as the classical idiom δίκην τίσουσιν ("will pay the penalty") is resumptive of διδόντος ἐκδίκησιν from v. 8. The penalty is specified as ὄλεθρον αἰώνιον ἀπὸ προσώπου τοῦ κυρίου καὶ ἀπὸ τῆς δόξης τῆς ἰσχύος αὐτοῦ ("eternal destruction from the presence of the Lord and the glory of his might"). Both ὄλεθρον ("destruction") and αἰώνιον ("eternal") are susceptible of several meanings. Going back to the OT, ὄλεθρον had an eschatological application in judgment pronouncements (cf. LXX Je. 28[51]:55; 31[48]:3, 8, 32; 32:17 [25:31]; Ezk. 6:14; 14:16). This eschatological dimension is characteristic of its usage in Paul (cf. 1 Cor. 5:5; 1 Thes. 5:3). But it can either denote destruction in a physical sense or possess a metaphorical connotation. If it were literal here it would imply the annihilation of the enemies of God. On the other hand it may have a more metaphorical signification. The problem is made more difficult by the qualifying adjective αἰώνιος. It can mean either something without end or something that is final or ultimate. The latter would accord with the sense of annihilation, while the former would fit with the idea of destruction in the metaphorical sense of punishment. As there is no evidence in Paul (or the rest of the NT for that matter) for a concept of final annihilation of the godless, the expression "eternal destruction" should probably be taken in a metaphorical manner as indicating the severity of the punishment awaiting the enemies of God (cf. 4 Macc. 10:15 where τὸν αἰώνιον τοῦ τύραννου ὄλεθρον ["the eternal destruction of the tyrant"] occurs), without seeking to specify its precise content beyond what Paul himself depicts in the following phrase.

This phrase, ἀπὸ προσώπου τοῦ Κυρίου καὶ ἀπὸ τῆς δόξης τῆς ἰσχύος αὐτοῦ ("from the presence of the Lord and from the glory of his might"), reproduces the LXX text of Is. 2:10b (= vv. 19b, 21b), except that Paul has dropped φόβος ("fear") from ἀπὸ προσώπου τοῦ φόβου κυρίου in order to fit the quotation into the structure of v. 9. This change has the further effect of personalizing the impersonal formulation of Isaiah 2. The choice of the imagery from Isaiah 2 was undoubtedly based on the judgment scene depicted there, though it is highly unlikely that Paul's readers would have caught the allusion. The two members of the formulation ("from the presence of the Lord" and "from the glory of his might") are part of the poetic synonymous parallelism used by the writer of Isaiah and should probably be understood in the same way in 2 Thes. 1:9. The presence of the Lord was traditionally associated with glory manifested as brilliant light (cf. Ezk. 1:26-28), and hence "the glory of his might" is simply a way of describing the glorious and majestic presence of the Lord from which the persecutors of the Thessalonians will forever be excluded. Paul does not describe the punishment of the godless here or anywhere else in graphic detail. Rather he focuses on exclusion from the glorious and majestic presence of the Lord with ἀπὸ having its normal spatial connotation here as in Is. 2:10.

For Paul exclusion from the glorious presence of the Lord constitutes the obverse of salvation, which is to be with the Lord always (1 Thes. 4:17) and to share in God's glory (Rom. 8:17f., 30; 2 Cor. 4:17; Phil. 3:21). The theme of glory is taken up again in vv. 10 and 12 in a positive way to explicate the blessed experience in store for the Thessalonians.

Marshall (179f.) notes that Paul has applied a Yahweh text to Christ in v. 9. The appropriation of texts originally written about God to describe Jesus as Lord was one of the most important developments of early christology and eventually led to the near-total identification of Christ with the nature and activities of God.

1:10 Having dealt with the punishment threatening those who refuse to acknowledge God and who disobey the gospel of the Lord Jesus, among whom are numbered the persecutors of the Thessalonian community, Paul returns to the theme of v. 7b, the parousia of Christ, with ὅταν ἔλθῃ ("when he comes"). Paul does so because the day of the Lord's coming will be the day of judgment when sentence will be passed and executed against the opponents of God and God's people. V. 10 emphasizes the identification of the Christian community with the coming Lord on the day of judgment and salvation without elaborating on the reward to be received by the followers of Christ for their faithfulness. Just as Paul is elusive about the nature of the vengeance to be inflicted by the Lord Jesus, he is also elusive about the nature of the reward to be bestowed.

Both of the two parallel infinitival purpose clauses, ἐνδοξασθῆναι ἐν τοῖς ἁγίοις αὐτοῦ ("to be glorified in the presence of his saints") and θαυμασθῆναι ἐν πᾶσιν τοῖς πιστεύσασιν ("to be wondered at in the presence of all those who have believed"), are probably derived from OT texts. Here they are used to express the purpose of the Lord's coming on the day of judgment, a purpose differing radically depending on whether one is a member of the faithful people of the Lord or an enemy of God.

The first clause was almost certainly constructed from the LXX version of Ps. 88:6 (89:7), which speaks of God ἐνδοξαζόμενος ἐν βουλῇ ἁγίων ("being glorified in the council of the saints"), since the combination of the rare compound form ἐνδοξάζεσθαι and ἅγιος only occurs here and in 2 Thes. 1:10 of the Christian Bible. Originally in Ps. 88:6 the βουλὴ ἁγίων referred to the angelic council (or at an even earlier stage to the gods of the nations around Israel, who are called the sons of God in Ps. 82:6f.). Like the people of Qumran, who referred to themselves, along with the angels, as the holy ones, Paul uses ἅγιοι ("holy ones" or "saints") of both Christians and angels (cf. 1 Thes. 3:13; 1 Cor. 1:2). Here it denotes the people of God rather than the angels, as the corresponding term, τοῖς πιστεύσασιν ("those who have believed"), in the second part of the verse reveals.

Aus (*Comfort*, 99) urges that the infinitives ἐνδοξασθῆναι and θαυμασ-θῆναι in v. 10 be given causal translations like "to show Himself [*sic*] glorious" and "to show Himself [*sic*] wonderful/marvelous." He bases this on the fact that the LXX often understands "δοξάζεσθαι in light of the Hebrew niphal construc-tion not as a true passive but simply as intransitive or causative." This would make good sense in the context. However, since Aus fails to explain how Paul's Greek-speaking Thessalonian converts would have known to understand the two infinitives in a causal sense, this suggestion must be rejected.

The compound form ἐνδοξάζεσθαι, found only here in the NT, means "to be glorified or honored," but a proper understanding of it in v. 10 depends on the interpretation of the prepositional phrase ἐν τοῖς ἁγίοις αὐτοῦ. The preposition ἐν ("in") can be viewed as instrumental, giving the meaning "by or through his saints"; as causal, leading to the translation "because of his saints" (so Frame, 237); or as locative, in the sense that the glory of Christ will be mirrored in the lives of his saints (so Morris, 207) or in the sense that his glorification will occur "in the presence of his saints." This last sense agrees with the meaning of ἐν in Ps. 88:6 (LXX), but more importantly it counterbalances the physical exclusion of the persecutors of the Thessalonian community from the presence of the Lord and his mighty glory when he comes (v. 9) by making clear that the Lord will be present in the midst of the community of his saints and that they will share in his glory. This interpretation seems to leave unanswered the question of who will glorify Christ, but it should not be forgotten that one important theme in the eschatological thought of Paul and other early Christians was that the enemies of Christ would ultimately be forced to honor or glorify him (cf. Phil. 2:10f.). If this thought lies behind v. 10, it makes the glorification of Christ in the midst of his saints by their persecutors an ironic reversal in which the Thessalonians will be vindicated by their very enemies. Although this interpretation would make good sense of v. 10, it reads rather more into the passage than can be determined from what is actually written.

The second purpose clause of v. 10 may have been derived from the LXX text of Ps. 67:36 (68:35), where θαυμαστὸς ὁ θεὸς ἐν τοῖς ἁγίοις αὐτοῦ ("God will be marveled at in the presence of his saints") appears, or perhaps from the LXX of Ps. 88:6 (89:5) through a compression and paraphrasing of the synonymous parallelism of the text, which includes a reference to τὰ θαυμάσια ("the wondrous deeds") of the Lord and to the ἐκκλησία ἁγίων ("congregation of the saints"). Whatever may be the case in this matter, this second purpose clause must be understood in the same general way as the first one. Just as v. 9 has a wider group in mind than the persecutors of the Thessalonians, so πᾶσιν τοῖς πιστεύσασιν ("all those who have believed") in v. 10 includes all Christians who come to faith in Christ. The aorist tense of the participle πιστεύσασιν is somewhat surprising. The present tense would seem more appropriate, but the participle probably has in view the actual coming to faith of Christians, which is antecedent to the coming of Christ as Lord.

The ὅτι clause that follows is a parenthetical remark evoked by the reference to faith in the preceding phrase. Best (266) observes that it is "the kind of thing which takes place so easily in dictation or in the revision of the copy." For example, 1 Cor. 1:6 provides a close parallel when Paul interjects the words καθὼς τὸ μαρτύριον τοῦ Χριστοῦ ἐβεβαιώθη ἐν ὑμῖν ("just as the testimony of Christ was established among you") into his opening thanksgiving. But with Aus (*Comfort*, 101f.) we can go further than this. If 2 Thessalonians were a carefully composed pseudonymous letter based on 1 Thessalonians, as is increasingly maintained, such an awkward parenthesis would be inexplicable, a point that has not received sufficient attention from those denying Pauline authorship.

The interruption of the flow of v. 10 by the insertion of this parenthetical remark about the origins of the Thessalonians' faith was probably intended to personalize the preceding statements to the situation of the Thessalonians.

μαρτύριον ("testimony") broadly takes in the whole preaching and teaching activity of Paul and his colleagues. It is followed by the subjective genitive ἡμῶν ("our") in correspondence with such Pauline expressions as "our gospel" (cf. 1 Thes. 1:5; 2 Cor. 4:3) and "my gospel" (cf. Rom. 2:16; 16:25). The content of the testimony directed toward the Thessalonians concerned Christ, as 1 Cor. 1:6 indicates, and was the basis of their faith. By this parenthetical remark Paul connects his readers with the saints, those who have believed in Christ, in whose presence Christ will stand on the day of judgment as their redeemer (cf. 1 Thes. 1:10) and vindicator.

The final words of the verse, ἐν τῇ ἡμέρα ἐκείνη ("on that day"), clearly referring to the coming day of the Lord (cf. 1 Thes. 5:2 and Is. 2:10f., 19f.), are separated from the rest of the temporal clause by the parenthetical clause and are unnecessary for the thought of the text. This suggests that Paul was working with pre-formed material into which he inserted his personalizing comment. This possibility is made the more likely by several other factors. (1) Vv. 7b-10 exhibit an inordinately high number of references to a variety of LXX texts without any formal citations. The common denominator between most of the references is the theme of divine judgment, showing that a conscious attempt was made to formulate a statement about divine judgment based on the OT. (2) A sudden change occurs in vv. 7b-10 as the second person pronouns and verbs predominating in vv. 3-7a and vv. 11f. cease except for Paul's parenthetical remark in v. 10 where he personalizes the depiction of the judgment in vv. 7b-10 for the readers. (3) The reference to those not knowing God and not obeying the gospel in v. 9 introduces a new and unexpected description of the Thessalonians' persecutors. (4) The repeated use of synonymous parallelism in vv. 7b-10 is not typical of Paul's normal epistolary style. This evidence argues forcefully that the material in vv. 7b-10 existed prior to its inclusion in 2 Thessalonians 1 (cf. Best, 266f.), though it is not possible to determine in what form it originally existed or whether it originated with Paul. Paul introduced this material into 2 Thessalonians because it addressed one of the major questions troubling the recipients of his letter in their time of persecution and affliction, namely, the question of God's justice. In conjunction with vv. 5-7a it is intended to indicate the character of God's righteous judgment for the Thessalonians.

1:11 The long opening sentence of the thanksgiving section, running from v. 3 through v. 10, is followed by an intercessory prayer report in vv. 11f. V. 11 is loosely connected to what precedes by εἰς ὅ ("to this end"), a mildly telic phrase (cf. Rigaux, 637), and takes up the thought of salvation for the persecuted Thessalonians, a theme dealt with initially in vv. 7 and 10. Frame (238) perhaps goes too far in relating it back to εἰς τὸ καταξιωθῆναι ὑμᾶς ("in order that you might be worthy") in v. 5 since this theme is re-introduced in the second part of v. 11 in its own right. The καί is probably not reciprocal as Frame (238) thinks. Either it indicates that thanksgiving as well as prayer is offered on behalf of the Thessalonians, as O'Brien (*Introductory Thanksgivings*, 178) suggests (cf. 1 Thes. 1:2), or it has no real translational value, as Best (268) appears to believe. Prayer for his converts was an important element of Paul's life, as Phil. 1:9 and Col. 1:3, 9 show. For this reason it is not surprising that he should say προσευχόμεθα πάντοτε περὶ ὑμῶν ("we always pray for you").

The ἵνα clause that follows may express either the purpose or the content of Paul's prayers for his readers, though the two cannot easily be distinguished in this passage. Paul's prayer for the Thessalonians is in the first instance ἵνα ὑμᾶς ἀξιώσῃ τῆς κλήσεως ὁ θεὸς ἡμῶν ("that our God may make you worthy of his call"). Paul uses κλῆσις ("call") on only three other occasions in his undisputed letters, each time with a different meaning determined by the context (cf. 1 Cor. 1:26; 7:20; Phil. 3:14), unless the two occurrences in 1 Corinthians both mean "station" or "position." In any case the Thessalonians would understand the word in terms of their normal linguistic usage unless Paul used it in a technical sense during his mission work among them. This possibility cannot be dismissed because in 1 Thes. 2:12 Paul employs the cognate verb καλεῖν ("to call") to describe God as τοῦ καλοῦντος ὑμᾶς εἰς τὴν ἑαυτοῦ βασιλείαν καὶ δόξαν ("the one who calls you into his own dominion and glory"). Here the idea of the call has a definite eschatological character (cf. 1 Thes. 5:24), and such an eschatological connotation would be most appropriate in 2 Thes. 1:11, since the preceding material deals with the parousia of the Lord and the coming judgment. For this reason we should probably see in the term κλῆσις an allusion to God's call to the Thessalonians to share in eschatological salvation.

This explanation receives additional support when we consider the verb ἀξιώσῃ. A number of scholars have asserted that this word means "to *make* worthy," in spite of the fact that with the possible exception of Ep. Diog. 9:1 no other examples of this sense are known (cf. von Dobschütz, 255; Best, 268f.; Trilling, 62). On account of this we should stay with the normal denotation of the word, "to *consider* worthy" (cf. Frame, 239f.). This interpretation is substantiated by v. 5, where the compound form καταξιωθῆναι has this meaning. That Paul prays that God may consider the Thessalonian Christians worthy of his call means simply that Paul prays for his readers' salvation on the day of judgment. This is probably how his readers would have understood his remark, especially in light of v. 5 where he speaks of them "being considered worthy of the dominion of God."

But Paul was aware that withstanding persecution was not the only activity required of the Thessalonians. Therefore his prayer for them extends to their moral conduct. He also prays that God πληρώσῃ πᾶσαν εὐδοκίαν ἀγαθωσύνης καὶ ἔργον πίστεως ἐν δυνάμει ("may complete every good intention [literally "good desire of goodness"] and work of faith in power") in his readers. Although εὐδοκία primarily refers to God's good desire in the LXX (forty of the fifty-six occurences, according to G. Schrenk, *TDNT* II, 743), in two of the three other occurrences in Paul's undisputed letters, and possibly all three, it relates to the human will (cf. Rom. 10:1; Phil. 1:15; and 2:13). Here it is unclear whether it has as its subject God or the Thessalonians since πᾶσαν εὐδοκίαν ἀγαθωσύνης ("every good intention") might apply equally to either. On the whole, however, it seems best to take it in connection with the readers because the parallel phrase ἔργον πίστεως ("work of faith") relates more naturally to the activity of the Thessalonians (cf. 1 Thes. 1:3) than to the work of God, a point not taken seriously enough by von Dobschütz (256) and Schrenk (*op. cit.*, 746). This conclusion is perhaps bolstered by πᾶσαν ("every"), a somewhat difficult idea to put together with εὐδοκίαν in relation to God because it requires us to think of God having a variety of desires for the Thessalonians. The verb πληρώσῃ carries in this passage the sense of completing or finishing something already begun. Paul's converts were not without good desires or intentions and works of faith in light of their willingness to suffer for their belief in Christ, but the apostle recognized that they must continue in their present course of behavior until the parousia.

By invoking God to complete the readers' good intentions and works of faith Paul reminds the community that they do not stand alone: God is at work in their lives. This point is made the more emphatic by the adverbial prepositional phrase ἐν δυνάμει ("in power"), which expresses Paul's wish that God should work "powerfully" in the lives of the Thessalonians.

V. 11, with its stress on the Christian behavior of the Thessalonians, points forward to the parenetic material of 2:13–3:15. As noted above, this outlining of the themes to be discussed in the letter is one of the important functions of the *exordium*.

1:12 Paul's prayer for the good intentions and works of faith of the Thessalonians has as its goal the reciprocal glorification of Christ in the community and of the community in Christ. Use of ὅπως ("in order that") to introduce a purpose clause is relatively uncommon in Paul's letters and was probably used for stylistic variation after ἵνα in v. 11 (cf. 1 Cor. 1:28f.; 2 Cor. 8:14 and see BDF §369.4).

Most commentators believe that Paul drew the words ἐνδοξασθῇ τὸ ὄνομα τοῦ κυρίου ("the name of the Lord may be glorified") from Is. 66:5. 2 Thes. 1:8 relies heavily on this chapter from Isaiah, and so the verse may have been in Paul's mind as he wrote v. 12. Against this is Paul's frequent use of "the name of the Lord" (cf. 2 Thes. 3:6; Rom. 10:13; 1 Cor. 1:2, 10; 5:4; 6:11; Col. 3:17) and that the phrase is necessitated here by the context, as will be seen in a moment. Furthermore, as I have observed, vv. 7b-10 almost certainly had an independent existence prior to their present usage so that a return to Is. 66:5 is less likely than most commentators realize. To this I would add the somewhat less weighty objection of Best (271) that Is. 66:5 employs the simple form δοξασθῇ rather than the compound form ἐνδοξασθῇ that we

1:12EXORDIUM

have here. However this matter is decided, it is certain that Paul intended the readers to recall v. 10 by virtue of his repetition of ἐνδοξάζειν, here in the passive.

As a result of this, Best (264f.) has argued that the prepositional phrase ἐν ὑμῖν ("in you") must have the same meaning as ἐν τοῖς ἁγίοις αὐτοῦ ("in his saints") in v. 10, but he fails to take account of the differences between vv. 10 and 12. Marshall (183) has observed that the element of reciprocity between the Lord Jesus and the Thessalonians in v. 12 creates a new theme, which requires the preposition to be understood differently from its use in v. 10. More importantly Paul is forced to make the name of the Lord his point of reference in v. 12, not the person of the Lord as in v. 10, because he is writing about the present glorification of the Lord who remains in heaven, not his future glorification, when he will be physically present with his people. The exclusively eschatological interpretation of v. 12 by Best and others ignores the present significance of the second part of the prayer request in v. 11 concerning the present behavior of the Thessalonians. The purpose of God completing every good intention and work of faith among the Thessalonians is to enable the name of the Lord Jesus to be glorified by means of their deeds. Thus ἐν ὑμῖν is employed instrumentally with the sense "because of you" and indicates that the readers through their actions cause the glorification of the name of the Lord Jesus (cf. Gal. 1:24, καὶ ἐδόξαζον ἐν ἐμοὶ τὸν θεόν ["and they were glorifying God because of me"]).

The phrase καὶ ὑμεῖς ἐν αὐτῷ ("and you in him") establishes that there is reciprocity between the Thessalonian believers and their Lord with regard to being glorified. Frame (242) maintains that αὐτῷ (which can be translated as either "him" or "it") refers back to the "name of the Lord," but the idea of Christians being glorified "in the name of the Lord Jesus" does not make very good sense in the context. The second ἐν has an identical function to the first one. Therefore the verse asserts that the readers' glorification is accomplished with the help of their Lord. The glorification of believers has both a present and a future component for Paul. The process of glorification begins through the Spirit working in the lives of Christians (cf. 2 Cor. 3:18) and culminates in the glorification of the believers' bodies at the parousia (cf. Rom. 8:18f.; Phil. 3:20f.). Either or both may be in view in v. 12 as the historical time reference of the purpose clause cannot be determined with any certainty.

The final phrase of v. 12 poses a major problem. The grammatical construction of κατὰ τὴν χάριν τοῦ θεοῦ ἡμῶν καὶ κυρίου Ἰησοῦ Χριστοῦ raises the question whether this passage, like such later texts as Jn. 20:28; Tit. 2:13 and 2 Pet. 1:11, speaks of Jesus as God as well as Lord. Certainly the text as it stands can easily mean this and would tend to suggest a post-Pauline origin, unless Rom. 9:5, which is problematic, is interpreted as designating Christ as God. Von Dobschütz (258) claims that only the assumption of a later interpolator who conformed the passage to his own understanding of Jesus as both

Lord and God by adding the words "the Lord Jesus Christ" could account for the obvious meaning of the construction in 2 Thes. 1:12. Given that no textual evidence exists to support his views and that an alternative explanation is possible, von Dobschütz's position should be rejected.

ἡ χάρις τοῦ θεοῦ ("the grace of God") appears frequently in Paul's writings, and almost invariably the article is found with θεοῦ (cf. Rom. 5:15; 1 Cor. 1:4; 3:10; 15:10; 2 Cor. 1:12; 6:1, etc.). Trilling (65) is therefore correct in saying that the designation "God" is not an isolated title in v. 12 but part of the formula "according to the grace of our God" (see 1 Cor. 3:10, where this formula recurs without "our"). To this was added the fixed expression κυρίου Ἰησοῦ Χριστοῦ ("[the] Lord Jesus Christ"), which is normally anarthrous in Paul (cf. 1 Thes. 1:1; Gal. 1:3; Phil. 1:2, etc., in the Greek text), without Paul noticing the problem the article with God created for the second member of the construction. As Best (272f.) has pointed out, this is the sort of thing that can easily happen in dictation. The focus of this concluding formulation is to identify God and the Lord Jesus Christ as together the source of the unmerited favor whereby the Thessalonians, unlike nonbelievers, enjoy the blessings of God.

PARTITIO: 2:1-2

Unlike 1 Thessalonians, 2 Thessalonians has no narration. This is typical of deliberative rhetoric, a simplified version of judicial rhetoric (Kennedy, *New Testament Interpretation*, 24). Vv. 1-2 function as a *partitio*. The *partitio* lists the propositions or headings to be discussed in the main body of the communication. V. 1 specifies the theme of the *probatio* or proof section of the argument, which is found in vv. 3-17. This theme concerns the parousia of Christ from heaven and the gathering of his followers at that time.

V. 2 enumerates two interrelated issues to be argued in the *probatio*. The first of these two proofs is a demonstration that the day of the Lord has not in fact occurred (vv. 3-12). It is difficult to know in what sense the Thessalonians may have thought that the day of the Lord had come, since clearly the coming of Jesus at the end of the age could not have happened. Perhaps, as I shall suggest below, they understood the day of the Lord not merely as the day of Jesus' parousia from heaven, but in a general way as the events of the end of the age. Possibly it was connected with their experience of oppression, but the text does not make this clear.

The second proof deals with what Hughes (57) calls "the notion of stability" in personal and doctrinal matters (vv. 13-15). Essentially the proof demonstrates why the readers should not be "quickly shaken in mind" (v. 2a) and concerns their election by God and perseverance in the faith. As a proof it challenges the readers to decide whether they should in fact be disturbed in mind and expects the obvious answer: No, they should not.

2:1 The transition to the *partitio* is marked by ἐρωτῶμεν δὲ ὑμᾶς, ἀδελφοί ("now, brothers [and sisters], we implore you"). Paul frequently employs δὲ ἀδελφοί ("now brothers [and sisters]") as a transitional phrase (cf. 3:6; 1 Thes. 2:17; 4:13; 5:1, 12) and occasionally uses ἐρωτῶμεν ("we implore"), as an alternative to the much more common παρακαλοῦμεν ("we exhort"), to introduce an exhortation (cf. 1 Thes. 4:1; 5:12).

The general subject of the exhortation is spelled out by ὑπὲρ τῆς παρουσίας τοῦ κυρίου ἡμῶν Ἰησοῦ Χριστοῦ καὶ ἡμῶν ἐπισυναγωγῆς ἐπ᾽ αὐτόν ("concerning the parousia of our Lord Jesus Christ and our assembling with him"). Since the Thessalonian Christians were a persecuted community with a powerful conviction that the end of the present order was at hand, it is not surprising that they raised questions regarding the public manifestation of

237

Christ and when it would occur. False starts have been a common phenomenon among movements predicting the imminent end of the age as people's expectations exceed their patience.

The coming of the Lord on the day of judgment was alluded to in 1:7 in the words "at the revelation of the Lord Jesus from heaven with his mighty angels." In 2:1 and again in 2:8 and 9, Paul employs the term παρουσία ("coming"), his customary term for the future coming of the Lord. Its cultic usage in Hellenistic religion included the idea of "the coming of a hidden deity who makes his presence felt by a revelation of his power" to the initiates of the cult (BAGD s.v., 2b). It is thus synonymous with the expression in 1:7 describing the coming of the Lord as a revelation. (For further discussion on the meaning and significance of "parousia" see the comments on 1 Thes. 2:19.) The inclusion of the full designation "our Lord Jesus Christ" with the reference to his coming adds solemnity to the statement and therefore to the subsequent discussion.

But Paul's theme is not merely the public manifestation of the Lord but also the disposition of Christians with respect to it. On account of this he proceeds to write the words "and our assembling with him." This is the only instance in Paul's letters of ἐπισυναγωγή or its cognate verb, but the idea is parallel to the one found in 1 Thes. 4:16f. The emphasis of the word lies on the act of the community's gathering together with the Lord at the time of his coming, though 1 Thes. 4:17f. suggests that the community is passive in the matter: The initiative for their being gathered or assembled comes from God.

The concept of an eschatological gathering goes back to the OT. The exilic prophets looked forward to God reassembling the nation of Israel after the exile in Babylon (cf. Is. 43:4-7; 52:12; 56:8; Je. 31:8; Ezk. 28:9; Ps. 106[LXX 105]:47, all of which use either ἐπισυνάγειν or its uncompounded cognate and synonym συνάγειν). They also warned of the assembling of the nations in judgment (cf. Joel 3:2). Since the followers of Jesus were a scattered group who could not come together as one single community, it became part of the eschatological hope of the early Christians that at the coming of the Lord they would be gathered together from the four corners of the earth to enter into their inheritance in God's dominion (cf. Mk. 13:27). This hope lies behind Paul's reference here to the gathering of believers to the Lord. The next verse gives some indication of the situation that led Paul to take up the theme of the parousia and the assembling of the community to be with the Lord.

2:2 When he wrote 2 Thessalonians, Paul feared that his converts were disturbed by their misunderstanding concerning the day of the Lord. He therefore explains the purpose of his entreaty to his readers: εἰς τὸ μὴ ταχέως σαλευθῆναι ὑμᾶς ἀπὸ τοῦ νοὸς μηδὲ θροεῖσθαι ("in order that you not be quickly shaken from your composure nor disturbed"). The expression "not be quickly shaken from your composure" stresses the need for the readers to be constantly vigilant against the possibility of being made to waver in their beliefs regarding the coming of Christ. νοῦς refers to the "mind" as the seat of thinking and understanding and has the connotation of mental composure in this passage (BAGD s.v., 1).

The second infinitive, θροεῖσθαι ("to be disturbed") is in the present tense and appears to designate a continuing state of mental disturbance that Paul feared had been precipitated by a misunderstanding in the community regarding the arrival of the day of the Lord. He mentions three possible sources of his readers' misunderstanding: διὰ πνεύματος, διὰ λόγου, and δι' ἐπιστολῆς ὡς δι' ἡμῶν ("through a 'spirit,' through an oral statement, or through a letter allegedly by us"). "Through a spirit" presumably means "through a spirit-inspired utterance" (cf. Bruce, 163 and Best, 279). ὡς δι' ἡμῶν ("allegedly by us") probably goes either with the last two of the preceding prepositional phrases or with all three, since in v. 15 "through an oral statement" and "through a letter" must refer to Paul's own speech and letter to the Thessalonians. Also, as Best (278) has pointed out, "oral statement" would make more sense with a qualifier and the words "allegedly by us" are the only available ones in the context in v. 2. If "allegedly by us" goes with the last two phrases then it seems likely that it should also go with the first, "by a 'spirit,'" to balance the sentence. ὡς in this context denotes a quality wrongly attributed to someone. This implies that Paul either believed or considered it possible that the Thessalonians' misunderstanding was *alleged* to be based on something prophesied, spoken, or written by himself or one of his colleagues.

Lindemann ("Abfassungszweck," 36-42) has argued that the reference to a letter purporting to be from Paul was intended by a later author to throw doubt on the Pauline authorship of 1 Thessalonians in order to discredit it in the church on account of its unacceptable teachings regarding the parousia. This is an ingenious thesis, but the ambiguity of the reference in 2:2 does not allow an identification of the possible letter in question with 1 Thessalonians. If the author of 2 Thessalonians had sought to displace 1 Thessalonians as the source of a misleading conception of the parousia, a more direct approach would have been required. In any case, as Trilling (24 n. 21) has pointed out, it is improbable that a writer would try to bring about the rejection of the whole letter because of dissatisfaction with 4:15, 17, as Lindemann asserts. Although Frame (247), Marshall (187), and Trilling (77) for various other reasons maintain that "through a letter as by us" probably refers to 1 Thessalonians, Best (279) is correct in pointing out that if Paul had thought that a passage in a previous letter was the source of the trouble he would have sought to explain his position more carefully.

The way in which 2:2 reads indicates that Paul probably did not know the origins of the Thessalonians' misconception. He appears to have been uncertain himself as to whether the problem was created by a letter, an oral statement of a rational nature, or a spirit-inspired prophecy. He merely wished to exclude the possibility that anything he or his missionary colleagues might have said or written could be construed as grounds for believing that the day of the Lord had already come.

The text does not provide us with sufficient information to know exactly why the Thessalonians maintained that ὡς ὅτι ἐνέστηκεν ἡ ἡμέρα τοῦ κυρίου ("the day of the Lord has come") or what precisely they meant by it. The ὡς preceding the dependent clause "that the day of the Lord has come" should probably be interpreted like the previous ὡς to refer to an incorrectly maintained fact. Von Dobschütz (268), Dibelius (29), and others interpret ἐνέστηκεν as meaning "to be about to take place" on the grounds that it is inconceivable that the Thessalonians could have believed that the day of the Lord had actually arrived as this would have entailed the coming of the Lord, something that had clearly not happened. The available evidence for the use of ἐνιστάναι, however, indicates that the word never has this sense when used in the past tenses, and so, with a majority of recent commentators, I accept that the word must have the meaning "has come."

Some, like Schmithals (*Paul and the Gnostics,* 202-208), claim that the Thessalonians believed that the day of the Lord had come in a spiritualized sense owing to Gnostic influence. This appears unlikely. Paul's argument in 2 Thes. 2:1-12 attempts to demonstrate that the events associated with the day of the Lord had not occurred. Such a line of argument would not make any impression on the Gnostics whom Schmithals describes, since they would have spiritualized both the day of the Lord and the parousia of the Lord (see Laub, *Eschatologische Verkündigung,* 138-140 and Best, 276f. for further criticism).

If the Thessalonians did in fact believe that the day of the Lord had come, they most likely understood it not as a literal twenty-four-hour period but as the final period of the present order culminating in the coming of the Lord Jesus. They may have believed in something similar to the Jewish idea of the "messianic woes," a period of severe distress before the appearance of the messiah, who would usher in the period of salvation. From this perspective they may have considered their own suffering as part of the final phase before the coming of the Lord (cf. Aus, "Relevance," 263f.).

Whatever their precise understanding may have been, it led to Paul's attempt in 2:3-15 to refute the notion that the day of the Lord was already present. Nevertheless, Paul's vagueness about the source of the misunderstanding may suggest that he was not well-informed about what was happening in Thessalonica. This would support my contention that 2 Thessalonians was a letter taken by Timothy on his initial visit as described in 1 Thes. 3:1-6. Paul mentions there that it was anxiety about the Thessalonians that caused him to send Timothy. He also tells us that he was concerned that nothing should shake (τὸ μηδένα σαίνεσθαι) his converts in their tribulation. This is probably an allusion to the problem dealt with in 2 Thes. 2:1-12. Undoubtedly when Timothy returned after the visit mentioned in 1 Thes. 3:1-6 he reported to Paul about the exact nature of the situation at Thessalonica. If I am correct that Paul was not well-informed about the situation when he wrote 2 Thessalonians, then the real problem disturbing his converts may have involved the participation of deceased Christians in the parousia and assumption to heaven as discussed in 1 Thes. 4:15-18. This possibility receives some corroboration from the reference to the gathering of Christians at the parousia of the Lord in 2 Thes. 2:1.

PROBATIO: 2:3-15

Jewett (*Thessalonian Correspondence,* 83f.) divides the *probatio* into two proofs, the first, in 2:3-12, demonstrating that the parousia has not yet occurred, the second, in 2:13–3:5, providing assurance that believers "will prevail until that time" if "they stand firm in the Pauline teachings and example." Jewett's inclusion of 3:1-5 in the second proof appears questionable. Giblin (*Threat to Faith,* 43) has convincingly argued that Paul regularly uses the phrase ἄρα οὖν ("therefore then"), found in 2:15, as a concluding phrase. The obvious allusions in v. 15 to v. 2 confirm that it is intended as a conclusion to the section. Vv. 16f. form a *peroratio* that both summarizes the argument and attempts to persuade the readers to act appropriately in light of the argument. For this reason it is best to understand the expression τὸ λοιπόν ("finally") in 3:1 as a transitional phrase to the exhortative section rather than inferentially, as Jewett thinks (see the discussion below of 3:1).

Jewett is also mistaken about the nature of the second proof. It is not a demonstration that Christians will persevere to the end, as Jewett suggests. Instead, it demonstrates why they should not be disturbed by what is happening around them and to them. The imperatives of v. 15 indicate that vv. 3-14 have a parenetic or hortatory function, as Giblin points out (*Threat to Faith,* 43).

FIRST PROOF: 2:3-12

The first proof divides into two parts and demonstrates that the day of the Lord cannot possibly have come. Paul begins his proof in vv. 3-7 by showing that the necessary events preceding the appearance of Jesus have not occurred. In vv. 8-12 he gives evidence to demonstrate that the events associated with the day of the Lord itself have not happened. On careful inspection this proof maintains that only two events will precede the parousia of Christ: (1) the removal of the one now prevailing (v. 7) and (2) the rebellion and public manifestation of Satan's emissary, the lawless one (vv. 3f., 8). Everything else in these verses is simply an amplification of these two events and the people involved in them. For this reason Hughes (58) gives a false impression of what is contained in the text when he speaks of "a timetable of apocalyptic events"

242

in vv. 3-12. His separation of the "rebellion" and "the public manifestation of the lawless one" into two distinct steps is crucial for creating the impression that Paul was providing a timetable, but it is exegetically unwarranted, as will be shown.

Vv. 10-12 move away from the question of the day of the Lord itself to those who will be condemned on that day. This shift in focus introduces a parenetic dimension into the discussion as the readers are implicitly warned not to be deceived by the anti-parousia of Satan's emissary. At the same time vv. 10-12 also offer an explanation as to why people reject the truth of the gospel and ultimately why the Thessalonians underwent persecution at the hands of their fellow citizens. The discussion of those who are perishing in vv. 10-12 also prepares for the second proof in vv. 13-15 regarding those who are being saved.

2:3 Apparently Paul did not know how or from where the misconception concerning the day of the Lord arose, because he warns his readers μή τις ὑμᾶς ἐξαπατήσῃ κατὰ μηδένα τρόπον ("do not let anyone deceive you in any way"). Had he known, he would probably have given some indication as to the source of the problem. This helps justify my view that he was not well-informed about the situation at Thessalonica when he wrote the letter. But v. 3a may also represent an example of Paul taking up a traditional apocalyptic theme regarding the forces opposing the community and God and seeking to deceive the faithful (cf. Mk. 13:5f.). This is a natural worry for a millenarian movement because such movements often manifest fear about internal corruption of their belief and behavior systems. New interpreters and their interpretations pose a threat to the original interpreters of the tradition. Paul's anxiety regarding such a possibility is shown in what follows.

The second clause of v. 3 continues into v. 4 and contains a grammatical difficulty of considerable importance. Paul begins a future probable conditional sentence with the protasis ὅτι ἐὰν μὴ ἔλθῃ ἡ ἀποστασία πρῶτον καὶ ἀποκαλυφθῇ ὁ ἄνθρωπος τῆς ἀνομίας ("for unless the rebellion comes first and the person of rebellion [literally "of lawlessness"] is revealed") but with no apodosis. The construction is first interrupted by the description of the person of rebellion, which begins in the last phrase of v. 3 and continues through verse 4, and is finally lost sight of because of the parenthetical remark in v. 5. Although πρῶτον ("first") in v. 3 could mark the beginning of a temporal sequence in which the apostasy would be followed by the revealing of the person of rebellion, in the absence of ἔπειτα ("then") or a similar term with ἀποκαλυφθῇ ("be revealed") it is more likely that the temporal adverb includes the whole of the protasis. This places the rebellion and the revelation of the person of rebellion on a similar footing. Their precise significance can only be determined after it is decided how the anacoluthon of the conditional sentence should be concluded.

Two possibilities exist. Either we derive the missing apodosis from what follows, as Giblin argues (*Threat to Faith,* 122-139), or from what precedes it, as do most commentators (cf. Frame, 250; Best, 280f.). Giblin (135) argues that the conclusion to the conditional sentence should be understood as something like " 'the judgment of God will not have been executed against the powers of deception, removing them once and for all,' " or " 'the Lord will not have come in judgment to end definitively the deception that is the work of Satan.' " By this interpretation he intends to stress what he calls the *"qualitative* aspects of the parousia" (the emphasis is his) and his belief that the rebellion and revelation mentioned in v. 3 are conditions for the manifestation of the coming judgment rather than signs of its imminence.

In spite of Giblin's elaborate argument, his version of the missing conclusion or apodosis is simply a description of what the day of the Lord will be like. Furthermore his contrast between conditions for its manifestation and signs of its arrival is overly subtle. Anyone reading vv. 1-4 would naturally identify the presence of the conditions for the manifestation of God's judgment, or the day of the Lord, as signs of its arrival when they occurred.

Thus we may assume that the missing conclusion to the conditional sentence was something like "the day of the Lord will not come." The absence of the conclusion to the conditional sentence in vv. 3f. represents yet another example of imprecision and carelessness which, while not unknown in Paul, who probably dictated most of his letters, appears very strange if the letter were intended as a theological correction or restatement of Paul's views by a later writer. A self-conscious literary forger would almost certainly have made his point with great care rather than allowing an anacoluthon with its inherent ambiguity to occur precisely at a key point in his argument.

Although ἀποστασία, signifying the state of apostasy or rebellion, was used in both a political and a religious sense, the latter dominates in the Greek Bible (cf. LXX Jos. 22:22; 2 Ch. 29:19; 33:19; Je. 2:19; 1 Macc. 2:15; and in the NT see Acts 21:21; see also the use of the cognate verb ἀφίσταναι in Lk. 8:13; 1 Tim. 4:1; Heb. 3:12). In the apocalyptic context of 2 Thessalonians 2, the rebellion referred to is a religious one directed against God. In all probability we may identify those whose rebellion is mentioned in v. 3 with those who are to be deceived in vv. 10-12. While Paul may have thought of certain Christians being involved (elsewhere he questioned the bona fides of some who purported to be Christians: cf. Gal. 2:4; 2 Cor. 11:12-15; Phil. 1:15-18), the reference to the temple in v. 4 suggests that he is working with a traditional apocalyptic understanding in which it was maintained that many of the people of God, that is the Jews, would rebel against God and the Law at the time of the end (cf. *Jub.* 23:14-23; 2 Esdr. 5:1-13; *1 Enoch* 91:3-10; 93:8-10; 1QpHab 2:1ff. and Mk. 13:5f.). Paul probably taught that the apostasy was to come about through the activity of the person of rebellion. According to vv. 9-12 that person's advent, as the agent of Satan, will deceive those perishing because they refuse to believe the truth. Whether this interpretation is correct or not, Paul certainly expected his readers to understand the meaning of what he was writing on the basis of what they had been taught previously regarding the end of the age (cf. v. 5).

The "revealing" of the person of rebellion should not be thought of as the making known of some formerly unknown or unidentified figure. Rather, just as Paul uses the noun ἀποκάλυψις to denote Christ's parousia in 1:7, so the cognate verb is employed here to refer to the public manifestation of the person of rebellion mentioned in vv. 9f. As those verses show, that person's manifestation is a deceptive parody or "anti-parousia" of Jesus' future coming. The distinctive designation ὁ ἄνθρωπος τῆς ἀνομίας ("the person of rebellion") is very probably derived from a Semitic genitive construct, as is the parallel expression ὁ υἱὸς τῆς ἀπωλείας ("the son of destruction"; see Turner, *Syntax*, 207f.). In both cases the nouns in the genitive indicate a particular quality of the individual referred to. Townsend ("II Thessalonians 2:3-12," 234f.) believes that these two Semitic construct phrases and "the mystery of rebellion" (v. 7), which has a Hebrew parallel in 1Q27 (= 1QMyst) 1, argue for 2 Thes. 2:3-12 being dependent upon either a Semitic language source or a highly Semiticized Greek language source. If this is correct, it would account for some of the unusual linguistic and conceptual features of the passage.

The designation "person of rebellion" describes this individual's blatant disregard for and opposition to the will of God. The term "son of destruction" probably denotes his role as an agent of destruction for Satan, as vv. 9f. imply (cf. Best, 284 and Marshall, 190, who maintain that it refers to the fate or doom of this person). (The reading ἀνομίας [א B 81, etc.] is to be preferred over the more widely attested reading ἁμαρτίας [A D G K L P, etc.] because in v. 8 the abbreviated term ὁ ἄνομος is used with the verb ἀποκαλυφθήσεται to refer to the same individual.) Ps. 88:23 (LXX) has the designation υἱὸς ἀνομίας. This has long been recognized as parallel to the two expressions in 2 Thes. 2:3 (cf. von Dobschütz, 272). Aus ("God's Plan," 538) believes that both of these expressions were, in fact, derived from Ps. 88:23. But this is far from certain.

What we probably have here in 2 Thessalonians is a traditional apocalyptic figure whose opposition to God was based on recollection of Pompey and his subjugation of Palestine. *Pss. Sol.* 17:11-22 records a pious Jewish interpretation of Pompey's campaign in 63 BC and possesses a striking similarity to 2 Thes. 2:3f. The text refers to Pompey as the lawless one (ὁ ἄνομος), describes his destruction of the land, and mentions the Jewish apostasy resulting from his activity. All three of these themes are brought together in 2 Thes. 2:3: the coming apostasy is associated with the person of rebellion (who in v. 8 is called ὁ ἄνομος) and the son of destruction. I will later indicate several other interesting parallels between *Psalms of Solomon* 17 and 2 Thessalonians 2, as well as connections with other apocalyptic texts showing that the imagery and eschatological schema employed in 2 Thessalonians

2, like parts of chap. 1, were already extant when Paul wrote and probably derived from an earlier stage of Christianity as it emerged in the apocalyptically-oriented environment of Palestine.

2:4 The person indicated in v. 3 is described in v. 4 as arrogating to himself divine status. The participles ἀντικείμενος ("opposing") and ὑπεραιρόμενος ("exalting [himself]") are governed by the same article and are used restrictively to spell out the distinctive activity of the person of rebellion. That person opposes and exalts himself ἐπὶ πάντα λεγόμενον θεὸν ἢ σέβασμα ("over every so-called god or object of worship"). The language here may well be drawn from Dn. 11:36, which speaks of a certain king, almost certainly Antiochus Epiphanes, who ὑψωθήσεται ἐπὶ πάντα θεόν ("will be exalted over every god"). Whether the creator of the eschatological scenario contained in 2 Thes. 2:3-8 was aware that the passage originally referred to Antiochus is doubtful. He was most likely a student of sacred literature who found in Daniel an unfulfilled prophecy regarding the end of the age and combined it with other ideas and images such as those in *Psalms of Solomon* 17. λεγόμενον ("so-called") was probably added by the Christian creator of the material to preserve the belief that there was only one true God in spite of the fact that pagans believed in many gods (cf. 1 Cor. 8:5f. where the expression λεγόμενοι θεοί ["so-called gods"] occurs in relation to the pagan deities). To it was also appended the term σέβασμα ("object of worship") to indicate that the person would arrogantly exalt himself above the sacred objects of the various religions to demonstrate his own superiority.

In the Jewish-Christian perspective from which the tradition originated, the arrogance of the person of rebellion toward religion in general would culminate or result in his usurpation of the temple of God to declare his own divinity, as ὥστε αὐτὸν εἰς τὸν ναὸν τοῦ θεοῦ καθίσαι, ἀποδεικνύντα ἑαυτὸν ὅτι ἔστιν θεός ("so that he takes his seat in the temple, proclaiming himself that he is God") demonstrate. ναός may refer to a temple in general, as does ἱερόν, but in the present context it probably refers to the inner sanctuary where the deity was thought to reside. The inner sanctuary in question is almost certainly the Holy of Holies in the Jerusalem temple where God was thought by the Jewish people from OT times to dwell. ναόν is made definite by the article and the possessive genitive τοῦ θεοῦ ("of God"), indicating that a specific building was intended. Although it is true that in 1 Cor. 3:16f. Paul employs ναός in a metaphorical sense to refer to the Christian as a temple of God (cf. 1 Cor. 6:19), in the present context where no mention is made of the believer and the indwelling of the Spirit of God as in 1 Corinthians, such an interpretation is highly unlikely. Jewish Christians as well as Gentile Christians undoubtedly would have understood it as a reference to the one true temple of God in Jerusalem, especially since the verse contains an allusion to Dn. 11:31-36 and the desecration of the temple at Jerusalem by Antiochus Epiphanes (see Townsend, "II Thessalonians 2:3-12," 235-237 for this and further evidence concerning the identification of "the temple of God" in v. 4 with the temple at Jerusalem).

The definite nature of this reference makes it impossible to believe that either the creator of the scenario, whether Paul or another, or the original readers of the letter would have understood the reference metaphorically, as Marshall (190-192) and Bruce (169) seem to favor. Marshall wishes to preserve the passage as a genuine piece of early Christian prophecy in spite of the destruction of the temple in AD 70. To do so he interprets the statement about the figure taking his seat in the temple sanctuary as a metaphor "to express the opposition of evil to God." While this explanation provides us with a way to maintain the abiding relevance of the passage today, it can hardly be taken as definitive for its interpretation during the lifetime of Paul. The apostle, after all, expected a relatively imminent end to the existing world order and had undoubtedly imbibed enough of the apocalyptic tradition of first-century Judaism to know that the defilement of the temple was part of eschatological expectation (cf. Dn. 9:27; 11:31; 12:11; Mk. 13:14). Bruce accepts that the reference is to the temple at Jerusalem but then claims that Paul and his companions meant it "in a metaphorical sense" on the grounds that the language was intended to denote the usurpation of divine authority. Bruce here confuses the symbolic meaning of the act of usurpation in the temple at Jerusalem with the language used to describe it, seeing a metaphor in the language instead of referring to the symbolic nature of the deed committed by the person of lawlessness.

In trying to give his readers a temporally oriented framework for understanding the coming of the day of the Lord, Paul appears to have intended that they think of a final act of hostility toward God by some powerful individual, which would precipitate the coming of Christ. The well-known attempt in AD 40 by Gaius Caesar to have his image erected in the temple at Jerusalem may well have given renewed substance to the belief that the temple would be desecrated by a usurper whom God would destroy in ushering in the new age. This event may well lie behind the circulation of the tradition found in Mk. 13:14-19 regarding "the abomination of desolation standing where it should not be." The idea itself was based on Dn. 9:27; 11:31; 12:11 and came into the apocalyptic tradition as a result of Antiochus Epiphanes' desecration of the temple in the second century BC (see Bruce, *New Testament History*, 256f.).

The final clause of v. 4 explains the meaning of the usurper's seating himself in the Holy of Holies in the temple at Jerusalem. By doing so, he is ἀποδεικνύντα ἑαυτὸν ὅτι ἔστιν θεός ("proclaiming himself, that he is God"). The idea of historical figures arrogating to themselves claims to be divine had a long history in Jewish thought. Ezk. 28:1-10 describes the king of Tyre being condemned by God for doing so, and Is. 14:4-20 describes the fate of the king of Babylon, who sought to elevate himself to the realm of the divine (cf. *Sib.*

Or. 5:33f., written about Nero). As mentioned above the Roman emperor Gaius was a contemporary example of someone who sought to assert his own deity specifically in connection with the temple at Jerusalem and therefore may have provided a paradigm for the activity described in v. 4. Best (288f.) may well be correct that 2 Thes. 2:3f. is related to the emergence of the tradition about false Christs who would appear and lead the faithful astray (Mk. 13:21f.) and to the development of the Antichrist motif (1 Jn. 2:18; 4:3), which emerged toward the end of the first century AD.

2 Thes. 2:3f. is of considerable importance for the understanding of early Christianity. It offers us one of our earliest windows on the imagery of apocalyptic eschatology as found in the initial period of the Christian movement and shows the historicizing description of the eschatological events, which served to make the imminent eschatological expectations of the primitive community realistic to its adherents. This historicized and realistic quality is what gives the passage its prophetic character and causes the chief problem for those who seek to find some abiding validity in the passage.

Much of the language found in various Jewish and Christian apocalypses from the period is highly symbolic and does not purport to be prophetic. 2 Thes. 2:3f., however, reads like prophecy about historical events to come, and it is almost certain that this is how Paul and his readers would have understood it. The passage can no longer be understood as valid, since the temple was destroyed in AD 70 without the manifestation of the person of lawlessness or the return of Christ occurring. In order to maintain the continuing validity of the passage, some deny the obvious reference to the historical temple at Jerusalem, as does Marshall (191f.; he mentions others who do so for less plausible reasons than his own). A more straightforward way of treating the problem is to admit that the passage meant something very different to Paul and his original readers than it can mean for us today. Once this is acknowledged, Marshall's conclusion (192) that the imagery of vv. 3f. expresses "the reality and menace of the power of evil which attempts to deny the reality and power of God" offers us a meaningful interpretation of the passage, since it is as true today as it was in Paul's day.

Paul and his contemporaries intuitively recognized that the type of evil that defies God and seeks to usurp his position derives from corrupt and unjust social and political institutions such as imperial rule under Gaius Caesar (cf. the attitude of the writer of Revelation toward Roman power). This insight informs the eschatological scenario of 2 Thes. 2:3-8 and reflects the sense of human powerlessness felt by the early Christians in the face of social and political processes that denied the truth of their beliefs in a good and just God and sometimes even led to their persecution, as at Thessalonica.

For Christians of today the problems are often more complex. Political figures and nation states arrogate to themselves Christian symbols to legitimate their unjust and oppressive practices such as apartheid, militarism, and imperialism (see *The Road to Damascus: Kairos and Conversion* for a discussion of this problem from the perspective of Third World Christians). Contemporary Christians must recognize in this a manifestation of the pervasive and arrogant evil described by Paul in 2 Thes. 2:4.

2:5 The conditional sentence begun in vv. 3 and 4 is interrupted by the interjection οὐ μνημονεύετε ὅτι ἔτι ὢν πρὸς ὑμᾶς ταῦτα ἔλεγον ὑμῖν; ("do you not remember that while I was still with you I used to tell you these things?"). Paul frequently appeals to his readers' knowledge or recollections in support of what he says in his letters (cf. 1 Thes. 2:9; 3:3f.; 4:2). V. 5 indicates that Paul's readers were familiar with the thought just expressed and therefore could be expected to complete the conditional sentence begun in v. 3. He momentarily lapses into the first person singular with ἔλεγον ("I used to tell"). This reflects the fact that he was primarily responsible for the composition of the letter and for the grounding of the Thessalonians in their new faith. (On the change from first person plural to first person singular cf. 1 Thes. 2:18; 3:5.)

Trilling (88), who claims that 2 Thessalonians is pseudepigraphic, maintains that v. 5 was intended to create the fiction that the Antichrist tradition went back to Paul's oral teaching even though it was not discussed in any of his letters. He further asserts that the appeal to the recollection of the readers was introduced "as a stylistic expedient of the pseudepigraphical technique" (my translation). His interpretation of v. 5, however, is highly unlikely. It is nearly impossible to conceive of the sophisticated forger whom Trilling presupposes being so careless as to disrupt his own thought at a crucial point by introducing an anacoluthon into his argument (see comments on v. 3). An intelligent forger would certainly have interjected a feigned appeal to his readers' knowledge or recollections after he had completed the conditional sentence. In addition Trilling (88 n. 333) notes that it is strange that the writer makes no reference to 1 Thes. 4:13-18, if 2 Thessalonians was written shortly after 1 Thessalonians. Marshall (192) argues that the theme of 1 Thessalonians was different in that it concerned the return of the Lord, but he is not altogether correct at this point since 2 Thes. 2:1-17 is also directed to the problem of the parousia of the Lord. If, however, as I have suggested, 2 Thessalonians was written before 1 Thessalonians, one of Trilling's main lines of attack against the authenticity of 2 Thessalonians collapses.

2:6-7 These two verses are among the most problematic texts in the whole of the Pauline corpus. They presuppose knowledge to which we do not have access, no fully convincing parallels have ever been suggested, and, beyond the likelihood that the material derives from the mythical world of apocalypticism, no one has put forward a satisfactory background for the verses. We must assume that Paul's original readers had the necessary knowledge, based on his oral teachings, to interpret the passage. Certainly

Paul thought they did, since he writes καὶ νῦν οἴδατε ("and now you know").
V. 5, it would seem, refers to what precedes it as well as to what follows. In
addition, if I am correct in my understanding of the external circumstances of
the letter, Timothy, as the bearer of the letter, would have explained anything
not fully understood when he brought the letter to Thessalonica.

The primary exegetical difficulties revolve around the meaning of the
neuter participle τὸ κατέχον in v. 6 and the masculine participle ὁ κατέχων in
v. 7, although there are other problems as well. The verb κατέχειν can be and
has been interpreted in several different ways leading to radically different
understandings of the text. Before I attempt to explain the passage, therefore,
a brief review of major approaches to the problem of τὸ κατέχον and ὁ κατέχων
will prove valuable.

1. From at least the days of Tertullian (ca. AD 200; see Best, 296) the
verb κατέχειν has been interpreted as meaning "to restrain." The neuter
participle is understood to refer to the Roman Empire and the masculine
participle is thought to allude to the emperor. This view is based on the belief
that Paul as a Roman citizen valued the protection that Roman law and the
emperor, as the chief arbiter of it, offered him against his Jewish opponents
and the general disorder which would have hindered his mission (see Findlay,
177-179 for a modern writer holding this position).

Several factors have led to the rejection of this view by recent commentators. In the first place, the passage is clearly not about civil rebellion, but
about opposition to God. Second, the imagery is drawn from the world of
apocalyptic with its mythical symbols and perspectives, not the everyday
world of public law and order in the Roman Empire. But apart from these
considerations, it is difficult to believe that Paul looked to the collapse of
Roman rule as a precondition for the final denouement of the present age.
Notwithstanding Rom. 13:1-7, Paul was no exponent of civil religion (that is,
religion used to legitimate the rule of the state), as this view would suggest.
He could, for example, accuse the earthly rulers of this age of collusion in the
crucifixion of the Lord (cf. 1 Cor. 2:8).

2. Another line of interpretation going back to Cullmann ("Caractère,"
210-245) and subsequently developed by Munck (*Paul*, 36-42) maintains that
the restraining factor (neuter participle) was the preaching of the gospel and
that the restrainer (masculine participle) was the apostle Paul himself whose
task was to preach the gospel to the Gentiles.

This interpretation is problematic. It presupposes that Paul would have
to be removed from the scene before the end could come, even though he
expected to survive to the parousia, according to 1 Thes. 4:13-18. Marshall
(198f.) is also correct in questioning whether Paul considered his own role as
decisive in the unfolding salvation of humankind, as this interpretation assumes.

Marshall himself has suggested a variation of this view. He believes

250

with Cullmann and Munck that the preaching of the gospel to the nations provides the reason that God has restrained the outbreak of evil. He differs from them, however, by claiming that it is not Paul but an angel of God who serves to restrain evil until God orders his withdrawal at the appropriate time. This explanation, like that of Cullmann and Munck, depends on an idea not set out in the passage, namely that Paul believed the preaching of the gospel to the Gentiles would have to occur before the end of the age could come. Such an approach should only be considered as a last resort. As I will show below, another understanding is possible and renders such speculative inter-pretations unnecessary.

3. A third and very different line of interpretation takes the two partici-ples to mean "delay," in light of Hab. 2:3, a passage dealing with God's delay of the end of the age. This approach views God (or one of the divine angelic agents) as the one who is delaying the end or more specifically the coming of Christ (see Strobel, *Untersuchungen,* 98-116; Trilling, 90-102).

Best (300f.) has demonstrated that this explanation has serious draw-backs. It assumes that the neuter participle is little different in meaning from the masculine participle (so Trilling, 92). This leaves unanswered the question of why the two different genders were employed in the first place. If the neuter refers to the will of God, one has to ask why Paul did not make this clear. This interpretation also falters on linguistic grounds. κατέχειν does not normally mean "delay" (Hab. 2:3 employs χρονίζειν to mean "to delay"). Moreover, Best is right to ask why such imprecise language was used to refer to the activity of God since there was no apparent need to be secretive.

4. Quite similar to the previous explanation in terms of its conclusions is one proposed by Aus ("God's Plan"). As with his study of 2 Thessalonians 1, Aus looks to Isaiah 66 to find the background for 2 Thes. 2:6f. According to him, the Hebrew term 'āṣar, found in Is. 66:9 and referring there to the possibility of God "shutting the womb" or "restraining birth" in a context speaking of God's restoration of Jerusalem, provided the source of the allusion in 2 Thes. 2:6f. He assumes that the creator of vv. 6f. was working with the Hebrew text of Isaiah 66 in mind and simply paraphrased it, since the LXX does not use κατέχον at this point.

Aus's explanation is more ingenious than credible for several reasons. In the first place, if the author of 2 Thes. 2:6f. had wished to use the image of the restraint of birth as found in Isaiah 66 to describe the delay of the coming of Christ, it is strange that he used only κατέχον, a possible translation of Hebrew 'āṣar, though not the most obvious, and not the image of the shut womb as well. Moreover, since the verb alone is used and not the image of the shut womb, there is no evidence that God is the one restraining, as is the case in Isaiah 66. Secondly, the final phrase of 2 Thes. 2:7, "until he/it is removed from the midst" logically has to refer to the removal of the κατέχων. If, as Aus maintains, the κατέχων is God, then his removal is impossible (as in 3. above). Aus is aware of this criticism. To get around it he argues that the author was careless in his excitement and this led him to be imprecise. What the author meant to say, according to Aus, was that God was restraining the mystery of rebellion until it reached its peak, at which time the mysterious aspect would be removed. In rejecting the obvious meaning of the text, Aus builds on a set of poorly supported suppositions regarding the hypothetical background of the text in Isaiah 66.

5. Another recent attempt to explain κατέχον is found in Giblin's *Threat to Faith* (224-242). He argues that the κατέχον is to be associated with the "person of rebellion" from v. 3 and exists as a threat to the faith of the Thessalonians. In keeping with this he claims that κατέχον means to "seize" or "possess" and that Paul refers to a function, namely prophetic seizure, (hence the neuter form of the participle in v. 6) and to some individual (hence the masculine form in v. 7) who was causing trouble in the community by his false prophecy concerning the imminent or present parousia while in a state of frenzy or ecstasy. This person's removal was a condition for the "parousia" of the person of rebellion.

This interpretation has received little support for several reasons. In the first place, the verb κατέχειν normally refers to seizure in a religious sense only in the passive, not in the active. Secondly, Giblin's very localized interpretation of the κατέχον seems to make the coming of Christ dependent upon the happenings in one small Christian community, whereas the event is actually to be cosmic. That Paul believed the coming of Christ would or could be held up until some local false prophet was out of the way seems highly unlikely.

6. A sixth major approach to the two participles holds that vv. 6f. concern an evil power and some evil person or other. In favor of this suggestion is that it can be derived from the context of vv. 3-12. It takes the two participles in the sense of "possessing," "ruling over," "holding sway," or "prevailing." Frame (259-262) takes the neuter participle as referring to the principle of rebellion and the masculine one as referring to Satan. Best (301f.) holds a somewhat similar view. He argues that the hostile figure involved must be an agent of Satan rather than Satan himself, though he does not give a reason for this. Townsend (240-242), without finally committing himself to a particular interpretation, argues that the κατέχων of v. 7 must be either God or the person of rebellion since no other figures are named in the passage prior to v. 7. As I shall show below, this approach, which views the two participles as referring to a power or principle and an individual hostile to God, offers the best solution to the enigma of vv. 6f.

2:6   καὶ νῦν ("and now") at the beginning of v. 6 almost certainly goes with οἴδατε ("you know"; see Bruce, 169f.) and has a temporal significance. Best (290), following Frame (262), argues that νῦν ("now") refers generally to the present situation of the readers in contrast to the future situation indicated by the καὶ τότε ("and then") in v. 8. The idea of a temporal sequence between the current knowledge of the readers and what will be revealed to them in the future makes good sense of the thought development of the passage. οἴδατε ("you know") probably denotes more than mere intellectual knowledge acquired at conversion. In Christianizing the Thessalonians, the process commonly referred to as catechization, Paul had given them new beliefs and values. These had transformed their perception of reality and of their own place in the world. As with converts to any new religious movement, the Thessalonians then began the process of reinterpreting the world and their own experience in it in terms of their newly acquired beliefs and values. Thus for Paul to say, "And now you know the κατέχον" is another way of saying that in the past they did not know or recognize the κατέχον but now, because they had been given the interpretative keys for doing so, they could recognize the effect of the κατέχον in the world (cf. Giblin, *Threat to Faith*, 159-166, who argues that οἴδατε concerns experiential knowledge).

The decisive issue for understanding this verse, as we have seen, revolves around the interpretation of the neuter participle κατέχον. Whatever conclusion we arrive at must account for the shift to the masculine participle of the same verb in v. 7. The simplest solution and the one making the best sense of the grammar is to take κατέχειν as meaning "to hold sway," "to rule," or "to prevail." All of these meanings are possible intransitive renderings of the verb and do not require us to supply an object, as do such renderings as "to restrain" or "to delay." The neuter form of the participle suggests that the writer has a principle in mind here, while the masculine form in v. 7 indicates that he has an individual in view. When it is asked what principle could now be "holding sway" or "prevailing" that would make sense in the passage, we need look no further than the mention of τὸ μυστήριον τῆς ἀνομίας ("the mystery of rebellion," literally "of lawlessness") in v. 7. The neuter form of the noun μυστήριον matches the gender of κατέχον in v. 6 and ἤδη ἐνεργεῖται ("now at work") indicate that the "mystery of rebellion" was a currently active force in the world perceivable by the Thessalonians in light of their Christian understanding. The explanatory γάρ ("for") of v. 7 indicates that v. 7a is intended to explain the meaning of τὸ κατέχον in v. 6.

The relation between εἰς τὸ ἀποκαλυφθῆναι αὐτὸν ἐν τῷ ἑαυτοῦ καιρῷ ("so that it may be revealed in its own time") and the words preceding it in v. 6 is problematic. The infinitival construction can depend either on τὸ κατέχον ("that which prevails") or on οἴδατε ("you know"), but both possibilities raise difficulties. According to Giblin (*Threat to Faith,* 206) the standard order of construction used by the writers of the NT, including Paul, demands that εἰς τὸ ἀποκαλυφθῆναι be taken with the verb οἴδατε. However, Best (291) points out that οἴδατε already has a direct object, that this verb is never followed by εἰς τό in Paul and only twice by an infinitive at all, and that where it occurs with a direct object followed by a dependent clause (see, e.g., Rom.

13:11; 1 Cor. 2:2; 16:15; 2 Cor. 9:2; 12:3; 1 Thes. 1:4f.; 2:1) the dependent clause is attached to the direct object and functions to explicate it further. In addition, Barnouin ("Problèmes," 484f.) maintains that because οἴδατε is not a verb of action, but refers to a cognitive process, it is not able to govern an articular infinitive. Paul may have placed the participle κατέχον forward in the sentence for emphasis rather than after the main verb as would normally be expected if a dependent articular infinitive construction was to follow. For this reason it appears better to agree with Best and Barnouin in favor of taking "so that it may be revealed in its own time" with "that which prevails."

The preposition εἰς with an articular infinitive following it can express either purpose or result. Here it is difficult to decide which is intended. In the end it is perhaps unnecessary to decide since the difference between a purpose clause and a result clause is often only a matter of perspective. Several other issues are of greater importance, such as to whom αὐτόν refers. The masculine gender of αὐτόν ("him") precludes the possibility of identifying it directly with κατέχον, a neuter, even though there is no other antecedent in the sentence. Since vv. 3 and 8 refer to the revealing of the person of rebellion it seems probable that αὐτόν in v. 6 is to be identified with the person of rebellion. ἑαυτοῦ ("his/its") can be either masculine or neuter, but it is perhaps best to relate it to the previous pronoun (some manuscripts like א A K P have the variant reading αὐτοῦ, which does this unambiguously) so that it is the person of rebellion who is to be revealed in his own time, that is, at the appointed time.

Normally we would assume that God is in control of time and thus determines when the person of rebellion will be revealed. In v. 9, however, it says that the "parousia" of the person of rebellion will be in conjunction with the activity of Satan. This may indicate that the "appointed time" of the person of rebellion is under the dominion of Satan rather than God because the person of rebellion is Satan's agent.

2:7 As indicated above, γάρ ("for") in v. 7 is explanatory, with the initial clause of the verse elucidating how τὸ κατέχον ("that which prevails") in v. 6 is to be understood. "That which prevails" is τὸ μυστήριον τῆς ἀνομίας ("the mystery of rebellion"), which ἤδη ἐνεργεῖται ("is already at work"). Since the masculine form ὁ κατέχων occurs in v. 7b, it evinces a close connection between the second part of the verse and v. 6a, where the neuter form τὸ κατέχον appears. The two halves of v. 7 should be understood together as explanatory of v. 6a, just as vv. 8f. are explanatory of v. 6b.

In Rom. 6:12-23 Paul describes the experience of Christians before coming to faith in Christ in terms of enslavement to the power of sin. From this it can be concluded that sin as a principle prevails over humanity before conversion. This does not appear to be what Paul has in mind here. The term ἁμαρτία ("sin") and its cognates are lacking in the context and the phrase ἤδη ἐνεργεῖτε ("it is now at work") implies that the "mystery of rebellion" has not always been active, but in the times leading to the end of the current age it has become active. Although parallels have been offered from Qumran, where the phrase "mysteries of sin" occurs (see 1QH 5:36; 1Q27 1:2, 7; 1QM 14:9), and from Josephus, where there is reference to "a mystery of evil" (*War* 1.470), the two are not exact parallels. Probably "the mystery of rebellion" is an ad hoc construction and denotes the secret or hidden workings of rebellion against God (cf. v. 3 on the meaning of ἀνομία). The process of rebellion was known to be at work already by the community of faith, but it would only become manifest with the revealing of the person of rebellion (cf. G. Bornkamm, *TDNT* IV, 823).

The voice of the verb ἐνεργεῖται is of some significance for exegesis. If it is passive it probably indicates that God is responsible for the activity of the mystery of rebellion (so Best, 293; cf. Marshall, 195). On the other hand, if the verb is middle, then the clause simply refers to the fact that rebellion against God is taking place. Lightfoot (*Galatians,* 204) claimed that ἐνεργεῖσθαι is never passive in Paul, and this view seems largely to have been accepted (see, e.g., BAGD s.v.). But Robinson in a detailed study of ἐνεργεῖν and its cognates (*Ephesians,* 241-247) has argued correctly, in my opinion, that there is no grammatical reason to take the verb as middle in our text because impersonal subjects do not require the middle voice of this particular verb, as BAGD suggests. Since v. 9 depicts the "parousia" of the man of rebellion as κατ' ἐνέργειαν τοῦ Σατανᾶ ("according to the working of Satan"), it may well be that in v. 7 it is Satan who has put in operation the secret rebellion currently underway (cf. Rigaux, 669f.).

The second part of v. 7 is by far more difficult to interpret, not only because of the problematic ὁ κατέχων, but also because the sentence does not seem to make grammatical sense as it stands. Many scholars believe that the sentence is elliptical (cf. Townsend, "II Thessalonians 2:3-12," 239); the question is how to make sense out of it. Three basic approaches are possible:

1. Barnouin ("Problèmes," 486-490), who receives some support from Townsend (*op. cit.,* 240), maintains that the unexpressed object of the participle κατέχων is the rebel of vv. 3f. This object of κατέχων is also the unexpressed subject of the temporal clause ἕως ἐκ μέσου γένηται ("until he comes from the midst"; cf. Aus, "God's Plan," 550f., who also holds that the "mystery of lawlessness" or "rebellion" is the subject of the temporal clause). This leads Barnouin (498) to understand v. 7b as meaning that someone holds back the rebel until the rebel departs from the place where he is restrained and comes.

But this approach does not really solve the problem of the missing verb in the main clause. Barnouin's attempt to find the object of κατέχων and the subject of the temporal clause is unnecessary in any case. κατέχων is intransitive in the context, as I have previously suggested, and is to be understood as the subject of the temporal clause, as most scholars believe.

2. With Frame (264f.), Giblin (*Threat to Faith,* 210-214), Best (294), and Trilling (94), among others, it is possible to supply a verb to go with ὁ

κατέχων, making v. 7b into a complete sentence and understanding κατέχων as the subject of the temporal clause. Here one could: (a) take κατέχων as essentially verbal and render v. 7b: "only the one who prevails prevails now until he is out of the way," or (b) provide a verb from the context, either ἐνεργεῖται from the previous clause, giving the translation "only the one who prevails is now at work until he is out of the way," or γένηται from what follows, giving the sense "only the one who prevails is (active) now until he is out of the way."

3. While thus supplying a verb from the context makes relatively good sense of the verse, an alternative is to preserve and even emphasize the close link between the first and second parts of the verse without resorting to understanding the verse as an ellipsis. It is possible that an inversion of the usual word order has taken place in v. 7 with ἕως occurring in the postpositive position (after ὁ κατέχων ἄρτι) in order to emphasize the subject of the subordinate clause that it introduces. This is characteristic of Paul (cf. Rom. 12:3; 1 Cor. 3:5; 6:4; 7:17; 9:15; 11:4; 2 Cor. 2:4; Gal. 2:10), and is the explanation suggested by BDF §475.1. This would yield a temporal clause dependent upon the clause in v. 7a and would read as follows: "only until the one who is now prevailing is out of the way." This, as the simplest interpretation of the existing text, is to be preferred, though as Best (294) points out, it does not differ significantly from taking the verse as an ellipsis and supplying either ἐνεργεῖται or γένηται.

The expression ἐκ μέσου γένηται is not found elsewhere in biblical Greek, but ἐκ μέσου implies separation or movement away from something. Bruce (170) adduces several examples from nonbiblical Greek where ἐκ μέσου plus a participial form of γενέσθαι occur with the sense of "be removed." This is the probable sense in our present text, and it indicates that the one who prevails will do so until he is removed. His close connection with the mysterious working of rebellion which continues in secret as long as he prevails indicates that the figure of the κατέχων is negative, even if he is not on a par with the person of rebellion who will be manifested after the former's removal according to v. 8.

The identity of the one who prevails was perhaps clear to the original readers, but we can only guess who it was. Since apocalyptic writings from the early Enoch literature and the Book of Daniel to the Book of Revelation often attempted to understand the political situations in their own world from the perspective of the divine world (on this theme see J. J. Collins, *Apocalyptic Imagination*), it is a reasonable possibility that Paul had in mind the political-religious conditions of his own day. The most likely possibility would seem to be the existing Roman emperor for three reasons: (1) The expression ὁ κατέχων could be used of a ruler. (2) ἤδη emphasizes that "the one who prevails" was doing so at the time Paul wrote. (3) The earlier image of the person of rebellion was probably based on such historical figures as the

Roman general Pompey and Gaius Caesar (see on v. 4). That Paul was critical of the political rulers of his day is clear from 1 Cor. 2:8, where they are condemned for having crucified the Lord of glory (cf. 1 Cor. 2:6).

The idea that the κατέχων would need to be removed before the person of rebellion would be revealed may have derived from several factors. In the first place the ruling emperor Claudius had not shown himself to be as egregious a ruler as his predecessor Gaius, even though the Christian community was convinced that rebellion against God was taking place, if not openly, at least in secret. The removal of the ruling figure may have been based on the fact that the praetorian guard had removed Gaius, and Paul expected that a similar removal of the present ruler would lead to the revealing of the final rebellious ruler whom Christ would destroy. Given 1 Cor. 2:8, Paul could easily have connected the Roman civil rulers with the working of Satan, as v. 9 suggests.

2:8 καὶ τότε ("and then") at the beginning of v. 8 indicates that what is about to be described will occur after the removal of "the one who now prevails." ἀποκαλυφθήσεται ὁ ἄνομος ("the rebel will be revealed") picks up the thought of vv. 3b and 6b. The Semitic expression "the person of lawlessness" (or "rebellion," as I have translated ἀνομίας) in v. 3b is replaced by the more typically Greek ὁ ἄνομος ("the lawless one" or "the rebellious one") here. The same person is, however, clearly in mind and the emphasis is upon his rebellious nature vis-à-vis God, which will lead to his destruction by God's agent, the Lord Jesus. The revealing of the rebel in the future is intended to contrast with the hidden workings of rebellion now taking place until the present "prevailer" is removed (v. 7) and matters come to a crisis. This crisis will result in the coming of the Lord Jesus. The revelation of the rebel is not a general revelation: it is directed to the members of the Christian community. God will make it clear to them when the final rebel appears on the scene, hence the passive voice of ἀποκαλυφθήσεται ("he will be revealed").

V. 8b and vv. 9f. are two relative clauses qualifying "the rebellious one" in v. 8a. The logical order of the two relative clauses has been reversed in order to emphasize that the fate of the rebel who defies God (cf. vv. 3f.) is certain destruction even though the rebel is the emissary of no less a person than Satan himself, God's greatest opponent.

According to v. 8b, ὁ κύριος [Ἰησοῦς] ἀνελεῖ τῷ πνεύματι τοῦ στόματος αὐτοῦ καὶ καταργήσει τῇ ἐπιφανείᾳ τῆς παρουσίας αὐτοῦ ("the Lord Jesus will slay [the rebel to be revealed] with the breath of his mouth and bring [the rebel] to an end at the sudden appearance of his manifestation"). The textual tradition of this verse shows considerable disruption. Several early texts (B Dᶜ K) and other early witnesses (copᵇᵒᵐˢ Origenᵍʳˡ/³ Ephraem Cyril-Jerusalem, etc.) omit the name "Jesus" after the designation "Lord." On normal text-critical grounds it is easier to explain how "Jesus" was added to the original text, rather than why it should have been left out. This is why the *UBSGNT* places the term in brackets indicating that it is disputed even though the textual evidence would seemingly favor its presence in the original text. The problem is not serious, however, because the context makes it clear that the title "Lord" refers to Jesus. The form of the verb ἀνελεῖ ("will slay") is also in doubt, but this too is a minor problem and does not affect the meaning of the passage in a serious way.

The first part of the relative clause is perhaps based on the LXX version of Is. 11:4, especially if we are to read ἀνελεῖ, "slay" (with A B P 81, etc.), rather than some form of ἀναλίσκειν, "consume" (with Dᶜ K Ψ syrᵖ˒ ʰ). ἀνελεῖ was probably changed to ἀνέλοι and then later ἀναλώσει (the latter in conformity with the future tense of καταργήσει in v. 8c) when the allusion to Is. 11:4 was no longer recognized, and it seemed more natural to some scribe to speak of the rebel being "consumed by the breath" rather than "slain by the breath" of the Lord (cf. Frame, 266; Best, 302f.). From Paul's point of view an allusion to Is. 11:4, probably from memory, was particularly appropriate. Isaiah 11 was an important messianic text in the early Church, and the judgment theme of Is. 11:4 was probably seen as awaiting its fulfillment with the parousia of Christ. Best (303) may well be correct that behind our present text is war imagery associated with the breath of God, but this cannot be adduced from the text as it now exists. If anything Paul seems to be economizing on his imagery in this passage, perhaps because he was simply seeking to remind his readers of his oral teaching on the subject.

The verb καταργήσει ("he will bring to an end") is parallel to ἀνελεῖ and is intended to emphasize the destruction of the rebel and in particular the breaking of his power by the Lord. This will occur τῇ ἐπιφανείᾳ τῆς παρουσίας ("at the sudden appearing of the coming") of the Lord. ἐπιφανεία and παρουσία are both used in the literature of the time as technical terms for the manifestation of a divine figure, either in personal form or through an act of power demonstrating his or her presence. Outside the Pastorals (cf. 1 Tim. 6:14; 2 Tim. 4:1, 8; Tit. 2:13, where it is used of Christ's return to judge the world, and 2 Tim. 1:10, where it refers to his human existence) ἐπιφανεία occurs only here in the NT. As it creates a pleonasm if both terms are given their technical meaning in this context, it seems likely that Paul chose ἐπιφανεία because it could connote a sudden appearance in a hostile situation (see LSJ s.v., I.1). Thus the rebel who arrogates for himself the claim to be divine (v. 4) will be overthrown at the unexpected appearance of Christ's public and powerful manifestation. Clearly from Paul's perspective the public manifestation of Christ would lead to the overthrow of all those rebellious toward God, of whom the rebel envisaged in this section is the archetypal figure.

2:9 The grammar of this verse is somewhat difficult, though the meaning is relatively clear. Paul describes the parousia of the rebel mentioned in v. 8. It has the quality of a parody on the true parousia of Christ. For this reason I refer to it as the anti-parousia. The grammatical problem is the identity of the predicate complement of οὗ ἐστιν ἡ παρουσία ("whose manifestation is"), since either κατ' ἐνέργειαν τοῦ Σατανᾶ ("according to the working of Satan"), or ἐν πάσῃ δυνάμει καὶ σημείοις καὶ τέρασιν ψεύδους ("with all power and deceptive miracles and wonders and with all wicked deception"), or τοῖς ἀπολλυμένοις ("to those being destroyed") in v. 10 might possibly provide the complement. The third possibility seems rather unlikely because τοῖς ἀπολλυμένοις would have to be understood as dative of disadvantage in the sense that the manifestation of the rebel would be to the disadvantage of the perishing. Since those who are perishing are already at an appreciable disadvantage this would be a fairly trivial point to make. Between the first and the second possibilities there is little to choose, but the first is perhaps to be preferred because of its proximity to the subject of the clause and because it tends to emphasize that the rebel's public manifestation is a work of Satan.

The choice of παρουσία to denote the coming of the rebel may well have been influenced by the use of the term in the previous verse for Christ's public manifestation. It is, however, singularly appropriate in that Paul probably has in mind the technical sense of the term for official visitations by the emperor to the provinces. According to v. 4 the rebel, who was probably thought of as a future emperor, would manifest himself at the temple in Jerusalem, where he would take his seat in order to assert his deity. Paul saw this as a work of Satan (κατ' ἐνέργειαν τοῦ Σατανᾶ) because the type of opposition to God envisaged in this passage could only emanate from God's ultimate opponent and because the power (δύναμις) mentioned here could only have its source in the power of Satan.

The phrase ἐν πάσῃ δυνάμει ("with all power") indicates that the parousia of the rebel is accompanied by a manifestation of Satan's power. Here, as on several other occasions in Paul, δύναμις is found in conjunction with σημεῖα ("signs" or "miracles") and τέρατα ("wonders"; cf. Rom. 15:19; 2 Cor. 12:12). This suggests that the terms have a natural connection with one another in Paul's mind. In Rom. 15:19 the "power" is what works the miracles and wonders, but the parallelism between δυνάμει καὶ σημείοις καὶ τέρασιν precludes this idea here in 2 Thes. 2:9. Undoubtedly σημείοις and τέρασιν are to be taken together, since these two terms are commonly juxtaposed in the writings of the Greek Bible to indicate miraculous activity (cf. Ex. 7:3; Dt. 4:34; 6:22; Is. 8:18; 20:3; Je. 39:21; Jn. 4:48; Acts 2:43; 4:30; 5:12; 6:8; 7:36; Heb. 2:4, etc.). In 2 Thes. 2:8, as in the tradition found in Mk. 13:22, these miraculous activities are the work of a figure who is opposed to God (cf. Rev. 13:13f.; 16:14; 19:20, where σημεῖα is used alone of miracles performed by Satan's emissaries).

Paul does not doubt the reality of the Satanic miracles, hence he uses the adjectival genitive ψεύδους (see Bruce, 173) to label them as deceptive. They imitate divine miracles in order to lead people away from the true God. V. 11 makes it clear, however, that even this work of deception is ultimately under the control of God and is used by God to achieve his own purposes.

Given the probable historical origin of the material in the crisis associated with Gaius Caesar's attempt to have his image erected in the temple, it is worth noting that the connection of "with all power and miracles and wonders" with the rebel in v. 9 may owe something to the fact that miracles were said to be performed by and in conjunction with various emperors (cf. Tacitus, *Ann.* 4.81).

2:10 The initial phrase of this verse, καὶ ἐν πάσῃ ἀπάτῃ ἀδικίας τοῖς ἀπολλυμένοις ("and with all deception of wickedness [or "unrighteousness"] to those who are perishing") is parallel to "with all power and deceptive miracles and wonders" in the previous verse. Paul has employed strongly condemnatory language in vv. 9f. to indicate the reprehensible character of Satan's activity conducted through the rebel. If the expression "with all power and deceptive miracles and wonders" describes the character of the deeds accompanying the rebel's "parousia," then "with all wicked deception" describes the effect of his activity in seducing people into their own destruction.

Rigaux (675f.) claims that ἀδικία is an eschatological term and is virtually synonymous with ἀνομία ("rebellion" or "lawlessness"). It is perhaps going too far, however, to press for this sense in the present context because an implied contrast exists here between the wickedness perpetrated by the rebel and the love of the truth that is mentioned in the second part of the verse. The contrast between ἀδικία ("wickedness") and ἀληθείας ("truth") is common in Paul (cf. Rom. 1:18; 2:8; 3:5, 7; 1 Cor. 13:6 and see G. Schrenk, *TDNT* I, 156), and in fact appears in v. 12, suggesting that the same interpretation should be made in v. 10 (cf. Trilling, 105). If Rigaux's view is accepted, this contrast is obscured.

What Paul wishes to say by the somewhat awkward expression "deception of wickedness" is that the wickedness or unrighteousness perpetrated by Satan's agent is deceptive in order to prevent those who are perishing (τοῖς ἀπολλυμένοις) from recognizing its true character. ἀπολλύμενοι (here used in the dative plural) occurs in three other places in Paul's letters (1 Cor. 1:18; 2 Cor. 2:15; 4:3). On each occasion it denotes those who are outside the community of faith, in distinction to those who are being saved because they belong to it. Although this might be understood in terms of predestination, the next clause in v. 10 makes it clear that those who are perishing chose the path of destruction for themselves. Therefore the "parousia" of the rebel will inevitably deceive them. As Trilling (109) puts it, τοῖς ἀπολλυμένοις "anticipates what can be shown at present as a result of their life's decision and direction" (my translation). V. 11 indicates that the working of God is present in their continuing deception and acceptance of the false "parousia."

The perishing find themselves in their predicament ἀνθ' ὧν τὴν ἀγάπην τῆς ἀληθείας οὐκ ἐδέξαντο εἰς τὸ σωθῆναι αὐτούς ("because they did not receive the love of the truth so that they should be saved"). ἀνθ' ὧν in the sense of "because" is somewhat unusual in the NT, appearing only here in Paul's letters and three times in Luke (Lk. 1:20; 19:44; Acts 12:23; cf. Lk. 12:3, where it has the meaning "wherefore"), but it is a classical usage that was carried over into Hellenistic Greek.

The phrase τὴν ἀγάπην τῆς ἀληθείας "the love of the truth" is also uncommon, occurring nowhere else in the Greek Bible, though it has formal parallels in Josephus (cf. *Ap.* 2.296; *War* 1.30). But these are of no value in understanding how it is used here. "Truth" in Paul is sometimes used as a virtual synonym for the "gospel" (2 Cor. 4:2; 13:8; Gal. 5:7; cf. Gal. 2:5, 14; Col. 1:5, 6), and it has this sense here and again in v. 12. ἀληθείας is an objective genitive with τὴν ἀγάπην; taken together the construction refers to love that has as its object the Christian gospel.

The aorist tense of ἐδέξαντο is difficult to interpret in relation to "the love of the truth." Best (307) thinks that the aorist is written from the point of view of the later parousia, but it is far more likely that Paul is referring to those who have already shown themselves to be perishing by virtue of their refusal to accept the gospel. These are the ones who will be deceived by the anti-parousia of the rebel. Within the context of 2 Thessalonians it is probable that Paul is alluding broadly to those who refused to accept the gospel at the time it was preached at Thessalonica and became the persecutors of the Christians (cf. 2 Thes. 1:8), though if the idea were a traditional one it would have originally referred to the Jewish people. (Best, 308, who is not sensitive to the traditional nature of this apocalyptic material, refers back to the apostasy mentioned in v. 3 and claims that Paul has the same group in mind in v. 10, namely the Jews.) The expression "they did not receive the love of the truth" is tantamount to saying that they did not accept or obey the gospel of Christ when they were called to Christian love when the gospel was preached. If they had received the gospel in obedience, then, instead of being in danger of destruction, they would have been saved because salvation results (εἰς τὸ σωθῆναι is a consecutive construction) from acceptance of the gospel.

This language has an interesting social function. If the gospel preached by Paul was true, why did not everyone in Thessalonica, and elsewhere for that matter, accept it in order to be saved? This was undoubtedly a question frequently asked by early Christians. While it may not be a satisfying answer, v. 10 does account for the existence of unbelief. The language also serves to define the "world" of the Christians over against the rest of humanity, who are doomed to destruction. In this sense the language reinforces the Christian identity of the readers and carries an implicit exhortation to remain faithful no matter what "miracles and wonders" might seem to refute their beliefs. Paul warns that such miracles and wonders are deceptions.

2:11 The words καὶ διὰ τοῦτο ("and for this reason") refer back to the second part of v. 10 (cf. 1 Thes. 2:13; Rom. 1:26), where Paul explains that people perish because they have not accepted the gospel. From this he draws an inference concerning God's dealings with these people, thus showing the correspondence between their guilt and its punishment by God (cf. Frame, 271).

The idea that πέμπει αὐτοῖς ὁ θεὸς ἐνέργειαν πλάνης ("[God] sends to them [i.e., those mentioned in v. 10] a deluding influence") may seem strange to readers today. How can God intentionally create a situation leading to people's delusion and ultimately to their condemnation? Both in the OT (cf. 2 Sa. 24:1; 1 Ki. 22:23; Ezk. 14:9) and elsewhere in Paul's letters (cf. Rom. 1:24-32) the idea is found that God actively intervenes in human experience to exacerbate situations of sin and disobedience among those who should know better. In our passage God's sending of the "deluding influence" appears to be a direct response to people's refusal to accept the gospel. In light of other biblical texts where God is said to compound the disobedience or wrongdoing of people who should have recognized the error of their ways, it may well be that Paul has in mind specifically those who heard the truth of the gospel and then wavered in their commitment. Paul may be implying that these people were never really converted to the faith, and as a result of their faithlessness God ensures that they will never be saved. Marshall (204) believes that the present tense of πέμπει ("send") should be understood as a future reference to God sending the power of deception at the time of the anti-parousia mentioned in v. 9. This seems unlikely, however, because the "deluding influence" is sent in response to people who have already refused to accept the gospel and therefore are perishing, as v. 10b indicates.

God's purpose in sending the power that leads to the deception of those rejecting the gospel is stated in the second half of the verse: εἰς τὸ πιστεῦσαι αὐτοὺς τῷ ψεύδει ("so that they may believe the lie"). Here, as in the next verse, Paul uses πιστεύειν ("to believe") with a dative object but no governing preposition. This is unusual and may serve to emphasize the absolute character of the "lie" here and the "truth" in the next verse. An obvious contrast exists between the two (cf. Rom. 1:25). To understand what the "lie" is we must look back to v. 9, where ψεῦδος first occurs and where it describes the nature of the miracles and wonders to be performed by Satan's emissary at his "parousia." The coming of the rebel is clearly intended to imitate the parousia of the Lord and is the final great lie perpetrated by Satan in an effort to delude those who are perishing. God ensures that this delusion, which those who are perishing have effectively chosen for themselves, is complete. The following verse provides the reason.

2:12 The goal of God's activity in v. 11 (ἵνα κριθῶσιν is final) is to bring about the condemnation of those who have not believed in the truth of the gospel. The verb κρίνειν in this verse means not only to judge, but to judge and pass an unfavorable verdict, to condemn someone (cf. Rom. 2:1; 14:3, 13; 1 Cor. 4:5). It is used here of the final judgment. The subject of the purpose clause is quite clear from the context, but it is made emphatic by the words πάντες οἱ μὴ πιστεύσαντες τῇ ἀληθείᾳ ἀλλὰ εὐδοκήσαντες τῇ ἀδικίᾳ ("all those who have not believed the truth but have taken pleasure in wickedness"). ἀλήθεια is the same word used in v. 10 of the Christian gospel in its broadest sense, and it should probably be understood in the same way here. Whether the aorist participle πιστεύσαντες ("those who have believed") should be understood from the perspective of the judgment, which is certainly possible (so Best, 309), or should be seen as a specific reference to the local situation in Thessalonica, where many who had heard the gospel had not believed in it, is not clear. As it agrees with the aorist ἐδέξαντο ("received") in v. 10, it is perhaps better to see Paul focusing a universally applicable observation on a local situation for which the aorist tenses of vv. 10 and 12 are particularly appropriate. The aorist participle εὐδοκήσαντες ("those who have taken pleasure") should be understood in a similar way as referring to those who have chosen to persecute the Christians at Thessalonica, thus acting in a wicked fashion when given the opportunity to be saved.

The apparent intention behind vv. 10b-12 is twofold. On the one hand, these verses offer an explanation for why people outside the community of faith are perishing: they have chosen to reject the truth of the gospel when it was presented to them, taking pleasure in wickedness instead. For this reason God has made certain that their own decision against the truth will result in their condemnation in the judgment, thereby sealing their destruction. Vv. 10-12 do not really speak to the question of the condition of those who have not heard the gospel. This is why the Thessalonians would have assumed that Paul was speaking about the situation in Thessalonica as they had experienced it. On the other hand, in true apocalyptic fashion these verses reinforce the inevitable separation between those who have loved the truth and those who prefer the great lie, resulting in their identification with Satan and his emissary, the rebel. The sentiments expressed in these verses could easily be turned against those who have once been attracted to the Christian faith but have then distanced themselves from it. They have not really loved the truth (v. 10b) nor have they believed the truth (v. 12). Instead they have taken pleasure in wickedness by maliciously turning away from the Christian community, and this will lead to their condemnation in the final judgment.

If my interpretation of this passage is correct, it has an interesting correlation with the situation at Thessalonica as I have depicted it in the Introduction. There, following the lead of Donfried and others, I sought to argue that the persecution of Christians in Thessalonica was related to the apparent sense of competition which the Christian movement engendered in some people who saw it as a threat to their own religion. What Paul says here could certainly be directed against Jewish instigators of opposition to Paul as well as those who sought to defend the civic cults of Thessalonica, including the imperial cult, against the inherently anti-imperial religion of Paul, which promised the public manifestation of the true Lord.

The allusive apocalyptic language of vv. 3-12 appears to serve a double function. On the one hand, it clearly demonstrates that the day of the Lord has not come, the primary issue calling forth the discussion in vv. 3-12. On the other hand, vv. 3-12 also address the situation of persecution experienced by the Thessalonian Christians. The passage does so by providing an argument predicting the destruction of those who have refused to receive the gospel of Christ and therefore have become persecutors of the Christian community. Naturally, this rhetoric provided considerable encouragement for Paul's converts to persevere, in spite of their experience of oppression, by ultimately promising their vindication. It is to this theme that Paul turns in vv. 13-17 since it completes the picture begun in vv. 10-12.

The historicizing detail of the apocalyptically oriented eschatology of vv. 3f., the somewhat obscure apocalyptic thought of vv. 6f., and the mythic-symbolic character of the apocalyptic language of vv. 8f. tell us a great deal about the thought world of the early Christians. This is not the natural thought world of First World Christians of today (though many such Christians have adopted the apocalyptic thought world of Paul at the level of their religious experience). But the human experience of powerlessness and alienation in the face of pervasive evil within the socio-economic and political structures of the day, which spawned the apocalyptic worldview of Paul and other early Christians, is not unknown to many Christians of today. Certainly Christians in South Africa, where this commentary has been written, experience these things. Just as the apocalyptic imagery of such texts as 2 Thes. 2:3-12 provided hope of divine victory in an oppressive and hostile environment for early Christians, so also contemporary Christians have to engage in their own quest(s) for new and contextually relevant symbols and imagery to provide divine hope and direction in their own oppressive and hostile environments. This is the real lesson to be learned from vv. 3-12.

SECOND PROOF: 2:13-15

In vv. 13-15 Paul moves to the second of the two interrelated proofs announced in the *partitio*. In 2:1 Paul mentioned two related issues: the parousia of Christ and the gathering of Christians to Christ at the parousia. Vv. 3-12 address the first of these issues. Vv. 13-15 address the second by referring to the readers' election to "salvation by means of the sanctification of the Spirit" in v. 13 and to their call to "obtain the glory of the Lord Jesus Christ" in v. 14. Paul seeks to demonstrate that the readers have no reason to be shaken in their beliefs regarding the day of the Lord and more particularly their own participation in the salvation to come with that day by virtue of their call and election. Since they have assurance of their future salvation, Paul directs them to stand firm and to hold fast to the traditions taught to them. This will ensure their victorious participation in Christ's parousia.

2:13 The particle δέ at the beginning of this section has been understood in three distinct ways by commentators. Some take it to be resumptive, referring back to 1:3 where the initial thanksgiving period begins (cf. Dibelius, 34); others view it as merely transitional (cf. Best, 311); and still others see it as contrastive, emphasizing the difference between the unbelievers of the previous few verses and the elect (cf. Rigaux, 681). The first possibility seems unlikely since 2:13 is very remote from 1:3, and in any case, as O'Brien (*Introductory Thanksgivings*, 184) maintains, "It does not form part of the opening thanksgiving of chap. 1:3ff., nor does it have an epistolary function." The second way of understanding δέ ignores the implied contrast between "those not believing in the truth" who will be condemned (v. 12) and those whom "God has chosen from the beginning for salvation by sanctification of the Spirit and belief in the truth" (v. 13). This then shows that a contrast is present, though the contrast does not pertain to Paul's obligation to give thanks for his converts (v. 13a), but to their election to salvation (v. 13b).

ἡμεῖς at the beginning of v. 13 may be emphatic, though it need not be (cf. von Dobschütz, 297, who sees the use of the first person pronoun as an affected stylistic feature of Paul's). ὀφείλομεν εὐχαριστεῖν τῷ θεῷ πάντοτε περὶ ὑμῶν, ἀδελφοί ("we are obligated to give thanks to God always concerning you, brothers [and sisters]") repeats what is found in 1:3, though the word order is slightly different. Here as there a ὅτι clause states the grounds for the thanksgiving, but, as I will show in a moment, the grounds have changed. To his commonly used term of address, "brothers [and sisters]," Paul adds ἠγαπημένοι ὑπὸ κυρίου ("beloved by the Lord"). "Lord" is somewhat unexpected, if it refers to Jesus, since in 1 Thes. 1:4 Paul writes ἀδελφοὶ ἠγαπημένοι ὑπὸ θεοῦ ("brothers [and sisters] beloved by God") and in 2 Thes. 2:16 God the father is said to be ὁ ἀγαπήσας ἡμᾶς ("the one who loves us"). Nevertheless, it must refer to Jesus because Paul almost always uses "Lord" in relation to Jesus rather than God, and in fact he does so in the following verse. In any case he probably would have used a pronoun for "God" in the subsequent ὅτι clause if the term "Lord" referred to God. The idea of the love of Christ for his followers is not unknown in Paul (cf. Rom. 8:35; 2 Cor. 5:14; Gal. 2:20) and is regularly associated with certainty regarding salvation. As vv. 13-14 deal with the assurance of salvation and in v. 14 salvation itself is associated with the Lord Jesus Christ, it has a similar function here.

The ὅτι clause gives the reason for Paul's thanksgiving, but its function is to reassure the readers of their salvation in the face of the eschatological dangers discussed in vv. 3-12. The basis of their certitude is their election by God. αἱρεῖσθαι ("to choose" or "elect" in the middle) is not very common in

Paul's letters, occurring only here and in Phil. 1:22, where it is used of a personal choice confronting Paul. In one text in the LXX, Dt. 26:18, the verb is used of God's election of Israel, but it is not possible to say that this is why it is employed here, since there are no other obvious connections between the two passages.

What Paul identifies as the purpose of God's election of Paul's converts is somewhat problematic because of a divided textual tradition. One set of texts (B F G^{gr} P 33 81 syr^h cop^{bo}, etc.) reads ἀπαρχὴν εἰς σωτηρίαν ("as firstfruits for salvation"). Another set (ℵ D K L Ψ 104 181 syr^p cop^{sa}, etc.) has ἀπ᾽ ἀρχῆς εἰς σωτηρίαν ("from the beginning for salvation"). As the textual evidence is not sufficient in itself to make a decision between the two possibilities (contra Bruce, 190), we must ask which is the more appropriate variant in the context and in terms of Paul's normal usage. This, however, poses its own difficulties.

On the one hand, Paul nowhere else uses ἀπ᾽ ἀρχῆς to denote "from the beginning of time," which is what it would have to mean here (cf. 1 Cor. 2:7; Col. 1:26; Eph. 1:4), and only on one occasion does he employ ἀρχή in a temporal sense at all (cf. Phil. 4:15). By way of contrast ἀπαρχή occurs six other times in Paul's letters (cf. Rom. 8:23; 11:16; 16:5; 1 Cor. 15:20, 23; 16:15), but only on one occasion without a qualifying genitive (Rom. 11:16). On the other hand, ἀπ᾽ ἀρχῆς makes good sense in the context, whereas it is difficult to find a satisfactory meaning for ἀπαρχήν. Two possibilities exist. It may have a temporal significance, but against this is the fact that the Thessalonians were not the first to believe in Macedonia and no other possibility seems to make sense. (Ellis, *Prophecy and Hermeneutic,* 20 tries to link it to his thesis that the "brethren" [*sic*] were Paul's coworkers who constituted the firstfruits of his activity, but as I have shown, his general thesis cannot be sustained.) Alternatively, it may have a qualitative significance, but it seems unlikely that Paul would wish to say that his readers were of greater value to God than other Christians without further ado. In light of the above, it is perhaps better on the whole to accept the reading ἀπ᾽ ἀρχῆς with a majority of commentators and to see it as a reference to the fact that from the beginning God's purpose was to save the elect.

The nature of the divine salvation for which the Thessalonians were chosen by God is not specified in this verse. Paul is generally reticent on this subject, though he does allude to one dimension of it in the next verse. The two phrases ἁγιασμῷ πνεύματος ("sanctification of the Spirit") and πίστει ἀληθείας ("faith in the truth") are governed by the preposition ἐν ("in") and describe the means by which salvation comes about. In the first place it is through the "sanctification of the Spirit." Although it is possible that πνεῦμα might refer to the human spirit (cf. 1 Thes. 5:23), sanctification in the end comes from God, not from the human spirit (cf. 1 Thes. 4:3-8; 5:23), and it is elsewhere attributed to the work of the Holy Spirit (Rom. 15:16; cf. 1 Cor.

6:11). For these reasons it is best to see πνεύματος as a subjective genitive referring to the work of God's Spirit in the sanctification of the people of God. (If Paul intended πνεύματος to be understood in terms of the human spirit, then it is objective genitive and the implied subject of the process of sanctification remains God through the agency of his Spirit.)

Just as salvation has a divine dimension, so also it involves a human response in the form of faith. ἀληθείας ("truth") is probably an objective genitive indicating that to which faith is directed. The choice of the word "truth" in this context is determined by its use in the previous section, where those who are perishing are said to have refused to believe in the truth, that is, in the gospel (cf. vv. 10, 12). Paul's thanksgiving is directed to God precisely because his readers have believed in the gospel and experienced the sanctifying activity of the Spirit as part of the process of their salvation.

2:14   The words εἰς ὅ ("to which") at the beginning of v. 14 probably have as their referent the whole of the expression "for salvation by sanctification of the Spirit and belief in the truth" in the previous verse, rather than any of the individual items. God is the subject of the relative clause εἰς ὅ [καὶ] ἐκάλεσεν ὑμᾶς διὰ τοῦ εὐαγγελίου ἡμῶν ("to which [also] [God] has called you through our gospel"), because God is the one who actually called the Thessalonians to their current experience of salvation. The aorist ἐκάλεσεν ("called") does not refer to some remote act on God's part, as does εἵλατο ("chose") in the preceding verse. The Thessalonians were called by God (cf. 1 Thes. 2:12; 4:7; 5:23) to share in salvation when Paul and his missionary colleagues were visiting their city to preach the gospel. For this reason Paul can specify that his readers were called διὰ τοῦ εὐαγγελίου ἡμῶν ("through our gospel"). By this he means that they experienced the call of God in a very real sense through the missionary preaching of the gospel; without this no call can exist (cf. Rom. 10:14). As Marshall (208) rightly points out, Trilling's assertion (122) that the real Paul could not have written v. 14a because he reserved the call of people to salvation exclusively for God is unconvincing. Logically the call of God had to be experienced through the preaching of the gospel, and in any case Gal. 1:6f. implies that a connection exists between the call of God and the preaching of the gospel.

The readers were called originally to share in God's salvation. The second half of v. 14 spells out one important aspect of that salvation. They were called εἰς περιποίησιν δόξης τοῦ κυρίου ἡμῶν Ἰησοῦ Χριστοῦ ("for obtaining the glory of our Lord Jesus Christ"). Interestingly, περιποίησις is found only one other time in the undisputed Pauline letters, in 1 Thes. 5:9, and there also it is used of the obtaining of salvation. What is to be obtained is, in 2 Thes. 1:14, "the glory of the Lord Jesus Christ." This idea is fundamental in Pauline thought, as Rom. 8:17, 29f.; 1 Cor. 15:43; 2 Cor. 3:18; Phil. 3:21; and 1 Thes. 2:12 show. According to Rom. 3:23, "All have sinned and lack the glory of God." This idea derived from the Jewish belief that Adam had lost his luster when he sinned, and that eschatological salvation would therefore include the return of the divine glory, that is, God's outward appearance of brilliance, to saved humanity (cf. 1QS 4:23; CD 3:20; 1QH 17:15; see also Scroggs, *Last Adam*, 26f.; 35f.; 73f.). Thus when Paul talks about obtaining the glory of Christ he has in mind the eschatological transformation of the people of God into the form of Christ's divine existence. In an ultimate sense this was associated with the resurrection for Paul, as 1 Cor. 15:43 and Phil. 3:21 demonstrate.

2:15 Paul moves from reassuring his readers regarding their salvation to an exhortation concerning how they should live their Christian lives in relation to the apostolic tradition that they have received. ἄρα οὖν ("so then") at the beginning of v. 15 shows that Paul is drawing an inference from what precedes. The content of v. 15 points to the inference being the real point of Paul's argument in chap. 2. It calls on the readers to adopt a correct understanding of Paul's teaching regarding the coming of Christ.

Paul begins by exhorting his readers, ἀδελφοί, στήκετε ("brothers [and sisters], stand firm"). Usually the imperative στήκετε is accompanied by an object indicating what those who are being exhorted are to stand firm in (cf. 1 Cor. 16:13, "in the faith"; Phil. 4:1 and 1 Thes. 3:8, "in the Lord"; Phil. 1:27, "in one spirit"). Here we are probably to see an allusion back to v. 2, where Paul expresses his worry that the Thessalonians might be disturbed through some false teaching or prophecy regarding the day of the Lord. In the face of this possibility they are exhorted to continue to stand firm (this is the implication of the present tense of the imperative).

The second present imperative, κρατεῖτε ("hold fast"), has the explicit object τὰς παραδόσεις ἃς ἐδιδάχθητε εἴτε διὰ λόγου εἴτε δι' ἐπιστολῆς ("the traditions that you were taught, whether through oral statement or this our letter"). The terms for tradition (παράδοσις), the passing on of tradition (παραδιδόναι), and the reception of tradition (παραλαμβάνειν) recur on several occasions in Paul's letters and demonstrate that the communication of tradition was a regular feature in Paul's missionary activity. Dunn (*Unity and Diversity*, 66-69) points out that three types of tradition may be isolated in Paul: (1) kerygmatic tradition, that is, tradition concerning the central gospel message (e.g., 1 Cor. 15:1-3); (2) Church tradition, that is, tradition passed on to govern the practice of the Church (e.g., 1 Cor. 11:23-25); and (3) ethical tradition, that is, tradition dealing with proper behavior for Christians (e.g., 1 Cor. 7:10; 11:2; 1 Thes. 4:1). If, as seems likely, we are to see v. 15 in terms of the broader context of chap. 2, then we probably have a reference specifically to the kerygmatic traditions associated with the parousia of Christ. The fact that the command to keep these traditions represents an inference drawn from the discussion of salvation in vv. 13f. implies that nothing less than the salvation of the Thessalonians depended on their holding to these traditions. (In 3:7 Paul refers to a different type of tradition which he had passed on to his readers and to which he expected them to adhere, namely, a tradition regarding proper Christian conduct.)

The traditions regarding the coming of Christ to which Paul wished the Thessalonians to hold fast had been taught to them in two ways, both equally authoritative and binding on them, as εἴτε . . . εἴτε ("whether . . . or") indicates. First, while he was with them he had taught them orally regarding the coming of Christ, when it would happen and what it would entail. This is the meaning of διὰ λόγου ("by word of mouth").

The meaning of δι' ἐπιστολῆς ("by our letter") is debatable. Most commentators see in them a reference to 1 Thessalonians (e.g., von Dob-schütz, 301; Frame, 285; Best, 318). In the second section of the Introduction to this commentary, however, I have demonstrated that this view is problematic for a variety of reasons, not least of which is the fact that anyone possessing 1 Thessalonians could not have believed that the day of the Lord had come. I also have shown that several factors related to v. 15 itself raise questions with the claim that the words "through our letter" refer to 1 Thessalonians. For the reasons discussed in the Introduction, the words "through our letter" probably refer to the present letter. In the context of 2 Thessonians 2 the intention of Paul's statement in v. 15 is to ensure that what he has just taught his readers regarding the events associated with the coming of Christ is treated as having the same authority as his oral teaching to them when he was present.

PERORATIO: 2:16-17

Hughes (62) observes that a number of *perorationes* take the form of prayers. In the case of 2 Thes. 2:16f. we have what Wiles *(Intercessory Prayer Passages)* describes as a wish-prayer (see the discussion of 1 Thes. 3:11-13). In effect the wish-prayer as a *peroratio* requests that God and the Lord Jesus Christ accomplish in the lives of the Thessalonians what the two proofs of vv. 3-15 have attempted to persuade the Thessalonians to think and do (Hughes, 62).

2:16 The wish-prayer formed by this and the next verse, like the one in 1 Thes. 3:11-13, is located after a thanksgiving and before a new section beginning with λοιπόν, ἀδελφοί ("finally, brothers [and sisters]"), though in this case the exhortation of v. 15 intervenes between the thanksgiving and the wish-prayer.

Here the wish-prayer begins with an emphatic αὐτός ("himself"), which seems to be a structural part of the wish-prayer (cf. 3:16; 1 Thes. 3:11; 5:23). The order of the invocation is somewhat unusual with the common designation ὁ κύριος ἡμῶν Ἰησοῦς Χριστός ("our Lord Jesus Christ") preceding that of [ὁ] θεὸς ὁ πατὴρ ἡμῶν ("God our father"), but this order is found elsewhere in Gal. 1:1 and 2 Cor. 13:13. Rigaux (690) may be correct when he proposes that Christ's name precedes that of God's here because the context is christological in its orientation. On balance, however, it is perhaps more likely that the long participial phrase attached to the name of God caused Paul to put God's name second (cf. Trilling, 131). One of the most unusual features of v. 16 is the order of the words used to invoke God since [ὁ] θεὸς ὁ πατὴρ ἡμῶν ("God our father") occurs nowhere else in Paul, though 1 Cor. 8:6 has the same order except that ἡμῶν, which would be inappropriate in the context, does not occur.

As indicated above, the long participial phrase in v. 16b, ὁ ἀγαπήσας ἡμᾶς καὶ δοὺς παράκλησιν αἰωνίαν καὶ ἐλπίδα ἀγαθὴν ἐν χάριτι ("who loved us and gave us eternal encouragement and good hope by grace") qualifies the reference to God by elaborating on his saving activity toward the followers of Christ. In this Paul identifies himself with his readers through the pronoun ἡμᾶς ("us"), the object of the participle ὁ ἀγαπήσας ("who loved us").

The aorist participle alludes to some particular act of God in the past, and for this reason (as well as for grammatical reasons—the participle is

270

singular) it cannot be maintained (contra Best, 286; Bruce, 196) that ἀγαπήσας refers to both God and Christ. The context may suggest that "who loved us" is a reference to God's choice or election of Christians to share in salvation (v. 13; cf. 1 Thes. 1:4). But it is also possible that Paul is thinking of God's love as demonstrated in the death of Jesus Christ. This for Paul is the ultimate evidence of God's love (cf. Rom. 5:8).

A logical connection exists between ὁ ἀγαπήσας and the second aorist participle, δούς ("who gave"), in that God gives gifts to the followers of Christ out of divine love for them. The "us" of the first participle should be understood with the second as well.

Two gifts are specified. First God gave παράκλησιν αἰωνίαν ("eternal encouragement"). Christians, faced with oppression and rejection for their new faith, receive from God encouragement to withstand the trials and distresses that attend them in this age. But this encouragement lasts through the judgment into the age to come, and hence it is eternal. ἐλπίδα ἀγαθήν ("good hope") adds little to the previous thought regarding the gift of eternal encouragement, though perhaps the idea is implied that God's gift of encouragement leads to hope for future life in those who receive it. The expression "good hope" was used in the Hellenistic world for life after death (cf. Otzen, " 'Gute Hoffnung,' " 283-285), and thus it is singularly appropriate in the present context.

The final words of v. 16, ἐν χάριτι ("by grace"), are adverbial, are to be taken with the two participles ἀγαπήσας and δούς, and are characteristic of Paul. They stress that God's love, as well as the divine gifts of encouragement and hope, are based on God's unmerited favor freely bestowed.

2:17 Paul's petition for his readers in this wish-prayer is twofold. First, he wishes for the Thessalonians that God παρακαλέσαι ὑμῶν τὰς καρδίας ("may encourage your hearts"). The verb παρακαλέσαι is an aorist singular optative, as is the second verb στηρίξαι ("may he strengthen"). These optatives are voluntive in force, and this is why the prayer is referred to as a wish-prayer. The singular form of the two verbs is problematic since they have two subjects, "our Lord Jesus Christ and God our father." Apparently Paul forgot that he had used a plural subject because of the long intervening participial phrase related to God alone.

The verb παρακαλέσαι is a cognate of the noun παράκλησις from the previous phrase and has the sense of "to encourage." Thus Paul wishes for God to encourage the hearts, or inner beings, of the Thessalonians in their particular situation of persecution (1:4) and pending eschatological distress (2:3-12), just as he has given them eternal encouragement and good hope in their conversion experience.

Paul's concern, however, is not only with the inward state of his converts, but also with their outward behavior. He therefore includes in his wish-prayer the request that God στηρίξαι ἐν παντὶ ἔργῳ καὶ λόγῳ ἀγαθῷ ("may establish [you] in every good deed and every good word"). The implied object of the στηρίξαι may be either "you" or a repetition of "your hearts."

The distinction Paul is making here between inward encouragement and outward behavior is lost by Best (321, see also 310) when he translates the whole clause in a comprehensive fashion: "may our Lord Jesus Christ himself and God our Father . . . encourage and strengthen your hearts in every good deed and word." Paul's desire is that inward encouragement in the face of external opposition be accompanied by godly behavior in whatever Christians say and do (cf. Col. 3:17, where a similar idea is expressed as an instruction). The connection of these words with v. 15 is obvious and serves to focus the readers' attention on the need for stability in their Christian thought and behavior, the goal of the *probatio.*

It is worth noting that in 1 Thes. 3:2 Paul tells the Thessalonians that his intention in sending Timothy to them was εἰς τὸ στηρίξαι ὑμᾶς καὶ παρακαλέσαι ὑπὲρ τῆς πίστεως ὑμῶν ("in order to establish you and encourage you concerning your faith") in the face of their situation of persecution. This lends support to the possibility that 2 Thessalonians was the letter carried by Timothy since the wish-prayer calling for the readers to be encouraged and established in 2 Thes. 2:17 reflects precisely the intention behind the sending of Timothy to Thessalonica described in 1 Thes. 3:2.

EXHORTATIO: 3:1-15

Jewett (*Thessalonian Correspondence*, 81-87) includes 3:1-5 in the *probatio* section of the letter, claiming that the *exhortatio* begins only in 3:6. In support of this view he claims that τὸ λοιπόν at the beginning of 3:1 should be understood inferentially ("therefore"). Against this claim is the fact that there are no clear examples of the inferential use of τὸ λοιπόν in Paul, and in any case nothing in the context indicates that the request for prayer support is an inference from what has preceded. On several occasions Paul uses τὸ λοιπόν ("finally") near the end of a letter to indicate the transition to his concluding remarks (cf. 2 Cor. 13:11; Phil. 4:8). On other occasions he employs it to mark a change of topic (cf. Phil. 3:1; 1 Cor. 4:2). 1 Thes. 4:1 is particularly interesting because τὸ λοιπόν signals the transition to the main parenetic section of the letter. For this reason von Dobschütz (305), Frame (288), and others are probably correct in maintaining that it marks the transition to the exhortative section of 2 Thessalonians.

The exhortative section divides into two parts: 3:1-5, having a general character, and 3:6-15, dealing with the issue of economic responsibility among members of the community. Rigaux (692f.) observes that vv. 1-5 are not well composed (vv. 1f. do not connect well with vv. 3f., and the latter are only loosely related to v. 5). On the other hand vv. 6-15 are much more clearly structured, focusing as they do on a particular aberration in the life of the church that requires correction.

GENERAL EXHORTATION: 3:1-5

The exhortative material in this subsection has a general character. As noted above, 3:1-5 is roughly composed. Trilling (134) maintains that the roughness of composition in 3:1-5 resulted from the inability of a later writer imitating 1 Thes. 4:1f. to provide a convincing specific occasion for the request for prayer in 2 Thes. 3:1. That an otherwise sophisticated forger would compose such a disjointed paragraph demands greater credulity than to accept that Paul was responsible for the awkwardness of 3:1-5. Perhaps he was interrupted in his composition of the letter after 2:17, and in returning to the letter did not give enough care to continuing his train of thought smoothly, or perhaps he originally intended to end the letter at v. 5 but then for some reason continued it. Whatever the reason for the disjointed character of 3:1-5, the exhortation to intercessory prayer in 3:1 and the preparation in vv. 3f. for the main issue requiring exhortation in vv. 6-15 mark the transition to the main hortatory section of the letter.

3:1 Paul begins the *exhortatio* section of the letter with an instruction to his readers to pray for him and his fellow missionaries. The words προσεύχεσθε, ἀδελφοί, περὶ ἡμῶν ("brothers [and sisters], pray for us") are identical to Paul's instruction in 1 Thes. 5:25. There, however, the content of the prayer is not specified. This would be easy to understand if 2 Thessalonians was written before 1 Thessalonians; the more generalized request of 1 Thes. 5:25 would presuppose the specific request found in 2 Thes. 3:1f.

The issues for which Paul desired intercession are specified in the two purpose clauses of vv. 1b and 2a. First, Paul wants prayer not directly for himself but for the progress of the gospel, as shown by the words ἵνα ὁ λόγος τοῦ κυρίου τρέχῃ καὶ δοξάζηται καθὼς καὶ πρὸς ὑμᾶς ("that the word of the Lord may spread quickly and be glorified, as indeed [it has] with you").

The expression "the word of the Lord" appears only in 1 and 2 Thessalonians among the Pauline letters (cf. 1 Thes. 1:8; 4:15). As in 1 Thes. 1:8 it is synonymous with the gospel of Christ, an expression recurring with a good deal more frequency in Paul's letters (cf. Rom. 15:19; 1 Cor. 9:12; 2 Cor. 2:12; 9:13; 10:14; Gal. 2:7; Phil. 1:27; 1 Thes. 3:2; 2 Thes. 1:8). Although Paul uses the verb τρέχειν ("to run") in several other passages (1 Cor. 9:24, 27; Gal. 2:2; 5:7; Phil. 2:16; Rom. 9:16), only in this text is it employed with a nonhuman subject. He may have derived the imagery from the races held in Hellenistic stadiums, as Frame (291) thinks, or, as seems more likely, given that it is unusual to use τρέχειν without a human subject, he may have been dependent on Ps. 147:4 (LXX; English Ps. 147:15), a text speaking of God's word running swiftly. Regardless of where the imagery came from, in 2 Thessalonians it is designed to evoke the idea of the rapid progress of the Christian mission. This was to become the object of the Thessalonians' prayers. To this Paul adds a second object of prayer, namely, that the word of the Lord might be held in honor or extolled (cf. Acts 13:48). This is the basic idea of δοξάζηται rather than "triumph," as the *RSV* translates it. Paul is balancing the idea of the rapid spread of the word of the Lord with its successful communication since the act of honoring or extolling the word of God refers to acceptance of it.

The phrase καθὼς καὶ πρὸς ὑμᾶς ("as indeed with you") probably qualifies the whole of the purpose clause. Because Paul has not included a temporal reference with "as indeed with you," it is unclear whether he is referring to the past or the present with respect to his readers. Frame (291f.) maintains that the phrase has a present reference and that it is intended to act as an encouragement in fulfilling the prayer in their own community. In a sense the turn of phrase left it up to the readers to understand it as present, past, or perfect in light of their experience at the time. But if 2 Thessalonians was written before Timothy's return visit mentioned in 1 Thes. 3:2, then Paul probably intended it to refer to his missionary work and its results, since he did not know the situation at Thessalonica when 2 Thessalonians was written.

3:2 Not only does Paul request prayer for the progress of the Christian mission but also for his own well-being and that of his colleagues. This entreaty for prayer must be understood from the perspective of the previous clause, and therefore it relates specifically to Paul and his colleagues' missionary activity. He asks for prayer ἵνα ῥυσθῶμεν ἀπὸ τῶν ἀτόπων καὶ πονηρῶν ἀνθρώπων ("in order that we may be delivered from wicked and evil people"). The verb ῥύεσθαι can be used of divine eschatological deliverance or salvation, as in 1 Thes. 1:10, but here, as in 2 Cor. 1:8-11, it has the sense of deliverance or preservation from human forces who oppose the progress of the Christian mission. The 2 Corinthians text is particularly interesting because it involves a similar request for prayer to expedite Paul's deliverance from his adversaries (cf. Rom. 15:31; on Paul's suffering at the hands of his opponents see 2 Cor. 11:23-25). The passive voice of ῥυσθῶμεν reflects the fact that it is actually God whom Paul relies upon to deliver him from his opponents.

Paul describes his antagonists as τῶν ἀτόπων καὶ πονηρῶν ἀνθρώπων. The terms ἄτοπος and πονηρός are virtually synonymous in this context and together castigate Paul's adversaries as morally depraved and malicious individuals. Various commentators, such as von Dobschütz (306), Best (325), and Marshall (214), think that for one reason or another Paul has used ἄτοπος as a replacement for ἄνομος ("lawless"), but there is no real evidence that this is the case, any more than that it can be demonstrated that Paul is specifically referring to Jewish opposition to his missionary work, as some have maintained. What is clear, however, is that Paul is engaging in vilification of his opponents. This has an important social function, as A. Y. Collins ("Vilification") has shown in relation to the Book of Revelation. As she puts it (314):

> Vilification or apocalyptic hatred expresses and reinforces a consciousness of a difference in values, in symbolic universes. It serves to demarcate and define a new group. Vituperation also serves to neutralize the opponent by casting doubt on the legitimacy of the rival group.

Paul appears to be doing precisely this toward those who oppose the preaching of the gospel.

Although an exact translation of the final clause in v. 2 is difficult because the genitive πάντων lacks a governing noun, οὐ γὰρ πάντων ἡ πίστις means something like "faith is not [the response] of all to the word of God." γάρ indicates that this is the reason that the wicked persecute the Christian missionaries and, as the next verse suggests, by extension the people of Thessalonica (cf. Jewett, *Thessalonian Correspondence*, 86). ἡ πίστις proba-

275

bly does not mean "the faith" in the sense of the peculiarly Christian set of beliefs. Rather, it refers to the act of believing or trusting in the gospel of salvation. As Best (326) points out, this interpretation of the word leads more naturally to v. 3, where πιστός is used in the sense of "faithfulness."

3:3 The transition from the thought of v. 2 to that of v. 3 seems somewhat abrupt even though a word link exists in the use of πίστις/πιστός ("faith-faithful"). Paul shifts from talking about human faith or trust in the gospel to the Lord's faithfulness. At the same time he moves from his own situation to that of his readers. The connection becomes clearer when we realize that Paul's awareness of his own need for divine deliverance from evildoers and their wicked designs causes him to assure his readers of divine protection from the evil deeds perpetrated by their opponents. δέ in the phrase πιστὸς δέ ἐστιν ὁ κύριος ("but the Lord is faithful") is genuinely adversative. The contrast in vv. 2b and 3a is between the faithlessness of non-Christians, who act maliciously toward believers, and the abiding faithfulness of the Lord, who protects and cares for his people.

As 1 Thes. 2:14 reveals, the Thessalonians encountered opposition from their own fellow citizens, or perhaps more precisely, as Meeks ("Social Function," 691) urges, from those "with whom they formerly shared ties of kinship and racial or local origins." Such an experience, as discussed above in connection with 1 Thes. 2:14, must have proved profoundly disturbing for recent converts. If this ordeal formed an undercurrent in the formulation of 2 Thes. 3:2f., then the stress on the faithfulness of the Lord, who in a sense was responsible for their suffering, served as a powerful contrast to the wickedness of people with whom they had formerly shared so much in common but who had subsequently turned against them.

Several commentators have noted that the more common Pauline expression is "God is faithful" (1 Cor. 1:9; 10:13; 2 Cor. 1:18; 1 Thes. 5:24), rather than "the Lord is faithful," which appears only here in 2 Thes. 3:3. This unusual reference to "the Lord" reflects Paul's belief that the Lord Jesus would at the time of his parousia render judgment against the enemies of the people of God (cf. 1:7f.). This was the basis for the Christian community's sense of confidence in the Lord regardless of the opposition they suffered.

Paul does not leave the idea of the Lord's faithfulness vague. He connects it to the Lord's role in the life of the community through the relative clause in v. 3b: it is the Lord ὃς στηρίξει ὑμᾶς καὶ φυλάξει ἀπὸ τοῦ πονηροῦ ("who will continue strengthening and guarding you from evil"). The verb στηρίξει is also used in 2:17, but here the emphasis is on the strengthening of Christians in the face of the evil one's machinations. στηρίξει and φυλάξει are probably to be understood as progressive futures; that is, the Lord "will continue strengthening and guarding them." Paul not only wants his readers strengthened, he also wants them protected against evil. Although this is the only passage in Paul where φυλάσσειν is used of divine protection, it is commonly used for this in the LXX, especially in the Psalms (cf. Pss. 11[12]:7; 15[16]:1; 40[41]:2; and esp. 120[121]:7).

The gender of τοῦ πονηροῦ, which may be either neuter or masculine, poses a difficulty. If it is taken as neuter, it refers to the general phenomenon of evil, but if it is understood as masculine, it denotes the evil one, that is, Satan (cf. Mt. 6:13, which has the same ambiguity in Greek). While the latter possibility cannot be ruled out because in several later NT writings πονηρός does refer to the evil one (cf. Mt. 13:19; Eph. 6:16; Jn. 17:15; 1 Jn. 2:13f.), Paul does not use it of the evil one (unless Eph. 6:16 is assumed to be Pauline), whereas he does use the neuter form of evil in general (cf. Rom. 12:9; 1 Thes. 5:22). Because Paul's own concern was that he should be rescued from πονηρῶν ἀνθρώπων ("evil persons," v. 2), and evil people are a danger because they do evil things, the implicit parallel between Paul's experience and the Thessalonians favors taking τοῦ πονηροῦ in the general sense of evil rather than of Satan.

3:4 This verse seems to take up a theme unrelated to the previous one. But on closer examination vv. 3f. appear to duplicate the thought pattern of 2:13-15. The pattern consists of an affirmation of divine care for the community (3:3 parallels 2:13-14), followed by an exhortation to obedience (3:4 parallels 2:15). Put somewhat differently, v. 3 assures the readers that the Lord is working in their presence while v. 4 indirectly requires obedience in response to what the Lord is doing.

Paul requires obedience by initially expressing his confidence in his readers: πεποίθαμεν δὲ ἐν κυρίῳ ἐφ᾽ ὑμᾶς ("and we have confidence in the Lord concerning you"). On several other occasions Paul states his confidence in his readers in respect to situations where he most probably had reservations about how his readers would respond or at least where he felt that the response he requested was imperative (cf. Gal. 5:10; 2 Cor. 2:3; Phm. 21). That he indirectly invokes the Lord at this point with the ἐν κυρίῳ formula may well reflect his reservations about the obedience of his converts. This point is substantiated by the divine sanction issued with the commands in vv. 6 and 12, the explicit indication that not everyone in the community was doing what Paul wanted in vv. 11f., and the institution of a procedure to deal with any refractory members of the community in vv. 14f.

The ὅτι clause expresses Paul's concern in a very general way, namely that ἃ παραγγέλλομεν [καὶ] ποιεῖτε καὶ ποιήσετε ("that what we command [also] you practice and will continue practicing"). παραγγέλλομεν ("command" or "instruct") clearly refers to ethical direction from Paul, as its use in the subsequent verses demonstrates (cf. vv. 6, 10, 12). Its present tense form here (as in vv. 6 and 12) most naturally refers to the instructions contained in the present letter. It may therefore be a reference back to 2:15, but it also clearly prepares for vv. 6-15.

On the one hand the present verb ποιεῖτε ("you practice") appears to imply that the Thessalonians were already carrying out Paul's commands before they received the letter. Vv. 6-15 belie this, however, at least with respect to one important matter. Similarly, the assertion of confidence in their future behavior implied by the progressive future ποιήσετε ("you will continue practicing") is belied by the institution of a disciplinary procedure against recalcitrants in vv. 14f. Vv. 6-15 thus make it clear that Paul was anything but confident about the current as well as the future obedience of his readers. Through the "praise" in v. 4 Paul seeks to create *pathos* in his readers in order to encourage them to accept and carry out his instructions in vv. 6-15. From Paul's perspective the social control in which he was engaged was absolutely essential for maintaining discipline and order within the community at Thessalonica. For Paul correct behavior was at least as important as correct beliefs.

3:5 The general exhortation begun at 3:1 ends with a benedictory wish-prayer. As with the thoughts in the preceding verses, the connection with what has come before is not immediately obvious, but on closer reflection it would appear that Paul intends the wish-prayer to support the indirect call for obedience in v. 4 and the explicit call for obedience in the following verses.

The opening phrase, ὁ δὲ κύριος κατευθύναι ὑμῶν τὰς καρδίας ("now may the Lord direct your hearts") is reminiscent of a number of LXX texts employing κατευθῦναι ("to direct") in a metaphorical sense. Particularly interesting in this respect are 1 Ch. 29:18; Pr. 21:2; and Sir. 49:3, which speak specifically of the Lord directing the heart. καρδίας ("heart") denotes the inner existence of individuals. In the present context it probably includes the thinking and willing dimension of human existence because Paul apparently wishes his readers to reflect on the love of God and the patience of Christ with a view to encouraging obedience in the area of Christian behavior.

The genitive τοῦ θεοῦ ("of God") goes with τὴν ἀγάπην ("the love") and may either be objective, referring to human love directed toward God, or subjective, denoting God's love for the followers of Christ. Most commentators, on the basis of normal Pauline usage (cf. Rom. 5:5; 8:39; 2 Cor. 13:13), maintain that τοῦ θεοῦ is subjective genitive after ἀγάπη (cf. Frame, 296; Rigaux, 699; Best, 330; Marxsen, 98). But Trilling (139), who rejects the Pauline authorship of 2 Thessalonians, argues that Paul's customary usage cannot serve as a criterion for determining the meaning of "the love of God" here. On the basis of the reference in 2:16 to God's love for the Thessalonians, he contends that in 3:5 the pseudonymous author of the letter wished to direct his readers' hearts to love for God. Trilling's position is, however, doubtful for three reasons: (1) The idea that the Lord should direct people to love for God seems somewhat unusual; love for God should be the response of individuals to God's prior love. Such a response should hardly require the direction of the Lord. (2) If the author, whoever he was, had wished to call his readers to love God, then it would have been much more natural and decisive to have employed the infinitive τὸ ἀγαπᾶν with the object τὸν θεόν. (3) The context necessitates that v. 5 encourage obedience in areas of Christian behavior. Reflection on the character of God's love and commitment to the followers of Christ would appear to be a stronger motivational force for Christian behavior than a call for Christians to love God without at the same time offering a precise reason for doing so. Trilling's reference to 2:16 is unconvincing as it is too distant to serve this purpose. Thus I would conclude with the majority of commentators that Paul is concerned in v. 5 to direct his readers to God's love for them as a motivating factor in proper Christian behavior (cf. Best, 330).

A similar grammatical complication exists with the second prepositional phrase εἰς τὴν ὑπομονὴν τοῦ Χριστοῦ ("to the perseverance of Christ") since the genitive τοῦ Χριστοῦ may be either objective or subjective. Scholars taking it as objective genitive have offered several different interpretations. Von Dobschütz (309) sees it as a reference to the need for the Thessalonians to have a patient expectation for the coming of Christ. Trilling (330f.) claims that it means steadfastness directed toward Christ in the face of "distress and disturbance" (cf. Turner, *Syntax,* 212). Two factors militate against either of these possibilities: (1) The two prepositional phrases should be grammatically parallel as they are linked by a coordinating conjunction. If the first genitive is subjective, then we should also expect τοῦ Χριστοῦ to be subjective. (2) Both von Dobschütz's and Trilling's interpretations necessitate amplifying the text with ideas not contained in the immediate context.

In light of τοῦ θεοῦ being subjective genitive, it seems probable that τοῦ Χριστοῦ should also be rendered as subjective genitive. Once this possibility is accepted it is still necessary to interpret the meaning of "the perseverance of Christ." Best (330) offers two possibilities. Either it refers to taking Christ's perseverance as an example (cf. Jas. 5:11; Pol. 8:2), or accepting the perseverance that comes from Christ (cf. Rom. 15:4f.). In keeping with the interpretation suggested above for the first prepositional phrase, the former seems the more likely possibility. The perseverance exercised by Christ is a more obvious topic for Christian reflection than the steadfastness given by Christ. Similarly, it is a more powerful force in motivating Christian behavior. Thus Paul's wish-prayer is for the Lord to direct the readers' hearts to God's love for them and to the perseverance which Christ demonstrated as a basis for encouraging what Paul considers proper Christian behavior.

PAUL'S EXHORTATION ON ECONOMIC SELF-SUFFICIENCY: 3:6-15

Unlike the exhortations in many of his other letters, that in 2 Thessalonians is mainly concerned with only one issue in the life of the community. This perhaps suggests that the letter was hastily written as an urgent response to, among other things, the problem addressed in the exhortation. This would explain its relative brevity and occasional looseness in composition in comparison to 1 Thessalonians. The issue in question involved the economic responsibility of the individual members of the community to provide for themselves and presumably their own families.

Most commentators who accept the Pauline authorship of 2 Thessalonians link this section with 1 Thes. 4:11f. and 5:14. They assume that the problem had intensified between the writing of the two letters (cf. von Dobschütz, 309; Frame, 297; Rigaux, 701; Best, 331). This conclusion is certainly not substantiated by a careful reading of 3:6-15. The lack of any allusion to what was written in the previous letter, when taken with the specific comment that Paul's instruction here corresponded to what he had commanded when he was still with them (v. 10), counsels that this was the first occasion after his departure on which he addressed the issue in question. While 3:6-15 is not amenable to the conclusion that Paul was taking up a problem dealt with in a previous letter, 1 Thes. 4:11 is. In 1 Thes. 4:11 Paul alludes to his past command regarding the responsibility of individual Christians to be economically independent. The reference could easily include 2 Thes. 3:6-15, if, as I contend, 2 Thessalonians was Paul's first letter to the community.

Trilling (141f., 151-153) sees in this section a post-Pauline attempt to deal in an authoritative way with the problem of laziness in the Christian community. His views on this matter do not stand up to careful scrutiny, as Marshall (219) demonstrates, and the same may be said of the thesis of Munro (*Authority,* 82-85). She holds that vv. 6-12 represent a "later stratum" or a post-Pauline addition to the letter. Apart from the absence of any evidence in the textual tradition for this, her criteria for isolating material contained in the so-called later stratum are ambiguous and open to alternative explanations. For example, she claims that the frequency of antithetical parallelism is indicative of the "later stratum," but this ignores the fact that the nature of the material itself determines whether antithetical parallelism is appropriate or not. In exhortative material such as vv. 6-15 this is a common feature (cf. 1 Thes. 4:1-12, another section that she claims is later stratum because of its antithetical parallelism).

Holmberg (*Paul and Power,* 111, 159; cf. Munro, *Authority,* 82f.) claims that vv. 6-12 may reflect a critique of charismatic authority figures demanding support from other members of the community, but this is hypothetical since he provides no substantial evidence to support this conclusion. Jewett (*Thessalonian Correspondence,* 105) holds a similar position. He maintains that Paul's argument in vv. 6-10 was directed toward the ἄτακτοι whom he says may have claimed apostolic privilege for receiving support from the community. The text certainly does not require this interpretation, nor can ἀτάκτως and its verbal form ἀτακτεῖν bear the weight of Jewett's interpretation. In particular his assertion that the ἄτακτοι were not motivated by laziness is simply not borne out by vv. 11f. In addition neither Holmberg nor Jewett offers any means for distinguishing between the leadership function of the ἄτακτοι and those whom Paul clearly supports in 1 Thes. 5:12f. As I will argue, a potentially serious problem had emerged, but it differed substantially from the one suggested by Holmberg and Jewett.

3:6 Having prepared his readers for the desired response of obedience in the preceding verses, Paul now addresses the second matter of paramount importance to him at the time of writing, namely, the problem of Christians living disorderly or idle lives. As so often in 1 and 2 Thessalonians, the words δὲ . . . ἀδελφοί ("now, brothers [and sisters]") mark this off as a new theme. Paul begins with the words παραγγέλλομεν δὲ ὑμῖν, ἀδελφοί, ἐν ὀνόματι τοῦ κυρίου [ἡμῶν] Ἰησοῦ Χριστοῦ ("now we command you, brothers [and sisters], in the name of [our] Lord Jesus Christ"). This introduction of the new theme in vv. 6-15 underscores the intensity of Paul's disquiet. Elsewhere Paul employs the formulas "in the name of the Lord Jesus" (1 Cor. 5:4) and "by the name of our Lord Jesus Christ" (1 Cor. 1:10) precisely where he is issuing emphatic commands regarding the behavior of the community. At a theological level the addition of "in the name of the Lord Jesus Christ" to a command implies that the command is not simply Paul's but that it has the sanction of the Lord Jesus Christ himself. At a functional level the formula makes failure to keep the command a matter of disobedience not merely to Paul but to the Lord himself. In other words it is one of the most powerful forms of theological coercion available to Paul. As the second part of the verse makes clear, Paul adds to his theological coercion the coercive power of the community to enforce the prescribed form of conduct. This gives some indication of just how seriously Paul viewed the situation.

In the first instance Paul's instruction is not directed toward the recalcitrant members of the community but toward the obedient members, whom he instructs στέλλεσθαι ὑμᾶς ἀπὸ παντὸς ἀδελφοῦ ἀτάκτως περιπατοῦντος καὶ μὴ κατὰ τὴν παράδοσιν ἣν παρελάβοσαν παρ' ἡμῶν ("that you keep away from every brother [or sister] living idly and not according to the traditions that they received from us"). As was mentioned previously in connection with 1 Thes. 5:14, the adverb ἀτάκτως, which appears in v. 6 and recurs in v. 11, and the verbal form ἀτακτεῖν, found in v. 7, may refer to disorderly behavior, but in the context of work it often has the sense of failure to fulfill one's duties or obligations. In such instances indolence is certainly one of the chief reasons for such a failure.

Spicq ("Les Thessaloniciens 'inquiets,'" 1-13), who is followed by Jewett (*Thessalonian Correspondence,* 104f.), claims that those living ἀτάκτως were resisting authority. This is perhaps implied in v. 6 since the people involved are said not to be living according to the traditions received from Paul. This, however, may not have been an intentional resistance of authority or act of disobedience on the part of the people involved. In any case

vv. 7f. and 11f. make it clear that the apostle was primarily exercised by their evasion of responsibility in providing for themselves through their own labors rather than their implied insubordination.

I will show later that Paul was also worried about idleness precipitating disorderly behavior since this might bring the community into disrepute with outsiders (vv. 11f.). The problem of indolence among the urban poor in the Roman world raises its own questions. Few people in the urban setting would have had any significant capital assets to fall back on, so how did Christians, who were not working, support themselves? The most likely answer appears to be that they lived off the largesse of the community, or more particularly its wealthier members, who functioned as traditional patrons in the Greco-Roman world (see comments on v. 10).

Since the community had it in its power to halt the abuse, Paul addresses the community at large in the first instance, charging its members with responsibility for ending the deviant conduct of those who would not work for their living by excluding them from Christian fellowship. This course of action would have three important consequences: (1) It would free those providing support to withdraw it. (2) It would force the indolent and irresponsible into line with Paul's teachings if they wished to enjoy the benefits that membership in the community offered in this age and the next. (3) It would provide an important statement to outsiders that the Christian community supported the best in traditional Greco-Roman moral values regarding work (cf. Hock, *Social Context,* 42-47).

Those living in irresponsible idleness were from Paul's perspective also not living κατὰ τὴν παράδοσιν ἣν παρελάβοσαν παρ' ἡμῶν ("according to the traditions that they received from us"). The textual tradition shows considerable disruption regarding the form of the verb παραλαμβάνω ("receive"). Was its original form third person plural (either παρελάβοσαν, an unusual dialectical form [ℵ* A 33 88 Basil] or παρέλαβον [ℵc Dc K L Ψ 81 104, etc.]; among the early versions vg syrp copsams favor either form) or second person plural (B Fgr G syrh copsa[bo])? The evidence is stronger for third person plural, and since it is a slightly unexpected reading in the context it should be taken as the original reading. A later scribe probably introduced the second person plural ending because the context was thought to require direct address of all the readers.

This third person plural verb has considerable significance. It focuses attention specifically on that segment of the community that was out of step with Paul's instructions and isolates such people from the mainstream of the community. Paul probably intended the whole phrase "not according to the traditions that they received from us" as a warrant for the responsible members of the community to withdraw from those living in an idle and irresponsible fashion.

The tradition to which Paul refers has a twofold character, as vv. 7-12 indicate. In vv. 7-9 the apostle elaborates on his and his colleagues' example as a guide for responsible behavior for their converts. The introductory words of v. 7 reveal that his and his fellow missionaries' behavior was intended to have the normative character of a received tradition. In addition, as a matter of course, Paul issued ethical instruction to new converts in order to regulate their behavior as Christians. In v. 10 he cites the specific tradition involved with regard to work.

3:7 The introductory formulation of v. 7 makes two points. First, γάρ ("for") implies that what Paul is about to say provides a motivation or reason for avoiding any Christian brother or sister who is living in idleness. Second, αὐτοὶ οἴδατε ("you yourselves know"; cf. 1 Thes. 2:1; 3:3; 4:2; 5:2) evinces that what follows is already recognized among Paul's readers, that is, it is part of the ethical tradition received from Paul. He and his missionary colleagues had furnished the Thessalonians with an example of self-sufficiency (see vv. 8f.) having the character of an ethical imperative. Thus Paul reminds them that they know πῶς δεῖ μιμεῖσθαι ἡμᾶς ("how [you] ought to imitate us"; cf. 1 Thes. 4:1 for the use of πῶς δεῖ in the sense of an ethical imperative). In 1 Thes. 1:6f. and 2:14 Paul notes the way in which the Thessalonians became imitators of the experience of suffering endured by various other Christians as well as Christ himself, but here he calls for ethical conformity to his own pattern of behavior, as he does in other texts, such as 1 Cor. 4:16; 11:1; and Phil. 3:17.

Trilling (145f.) argues that 2 Thes. 3:7 and 9 represent the emergence of a new attitude toward Paul in the post-Pauline period. The apostle was considered to have provided an authoritative measure for what Christian conduct should be. Trilling's position is based on his claim that in the other Pauline texts dealing with imitation Paul never required imitation of himself in an unqualified manner. Trilling appears to have overlooked 1 Cor. 4:16, in which Paul exhorts his converts at Corinth to become imitators of him without qualification. But even without 1 Cor. 4:16 Trilling's views are without foundation. He fails to take cognizance of the content of 2 Thes. 3:7-9, which of necessity had to center on Paul's (and his colleagues') behavior as the model to be imitated. In addition Paul's use of himself and his coworkers as examples for ethical imitation reflects a common convention among the moralists of the period, who, according to Malherbe (*Moral Exhortation,* 135; cf. Hock, *Social Context,* 47f.), preferred such personal examples "because they were regarded as more persuasive than words and as providing concrete models to imitate."

The ὅτι clause begins to spell out the behavior to be imitated by the readers. According to Paul, he and his fellow missionaries were not idle or irresponsible in maintaining themselves. The verb ἀτακτεῖν ("to be idle or negligent") is related to the adverb employed in v. 6 and with the negative particle οὐκ ("not") contrasts the missionaries' manner of life with that of the refractory members of the community at Thessalonica.

3:8 In this verse Paul amplifies his assertion that he and his fellow missionaries were not indolent with respect to caring for their own needs while working among the Thessalonians. First, he maintains, οὐδὲ δωρεὰν ἄρτον ἐφάγομεν παρά τινος ("nor did we eat bread from anyone without payment"). As has long been recognized (see von Dobschütz, 311), ἄρτον ἐφάγομεν may well be derived from a Semitic idiom, 'ākal lehem. This expression was given a literal translation in the LXX (cf. Gn. 3:19) and could have the general sense of receiving maintenance from someone (cf. 2 Sa. 9:7; 2 Ki. 4:8; Ezk. 12:18f.). It has this sense in v. 8. Paul's refusal to accept material support (οὐδὲ δωρεάν) would appear to have formed part of his missionary strategy (cf. 1 Cor. 9:1-18; 2 Cor. 11:7). Not only was this policy intended as an example to be imitated, but, as we have seen before, it also served to distinguish Paul himself and his message from that of the many charlatan preachers who made a living hawking their messages (cf. 1 Thes. 2:4f.; see Malherbe, "'Gentle as a Nurse,'" 217; Hock, *Social Context*, 47-49).

The second part of v. 8 specifies what Paul did to avoid dependence upon his converts, namely, ἐν κόπῳ καὶ μόχθῳ νυκτὸς καὶ ἡμέρας ἐργαζόμενοι πρὸς τὸ μὴ ἐπιβαρῆσαί τινα ὑμῶν ("with toil and exertion working night and day in order not to burden any of you"). It is generally assumed that the participle ἐργαζόμενοι ("working") is parallel to the verbs ἠτακτήσαμεν and ἐφάγομεν from vv. 7b and 8a and therefore is rendered as a finite verb (see, e.g., *RSV, NIV,* and most commentators). This represents yet another example of a grammar fault in the letter and adds to the impression that the letter was composed in a hurried fashion, a point we have observed before.

Both κόπος ("toil") and μόχθος ("exertion") are also found in 1 Thes. 2:9 and 2 Cor. 11:27. Here, as in 1 Thes. 2:9, they stress the fact that Paul's policy of self-support required considerable effort on his part. This point is made even more emphatic by his statement that he and his fellow missionaries worked νυκτὸς καὶ ἡμέρας, that is, both at night and during the day. The infinitive construction "in order not to burden any of you" expresses the purpose of the missionaries' toil and exertion. (See the discussion of the previous verse for this purpose.)

The whole expression νυκτὸς καὶ ἡμέρας ἐργαζόμενοι πρὸς τὸ μὴ ἐπιβαρῆσαί τινα ὑμῶν is found word for word in 1 Thes. 2:9, which has led some scholars to conclude that 2 Thes. 3:8 is dependent upon 1 Thes. 2:9. If this were true, it would be strange that there is not more direct literary dependence between the two letters, and even Trilling (147), who believes that 2 Thessalonians is dependent on 1 Thessalonians, acknowledges that it is possible that if the two letters were from Paul and were both written within a short period of time then the same expression might recur. What has gone unnoticed is that the broken grammatical construction of v. 8 is inexplicable if the writer had direct access to 1 Thes. 2:9, where Paul makes good grammatical sense with the words "night and day working in order not to burden any of you, we preached the gospel of God to you."

3:9 Through a parenthetical remark Paul distinguishes between his and his colleagues' rights and their actual practice as an example for their converts to follow. The first part of his statement, οὐχ ὅτι οὐκ ἔχομεν ἐξουσίαν, is elliptical and means "(it is) not that we did not have the right (to be supported)." In 1 Cor. 9:4-18 Paul appeals to the law of Moses and to temple practices for warrants to substantiate his right to support in the sight of God. At the same time he denies ever having invoked this right in his dealings with the Corinthians. From 1 Cor. 9:4-6 it would appear that Paul was exceptional among apostolic missionaries in not exercising this right. His reason, as mentioned above, was twofold: First, as 1 Thes. 2:4f. and 9f. suggest, he did not exercise his right to maintenance as a matter of principle; he did not wish anyone to think that he preached out of an impure motive or for his own gain. Second, as he indicates in the purpose clause of the second part of 2 Thess. 3:9, he did it ἵνα ἑαυτοὺς τύπον δῶμεν ὑμῖν εἰς τὸ μιμεῖσθαι ἡμᾶς ("in order that we might give ourselves as an example to you in order that we might be imitated"). Once again the expression is elliptical, but the context makes it clear that Paul's ethical example was intended to teach his converts to be self-sufficient. The reason for having inculcated this type of behavior is explained in v. 12.

3:10 Not only had Paul furnished them with an example to follow, but as καὶ γάρ ("for indeed") indicates, he had also given his readers an explicit command about their responsibility to provide for themselves. The way in which Paul puts the matter in v. 10 makes it seem unlikely that he had already written 1 Thes. 4:11f. to his readers. Paul states explicitly that it was ὅτε ἦμεν πρὸς ὑμᾶς, τοῦτο παρηγγέλλομεν ὑμῖν ("when we were with you, we used to give you this command"). Since 1 Thes. 4:11f. deals with the same general issue treated in 2 Thes. 3:6-15, the lack of reference to it in v. 10 and in the next two verses, where a reference would both have been appropriate and have strengthened Paul's case, supports my claim that 2 Thessalonians was the first letter to the church at Thessalonica.

The imperfect form of παρηγγέλλομεν ("we used to command") underscores that Paul did not simply mention the need to be self-sufficient in passing when he was with the Thessalonians but that he had repeatedly instructed them with respect to the necessity of working to provide for their own material requirements (cf. v. 6). The ὅτι at the beginning of the command probably indicates that Paul is quoting what he used to say to his converts verbatim in the words εἴ τις οὐ θέλει ἐργάζεσθαι μηδὲ ἐσθιέτω ("If anyone does not wish to work, neither let that person eat"). The command itself has the character of a maxim about it, although it is not known in the form that it has here from any other source (cf. Pr. 10:4; *Gn. Rab.* 2:2).

Three important points need to be noted about the command: (1) The command is qualified by the use of the verb θέλει ("wish"). Paul recognized that the important question was whether or not people were prepared to work for their living. His command, therefore, was not directed to those who were unable to work or who could not find work, but to those who refused to work. (2) The sanction against those refusing to work is that they should not be allowed to eat. Clearly it was the community's responsibility to see that Paul's imperative, μηδὲ ἐσθιέτω ("neither let that person eat"), was carried out in the case of anyone who was unwilling to work (cf. Did. 12:2-5). (3) By reminding the community of his instructions regarding work, Paul provided the community with the justification for stopping support to those who preferred to rely on the largesse of the wealthier members of the community rather than work themselves.

3:11 The opening words of this verse, ἀκούομεν γὰρ τινας περιπατοῦντας ἐν ὑμῖν ἀτάκτως ("for we hear that some among you are living in an idle manner") suggest that Paul had received a report regarding the indolent who were forcing the community to care for them through their own refusal to work. Paul does not specify that the whole church sent him word about the situation. Possibly someone representing a patron of the community had come with word of the emerging problems, as happened in the case of the Corinthian church (see 1 Cor. 1:11; 16:17). Alternatively, Paul may have received a secondhand report regarding the situation, perhaps from someone from another church in the region. This latter suggestion would account for Paul's lack of clarity about the origin of the misunderstanding regarding the day of the Lord in chap. 2. The phrase περιπατοῦντας ἀτάκτως ("living in an idle manner") has been picked up from v. 6 and has the same meaning here.

Paul gives some specificity to the meaning of "living in an idle manner" in the wordplay μηδὲν ἐργαζομένους ἀλλὰ περιεργαζομένους ("not working but meddling" or, as the *NIV* renders it in idiomatic English: "they are not busy; they are busybodies"). (For other wordplays in Paul see Rom. 12:3; 1 Cor. 11:29-34; 2 Cor. 1:13; 3:2; 6:10; Phil. 3:2f.) This amplification of the phrase "living in an idle manner" demonstrates that the fundamental issue was, from Paul's perspective, one of indolence, not of rebelliousness, as some have suggested (cf. Spicq, "Les Thessaloniciens 'inquiets,' "; Jewett, *Thessalonian Correspondence,* 105). The term περιεργαζομένους, found only here in Paul, probably requires the meaning "meddling" or "interfering," with the sense of people being busybodies involved in affairs that are none of their business (cf. the admonition in 1 Thes. 4:11 for the readers to live quietly and mind their own affairs).

What precisely led to this criticism is impossible to say. Paul may have simply intended the criticism in a general way, since idle people are more likely to interfere in other people's affairs than those who are busily engaged in their own affairs and earning a living for themselves. Such people were either potentially or actually disruptive for the community and needed to be disciplined. In addition, as Bruce (207) notes, the type of behavior described by Paul in this passage might also have brought the community into disrepute with outsiders and might therefore have needed to be brought under control (cf. 1 Thes. 4:12).

3:12 Having begun by instructing the responsible members of the community about how they should deal with their aberrant fellow believers, Paul now turns to those leading indolent and irresponsible lives in order to give them specific instructions. Paul employs strong and coercive language (cf. v. 6) when he says τοῖς δὲ τοιούτοις παραγγέλλομεν καὶ παρακαλοῦμεν ἐν κυρίῳ Ἰησοῦ Χριστῷ ("but we command and require such people in the Lord Jesus Christ"). The relation between παραγγέλλομεν and παρακαλοῦμεν necessitates comment. Some commentators detect a softening of the more forceful expression παραγγέλλομεν ("we command") by παρακαλοῦμεν understood in the sense of "we exhort" or "we beg" (cf. Frame, 306; Morris, 256; Best, 340). This interpretation seems somewhat doubtful. παρακαλοῦμεν can also mean "we demand" or "we require," and in the context this seems the more probable sense because Paul implicitly threatens the indolent members of the community with exclusion through his directives to the responsible members of the community in vv. 6 and 14. Moreover, "in the Lord Jesus Christ" is parallel to "in the name of the Lord Jesus Christ" in v. 6. This means that it expresses the idea of personal agency, namely, that the full authority of the Lord stands behind the command (on the use of the expression "in the Lord" in such situations see 1 Thes. 3:8 and Moule, *Origin of Christology*, 58-60). If this is the case, then the command has coercive power: to reject it is to reject the Lord Jesus Christ himself and therefore to exclude oneself from the community.

The command itself is contained in the ἵνα clause: ἵνα μετὰ ἡσυχίας ἐργαζόμενοι τὸν ἑαυτῶν ἄρτον ἐσθίωσιν ("that working with quietness they eat their own bread"). The verbal cognate ἡσυχάζειν ("to be quiet") of the noun ἡσυχία ("quietness") appears in 1 Thes. 4:11 and is directed there to the same general theme. Paul undoubtedly intended the practice of "working with quietness" as an alternative to the indolent members' tendency to meddle in other people's business (v. 11). Best (341) argues that the reference to working quietly probably indicates that it was to calm the "excitement" caused by the expectation of the parousia, but Marshall (225) points out that a more general reference is intended since in neither 1 nor 2 Thessalonians does Paul ever directly connect his commands about living quietly with the issue of the parousia. In light of 1 Thes. 4:11f. and Rom. 13:1-7, the claim of Trilling (151) that the instruction to work quietly reflects a later middle-class form of Christianity not typical of Paul's day is untenable. The ultimate goal of people working quietly is that they should provide for themselves (on the meaning of "eat their own bread" cf. v. 8) and stop being a drain on the resources of either the community as a whole or more likely its wealthier members. Ironically, Paul's emphasis upon familial love and commitment among the members of the community may have given rise to the situation. The order that the idle must work was not only in their interest, but also in the interest of the wealthier members of the community who would have increasingly found themselves burdened by the indolent if Paul had not intervened.

3:13 The initial words of v. 13, ὑμεῖς δέ, ἀδελφοί ("but you, brothers [and sisters]"), are taken by some (e.g., Trilling, 153f.; Marxsen, 102) as introducing a new section. Trilling, however, sees only a very loose connection between v. 13 and vv. 14f. He maintains that vv. 14f. refer to the whole of the epistle rather than to the immediate context of vv. 6-12. Trilling's view is unconvincing. The only issue addressed in the letter that could be construed as serious enough to warrant the disciplinary action described in vv. 14f. is the problem discussed in vv. 6-12, and in fact vv. 14f. are probably intended as a clarification of v. 6.

Even the seemingly general direction of v. 13 is best understood against the backdrop of vv. 6-12. The reason for the direct address of the readers in v. 13 is that in vv. 11f. Paul was speaking to the indolent members of the community indirectly, but in v. 13 he turns again to the responsible members of the community with further directions.

He exhorts them μὴ ἐγκακήσητε καλοποιοῦντες ("do not grow weary of doing good"). How specific we should understand this exhortation to be is difficult to determine. A virtually identical direction in Gal. 6:9 (τὸ δὲ καλὸν ποιοῦντες μὴ ἐγκακῶμεν ["let us not grow tired of doing good"]) is very general in scope. But here the situation is somewhat different. The aorist subjunctive ἐγκακήσητε would appear to allude to a specific situation in which the readers are not to grow weary. As vv. 6-12 and 14f. concern the problem of the indolent, it seems likely that the direction in v. 13 relates to this.

Commentators have suggested two possible meaning for the rare compound καλοποιοῦντες. It may mean either "to do the right" (cf. Frame, 308; Morris, 257) or "to confer benefits" (cf. von Dobschütz, 315; Best, 342). Most commentators, whichever translation they accept, assume that Paul was trying to ensure charitable behavior on the part of the responsible members of the community either toward the needy in the community except for the idle or toward all including the idle. Although Paul may have feared that his instruction regarding the idle might be construed as grounds for withholding charity from the truly needy, he does not specify this. As the text stands, it is much more probable that the apostle is exhorting his readers not to behave like the irresponsible members of the community.

3:14 In this verse Paul returns to the question of how to go about disciplining the refractory members of the community, a problem first addressed in v. 6. The initial statement, εἰ δέ τις οὐχ ὑπακούει τῷ λόγῳ ἡμῶν διὰ τῆς ἐπιστολῆς ("but if anyone does not obey our instruction through this letter"), suggests that Paul hoped for a change of behavior as a result of the letter. If a voluntary transformation did not occur, however, then the community must act decisively. λόγος is used here in the sense of a rule of conduct, a usage rooted both in classical Greek and in Paul's understanding of the

Torah, as Rom. 13:9 and Gal. 5:14 indicate. The singular form of the term shows that Paul is thinking specifically of the theme found in vv. 6-12, and in particular the regulation given in v. 12. Hence his reference to the rule of conduct διὰ τῆς ἐπιστολῆς ("through this letter"). The use of "our" with "rule of conduct" interjects a note of apostolic authority into the passage (cf. Bruce, 209), making noncompliance with the regulation regarding work a rejection of God's messenger.

Paul directs the obedient members of the community, τοῦτον σημειοῦσθε ("take special notice of this one"), referring to anyone who fails to comply with his injunction regarding work. Having taken note of such a person, the community is then μὴ συναναμίγνυσθαι αὐτῷ ("not to associate with the person"). συναναμίγνυσθαι occurs elsewhere in Paul's letters (and for that matter the NT) only in 1 Cor. 5:9-11, where it is found twice. In that text Paul directs the church at Corinth to dissociate itself from anyone who claims to be a fellow Christian but is guilty of immorality. H. Greeven (*TDNT* VII, 855) argues that the words "not even to eat with such a person" found in 1 Cor. 5:11 are intended to exclude the person involved from the Lord's Supper because it was central to the life of the community. Paul does not specify this in 2 Thes. 3:14, but he undoubtedly meant for the exclusion to include any form of participation in the common meals of the community where the Lord's Supper took place.

But the command was wider than this. As it stands it "restrains members of the community from dealings with the person concerned" (Greeven, 855); that is, Paul calls for their excommunication. He indicates in v. 14 that the primary purpose of the debarment was ἵνα ἐντραπῇ ("in order that the person may be ashamed"). The apostle hoped that exclusion would have a salutary effect on the individual, leading ultimately to his or her reintegration into the community as a chastened brother or sister (cf. v. 15). But quite apart from this explicit intention, the act of debarring refractory members also served to purge the community of corrupting influences (cf. Meeks, *First Urban Christians*, 130) that might affect other members and lead to opprobrium from outsiders.

3:15 Although Paul calls for excommunication of anyone who refuses to heed his instructions regarding work, at the same time he hastens to define more clearly what attitude the members of the community should have toward someone whom they have banned from their fellowship. First he exhorts them, καὶ μὴ ὡς ἐχθρὸν ἡγεῖσθε ("and do not consider [such a person] as an enemy"). Paul recognized that if someone were debarred from the church community, then in many people's minds this would be tantamount to having declared that person an enemy of the community. This in turn would lead to behavior predicated upon this assumption. This was not Paul's intention; rather, he appears to have hoped that if the people concerned were shunned by the community it would bring them to their senses. For this reason such people should not be treated as enemies. This would more than likely result in their complete alienation from the community.

Instead Paul urges, ἀλλὰ νουθετεῖτε ὡς ἀδελφόν ("but admonish [the person] as a brother [or sister]"). Exactly how this was to take place poses a difficulty. Best (343f.) believes that it can only refer to action to be taken while the community was assembled. If this were the case then the direction to dissociate from the individual involved was limited only to the Lord's Supper and the common meal associated with it. Nothing in the context, however, suggests such a limited significance for the command in v. 14 (cf. v. 6 as well). There is no reason to think that admonishing someone excluded from the community could not take place outside the communal meeting. The point Paul wishes to make does not include precise details about how to deal with a recalcitrant individual or where admonition should take place. Instead Paul attempts to moderate the attitudes of the community toward the person and give the community a positive action to carry out in an effort to restore the individual to fellowship. Thus Paul implies that exclusion from the community should not be understood as irrevocable.

EPISTOLARY CLOSING: 3:16-18

Commentators are generally divided about whether v. 16 should be seen as the conclusion to 3:6-15 or as part of the letter's conclusion or postscript (see Jewett, *Thessalonian Correspondence,* 222-225). On the grounds that the previous section closed with a wish-prayer (see comments on 2:16-17), it is possible to take v. 16 as the conclusion of the main exhortative section. This possibility is perhaps strengthened by the fact that the wish-prayer is a prayer for peace. The community was clearly being disturbed by the problem of indolent members, so a prayer for peace in the community might well be appropriate (cf. Marshall, 230). Against this, however, is the fact that the problem of peace for the community at Thessalonica involved other factors, such as an end to external oppression. In addition the contents of v. 16 do not allow us to limit the request for peace simply to the problem of the indolent (see the discussion below). The way in which v. 16 ends with a benediction and then is followed in vv. 17f. by Paul's remark about his signature and another benediction suggests that v. 16 was the original conclusion to the letter as it was written by Paul's amanuensis and that Paul then penned vv. 17f. himself. (This point seems to have escaped Longenecker's notice in his discussion of this passage in his article on ancient amanuenses ["Ancient Amanuenses," 290f.]).

Jewett (*Thessalonian Correspondence,* 87) describes vv. 16-18 as the *peroratio* of the letter. This designation is less appropriate for this section of this letter than it is for 1 Thes. 5:23-28 since 2 Thes. 3:16-18 does not serve as a direct and emphatic summary of the letter, as we should expect a *peroratio* to do. Only v. 16 can be construed as a summary at all, and it is a very general summary at best. For this reason I have chosen to describe vv. 16-18 simply as the epistolary closing.

3:16 The expression αὐτὸς δὲ ὁ κύριος τῆς εἰρήνης ("and the Lord of peace himself") is unusual because it is the only instance in the NT writings where Christ is designated as "the Lord of peace." The normal expression in Paul is "the God of peace" (cf. 1 Thes. 5:23; Rom. 15:33; 16:20; 2 Cor. 13:11; Phil. 4:7, 9), though in the salutations of most of his letters he connects peace both with "God our father" and "our Lord Jesus Christ" (cf. 2 Thes. 1:1; Rom. 1:7; 1 Cor. 1:3; 2 Cor. 1:2; Gal. 1:3; Phil. 1:2), and in Col. 3:15 he refers to "the peace of Christ."

The Lord of peace is called upon to give peace to the readers: δῴη ὑμῖν τὴν εἰρήνην διὰ παντὸς ἐν παντὶ τρόπῳ ("may he give to you peace at all times, in every way"). The peace that Paul requests from the Lord here is more than the absence of conflict within the community. The Christians at Thessalonica were also troubled by external oppression (cf. 1:4-10). Even this may not be as inclusive as Paul intended. Peace was virtually synonymous in Jewish circles with the idea of the total well-being of individuals and the community. Such peace could only come from God. The breadth of its application in v. 16 is shown by the words "at all times, in every way." (The textual variant τόπῳ for τρόπῳ found primarily in witnesses of the Western tradition [cf. A* D* F G it^(ar, c, d, dem, etc.) vg Ambrosiaster] probably arose in an attempt to bring the passage into conformity with such other Pauline texts as 1 Cor. 1:2; 2 Cor. 2:14; 1 Thes. 1:8.)

V. 16b is the first of two benedictions. Just as "the Lord of peace" in the first part of the verse is unique in Paul's letters, so also is the benediction "the Lord be with all of you." Both Rom. 15:33 and Phil. 4:9 speak of "the God of peace" being with the readers. In all probability the use of "the Lord of peace" in the first part of the verse led to the slightly unusual benediction in the second part of the verse. Whatever may be the reason for the unique formulation, Paul's wish-prayer had the effect of reassuring the readers of the presence of their Lord with all of them.

3:17 As in several of his other letters Paul took up the pen to write his own greeting and noted this point for his readers (cf. 1 Cor. 16:21; Col. 4:18; see also Phm. 19 and Gal. 6:11-18 where Paul identifies himself as writing the conclusion of the letter). Best (347) maintains that v. 16 is the greeting to which Paul refers in v. 17, but on the basis of both 1 Cor. 16:21 and Col. 4:18 this is incorrect. As Marshall (231) points out, the actual greeting is contained in the words ὁ ἀσπασμὸς τῇ ἐμῇ χειρὶ Παύλου ("greeting, with my own hand, from Paul"). The clear implication of this notice by Paul is that a change of handwriting occurred at this point in the autograph copy. This in turn means that he employed an amanuensis or secretary in the writing of the letter (see Longenecker, "Ancient Amanuenses," for the role of the amanuensis).

To his greeting Paul adds: ὅ ἐστιν σημεῖον ἐν πάσῃ ἐπιστολῇ· οὕτως γράφω ("which is a sign in every letter [of mine]; this is the way I write"). Lindemann ("Abfassungszweck," 39-40) claims that the author of 2 Thessalonians, someone writing after Paul's time and seeking to replace 1 Thessalonians with his own letter, intentionally sought to call into question the authenticity of 1 Thessalonians by means of 2 Thes. 3:17 (as well as 2:2). Lindemann asserts that 1 Thessalonians lacked the mark of Pauline authenticity as described in v. 17. The author of 2 Thessalonians intended this to cast doubt on 1 Thessalonians.

Lindemann's position is based on a misunderstanding of the "sign." The sign to which Paul refers is not his signature (signatures were not normally written at the end of letters in any case; cf. Spicq, *Épîtres pastorales,* 17). The sign was, rather, the fact that the greeting itself was written in Paul's hand. He did this, undoubtedly, because like many other letter writers of the time Paul dictated each of his letters to an amanuensis and then added the greeting and end of the letter in his own hand as an authenticating mark (see Deissmann, *Light,* page facing 170 for an example of the change in handwriting in the greeting based on a photograph of an original letter). For this reason we should not expect to find the "mark" in 1 Thessalonians as we do not possess the autograph copy which would have ostensibly shown the change in handwriting. That the first person singular suddenly appears in 1 Thes. 5:27, however, gives credence to the possibility that the original did in fact contain a greeting written in Paul's hand. The comment in 2 Thes. 3:17 that "this is the way I write" identified the particular handwriting appearing in the autograph as Paul's own. Thus if a question arose about any letter being from Paul (cf. 2:2), the greeting and conclusion of this letter provided a way of authenticating it. Marshall (232) may also be correct that Paul wrote v. 17 to underscore the authority of the letter for its recipients.

3:18 The concluding benediction is typically Pauline even though it is not identical with any found in Paul's other letters (cf. 1 Cor. 16:23; Gal. 6:18; Phil. 4:23; 1 Thes. 5:28; Phm. 25). The wording of this benediction, ἡ χάρις τοῦ κυρίου ἡμῶν Ἰησοῦ Χριστοῦ μετὰ πάντων ὑμῶν ("may the grace of our Lord Jesus Christ be with all of you"), is closest in wording to 1 Thes. 5:28 and 1 Cor. 16:23, though both of those texts lack the πάντων ("all"). But this is only a minor variation. If any theological point is to be made from the inclusion of "all," it is perhaps that Paul asked for Christ's grace even on those who were not holding to the Christian pattern of behavior regarding work.

INDEX OF MODERN AUTHORS

295

INDEX OF SUBJECTS

INDEX OF BIBLICAL AND OTHER ANCIENT WORKS

311